Lecture Notes in Computer Science 13211

More information about this series at https://link.springer.com/bookseries/558

Josep Balasch · Colin O'Flynn (Eds.)

Constructive Side-Channel Analysis and Secure Design

13th International Workshop, COSADE 2022 Leuven, Belgium, April 11–12, 2022 Proceedings

Editors
Josep Balasch
KU Leuven
Leuven, Belgium

Colin O'Flynn
Dalhousie University
Halifax, NS, Canada

ISSN 0302-9743 ISSN 1611-3349 (electronic)
Lecture Notes in Computer Science
ISBN 978-3-030-99765-6 ISBN 978-3-030-99766-3 (eBook)
https://doi.org/10.1007/978-3-030-99766-3

This Springer imprint is published by the registered company Springer Nature Switzerland AG
The registered company address is: Gewerbestrasse 11, 6330 Cham, Switzerland

Preface

The 13th International Workshop on Constructive Side-Channel Analysis and Secure Design (COSADE 2022), was held in Leuven, Belgium, during April 11–12, 2022. The COSADE series of workshops began in 2010 and provides a well-established international platform for researchers, academics, and industry participants to present their current research topics in implementation attacks, secure implementation, implementation attack-resilient architectures and schemes, secure design and evaluation, practical attacks, test platforms, and open benchmarks.

COSADE 2022 was organized by KU Leuven. This year, the workshop received 25 papers from authors in 14 countries. Each paper was reviewed in a double-blind peer-review process by four Program Committee members. The Program Committee included 31 members from 15 countries, selected among experts from academia and industry in the areas of secure design, side channel attacks and countermeasures, fault injection attacks, efficient implementations, and architectures and protocols. Overall, the Program Committee returned 94 reviews with the help of 11 additional reviewers. During the decision process, 12 papers were selected for publication. These manuscripts are contained in these proceedings and the corresponding presentations were part of the COSADE 2022 program. We would like to express our gratitude to the Program Committee members for their timely reviews, their active participation in the paper discussion phase, and their willingness to contribute to the shepherding of conditionally accepted papers.

In addition to the 12 presentations of selected papers, the program was completed by two keynotes and an industrial session. The first keynote entitled "Abstractions and Tooling for Leakage Evaluation" was given by Dan Page from the University of Bristol. The talk gave an overview of support for cryptography on the RISC-V ISA, as well as current research directions related to tooling for high-level leakage evaluation tasks. The second keynote entitled "Repurposing Wireless Stacks for In-Depth Security Analysis" was given by Jiska Classen from the Secure Mobile Networking Lab at TU Darmstadt. The talk presented recent research related to the exploration of closed-source wireless ecosystems, and demonstrated practical tools and discovered vulnerabilities. The industrial session included three talks from industry players in the field of hardware security.

We would like to thank the general chair, Benedikt Gierlichs, and the local organizers of KU Leuven for the organization, which made this workshop a memorable event. We are very grateful for the financial support received from our generous sponsors Riscure, Secure-IC, NewAE Technology, PQShield, Rambus, Texplained, and NXP. We would also like to thank the authors who submitted their work to COSADE 2022, without whom the workshop would not have been possible.

April 2022

Josep Balasch
Colin O'Flynn

Organization

Steering Committee

Jean-Luc Danger	Télécom ParisTech, France
Werner Schindler	Bundesamt für Sicherheit in der Informationstechnik (BSI), Germany

General Chair

Benedikt Gierlichs	KU Leuven, Belgium

Program Committee Chairs

Colin O'Flynn	NewAE Technology Inc., Canada
Josep Balasch	KU Leuven, Belgium

Program Committee

Diego F. Aranha	Aarhus University, Denmark
Victor Arribas	Rambus Cryptography Research, The Netherlands
Alessandro Barenghi	Politecnico di Milano, Italy
Shivam Bhasin	Nanyang Technological University, Singapore
Jakub Breier	Silicon Austria Labs, Austria
Olivier Bronchain	Université Catholique de Louvain, Belgium
Chitchanok Chuengsatiansup	University of Adelaide, Australia
Fabrizio De Santis	Siemens AG, Germany
Jean-Max Dutertre	Ecole Nationale Superieure des Mines de Saint-Étienne (ENSMSE), France
Wieland Fischer	Infineon Technologies, Germany
Fatemeh Ganji	Worcester Polytechnic Institute, USA
Annelie Heuser	CNRS/IRISA, France
Johann Heyszl	Fraunhofer AISEC, Germany
Naofumi Homma	Tohoku University, Japan
Jens-Peter Kaps	George Mason University, USA
Juliane Krämer	University of Regensburg, Germany
Victor Lomne	NinjaLab, France
Patrick Longa	Microsoft Research, USA
Roel Maes	Intrinsic ID, The Netherlands
Marcel Medwed	NXP Semiconductors, Austria

Thorben Moos	Université Catholique de Louvain, Belgium
Daniel Page	University of Bristol, UK
Michael Pehl	Technical University of Munich, Germany
Stjepan Picek	Delft University of Technology, The Netherlands
Chester Rebeiro	Indian Institute of Technology Madras, India
Francesco Regazzoni	University of Amsterdam, The Netherlands, and Università della Svizzera italiana, Switzerland
Sujoy Sinha Roy	TU Graz, Austria
Marc Stöttinger	RheinMain University of Applied Sciences, Germany
Ruggero Susella	STMicroelectronics, Italy
Lennert Wouters	KU Leuven, Belgium
Fan Zhang	Zhejiang University, China

Additional Reviewers

Reetwik Das
Lukas Giner
Mustafa Khairallah
Soundes Marzougui
Tim Music
Antoon Purnal
Martin Rehberg
Thomas Schamberger
Nikhilesh Singh
Emanuele Strieder
Lars Tebelmann

Contents

Machine/Deep Learning

Machine-Learning Assisted Side-Channel Attacks on RNS ECC Implementations Using Hybrid Feature Engineering 3
Naila Mukhtar, Louiza Papachristodoulou, Apostolos P. Fournaris, Lejla Batina, and Yinan Kong

Focus is Key to Success: A Focal Loss Function for Deep Learning-Based Side-Channel Analysis 29
Maikel Kerkhof, Lichao Wu, Guilherme Perin, and Stjepan Picek

On the Evaluation of Deep Learning-Based Side-Channel Analysis 49
Lichao Wu, Guilherme Perin, and Stjepan Picek

Tools and References

A Second Look at the ASCAD Databases 75
Maximilian Egger, Thomas Schamberger, Lars Tebelmann, Florian Lippert, and Georg Sigl

FIPAC: Thwarting Fault- and Software-Induced Control-Flow Attacks with ARM Pointer Authentication 100
Robert Schilling, Pascal Nasahl, and Stefan Mangard

Body Biasing Injection: To Thin or Not to Thin the Substrate? 125
G. Chancel, J.-M. Galliere, and P. Maurine

Attacks

On the Susceptibility of Texas Instruments SimpleLink Platform Microcontrollers to Non-invasive Physical Attacks 143
Lennert Wouters, Benedikt Gierlichs, and Bart Preneel

Single-Trace Clustering Power Analysis of the Point-Swapping Procedure in the Three Point Ladder of Cortex-M4 SIKE 164
Aymeric Genêt and Novak Kaluđerović

Canonical DPA Attack on HMAC-SHA1/SHA2 193
Frank Schuhmacher

Masking

Provable Secure Software Masking in the Real-World 215
Arthur Beckers, Lennert Wouters, Benedikt Gierlichs, Bart Preneel, and Ingrid Verbauwhede

Systematic Study of Decryption and Re-encryption Leakage: The Case of Kyber 236
Melissa Azouaoui, Olivier Bronchain, Clément Hoffmann, Yulia Kuzovkova, Tobias Schneider, and François-Xavier Standaert

Handcrafting: Improving Automated Masking in Hardware with Manual Optimizations 257
Charles Momin, Gaëtan Cassiers, and François-Xavier Standaert

Author Index 277

Machine/Deep Learning

Machine-Learning Assisted Side-Channel Attacks on RNS ECC Implementations Using Hybrid Feature Engineering

Naila Mukhtar[1], Louiza Papachristodoulou[2(✉)], Apostolos P. Fournaris[3], Lejla Batina[4], and Yinan Kong[1]

[1] School of Engineering, Macquarie University, Sydney, Australia
naila.mukhtar@students.mq.edu.au, yinan.kong@mq.edu.au
[2] Fontys University of Applied Sciences, Eindhoven, The Netherlands
louisa.pap@gmail.com
[3] Industrial Systems Institute/R.C. Athena, Athens, Greece
fournaris@isi.gr
[4] Institute for Computing and Information Sciences (ICIS), Radboud University, Nijmegen, The Netherlands
lejla@cs.ru.nl

Abstract. Machine learning-based side-channel attacks have recently been introduced to recover the secret information from protected software and hardware implementations. Limited research exists for public-key algorithms, especially on non-traditional implementations like those using Residue Number System (RNS). Template attacks were proven successful on RNS-based Elliptic Curve Cryptography (ECC), only if the aligned portion is used for templates. In this study, we present a systematic methodology for the evaluation of ECC cryptosystems with and without countermeasures (both RNS-based and traditional ones) against ML-based side-channel attacks using two attack models on full length aligned and unaligned leakages. RNS-based ECC datasets are evaluated using four machine learning classifiers and comparison is provided with existing state-of-the-art template attacks. Moreover, we analyze the impact of raw features and advanced hybrid feature engineering techniques. We discuss the metrics and procedures that can be used for accurate classification on the imbalanced datasets. The experimental results demonstrate that, for ECC RNS datasets, the efficiency of simple machine learning algorithms is better than the complex deep learning techniques when such datasets are limited in size. This is the first study presenting a complete methodology for ML side-channel attacks on public key algorithms.

Keywords: Elliptic curve cryptography · Side-channel attacks · Machine learning · Feature engineering

1 Introduction

Side-channel attacks (SCAs) constitute an ever evolving technique of recovering secret information by exploiting the physical leakage of cryptographic implemen-

J. Balasch and C. O'Flynn (Eds.): COSADE 2022, LNCS 13211, pp. 3–28, 2022.
https://doi.org/10.1007/978-3-030-99766-3_1

tations e.g. power consumption, electromagnetic emanations, timing and vibrations leakage [20,27,39]. From an information-theoretic point of view, profiled template attacks are one of the most powerful SCAs. The attacker is assumed to have an access to the open copy of the target device, which allows her to create a leakage profile from the collected leakage traces in the profiling phase. The leakage profile can be later used to retrieve an unknown secret (not under her control) from the device under test [15].

Recently, machine learning (ML) based side-channel attacks are proposed, as an extension of template attacks, as they provide more accurate results for secret information predictions [28,43,44]. Several researchers showed that machine learning and deep learning (DL) techniques, like Convolutional Neural Networks (CNNs), outperform traditional SCAs since they are able to learn from misaligned data and, therefore, eliminate the need of pre-processing [13,38].

While CNNs can improve the performance of the attacks, various factors can affect the accuracy of the classification using DL algorithms. Firstly, a huge amount of leakage traces (samples/instances) are required for training such a model. Secondly, the traces are collected using high sampling rate to capture the minor details in the leakage, which results in high-dimensional noisy data traces that might contain redundant features. Research so far was focused on reducing the number of traces required to retrieve the secret information while applying ML to SCA. However, the optimal number of samples required to achieve desired accuracy, known as sample complexity, grows rapidly (exponentially in some scenarios) with the high number of noisy instances containing irrelevant features [41]. Extracting a small subset of features, can indeed reduce the sample size required to achieve a good problem generalization with the particular ML algorithm. Picek et al. [50] evaluated the impact of various feature engineering techniques on the profiled SCA on AES. Mukhtar et al. [47] presented side-channel leakage evaluation on protected and unprotected ECC Always-double-and-add algorithm using ML classifiers and proposed to use signal properties as features. Zaid et al. [56] showed the insights for the selection of features while building an efficient CNN architecture for SCAs.

There is a considerable amount of research focusing on ML and DL SCAs for symmetric-key algorithms. The recent work of Masure et al. [46] deals with the soundness and effectiveness of classical SCA countermeasures in symmetric algorithms and presents the work in this field in a complete way. However, only few researchers have tumbled with the increased complexity and high number of samples in traces derived from implementations of public-key cryptosystems. Only recently, researchers have turned their interest to public-key cryptography ML/DL SCAs [14,38,55]. The few ML/DL based evaluation analyses that exist for public-key cryptography, do not yet consider the evaluation of cryptosystems under the presence of strong SCA countermeasures.

Elliptic curve cryptographic primitives have been widely studied for the efficiency and SCA resistance. Therefore, many performance enhancement techniques and SCA countermeasures have been devised. Among them, several researchers have proposed using Residue Number System (RNS) arithmetic representation as a way to boost the scalar multiplication computation [32,45] by transforming all parameters to the RNS domain before performing all finite field operations [7]. In addition, RNS can be used for producing strong SCA countermeasures that can withstand simple and advanced SCAs [7] using the Leak Resistant Arithmetic (LRA) technique. Recently, a comprehensive study on RNS ECC implementations for Edwards Curves [48], using the Test Vector Leakage Assessment (TVLA) techniques [30], showed that the combination of traditional SCA countermeasures like Base Point randomization, scalar randomization etc. when combined with LRA-based RNS countermeasures can considerably reduce information leakage. It was shown that profiled template attacks on RNS SCA protected implementation is partially successful, implying that more powerful attacks might be able to compromise the RNS SCA countermeasures [25,48].

All the above issues highlight the need for a methodology to analyze ECC implementation datasets for ML-based profiling SCAs with dedicated countermeasures. In this paper, a concrete methodology for ML SCA resistance of RNS-based ECC cryptosystems is proposed, realized in practise and analyzed in depth using various ML model algorithms and feature engineering techniques. This study could serve as a guideline for RNS-based RSA implementations as well. The methodology is able to retrieve attack vulnerabilities against noisy RNS-based implementations that include RNS and traditional SCA countermeasures. More specifically, the contributions of this work are listed below.

- A six stage methodology for launching a practical ML-based side-channel attack is proposed. Our analysis is based on assessing the SCA resistance of an RNS-based ECC implementation with and without countermeasures. For the first time in research literature, the effectiveness of a combination of RNS and traditional SCA countermeasures on an RNS ECC implementation against ML-based side-channel attacks is presented.
- ML-based side-channel attacks are presented for location and data dependent leakage models using four ML classifiers. We used Support Vector Machine (SVM), Random Forest (RF), Multi-Layer Perceptron (MLP) and Convolutional Neural Networks (CNN) to create the training leakage model. For each classifier, hyperparameter tuning has been performed to extract the best-trained model for the underlying problem. Results are presented using standard ML evaluation metrics. The implications of relying on the classification accuracy alone, in case of imbalance data, are also discussed.
- Various state-of-the-art hybrid feature engineering techniques are tested on side-channel leakage traces from RNS-based ECC implementations. Three hybrid feature engineering approaches are proposed, in order to handle the complexity of public-key cryptographic trace. A comparative analysis is performed to show the performance improvement of the proposed hybrid method as compared to the filter, wrapper and dimensionality reduction methods.
- An RNS-based ECC implementation is one challenging dataset, due to the RNS operation intrinsic parallelism. For RNS-based implementations, existing traditional template attacks are successful only if the aligned portion of the traces is used for the attack. This limitation makes the attack complicated

to launch. We perform a quantitative analysis of the success of the ML-based attack when using the full trace length for training the model.

The rest of the paper is organized as follows. Section 2 presents the classifiers used for evaluation along with the algorithm under attack. Section 3 explains the attack methodology along with other evaluation strategies and datasets used for evaluation. Section 4 presents the results on RNS-based ECC leakage datasets. Section 5 concludes the paper.

2 Preliminaries and Related Literature

2.1 RNS as Side-Channel Attack Countermeasure

The Residue Number System (RNS) is a non-positional arithmetic representation, where a number X is represented by a set of individual n moduli x_i ($X \rightarrow^{RNS} X : (x_1, x_2, ...x_n)$) of a given RNS basis $\mathcal{B} : (m_1, m_2, ...m_n)$ as long as $0 \leq x < M$, where $M = \prod_{i=1}^{n} m_i$ is the RNS dynamic range and all m_i are pair-wise relatively prime. Each x_i can be derived from x by calculating $x_i = \langle x \rangle_{m_i} = x \pmod{m_i}$. Since it can effectively represent elements of cyclic groups or finite fields there is a merit in adopting it in elliptic curve finite field operations. RNS hardware implementations of Montgomery multiplication for elliptic curves cryptography [5] and RSA [18] showed that it can improve the performance of scalar multiplication, mainly due to parallelism. Furthermore, RNS can be used to design SCA countermeasure as is observed in several research papers [6,7,23,24,32]. RNS parallel processing of finite field operations apart from speed offers also different representation of the elliptic curve points, which may reduce SCA leakage. Also, a single bit change in an RNS number's moduli can lead to considerable changes in the binary representation of finite field element, which intrinsically increases noise in the computational process [45]. The Leak Resistant Arithmetic [7] has been applied to modular exponentiation designs and can be extended in RNS-EC scalar multiplication in two ways, either by choosing a new base permutation once at the beginning of each scalar multiplication or by performing a random base permutation once in each scalar multiplication round [24]. In this paper, the latter is adopted.

The ECC scalar multiplication algorithm evaluated is based on a variation of Montgomery Power Ladder (MPL) for Elliptic Curves on $GF(p)$ [37]. Algorithm 1 uses the LRA technique by choosing a random base γ_i permutation and transforming all $GF(p)$ elements in this permutation in each MPL round i. After the end of the round the algorithm chooses a different base point permutation for the next round. This RNS SCA countermeasure is enhanced with the base point V randomization technique using an initial random point R [25]. All $GF(p)$ multiplications used in EC point addition and doubling are done using the RNS Montgomery multiplication [7]. Apart from the above countermeasures as proposed in [48], an RNS operation random sequence approach is followed.

In order to evaluate the potential of the above countermeasures, four variants of the algorithm were implemented, with different countermeasures activated each time.

Algorithm 1: LRA SCA-FA Blinded MPL [22]

Input: V, $R \in E(GF(p))$, $e = (e_{t-1}, e_{t-2}, ...e_0)$
Output: $e \cdot V$ or random value (in case of faults)

Choose random initial base permutation γ_t. ;
Generate random r integer and randomize scalar $s = [e + r\#E]$;
Transform V, R to RNS format using γ_t permutation;
$R_0 = R$, $R_1 = R + V$, $R_2 = -R$;
Convert R_0,R_1,R_2 *to Montgomery format*
for $i = t - 1$ **down to** 0 **do**
    $R_2 = 2R_2$, performed in permutation γ_t ;
    Choose a random base permutation γ_i;
    Random Base Permutation Transformation from γ_{i+1} to γ_i for R_0 and R_1 ;
    $b = \hat{s_i}$ (where the hat symbol is logical inverse);
    $R_b = R_b + R_{s_i}$ and $R_{s_i} = 2R_{s_i}$ in permutation γ_i;
end
Random Base Permutation Transformation from γ_i to γ_t for V;
if *(i, e not modified and* $R_0 + V = R_1$*)* **then**
    Random Base Permutation Transformation from γ_0 to γ_t for R_0;
    return $R_0 + R_2$ *in permutation* γ_t ;
end
else
    return *random value*
end

2.2 Feature Engineering Techniques

Features play a key role in accurate ML analysis. Sample values in a trace T represent the features. Generally, machine learning model can be represented with the Eq. (1), where F represents the feature matrix and w represents the weights learnt during learning steps that are used for predicting the class on unseen values.

$$y_i = w_0 + \sum_{j=1}^{F_n} F_{ij} w_j \tag{1}$$

It is evident from previous research that more is not better when it comes to features in the training dataset. The massive dataset containing irrelevant redundant features, probably due to the noise in side channel leakage traces, can confuse the model during the learning process and offer several problems. It can degrade the performance of the resulting ML model as the model learns from real and noisy data. It can elevate the sample complexity problem and computational processing requirement by increasing the requirement of sample size to achieve the desired accuracy for a particular cryptographic algorithm under attack. Finally, it can introduce over-fitting leading to poor generalization and inaccurate analysis. Feature engineering techniques can play a distinct role in eliminating the irrelevant unnecessary features from the cryptographic dataset

[11]. In this paper, our goal is to reduce the large number of irrelevant features and create an efficient, effective and accurate ML model for RNS ECC data. In all cases, number of features F_m are selected/extracted from a pool of features F_n, where inequality $F_m < F_n$ holds. The focus of this study is to utilize existing feature engineering techniques and propose an efficient hybrid feature engineering scheme (Sect. 3.4). The effect of dimensionality reduction and other feature selection techniques has not been analyzed on RNS-based ECC implementation datasets before.

Feature Extraction. As mentioned before, side channel dataset consists of high-dimensional data due to high sampling rate. In the classical side channel analysis, Principal Component Analysis (PCA) and Linear Discriminant Analysis (LDA) are used to reduce the data dimensionality [4,8,26,29]. In ML context, these techniques are grouped and named as feature extraction techniques. A new feature subset is formed by reducing the dimensionality of the existing feature dataset. Based on the transformation method being used, feature extraction can be further categorized into linear transformation and nonlinear transformation.

- Principal Component Analysis is a statistical procedure for data dimensionality reduction using orthogonal transformation, while retaining the maximum variance and internal structure of the sample [36]. However, since PCA does not involve sample classes, the subspace vectors in low dimensional space might not be optimal. Technically, new variables are formed in a subspace, known as principal components (PCs), which are uncorrelated to each other and contain the maximum useful information about the underlying dataset.
- LDA is a supervised learning dimensionality reduction technique, in which distance between mean of each class is maximized by projecting the input data to a linear subspace [9,54]. This helps in reducing the overlap between the target classes by minimizing the intra-class variance.

Feature Selection. In the feature selection techniques, a new feature dataset is formed by selecting the most contributing relevant features from the existing features dataset. They are split into three main categories: filter, wrapper and embedded methods. Generally, in all selection methods an empty subset is selected and then features that are not used before are added one-by-one from the pool of the existing features. In filter methods, intrinsic properties of the features are selected, based on the relevance between the features and the target class, using uni-variate statistical analysis [35]. In wrapper methods, each subset of features is used to train the model using a classifier algorithm and is cross-validated to check the performance. Optimal features are selected based on the algorithm performance by iteratively using a search algorithm [40]. Due to the k-fold cross-validation and huge learning steps, wrapper methods are more computationally expensive as compared to filter methods and take longer to select the feature from multi-dimensional data. In the proposed hybrid method, the characteristics of both filter and wrapper methods are combined.

In this study, the following filter and wrapper methods are used for analysis.

- *Chi-Square Test* (Chi2) measures the deviation between the expected and observed value of the feature and response key class. Based on this value, it is decided if the feature is dependent on the response key class.
- *Pearson's Correlation Coefficient* (PCorr) measures the degree of association between the features or between features and the response class. It returns a co-variance matrix, which holds correlation values. Correlation measures help in finding the classifier to be used, for example, for non-linear correlations, algorithms like SVM, and RF would be the best choice.
- *Ftest* measures the significance of each feature in the dataset with the help of hypothesis testing. Two models X and Y are created. Model X is created with a constant only, and model Y with a constant and a feature. The least-square errors of both models are calculated and compared. The difference between model errors helps in deciding if the feature is significant or not. Ftest shows poor performance for non-linear relationships.
- *Mutual Information* (MI) measures the dependence of features on the response class. If the feature and the response class are independent, then MI will be 0. If the response class is a deterministic function of features, then response class can be determined from the feature function, with MI $=$ 1. MI works well for non-linear relationships.
- *T-test* is a correlation test that measures the statistical significance between the features and the target class. It is used in side-channel analysis to evaluate if two sets of measured data are significantly different.
- *Recursive Feature Elimination* (RFE-RF) - This method follows backward brute force approach for feature selection. A model is created on an entire feature dataset and an importance score is calculated for each feature predictor. Feature predictors are ranked based on their score and least important predictors are removed. The model is re-built and procedure is repeated again for the desired number of cycles. It is seen that random forest works best in combination with recursive feature elimination [53].
- *Sequential Feature Selection* using Random Forest (RF-Imp) is a wrapper method, where a subset from the features set is selected and evaluated using the chosen algorithm. Step forward approach is followed in which empty pool is filled with best performing features one-by-one. For evaluation, k-fold validation is used. Random forest is selected as an induction algorithm, because of its easy interpretability, low over-fitting and better predictive performance.

3 Machine Learning Based Evaluation Methodology for ECC RNS Scalar Multiplication

The need for a tailored methodology to access RNS-ECC SM implementation stems from the unique characteristics of the algorithm under attack combined with the fact that ML models are adapted to the problem at hand. An overview of the complete methodology is given in Fig. 1 and is split into six distinct stages.

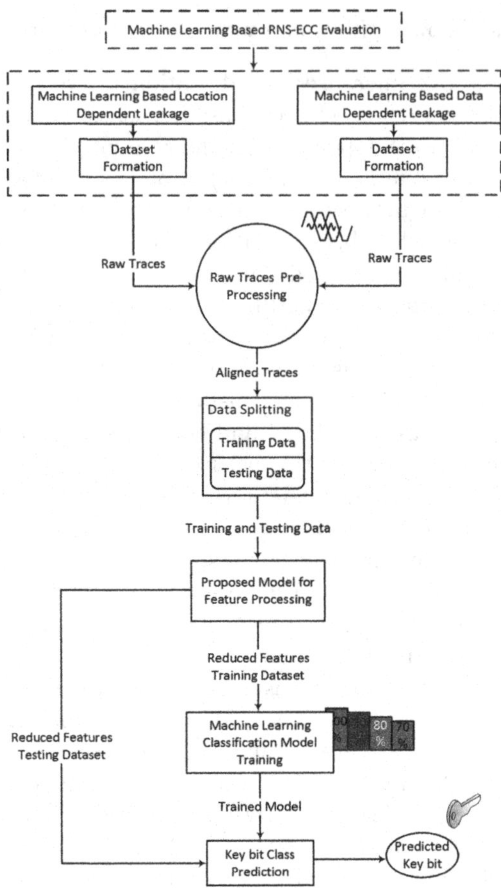

Fig. 1. Machine learning based evaluation methodology for RNS-ECC

3.1 Attack Scenario Specification

At first, the possible targets on the RNS-ECC SM algorithm are identified. More specifically, the most evident information leakage can be observed from the difference on the scalar bit when the registers R_0 or R_1 are updated. We note here that the RNS structure of the numbers makes the EM variations due to memory storage more complex, since the point coordinates are no longer single numbers handled by a big number software library (that may lead to R_0 or R_1 storage in contiguous memory blocks) but, small numbers that may be stored independently in memory for each moduli. Following the approach, carried in [48], two attack scenarios can be identified for ML SCAs: data-dependent attacks and location-dependent attacks.

In **ML-based data-dependent leakage attacks** ($MLDA$), the adversary can monitor the EM fluctuations due to the processing of a different value of the ith scalar bit e_i. This is reflected in processor instructions corresponding to line 10 of the ECC scalar multiplication algorithm (Algorithm 1), where the operations depend on the value of secret key bit e_i resulting in registers R_0 and R_1 updated differently depending on the value b. R_0 contains the addition result and R_1 contains the doubling result if the scalar secret key bit e_i = 1 and in reverse order if $e_i = 0$ (R_1: addition, R_0: doubling). Such data leakages should also be observable using protected scalar bit countermeasures if the scalar bits under attack are retrieved from a memory location in a clear view. We collected leakage traces of the first few rounds for a $233 - bit$ scalar. Data leakage LD is labeled as '1' if the scalar e_i = '1' and is labeled '0' otherwise. Only the instructions corresponding to step 10 of Algorithm 1 were observed and 50k traces, each of 700 samples, were collected; out of which around 3k–7k were utilized after alignment in the other stages of the proposed methodology.

In **ML-based Location-dependent leakage Attacks** ($MLLA$), it is assumed that key-dependent storage gives distinguishable leakage for a particular operation. In each round of Algorithm 1 only two operations have key-dependent instructions, addition and doubling. Both operations are performed in the same order, irrespective of the value of the scalar key bit e_i. However, the storage content differs according to the scalar bit value. The register R_0 is doubled when the scalar key bit is '0', otherwise R_1 is doubled. Since there is no memory address randomization, we can exploit this vulnerability by collecting leakage data for the doubling operation.Note that RNS base permutation described in Algorithm 1 can have an important role in the resistance against such an exploitation.The data will be labeled and classified by monitoring where the content of the doubling operation is accessed from in memory. Such memory access leakage has also been exploited for RNS-based RSA in [31]. Papachristodoulou et al. in [48] exploited a similar vulnerability for ECC SM by utilizing a small sample window of 451 samples (out of 3k samples per trace) for training and classification for template SCAs. Identifying the specific samples for training purposes requires more in-depth knowledge of the underlying system and requires a lot of signal processing, which might be discouraging for the attacker. Andrikos et al. performed location-based attacks using machine/deep learning, but those were focused on accessing different SRAM locations and are not algorithm-specific [3]. In our work, we used the ML approach to classify the scalar key bit e_i, exploiting the doubling operation leakage, by using the whole trace rather than the small sample portion of 451 samples. We achieved similar results, which proves that the ML attack is realistic and practical from an attacker point of view. For the location-based analysis, we labeled leakage data LD as '0' if R_0 is doubled and labeled LD as '1' if R_1 is doubled. We collected 50k traces (each of 3k samples long), out of which 14k traces are used after stage 2 (preprocessing) of the proposed methodology.

For a detailed evaluation of RNS-ECC SM against the above two ML-based attack scenarios, all potential countermeasures should be evaluated using the proposed methodology. To achieve that, two implementation variants of Algorithm 1 SM can be identified for each scenario, one with all SCA countermeasures enabled (protected version) and one with all SCA countermeasures disabled (unprotected version). In line with the above rationale, for the evaluation of Algorithm 1 the trace datasets of Table 1 can be identified, denoted and collected.

Table 1. Trace dataset categories

Name	Countermeasures	Notation
Protected data dependent leakages	RNS LRA technique, base point randomization, scalar randomization countermeasure and random RNS operation sequence	DD_P
Unprotected data dependent leakages	No countermeasure	DD_{UP}
Protected location dependent Leakages	RNS LRA technique, base point randomization, scalar randomization countermeasure and random RNS operation sequence	DL_P
Unprotec. Location dependent leakages	No countermeasure	DL_{UP}

3.2 Raw Trace Preprocessing

The fact that Algorithm 1 has several powerful SCA countermeasures and that software implementations lead to noisy and misaligned traces, highlight the need for trace preprocessing. In raw leakage samples each data point is treated as a feature and the feature columns are used to train the model. Having misaligned features might scatter the useful feature information all across the columns, hence making it difficult for the ML classifier to learn from the scattered data. Misalignment is related to the relative time of execution of specific operations with respect to the reference point (i.e., trigger). This is affected by the clock jitter and non-constant time execution of some operations or countermeasures. In some cases, noise is intentionally induced to the system as a countermeasure to increase side-channel attack resistance. Common signal processing techniques can be used in order to reduce the noise like low pass or band pass filter. The dominant frequencies in our traces are measured using Fast Fourier Transform (FFT), as shown in the Fig. 2, and it is observed that the maximum energy lies between 0–300 MHz, with the highest frequency at 1 GHz. Based on this observation, a low-pass filter is applied and the resulting clear patterns are used for alignment.

For a good performing trained model, it is imperative to have a balanced dataset. Skewed or imbalanced dataset is the one in which the traces for one class label are more than the other. The trained model will be biased due to the dominating class and will not be able to classify the unseen data accurately. To emulate the problem of imbalance for the RNS-ECC SM assessment, after alignment of the traces, we got both balanced and unbalanced dataset outcomes. Datasets DD_P, DD_{UP} and DL_P were almost balanced, having approximately 1050, 1500, and 3800 traces (for both 1's and 0's), respectively. These three

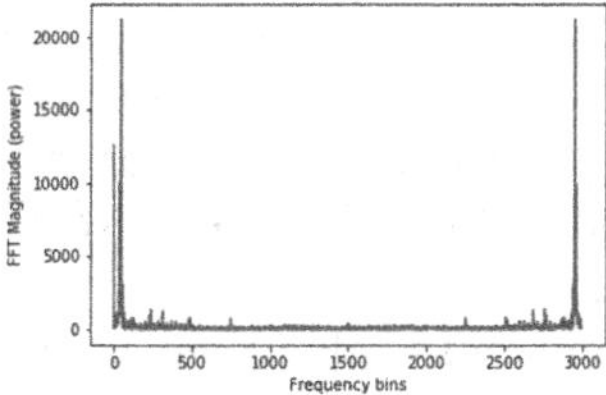

Fig. 2. Fast Fourier (FFT) of the leakage samples

datasets had ideal balanced data for modeling. However, dataset DL_{UP} traces were highly skewed. i.e. the number of traces for class key bit '0' was higher compared to class key bit '1' (10150 and 42 traces respectively)[1]. To handle the skewness and minimize its impact, Synthetic Minority Oversampling Technique (SMOTE) was used as it outperformed for other cryptographic datasets [51]. SMOTE synthesizes new instances for the minority class traces and balances the data [16].

3.3 Data Splitting

At this stage, the preprocessed raw data are split into separate training and testing datasets. Similar to template attacks, in ML SCAs the leakage data set LD is divided into the training dataset, D_{Train}, which is used to train the ML model and the test D_{Test} dataset. An extra dataset is introduced in ML analysis known as Validation D_{Val} dataset. At this stage of the methodology, the dataset splitting and its role is analyzed below:

- D_{Train} dataset is used during the model fitting process and helps model learn the patterns from data.
- During the evaluation, D_{Val} is used to fine-tune the model using model hyperparameters. The model never directly learns from the validation data, but it can occasionally see the data during the learning process. Hence it provides biased evaluation and changes the model structure based on the validation data results.
- D_{Test} dataset is completely unknown to the system and is never used in the training process. D_{Test} provides an unbiased evaluation of the model.

One important aspect in ML is to decide the dividing ratio of the training, validation, and testing sets. The bigger the dataset, the better the trained model. In side-channel analysis, the available leakage traces (instances) might be limited. Splitting data with 50-50 ratio produces a very small training dataset.

[1] We note here that the unbalanced dataset was not created on purpose, it was caused due to signal processing applied on the traces. The unbalanced dataset reflects real-life situations, and by using SMOTE we show that it is possible to get valid conclusions. Therefore, our methodology is validated even when there are unbalanced datasets.

Insufficient training datasets result in under-fitted model. A trade-off value is required to train and test the model. To evaluate the effect of data division on secret information recovery, we test three ratios for training and testing datasets, namely 90-10%, 80-20%, and 50-50%. Datasets are shuffled before splitting for spreading the instances in the space.

We suggest the use of k-fold cross-validation, which is a resampling procedure used for evaluation of ML trained model. After the initial dataset split into two sets, the training dataset is further split using k-fold validation scheme into training and validation. In this validation procedure, data samples are split into k-groups. One group is a holdout or validation dataset and rest of the data is used for training the model. Model is fitted on the training group set and evaluated on the holdout/validation set. This ensures that the whole dataset undergoes a proper validation process. For the k-fold validation, 5 and 10 folds are the most recommended values as they neither give high variance nor high bias in the resulting error estimate [34]. However, high number of validation folds lead to increased training time. This processing time can be reduced by using an optimal number of folds, yet still achieving a reliable trained model.

3.4 Feature Selection and Processing

At this stage, appropriate feature engineering techniques and feature processing combination models are proposed, in order to choose the optimal features for ML model training. Redundant features can lead to over-fitting and curse of dimensionality, which ultimately results in an inaccurate model. We propose an approach to deduce the impact of feature selection/extraction techniques (Sect. 2.2) on ML classification of RNS-based ECC dataset. Our hybrid approach combines the characteristics of two or more feature extraction/selection techniques to improve the learning performance and efficiency. To provide a comparison with the application of the classical feature techniques only (which is not tested for RNS-ECC dataset before), we have explicitly split the analysis into three sections as explained below.

- **Approach A:** In the first approach, features dataset is processed using the feature selection and extraction methods as explained in Sect. 2.2, that is, Ftest, T-test, Chi2, MI, P_Corr, PCA, LDA, RFE-RF, and RF-Imp. There are total F_n features for location-dependent leakages ($MLLA$) and data-dependent leakages ($MLDA$). Out of F_n, F_m features are selected. The selected output features are directly given as input to the ML models for training.
- **Approach B:** In the second approach, features datasets are processed (Tier 1) using filter methods (Ftest, T-Test, Chi2, MI, P_Corr), and the output features are further reduced (Tier 2) using PCA and LDA dimensionality reduction techniques. For Tier 1 feature selection, F_m features are selected from F_n pool of features, for both $MLLA$ and $MLDA$. However, for Tier 2, F_o PCA components (features) are selected from F_m features dataset. For binary classification, LDA projects F_m features onto one dimension.

- **Approach C**: In the third approach, in Tier 1 features F_n are ranked according to the relevance, resulting in a subset of features consisting of F_m features. In Tier 2 processing, features are further selected based on the classifier algorithm performance using RFE-RF and RF-Imp, and are reduced to feature subset consisting of F_o, for both $MLLA$ and $MLDA$. The RFE-RF and RF-Imp methods recursively eliminate the redundant features which do not contribute towards classification.

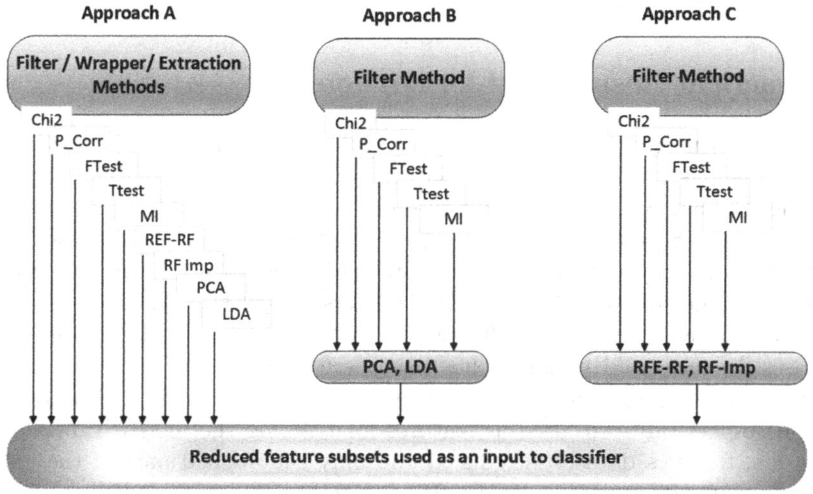

Fig. 3. Hybrid feature engineering approaches

Our proposed approaches help in tackling the drawbacks of filter and wrapper methods. In filter methods, the target response class is not involved in the selection process. To involve the target class, the relevant uncorrelated features are selected using filter methods and are further reduced by recursively searching through the feature pool or by using dimensionality reduction. Moreover, directly applying the wrapper methods or the dimensionality reduction techniques is computationally expensive due to the huge number of features in the dataset. This approach helps in eliminating the least correlated redundant feature, thus reduces the time required for processing, whereas preserves the overall useful information in the leakage dataset. The graphical description of the proposed approaches is presented in Fig. 3.

3.5 ML Classification Model Training

At this stage, the ML classifier models are trained using an optimal set of parameters selected from the hybrid feature extraction process to achieve the best performance. The ML algorithms, described in Sect. 5, are used to evaluate the effectiveness of the location-dependent and data-dependent attacks. For the systematic evaluation of RNS-ECC SM, the hyperparameters are tuned using gridsearch to obtain the best possible trained model. For the interested reader, the exact values are shown in Table 2 in Appendix.

3.6 Key Prediction

The final stage of the methodology is devoted to the usage of the ML-trained models on the testing dataset, in order to evaluate the SCA resistance of the RNS ECC SM implementation against ML profiling attacks. This stage is thoroughly analyzed in the next section.

4 Practical Results and Discussion

Here we present the results starting with our setup in Sect. 4.1. Section 4.2 presents the classifier's performance on raw features, without applying any feature engineering, Sect. 4.3 presents results after applying feature engineering techniques, and Sect. 4.4 exhibits comparison results for Sect. 3.4 approach A, B and C. For the sets of experiments conducted in Sect. 4.2–4.4, the models are trained with the raw traces using four classifiers, for all four datasets.

For comparative analysis with existing studies, analysis is divided into two sub-cases. In case a, ML analysis has been performed on the full length traces that is, all the trace samples (trace length 0–699 and 0–2999 for $MLDA$ and $MLLA$, respectively) are used as features for training the model. However, in the case b, features dataset is reduced and only the aligned part of the traces (precisely, 550–900 for DD_P, 1150–1950 for DD_{UP}, 80–250 for DL_P, 190–250 for DL_{UP},) is used for training the models.

4.1 Trace Collection and Experimental Setup

All datasets of traces for our analysis are collected by executing Algorithm 1 on a BeagleBone Black with an ARM Cortex A8 processor operating at 1 GHz. Samples were collected using EMV Langer probe LF B-1, H Field (100 KHz–50 MHz), and Lecroy Waverunner 8404M-MS with 2.5 GS/s sampling rate. The RNS-ECC SM implementation was taken from a public repository [22] and was customized according to the requirements for data collection and attack scenarios. For data collection and formatting, Matlab R2019 and Riscure Inspector 4.12 was used [1]. For ML analysis, a Python environment with Keras and Scikit learn libraries has been used [17]. All features selection/extraction methods have been taken from Scikit learn [49] except T-test which was implemented in-house.

To meet computation extensive needs of ML algorithms, NCI (National Computational Infrastructure) Australia high-performance supercomputing server has been used [2].

4.2 Classifier's Performance on Raw Features

Figure 4a and b show the accuracy of the trained classifiers for the case a and case b, respectively. The plotted accuracy is achieved by tuning the hyperparameters for each classifier. The hyperparameters which are tuned and the best selected parameters are given in the Table 2 and Table 3. Both tables are given in the Appendix for the purpose of reproduction of the results. It can be observed that for location-dependent attacks ($MLLA$) in case a, the secret can be recovered with 94–100% accuracy for the protected and unprotected implementations. However, for data-dependent attacks ($MLDA$), the best accuracy achieved is only 54% with RF. In some cases, imbalanced datasets are created and SMOTE is applied before applying ML classifiers. In addition to accuracy, recall, precision, and F1 score has been closely monitored as well, which is less than 0.5 in case of CNN, but greater than 0.9 for other classifiers.

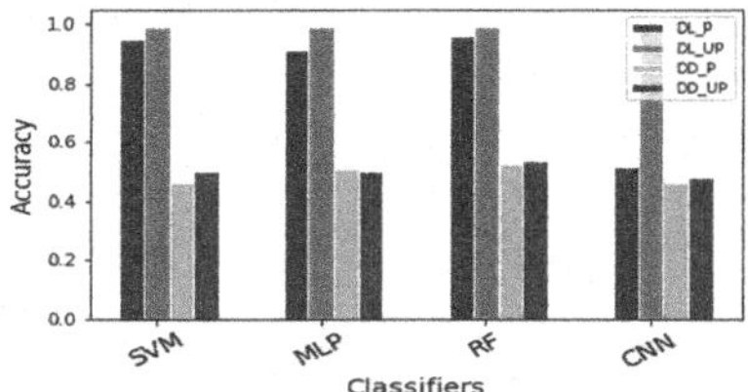

(a) Trace Dataset with all samples

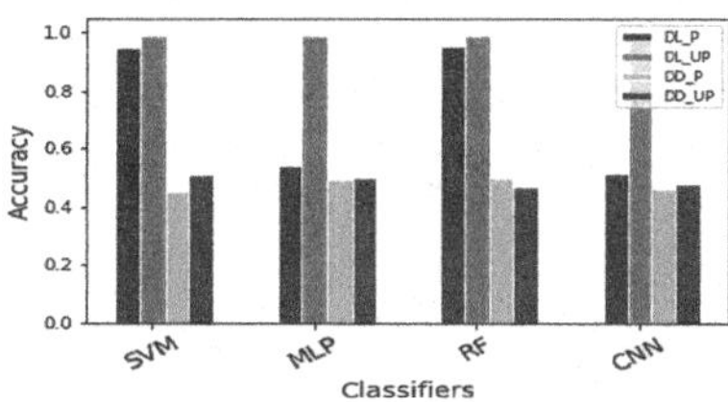

(b) Traces with aligned reduced samples

Fig. 4. Accuracy of classifiers without feature processing

It has also been observed that the complex deep learning model (CNN) did not perform well for all the datasets, which was the expectation because of the small number of traces and the large number of irrelevant features. It is expected that with a huge dataset, the performance, using complex networks like CNN might improve, but the collection of the huge dataset and high computational cost, might be highly discouraging for the attacker. Scope of this study is to analyze the affect of limited size datasets with computationally efficient classifiers. An important results is that a simple neural network like MLP gives good accuracy if the complete trace length is used. However, it cannot classify the target key bit with the reduced trace length, see the 53% accuracy for case b. This shows that an amount of useful information is contained in the unaligned portion of the trace as well.

RF, by design, constructs unpruned trees and removes the unnecessary redundant features during the training process, hence produces an efficient model without using any feature engineering technique. In SVM, Radial Bias Function (RBF) kernel transforms the data and creates new features that are separable in high dimensional space. So by design it retains the most contributing features and eliminates unnecessary ones. It appears that the RNS-ECC SM location-based leakage is linearly separable in higher dimension space. However, this is not the case with RNS-ECC SM data-dependent leakages.

To analyze the possibility of under-fitting and over-fitting, training, validation and testing accuracy are closely monitored. For SVM with RBF, it is observed that lower values of parameter 'C' and higher values of parameter 'gamma' provide the best results. The validation curve for gamma parameter tuning is given in Fig. 5. For RF, 50 and 100, trees along with varying tree depth of 5–20 present good results. For MLP, batch size 32, activation function 'relu' and optimizer 'adam' give the best results for $MLLA$ analysis. However, for $MLDA$ analysis, activation function 'tanh' and optimizer 'sgd' and 'adam' provide the best results for protected and unprotected leakage datasets, respectively.

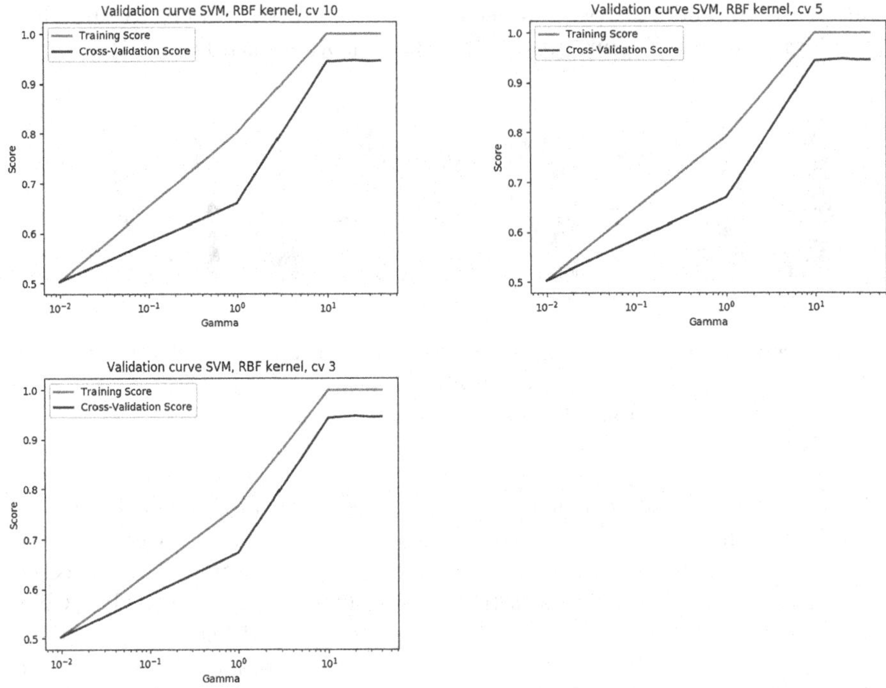

Fig. 5. Gamma parameter tuning

At this stage, a comparison between our work on ML analysis and the work of Papachristodoulou et al. [48] can be made. Steps explained in [21], are followed to estimate the perceived information (PI) of RNS implementation leakages from BeagleBone. As it is common for template attacks, PI utilizes practical leakages to estimate the Probability Density Function (PDF) of Algorithm 1. The leakage model is estimated based on profiling traces and then PI is estimated for the collected test traces. The estimation and assumption errors are calculated to evaluate the attacking model. It is observed that ML performs better than the template profiling attacks on the RNS-ECC SM implementation datasets. The authors of [48] report that the classification success rate for the location-based template attacks is 87–99% for unprotected implementation and for implementations with one countermeasure activated. When a combination of countermeasures is used, then this percentage drops to 70–83%. In our ML analysis the classification accuracy is 95% and 99.5% for protected (DL_P) and unprotected (DL_{UP}) RNS-ECC SM implementations, respectively. In [48], the template attack on RNS-ECC is successful only if the specific sample window from each trace is selected for training. However, in ML-based SCA, the model trained with the complete trace length gives equal or better results. Isolating and selecting the aligned part only for the training phase, might not be an easy task for an attacker thus making the template attack difficult. However, it is more convenient to train with the complete raw trace, which implies that ML attacks are less complex from an attacker perspective.

4.3 Impact of Feature Engineering

In this section, advanced feature engineering techniques based on wrapper and filter methods are applied to analyze the impact of feature reduction on the performance of the trained model. $F_n = 50$ features have been selected from the full length (features $F_m = 3k$ and $F_m = 700$ respectively) and reduced length traces. For T-test, the threshold is set to 0.5 and the resulting 1 299 features are selected for further analysis. Results for SVM trained model on RNS-ECC protected datasets ($MLLA$) are shown in Fig. 6.

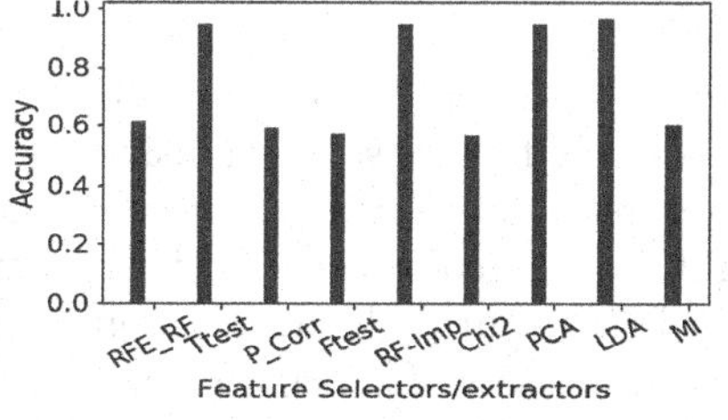

(a) Trace Dataset with all samples

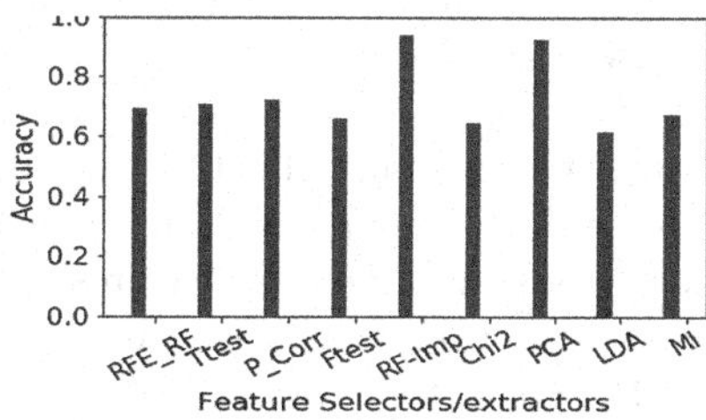

(b) Traces with aligned reduced samples

Fig. 6. $MLLA$ performance comparison using SVM with feature extraction techniques

The purpose of applying feature engineering techniques is to find the optimal numbers of features for the bias-variance trade-off. Variance in ML is the type of error that occurs due to the model's sensitivity to small fluctuations in the training dataset. High variance leads to over-fitting as the model might learn from the noise in the data. Bias, on the other hand, is the type of error that occurs due to erroneous assumptions in the learning algorithm. High bias leads to under-fitting as a model might miss relevant information between features and the target key class. Both errors are inter-linked, minimizing one error will increase the other one. Neural nets (high capacity models) can lead to high variance problems as they might learn from the noise in the data. Regularization, early stopping, and drop-out has been used to avoid the problem in our evaluation. For RF, pruning deals with the above issues, so feature engineering is not required. However, for SVM finding an optimal number of features will improve the model's accuracy.

In the case of RNS-ECC datasets, there is a higher bias than a variance. When PCA is applied, the variance is increased thus bias is reduced, up to a level where the model does not overfit. The suitable variance threshold (with classification accuracy 100%) is achieved when a number of features are selected to be $F_m = 50$ for PCA. For case a, model performance stays same or has improved by using T-test, RF-Imp, PCA and LDA. For case b, improvement is observed for RF-Imp and PCA. However, performance decreases when analysis is performed after reducing features using LDA. LDA uses classifier and fails to extract the relevant features as some of the information, required to identify the relationship between the target class and the feature dataset, is lost while the traces are trimmed during the alignment process.

4.4 Hybrid Feature Selection Techniques

In this section, a comparative analysis is performed, based on the evaluation results of the hybrid approaches of the proposed methodology on $MLLA$, as explained in Sect. 3.4 (approach B and C). For all hybrid methods, feature selection filter methods have been applied to reduce the bias in the input data by selecting the independent $f_n = 300$ features from the complete pool of the features $f_m = 3k$ ($MLLA$) and $f_m = 700$ ($MLDA$) and then only $f_o = 50$ features are selected from the reduced pool of features using extraction techniques, for both case a and case b.

For case a (Fig. 7a), T-test gives best results using approach A and B. Generally, the trend observed is that the combination of feature selection using filter method with the recursive feature elimination, reduces the model accuracy. One of the reasons could be that features are highly correlated with each other rather than with the target class. Approach 2 with PCA returns the accuracy greater than 80%. For F-test, MI, and Chi2, there is an increase of 13–30% in the resultant accuracy using hybrid approach C. For case b, some of hybrid methods have shown improvement in accuracy as compared to the Fig. 7b.

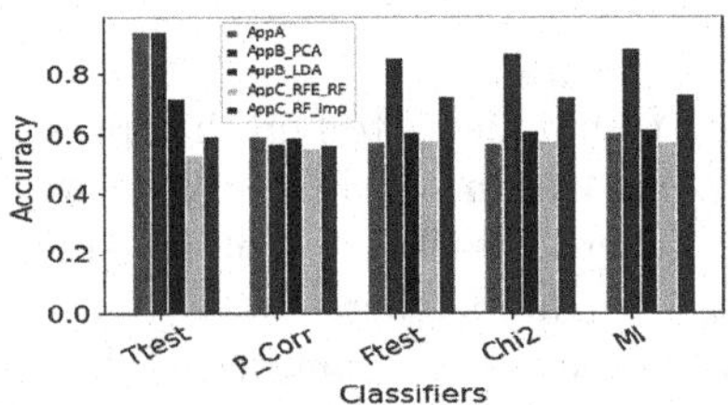

(a) Trace Dataset with all samples

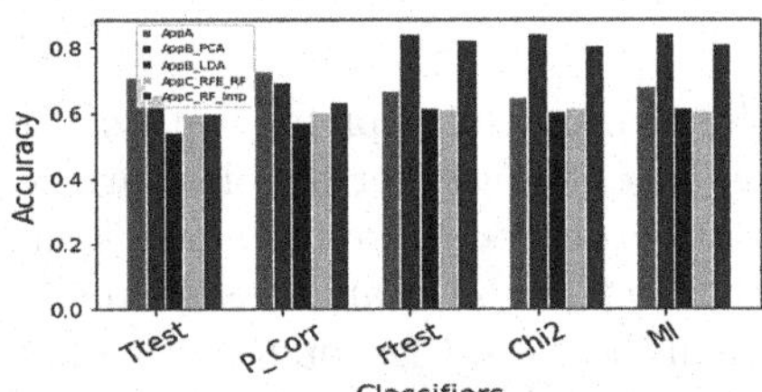

(b) Traces with aligned reduced samples

Fig. 7. Performance comparison of hybrid feature processing approaches

In [10], for symmetric ciphers, 60 000 instances are used, out of which 50 000 are for training and 10 000 are for testing. As expected, the huge set of traces is ideal for training with DL algorithms like CNN. However, the required training time in this case will be substantial too. In this study, we evaluated the effect of having a small number of traces used for key retrieval. We have shown that location dependent attack is successful in recovering the key with a few traces in less time using validation folds as low as 3.

5 Conclusion

In this paper, we presented the evaluation methodology of ML-based side-channel attacks on an elliptic curve RNS-based scalar multiplication implementation with and without countermeasures. Each stage of the methodology was described in detail and supported by practical experiments. A comprehensive analysis of the methodology was also provided for four different phases. A thorough comparison with the state-of-the-art template attacks on RNS-ECC balanced and imbalanced datasets was done. It can be concluded that the ML-based side-channel attacks require less prepossessing and give better performance results for location-based profiling attacks. Hence, leading to a time-efficient and realistic attack scenario. The secret key can be recovered from unprotected and protected RNS ECC SM, using location-based attacks, with 99% and 95% accuracy, respectively. The impact of advance feature engineering techniques has been analyzed using feature extraction and feature selection methods. Moreover, several hybrid approaches were evaluated. It has been observed that PCA, LDA, T-test and RF-based feature selection provides improved accuracy.

Furthermore, we evaluated the effect of training the model with a small dataset, to classify RNS-ECC key bits using ML-based side-channel attacks. Here with *small* dataset we mean in the order of thousands of traces, since for public-key implementations, and for RNS-ECC in particular, we cannot obtain millions of traces due to storage and time limitations. We observed that for location based attacks, SVM and RF can successfully distinguish the scalar key bit with more than 95% accuracy for both full length and reduced length aligned datasets. Trace sample window does not affect the classification results using SVM and RF, due to their inherent characteristics of eliminating redundant features during the training process. However, MLP can distinguish and classify the scalar key bit correctly only if the full-length traces are used. If the reduced aligned traces are used for training an MLP network, then some useful information is lost during the alignment process and the model fails to classify the scalar key bit. This reduces the complexity of the attack and increases the attack success rate in real world scenario. RNS-ECC implementations showed resistance against ML-based data dependent attacks.

To conclude, ML-based side-channel attacks on public key cryptography offer a realistic and viable attack scenario to recover the secret information, as they require less pre-processing compared to template attacks.

Acknowledgments. We would like to thank the COSADE reviewers for their useful comments and feedback. This work is partially supported by international Macquarie University Research Excellence Scholarship. This research received funding from the

Dutch Research Council (NWO) in the framework of the NWA-Cybersecurity Call for the project Physical Attack Resistance of Cryptographic Algorithms and Circuits with Reduced Time to Market (PROACT, project number: NWA.1215.18.014). Also, the work has received funding from the European Union's Horizon 2020 research and innovation programme CPSoSaware under grant agreement No. 871738 and also from the European Union's Horizon 2020 research and innovation programme CONCORDIA under grant agreement No. 830927.

A Appendix

Machine Learning Algorithms

In this paper, four different classifiers are used to create the training model for the leakage information of a device under test. Hereby, each classifier is described in brief and the important parameters for profiling SCAs are specified.

Support Vector Machine (SVM). Support Vector Machines are one of the most popular algorithms used for classification problems in different application domains, including side-channel analysis [19,33,57]. In SVM, n-dimensional data is separated using a hyperplane, by computing and adjusting the coefficients to find the maximum-margin hyperlane, which best separates the target classes. Often, real-world data is very complex and cannot be separated with a linear hyperplane. For learning hyperplanes in complex problems, the training instances or the support vectors are transformed into another dimension using kernels. There are three widely used SVM kernels; linear, radial and polynomial. To tune the kernels, hyperparameters like 'gamma' and cost 'C' play a vital role. Parameter 'C' acts as a regularization parameter in SVM and helps in adjusting the margin distance from the hyperplane. Thus, it controls the cost of misclassification. Parameter 'gamma' controls the spread of the Gaussian curve. Low values of 'C' reflect more variance and lower bias; however, higher values of 'C' show lower variance and higher bias. However, higher gamma leads to better accuracy but results in a biased model. To find an optimum value of 'C' and 'gamma', gridsearch or other optimization methods are applied.

Random Forest (RF). In Random Forest, data is formed by aggregating the collection of decision trees [12]. The results of individual decision trees are combined together to predict the final class value. RF uses unpruned trees, avoids over-fitting by design, and reduces the bias error. Efficient modeling using random forests, highly depends on the *number of trees* in the forest and the *depth* of each tree. These two parameters are tuned for an efficient model in this study.

Multi-layer Perceptron (MLP). Multi-Layer Perceptron is a basic feed-forward artificial neural network that uses back-propagation for learning and consists of three layers: input layer, hidden layer, and a output layer [52]. Input layer connects to the input feature variables and output layers return back the predicted class value. To learn the patterns from the non-linear data, non-linear activation function is used. Due to the non-linear nature of side-channel leakages, MLP appears to be the best choice, in order to recover secret information from learning patterns of the signals.

Convolutional Neural Network (CNN). Convolutional Neural Network is a type of neural network which consists of convolutional layers, activation layers, flatten layer, and pooling layer. Convolutional layer performs convolution on the input features, using filters, to recognize the patterns in the data [42]. The pooling layer is a non-linear layer, and its functionality is to reduce the spatial size and hence the parameters. Fully connected layers combine the features back, just like in MLP. There are certain hyperparameters related to each layer, which can be optimized for an efficient trained model. These parameters include learning rate, batch size, epochs, optimizers, activation functions, etc. In addition to these, there are a few model hyperparameters which can be used to design an efficient architecture. It should be noted that the purpose of this study is not to propose the architecture design of the CNN, but to analyze and test the existing CNN design on the RNS-based ECC dataset. Therefore, the focus is on tuning the optimized hyperparameters rather than modeling hyperparameters.

Hyperparameters Tuning for SVM, RF, MLP, CNN

For the training phase, we tuned the hyperparameters for SVM, RF, MLP and CNN using gridsearch to obtain the best possible model, as shown in Table 2.

Table 2. Parameter tuning for SVM, RF, MLP and CNN

Classifier	Parameter	Value range
SVM	C	[0.1, 0.01, 0.5, 1.0]
	Gamma	[1, 10, 30, 40, 50]
	Kernel	[Poly, Sigmoid, RBF]
MLP	Learning rate	[0.001, 0.0001]
	Solver	[adam, sgd]
	Batch size	[32]
	Activation function	[tanh, relu, identity, logistic]
	Epochs	[200]
RF	Trees depth	[5, 10, 20, 30]
	Number of trees	[10, 50, 100, 200]
CNN	Learning rate	[0.001, 0.01, 0.1, 0.5]
	Epochs	[300]
	Activation function	[relu, selu, elu]
	Optimizer	[Adam, Nadam, RMSprop, Adamax]
	Init mode	[uniform, normal]
	Batch size	[32, 100, 400]

The best parameters are chosen for each classification method and they are shown in Table 3.

Table 3. Best parameters for SVM, RF, MLP and CNN

DataSet	Classifier	Feature No.	Parameters
DL_P	SVM	All	`C: 1.0, gamma: 40, kernel: rbf`
	MLP	All	`activation: relu, batch_size: 32, solver:adam`
	RF	All	`max_depth: 20, n estimators: 100`
	CNN	All	`Act: Relu, Optimizer: Adam, Learning_Rate:0.001`
	SVM	Reduced	`C: 0.1, gamma: 40, kernel: poly`
	MLP	Reduced	`activation: relu, 'batch_size: 32, solver: adam`
	RF	Reduced	`max_depth: 30, n_estimators: 50`
	CNN	Reduced	`Act: Relu, Optimizer: Adam, Learning Rate:0.001`
DL_{UP}	SVM	All	`C: 0.1, gamma: 1, kernel: rbf`
	MLP	All	`activation: relu, batch_size: 32, solver: adam`
	RF	All	`max_depth: 5, n estimators: 50`
	CNN	All	`Act: Relu, Optimizer: Adam, Learning Rate:0.001`
	SVM	Reduced	`C: 0.01, gamma: 10, kernel: poly`
	MLP	Reduced	`activation:relu, batch_size: 32, solver: adam`
	RF	Reduced	`max_depth: 5, n_estimators: 10`
	CNN	Reduced	`Act: Relu, Optimizer: Adam, Learning Rate:0.001`
DD_P	SVM	All	`C: 0.5, gamma: 50, kernel: rbf`
	MLP	All	`activation: logistic, batch_size: 32, solver: sgd`
	RF	All	`max_depth: 20, n estimators: 100`
	CNN	All	`Act: Relu, Optimizer: Adam, Learning_Rate:0.001`
	SVM	Reduced	`C: 0.5, gamma: 10, kernel: rbf`
	MLP	Reduced	`activation: tanh, batch_size: 32, solver: adam`
	RF	Reduced	`max_depth: 20, n_estimators: 10`
	CNN	Reduced	`Act: Relu, Optimizer: Adam, Learning Rate:0.001`
DD_{UP}	SVM	All	`C: 0.5, gamma: 1, kernel: sigmoid`
	MLP	All	`activation: tanh, batch_size: 32, solver: sgd`
	RF	All	`max_depth: 20, n estimators: 100`
	CNN	All	`Act: Relu, Optimizer: Adam, Learning Rate:0.001`
	SVM	Reduced	`C: 0.5, gamma: 1, kernel: rbf`
	MLP	Reduced	`activation: logistic, batch_size: 32, solver: adam`
	RF	Reduced	`max_depth: 10, n_estimators: 10`
	CNN	Reduced	`Act: Relu, Optimizer: Adam, Learning Rate:0.001`

References

1. Inspector SCA tool. https://www.riscure.com/security-tools/inspector-sca. Accessed 08 Feb 2022
2. National Computational Infrastructure Australia. https://nci.org.au/our-services/supercomputing. Accessed 08 Feb 2022
3. Andrikos, C., et al.: Location, location, location: revisiting modeling and exploitation for location-based side channel leakages. In: Galbraith, S.D., Moriai, S. (eds.) ASIACRYPT 2019, Part III. LNCS, vol. 11923, pp. 285–314. Springer, Cham (2019). https://doi.org/10.1007/978-3-030-34618-8_10
4. Archambeau, C., Peeters, E., Standaert, F.-X., Quisquater, J.-J.: Template attacks in principal subspaces. In: Goubin, L., Matsui, M. (eds.) CHES 2006. LNCS, vol. 4249, pp. 1–14. Springer, Heidelberg (2006). https://doi.org/10.1007/11894063_1
5. Bajard, J.-C., Duquesne, S., Meloni, N.: Combining Montgomery Ladder for Elliptic Curves defined over Fp and RNS Representation. In Research Report 06041 (2006)
6. Bajard, J.-C., Eynard, J., Gandino, F.: Fault detection in RNS Montgomery modular multiplication. In: IEEE 21st Symposium on Computer Arithmetic, pp. 119–126. IEEE (2013)
7. Bajard, J.-C., Imbert, L., Liardet, P.-Y., Teglia, Y.: Leak resistant arithmetic. In: Joye, M., Quisquater, J.-J. (eds.) CHES 2004. LNCS, vol. 3156, pp. 62–75. Springer, Heidelberg (2004). https://doi.org/10.1007/978-3-540-28632-5_5
8. Batina, L., Hogenboom, J., van Woudenberg, J.G.J.: Getting more from PCA: first results of using principal component analysis for extensive power analysis. In: Dunkelman, O. (ed.) CT-RSA 2012. LNCS, vol. 7178, pp. 383–397. Springer, Heidelberg (2012). https://doi.org/10.1007/978-3-642-27954-6_24
9. Belhumeur, P., Hespanha, J., Kriegman, D.: Eigenfaces vs. Fisherfaces: recognition using class specific linear projection. IEEE Trans. Pattern Anal. Mach. Intell. **19**, 711–720 (1997)
10. Benadjila, R., Prouff, E., Strullu, R., Cagli, E., Dumas, C.: Deep learning for side-channel analysis and introduction to ASCAD database. J. Cryptogr. Eng. **11**, 163–188 (2019)
11. Blum, A.L., Langley, P.: Selection of relevant features and examples in machine learning. Artif. Intell. **97**(1–2), 245–271 (1997)
12. Breiman, L.: Random forests. Mach. Learn. **45**(1), 5–32 (2001). https://doi.org/10.1023/A:1010933404324
13. Cagli, E., Dumas, C., Prouff, E.: Convolutional neural networks with data augmentation against jitter-based countermeasures. In: Fischer, W., Homma, N. (eds.) CHES 2017. LNCS, vol. 10529, pp. 45–68. Springer, Cham (2017). https://doi.org/10.1007/978-3-319-66787-4_3
14. Carbone, M., et al.: Deep learning to evaluate secure RSA implementations. IACR Trans. Cryptogr. Hardw. Embed. Syst. **2019**(2), 132–161 (2019)
15. Chari, S., Rao, J.R., Rohatgi, P.: Template attacks. In: Kaliski, B.S., Koç, K., Paar, C. (eds.) CHES 2002. LNCS, vol. 2523, pp. 13–28. Springer, Heidelberg (2003). https://doi.org/10.1007/3-540-36400-5_3
16. Chawla, N., Bowyer, R., Hall, L., Kegelmeyer, W.: SMOTE: synthetic minority over-sampling technique. J. Artif. Intell. Res. (JAIR) **16**, 321–357 (2002)
17. Chollet, F.: Keras (2015). https://keras.io
18. Ciet, M., Neve, M., Peeters, E., Quisquater, J.-J.: Parallel FPGA implementation of RSA with residue number systems - Can Side-channel threats be avoided? In Cryptology ePrint Archive, Report 2004/187 (2004)

19. Cortes, C., Vapnik, V.: Support-vector networks. Mach. Learn. **20**(3), 273–297 (1995)
20. De Mulder, E., Örs, S.B., Preneel, B., Verbauwhede, I.: Differential power and electromagnetic attacks on a FPGA implementation of elliptic curve cryptosystems. Comput. Electr. Eng. **33**(5–6), 367–382 (2007)
21. Durvaux, F., Standaert, F.-X., Veyrat-Charvillon, N.: How to certify the leakage of a chip? In: Nguyen, P.Q., Oswald, E. (eds.) EUROCRYPT 2014. LNCS, vol. 8441, pp. 459–476. Springer, Heidelberg (2014). https://doi.org/10.1007/978-3-642-55220-5_26 https://www.iacr.org/archive/eurocrypt2014/84410138/84410138.pdf
22. Apostolos P. Fournaris. RNS_LRA_EC_scalar Multiplier (2018). https://github.com/afournaris/RNS_LRA_EC_Scalar_Multiplier
23. Fournaris, A.P., Klaoudatos, N., Sklavos, N., Koulamas, C.: Fault and power analysis attack resistant RNS based edwards curve point multiplication. In: Proceedings of the 2nd Workshop on Cryptography and Security in Computing Systems, CS2 at HiPEAC 2015, Amsterdam, Netherlands, 19–21 January 2015, pp. 43–46 (2015)
24. Fournaris, A.P., Papachristodoulou, L., Batina, L., Sklavos, N.: Residue number system as a side channel and fault injection attack countermeasure in elliptic curve cryptography. In: 2016 International Conference on Design and Technology of Integrated Systems in Nanoscale Era (DTIS), pp. 1–4 (2016)
25. Fournaris, A.P., Papachristodoulou, L., Sklavos, N.: Secure and efficient RNS software implementation for elliptic curve cryptography. In: 2017 IEEE European Symposium on Security and Privacy Work., pp. 86–93. IEEE (2017)
26. Standaert, F.-X., Archambeau, C.: Using subspace-based template attacks to compare and combine power and electromagnetic information leakages. In: Oswald, E., Rohatgi, P. (eds.) CHES 2008. LNCS, vol. 5154, pp. 411–425. Springer, Heidelberg (2008). https://doi.org/10.1007/978-3-540-85053-3_26
27. Genkin, D., Shamir, A., Tromer, E.: RSA key extraction via low-bandwidth acoustic cryptanalysis. In: Garay, J.A., Gennaro, R. (eds.) CRYPTO 2014. LNCS, vol. 8616, pp. 444–461. Springer, Heidelberg (2014). https://doi.org/10.1007/978-3-662-44371-2_25
28. Gilmore, R., Hanley, N., O'Neill, M.: Neural network based attack on a masked implementation of AES. In 2015 IEEE International Symposium on Hardware Oriented Security and Trust (HOST), pp. 106–11. Institute of Electrical and Electronics Engineers (IEEE) (2015)
29. Golder, A., Das, D., Danial, J., Ghosh, S., Sen, S., Raychowdhury, A.: Practical approaches toward deep-learning-based cross-device power side-channel attack. IEEE Trans. Very Large Scale Integr. (VLSI) Syst. **27**, 2720–2733 (2019)
30. Goodwill, G., Jun, B., Jaffe, J., Rohatgi, P.: A testing methodology for side channel resistance validation. In: NIST Noninvasive Attack Testing Workshop (2011)
31. Perin, G., Imbert, L., Torres, L., Maurine, P.: Attacking randomized exponentiations using unsupervised learning. In: Prouff, E. (ed.) COSADE 2014. LNCS, vol. 8622, pp. 144–160. Springer, Cham (2014). https://doi.org/10.1007/978-3-319-10175-0_11
32. Guillermin, N.: A Coprocessor for Secure and High Speed Modular Arithmetic. IACR Cryptology ePrint Archive (2011)
33. Hospodar, G., Gierlichs, B., De Mulder, E., Verbauwhede, I., Vandewalle, J.: Machine learning in side-channel analysis: a first study. J. Crypt. Eng. **1**(4), 293 (2011)
34. James, G., Witten, D., Hastie, T., Tibshirani, R.: An Introduction to Statistical Learning: With Applications in R, August 2013

35. John, G.H., Kohavi, R., Pfleger, K.: Irrelevant features and the subset selection problem. In: Proceedings of the Eleventh International Conference on International Conference on Machine Learning, ICML 1994, pp. 121–129, San Francisco, CA, USA. Morgan Kaufmann Publishers Inc. (1994)
36. Jolliffe, I.: Principal Component Analysis, pp. 1094–1096. Springer, Heidelberg (2011). https://doi.org/10.1007/978-3-642-04898-2_455
37. Joye, M., Yen, S.-M.: The Montgomery powering ladder. In: Kaliski, B.S., Koç, K., Paar, C. (eds.) CHES 2002. LNCS, vol. 2523, pp. 291–302. Springer, Heidelberg (2003). https://doi.org/10.1007/3-540-36400-5_22
38. Kim, J., Picek, S., Heuser, A., Bhasin, S., Hanjalic, A.: Make some noise. unleashing the power of convolutional neural networks for profiled side-channel analysis. IACR Trans. Crypt. Hardw. Embed. Syst. **2019**(3), 148–179 (2019)
39. Kocher, P., Jaffe, J., Jun, B.: Differential power analysis. In: Wiener, M. (ed.) CRYPTO 1999. LNCS, vol. 1666, pp. 388–397. Springer, Heidelberg (1999). https://doi.org/10.1007/3-540-48405-1_25
40. Kohavi, R., John, G.H.: Wrappers for feature subset selection. Artif. Intell. **97**(1–2), 273–324 (1997)
41. Langley, P., Iba, W.: Average-case analysis of a nearest neighbor algorithm. In: Proceedings of the 13th International Joint Conference on Artificial Intelligence - Volume 2, IJCAI 1993, pp. 889–894, San Francisco, CA, USA (1993). Morgan Kaufmann Publishers Inc
42. LeCun, Y., Haffner, P., Bottou, L., Bengio, Y.: Object recognition with gradient-based learning. In: Shape, Contour and Grouping in Computer Vision. LNCS, vol. 1681, pp. 319–345. Springer, Heidelberg (1999). https://doi.org/10.1007/3-540-46805-6_19
43. Maghrebi, H., Portigliatti, T., Prouff, E.: Breaking cryptographic implementations using deep learning techniques. IACR Cryptology ePrint Archive 2016, p. 921 (2016)
44. Markowitch, O., Lerman, L., Bontempi, G.: Side channel attack: an approach based on machine learning. In: Constructive Side-Channel Analysis and Secure Design, COSADE (2011)
45. Martins, P., Sousa, L.: The role of non-positional arithmetic on efficient emerging cryptographic algorithms. IEEE Access **8**, 59533–59549 (2020)
46. Masure, L., Dumas, C., Prouff, E.: A comprehensive study of deep learning for side-channel analysis. IACR Trans. Crypt. Hardw. Embed. Syst. 348–375 (2020)
47. Mukhtar, N., Mehrabi, A., Kong, Y., Anjum, A.: Machine-learning-based side-channel evaluation of elliptic-curve cryptographic FPGA processor. Appl. Sci. **9**, 64 (2018)
48. Papachristodoulou, L., Fournaris, A.P., Papagiannopoulos, K., Batina, L.: Practical evaluation of protected residue number system scalar multiplication. IACR Trans. Crypt. Hardw. Embed. Syst. **2019**(1), 259–282 (2018)
49. Pedregosa, F., et al.: Scikit-learn: machine learning in Python. J. Mach. Learn. Res. **12**, 2825–2830 (2011)
50. Picek, S., Heuser, A., Jovic, A., Batina, L.: A systematic evaluation of profiling through focused feature selection. IEEE Trans. Very Large Scale Integr. (VLSI) Syst. **27**, 2802–2815 (2019)
51. Picek, S., Heuser, A., Jovic, A., Bhasin, S., Regazzoni, F.: The curse of class imbalance and conflicting metrics with machine learning for side-channel evaluations. IACR Trans. Cryptogr. Hardw. Embed. Syst. **2019**(1), 209–237 (2019)
52. Schmidhuber, J.: Deep learning in neural networks. Neural Netw **61**(C), 85–117 (2015)

53. Svetnik, V., Liaw, A., Tong, C., Christopher Culberson, J., Sheridan, R.P., Feuston, B.P.: Random forest: a classification and regression tool for compound classification and QSAR modeling. J. Chem. Inf. Comput. Sci. **43**(6), 1947–1958 (2003)
54. Swets, D.L., Weng, J.: Using discriminant eigenfeatures for image retrieval. IEEE Trans. Pattern Anal. Mach. Intell. **18**(8), 831–836 (1996)
55. Weissbart, L., Picek, S., Batina, L.: One trace is all it takes: machine learning-based side-channel attack on EdDSA. In: Bhasin, S., Mendelson, A., Nandi, M. (eds.) SPACE 2019. LNCS, vol. 11947, pp. 86–105. Springer, Cham (2019). https://doi.org/10.1007/978-3-030-35869-3_8
56. Zaid, G., Bossuet, L., Habrard, A., Venelli, A.: Methodology for efficient CNN architectures in profiling attacks. IACR Trans. Crypt. Hardw. Embedd. Syst. **2020**(1), 1–36 (2019)
57. Zeng, Z., Gu, D., Liu, J., Guo, Z.: An improved side-channel attack based on support vector machine. In: 2014 Tenth International Conference on Computational Intelligence and Security, pp. 676–680, November 2014

Focus is Key to Success: A Focal Loss Function for Deep Learning-Based Side-Channel Analysis

Maikel Kerkhof[1], Lichao Wu[1], Guilherme Perin[1], and Stjepan Picek[1,2(✉)]

[1] Delft University of Technology, Delft, The Netherlands
stjepan@computer.org

[2] Radboud University, Nijmegen, The Netherlands

Abstract. The deep learning-based side-channel analysis represents one of the most powerful side-channel attack approaches. Thanks to its capability in dealing with raw features and countermeasures, it becomes the de facto standard approach for the SCA community. The recent works significantly improved the deep learning-based attacks from various perspectives, like hyperparameter tuning, design guidelines, or custom neural network architecture elements. Still, insufficient attention has been given to the core of the learning process - the loss function.

This paper analyzes the limitations of the existing loss functions and then proposes a novel side-channel analysis-optimized loss function: Focal Loss Ratio (FLR), to cope with the identified drawbacks observed in other loss functions. To validate our design, we 1) conduct a thorough experimental study considering various scenarios (datasets, leakage models, neural network architectures) and 2) compare with other loss functions used in the deep learning-based side-channel analysis (both "traditional" ones and those designed for side-channel analysis). Our results show that FLR loss outperforms other loss functions in various conditions while not having computational overhead like some recent loss function proposals.

Keywords: Deep learning · Focal loss · Loss function · Side-channel analysis

1 Introduction

Side-channel analysis (SCA) is one of the most popular tools to exploit the implementation weaknesses of an algorithm [11]. Commonly, SCA attacks can be divided into two categories: direct attacks and profiling attacks. The first attack method analyzes the leakages from the target device directly, while the second one requires a copy of the target device. There, an attacker would first learn the characteristic of the copied device (profiling phase) and then launch an attack on the target device (attack phase).

With stronger attack assumptions, profiling attacks are considered more powerful than their counterpart. In recent years, the rise of deep learning further

J. Balasch and C. O'Flynn (Eds.): COSADE 2022, LNCS 13211, pp. 29–48, 2022.
https://doi.org/10.1007/978-3-030-99766-3_2

increased the profiling attacks' capability. Specifically, such attacks can break targets protected with countermeasures by relaxing the assumptions of knowledge from target implementations [7,25,29]. Moreover, compared with the conventional profiling attack (i.e., template attack [22]) that relies upon points of interest selection, deep learning-based SCA has softer restrictions on data preprocessing/feature engineering.

Deep learning-based SCA still requires a significant effort to reach its full potential. There are many open questions when applying such attacks, such as network architecture design [18,24,29], evaluation metric design [30], as well as the interpretability and explainability of models [26]. Unfortunately, those issues represent only a part of the problem. A perspective that cannot be neglected is that classical machine learning metrics/loss functions do not necessarily give an accurate representation of the performance of an SCA model [16,30]. On the other hand, launching practical attacks and averaging the key rank to estimate the guessing entropy is computationally costly (especially if also done during the training phase, see, e.g., [14,19]). Consequently, the SCA community put a significant attention on developing SCA-specific metrics and loss functions, such as Cross-Entropy Ratio loss (CER) [30] and ranking loss (RKL) [28].

The CER loss is one of the recently developed methods to improve the performance of deep learning models in the SCA domain. When comparing the CER loss and the conventional categorical cross-entropy (CCE) loss, the CER loss introduces a denominator to the CCE loss that calculates the correlation between multiple traces and incorrect labels so that the difference between the target cluster and other clusters can be maximized. Similar implementations are proved to be efficient in the machine learning domain as well [31]. However, CER loss has two limitations. The CER's denominator calculation can be a challenging task since even for the traces that belong to the same cluster, the classification difficulties of each trace can be different. The easily classified traces can significantly increase the denominator's value for CER loss, thus reducing the overall loss. From a higher level, when performing the classification tasks, learning from easy samples is not helpful but could easily trigger model overfitting. The hard samples, on the contrary, help the classifiers learn the underlying data's properties, thus could lead to better classification performance.

Returning to the CER loss, although one can include more traces to increase the possibility of picking up hard samples 1) since the samples are randomly selected, the samples' difficulties are uncertain; 2) including too many samples would significantly slow down the training process. Using, e.g., ten traces for the denominator calculation significantly slows down the training time compared to the CCE loss.

To overcome the limitations mentioned before and inspired by the focal loss [9], we propose a novel loss function for SCA: Focal Loss Ratio (FLR). The main contributions of this paper are:

- We design a novel loss function that enables deep learning models to learn from noisy or imbalanced data efficiently.
- As FLR requires tuning of additional hyperparameters, we discuss the appropriate hyperparameter tuning strategies.

- We perform systematic evaluation and benchmark on commonly used and recently proposed SCA-based loss functions.

We provide the source code in a Github repository: https://github.com/AISyLab/focal_loss.

2 Background

This section provides an introduction to deep learning-based profiling side-channel attacks. Afterward, we discuss various loss functions and the datasets used in our experiments.

2.1 Deep Learning-Based Side-Channel Analysis

Supervised machine learning aims to learn a function f mapping an input to the output based on examples of input-output pairs. The function f is parameterized by $\boldsymbol{\theta} \in \mathbb{R}^n$, where n denotes the number of trainable parameters. Supervised learning consists of two phases: training and test. Moving to the profiling side-channel attacks, those two phases are commonly denoted as the profiling and attack phase. In the deep learning-based SCA, the function f is a deep neural network with the Softmax output layer. We encode classes in one-hot encoding, where each class is represented as a vector of c values (that depends on the leakage model and the considered cipher), with zero on all the places, except one, denoting the membership of that class. Our work considers two commonly used deep learning models: multilayer perceptron and convolutional neural networks.

The **multilayer perceptron** (MLP) is a feed-forward neural network that maps sets of inputs onto sets of appropriate outputs. MLP consists of multiple layers (at least three: an input layer, an output layer, and hidden layer(s)) of nodes in a directed graph, where each layer is fully connected to the next one, and training of the network is done with the backpropagation algorithm [4].

Convolutional neural networks (CNNs) commonly consist of three types of layers: convolutional layers, pooling layers, and fully connected layers. The convolution layer computes the output of neurons connected to local regions in the input, each computing a dot product between their weights and a small region they are connected to in the input volume. Pooling decrease the number of extracted samples by performing a down-sampling operation along the spatial dimensions. The fully connected layer computes either the hidden activations or the class scores.

A dataset is a collection of side-channel traces (measurements), where each trace $\mathbf{t}_i$ is associated with an input value (plaintext or ciphertext) $\mathbf{d}_i$ and a key value $\mathbf{k}_i$. Similar to the conventional machine learning process, the dataset is divided into disjoint subsets where the training set has M traces, the validation set has V traces, and the attack set has Q traces.

1. The goal of the profiling phase is to learn $\boldsymbol{\theta}$ (vector of parameters) that minimizes the empirical risk represented by a loss function L on a training dataset of size M.

2. In the attack phase (also known as test or inference), predictions are made for the classes

$$y(x_1, k^*), \ldots, y(x_Q, k^*),$$

where x denotes leakage traces and k^* represents the secret (unknown) key on the device under the attack. The outcome of predictions with a model f on the attack set is a two-dimensional matrix P with dimensions equal to $Q \times c$. The cumulative sum $S(k)$ for any key candidate k is then used as a maximum log-likelihood distinguisher:

$$S(k) = \sum_{i=1}^{Q} \log(\mathbf{p}_{i,y}). \tag{1}$$

The value $\mathbf{p}_{i,y}$ is the probability that for a key k being used to generate leakage d_i, we obtain the class y. A specific class y is obtained from the key and input through a cryptographic function and a leakage model.

In SCA, an adversary aims at revealing the secret key k^*. More specifically, given Q traces in the attack phase, an attack outputs a key guessing vector $\mathbf{g} = [g_1, g_2, \ldots, g_{|\mathcal{K}|}]$ in decreasing order of probability. Thus, g_1 is the most likely and $g_{|\mathcal{K}|}$ the least likely key candidate. The attack performance is evaluated by standard performance metrics such as success rate (SR) and guessing entropy (GE) [21]. Guessing entropy is the average position of k^* in $\mathbf{g}$. The success rate is the average empirical probability that g_1 is equal to the secret key k^*. In this work, both metrics are considered.

2.2 Loss Functions

In machine learning, the loss indicates the difference between the predicted outputs of the model and the ground truth labels belonging to the input. The result of a loss function L is used to update the weights in the network with gradient descent, finally reducing the deviation between the predicted and true labels.

For classification, the common loss function is the categorical cross-entropy (CCE), and it has been used in various classification tasks [5,8,27]. Since side-channel attack can be considered as a classification task as well, CCE is also usually adopted in SCA [1,7,10]. Cross-entropy is a measure of the difference between two distributions. Minimizing the cross-entropy between the distribution modeled by the deep learning model and the true distribution of the classes would improve the predictions of the neural network:

$$CCE(y, \hat{y}) = -\frac{1}{n} \sum_{i=1}^{n} \sum_{j=1}^{c} y_{i,j} \cdot \log(\widehat{y_{i,j}}), \tag{2}$$

where c is the number of classes, y is the true value, and $\hat{y}$ is the predicted value.

Categorical cross-entropy loss has several variants depending on usage cases. Focal loss is one of the popular ones in dealing with class imbalance problems as well as improving learning speed [9]:

$$FOCAL(y, \hat{y}) = -\alpha(1 - \hat{y})^{\gamma} CCE(y, \hat{y}), \tag{3}$$

where CCE is the categorical cross-entropy function, α is a vector of weights for each class, and γ is the parameter that increases the loss for correctly classified examples with low confidence.

More recently, two SCA-specific loss functions have been proposed. One of them is the ranking loss (RKL) proposed by Zaid et al. [28]. The ranking loss uses both the output score of the model and the probabilities produced by applying the Softmax activation function to these scores. The idea behind the ranking loss is to compare the rank of the correct key byte and the other key bytes in the score vector before the Softmax function is applied:

$$RKL(s) = \sum_{\substack{k \in \mathcal{K} \\ k \neq k^*}} \left(\log_2 \left(1 + e^{-\alpha(s(k^*) - s(k))} \right) \right), \tag{4}$$

where s is the predicted vector with scores for each key hypothesis, $\mathcal{K}$ is the set of all possible key values, k^* is the correct key, and $s(k)$ is the score for key guess k, calculated by looking at the rank of k in the list of all possible keys. Finally, α is a parameter that needs to be set dependent on the size of the used profiling set. The implementation of the ranking loss function is provided by the authors [28] on Github[1].

Zhang et al. proposed the cross-entropy ratio (CER) [30]. CER can be used as a metric to estimate the performance of a deep learning model in the context of SCA, which can be further extended as a loss function:

$$cer(y, \hat{y}) = \frac{CE(y, \hat{y})}{\frac{1}{n}\sum_{i=1}^{n} CE(y_{r_i}, \hat{y})}, \tag{5}$$

where CE is the categorical cross-entropy, and y_{r_i} denotes the one-hot encoded vector with the incorrect labels. Here, the variable n denotes the number of incorrect sets to use. The authors do not provide a value for n, but state that increasing n should increase the accuracy of the metric. We use $n = 10$ to balance computational complexity and attack performance in our experiments.

2.3 Datasets

Our experiments consider three publicly available datasets representing a typical sample of commonly encountered scenarios. These datasets are a common choice for evaluating the performance of deep learning-based SCA. For all datasets, we consider the Hamming weight (HW) and Identity (ID) leakage models.

ASCAD Datasets. The ASCAD datasets are generated by taking measurements from an ATMega8515 running masked AES-128 and are proposed as the benchmark datasets for SCA [1]. There are two versions of the dataset. The first

[1] https://github.com/gabzai/Ranking-Loss-SCA.

version consists of 50 000 profiling traces, and 10 000 attack traces, each trace consisting of 700 features. The profiling and attacking sets use both the same fixed key. We denote this dataset as ASCAD_fixed.

The second version of the ASCAD dataset uses random keys to build the profiling traces. The dataset consists of 200 000 profiling, and 100 000 attack traces, each consisting of 1 400 features. We denote this dataset as ASCAD_variable. For our experiments on the ASCAD datasets (both versions), 50 000 profiling traces are used. 2 000 traces for the ASCAD_fixed dataset and up to 3 000 traces for the ASCAD_variable are used in the attack phase. For both versions, we attack the first masked key byte, which is key byte 3. The ASCAD datasets are available on the ASCAD GitHub repository[2].

CHES CTF Dataset. The CHES CTF dataset was released in 2018 for the Conference on Cryptographic Hardware and Embedded Systems (CHES). The traces consist of masked AES-128 encryption running on a 32-bit STM microcontroller. In our experiments, we use 45 000 traces for the training set, which contains a **fixed key**. The validation and test sets consist of 5 000 traces each, where we used 3 000 traces for the attack phase. Unlike the ASCAD dataset, the key used in the training and validation set is different from the key for the test set. We attack the first key byte. This dataset is available at https://chesctf.riscure.com/2018/news. In our case, we considered a pre-processed version of the dataset where each trace consists of 2 200 features. The pre-processed dataset is available at http://aisylabdatasets.ewi.tudelft.nl/.

3 Related Works

To improve the side-channel attack performance, in recent years, deep learning has received more attention within the SCA community, see, e.g., [2,7,10,12,17,18,23,29]. MLP and CNNs have become the most popular candidates to launch such attacks. The results show that by carefully tuning the model's hyperparameters, the required number of attacks traces can be dramatically reduced to obtain the secret key. For instance, [29] proposed a methodology to find well-performing architectures for SCA, while [7] also researched different architectural choices and the influence of noise. More recently, [15] showed how ensembles of deep learning models can be used for SCA.

Although the model design methodologies have been widely studied, less attention has been put on the loss function. [10] first explored the usage of convolutional neural networks for SCA and mentioned the categorical cross-entropy and the mean squared error loss functions, which is followed by later works on deep learning-based SCA [1,13,15,23,29].

More recently, two novel loss functions optimized for SCA have been proposed [28,30]. More details are presented in Sect. 2.2. Finally, Kerkhof et al.

[2] https://github.com/ANSSI-FR/ASCAD/tree/master/ATMEGA_AES_v1.

recently conducted a systematic evaluation of several loss functions ("traditional" machine learning ones like categorical cross-entropy and mean squared error) but also the SCA-related ones (CER and ranking loss) [6]. Their analysis showed that CER performs the best for SCA, followed by categorical cross-entropy. Interestingly, the reported results for ranking loss indicate significant issues with that loss function.

4 A Novel Loss Function for SCA

In this section, we introduce our novel loss function. First, we provide a formal problem statement, followed by a discussion about the FLR loss function and how to tune its hyperparameters.

4.1 Problem Statement

Before introducing the Focal Loss Ratio, we first formally define the easy and hard samples [20]. Let a, p, and n denote *anchor* (i.e., ground truth), *positive* (with a label same as the anchor), and *negative* samples (with a label different from the anchor). In general, the anchor can be the data of any label, and the positive and negative samples are based on the anchor's label. We can categorize the positive samples p into two categories based on their similarity S to the anchor sample: 1) easy samples, where $S(a,p) < S(a,n)$; 2) hard samples, where $S(a,n) < S(a,p)$. The way of calculating the similarity depends on the selection of the loss function. Nevertheless, the samples closer to the anchor have higher confidence to be classified to the corresponding clusters. Following this, based on the classification outcomes, we define:

- Easy positives/negatives: samples classified as positive/negative examples.
- Hard positives/negatives: samples misclassified as negative/positive examples.

Recall that the CER loss takes advantage of samples with incorrect labels to increase the attack performance. However, the training would become inefficient if most samples are easy negatives that have limited contribution to the learning process. The bias introduced by easy negatives makes it difficult for a network to learn rich semantic relationships from samples: cumulative easy negatives loss overwhelms the total loss, which degenerates the model. Moreover, one should notice that the class imbalance can be introduced based on the leakage model. For instance, when using the Hamming weight leakage model, information related to middle classes (i.e., $\mathrm{HW} = 4$) in a dataset or mini-batches used in training is over-represented compared to the other classes. Indeed, training a network on an imbalanced dataset will force the network to learn more representations of the data-dominated class than other classes. Unfortunately, besides re-balancing from the dataset level, there are no special measures to address this problem during the training process. Finally, the accurate estimate of CER requires a sufficient number of negative samples (infinite in the ideal case), but it would reduce the training efficiency as a trade-off.

4.2 Focal Loss Ratio

Two actions are essential to address the problems identified in the previous section. First, the hard samples should be prioritized in the training process compared to the easier ones. Second, the weight of each class should be parameterized. Following this, we propose the Focal Loss Ratio (FLR):

$$FLR(y,\hat{y}) = \frac{-\alpha(1-\hat{y})^{\gamma}CE(y,\hat{y})}{\frac{1}{n}\sum_{i=1}^{n} -\alpha(1-\hat{y})^{\gamma}CE(y_{s_i},\hat{y})}, \tag{6}$$

where y are the true labels, y_s are the shuffled labels, CE is the categorical cross-entropy, and n is the number of negative samples to use. In Eq. 6, α and γ are introduced to weight the classes and emphasize hard samples for both numerator and denominator, respectively. When looking at the numerator, aligned with the focal loss, the samples with lower prediction probability (hard samples) have a greater impact on the loss function, which is further controlled by the α value. The same statement holds for the denominator as well. Besides, the introduction of the denominator further separates the prediction distribution between the correct cluster and other clusters. Indeed, compared with other loss functions, FLR introduces additional benefits to efficient learning: 1) concentrating on the samples that are difficult to classify (hard samples) and 2) balancing the dataset. Finally, FLR can be seen as an improved version of CER loss, focusing on learning efficiency. Since the theoretical evidence from the CER loss also applies to our FLR loss, we do not repeat it in this work.

Figure 1 demonstrates the above mentioned effects. Given that input in the prediction probability $\hat{y}$ ranges from zero to one and the ground truth y equals zero, as shown in the left graph, FLR ($\alpha = 0.5$) introduces the greatest penalty to the hard samples compared to others. When y_{pred} is getting closer to y_{true}, the FLR value is neglectable, thus reducing the contribution of the easy negatives. The effect of α is shown on the right graph: the influence of the hard samples is reduced when α decreases. Consequently, the FLR loss could be a good candidate when the classes are imbalanced (i.e., the HW leakage model). Moreover, since α can effectively control the hard sample's influence, then the improvement of the model's performance can be realized by different tuning strategies. More discussions are presented in Sect. 6.

4.3 Hyperparameter Tuning

Compared with other loss functions, FLR loss introduces additional hyperparameters. Thus, it requires careful tuning. We consider three strategies for α and γ selection to investigate their influence and reach the top performance in the considered testing scenarios. For the first strategy, we use the values given by [9], namely $\alpha = 0.25$ and $\gamma = 2.0$. Models with these settings are denoted as FLR. The second strategy optimizes both α and γ via random search, denoted as FLR_optimized. The search ranges are defined in Table 1.

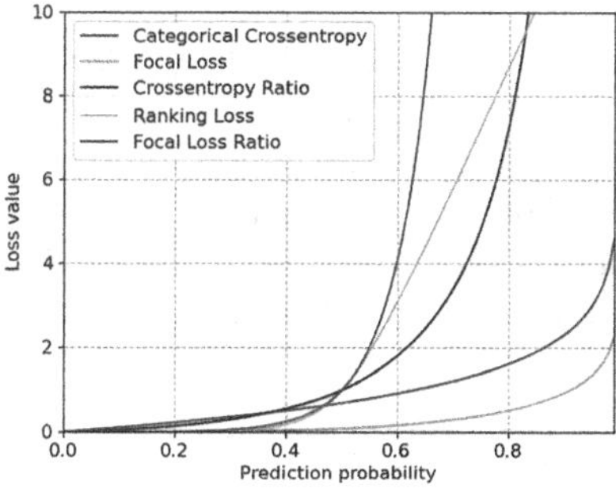

(a) Comparison between loss functions.

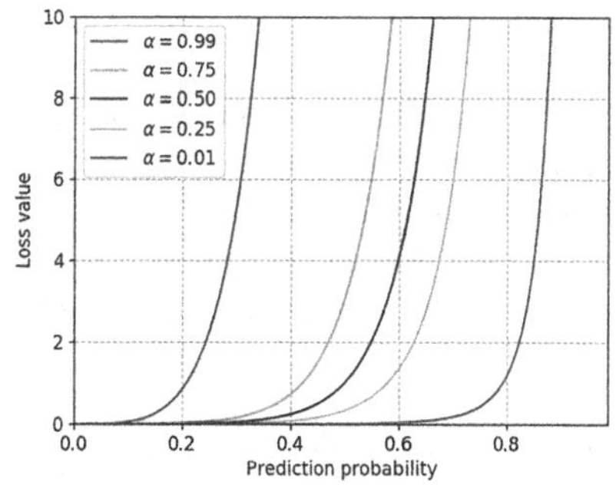

(b) The influence of α towards the FLR.

Fig. 1. Demonstration of different loss functions.

Table 1. Hyperparameter space for FLR_optimized.

α	0.1,	0.25,	0.5,	0.75,	0.9
γ	0,	0.5,	1.0,	2.0,	5.0

Finally, we introduce class re-balancing into our loss function [3]. With class balancing, the weights for each class (α) are set based on the classes' size. For each class, the corresponding weight is calculated as shown in Eq. 7.

$$\alpha_i = \frac{1-\beta}{1-\beta^{n_y}}, \tag{7}$$

where α_i is the weight for class i, n_y is the number of samples in the considered class in the profiling set, and β is a new parameter to be tuned. In this paper, aligned with [3], we set $\beta = 0.999$. Models trained with these settings are referred to as focal_balanced.

We conducted a preliminary search to determine the optimal value of n (ranges from 1 to 20). Our experiments showed the best attack performance when n equals three. This observation also holds when tested on the other datasets. Also, the impact on training time of using $n = 3$ is negligible compared to $n = 1$. Therefore, we set n to three for our experiments with FLR.

5 Experimental Results

In this section, we provide the experimental results for our new loss function. First, we provide details about the experimental setup. Afterward, we provide results for all considered datasets and loss functions.

5.1 Setup

Regarding model architecture tuning, using one or a few optimized models from the literature may introduce bias as they are optimized for a specific dataset-loss function combination. Besides, the model's performance may fluctuate with each training due to the random weight initialization. Therefore, we follow Algorithm 1 to tune the model's hyperparameters for each loss function.

Algorithm 1. Model tuning and the evaluation strategy.

1: Generate, train, and test Z models sampled from range S with loss function L.
2: Select the **best** performing model T_b.
3: Train and test the model T_b N times.
4: Select the **median** performing model T_{bm}.
5: Evaluate T_{bm} with evaluation metrics.

This paper compares our function against the CER loss, categorical cross-entropy, ranking loss, and focal loss. The selection of "traditional" loss functions is based on the results from [6]. Note that for the RKL's α value, the original paper selected 0.5 for the ASCAD dataset and did not provide values for the other datasets. Since the number of profiling traces we used was almost the same for all datasets, $\alpha = 0.5$ was used for every dataset and model. Although this value can be further optimized, we argue that tuning α for all of the scenarios and architectures is not viable and practical for real-world usages, considering the number of different scenarios/architectures that are relevant.

For each loss function, we set Z to 100 with hyperparameters sampled from Tables 2 and 3. n is set to be 10. We use guessing entropy to evaluate the model's performance during the tuning process (steps 2 and 4). For the evaluation (step 5), we look at the guessing entropy and success rate. In some of the plots in the following sections, the x-axis is reduced to increase visibility.

Table 2. Hyperparameter space for multilayer perceptrons.

Hyperparameter	Options
Dense layers	2 to 8 in a step of 1
Neurons per layer	100 to 1 000 in a step of 100
Learning rate	1e−6 to 1e−3 in a step of 1e−5
Batch size	100 to 1 000 in a step of 100
Activation function (all layers)	ReLU, Tanh, ELU, or SeLU
Loss function	RMSprop, Adam

Table 3. Hyperparameter space for convolutional neural networks.

Hyperparameter	Options
Convolution layers	1 to 2 in a step of 1
Convolution filters	8 to 32 in a step of 4
Kernel size	10 to 20 in a step of 2
Pooling type	Max pooling, Average pooling
Pooling size	2 to 5 in a step of 1
Pooling stride	2 to 10 in a step of 1
Dense layers	2 to 3 in a step of 1
Neurons per layer	100 to 1 000 in a step of 100
Learning rate	1e−6 to 1e−3 in a step of 1e−5
Batch size	100 to 1 000 in a step of 100
Activation function (all layers)	ReLU, Tanh, ELU, or SeLU
Loss function	RMSprop, Adam

5.2 ASCAD_fixed

Figures 2 and 3 show the guessing entropy and success rate metrics with different attack models and leakage models. From the results, models trained with FLR loss outperform the CCE and focal loss in all test scenarios. Specifically, when the HW leakage model is considered, the FLR model halves the required attack traces compared with categorical cross-entropy or focal loss to reach a GE of 1. Surprisingly, ranking loss performs mediocre in most cases, indicating its low generality towards different deep learning models and test scenarios. Note that we tested on the same datasets as the RKL paper does, and the poor performance mainly comes from the variation of the attack model (recall, we use models created via random search). Unfortunately, although RKL may work well with some specific settings (like the one in [28]), the general applicability of that loss function is relatively poor based on our results.

On the other side, FLR loss and CER loss perform comparably. Still, as shown in Table 4, when the median $\overline{N}_{T_{GE}}$ is evaluated, the models trained with FLR outperform the CER loss in three out of four of the test scenarios. Interestingly, all three FLR tuning strategies (for α and γ) work well and lead to successful attacks with a limited number of traces. Although optimal strategy differs per scenario, their variation is limited.

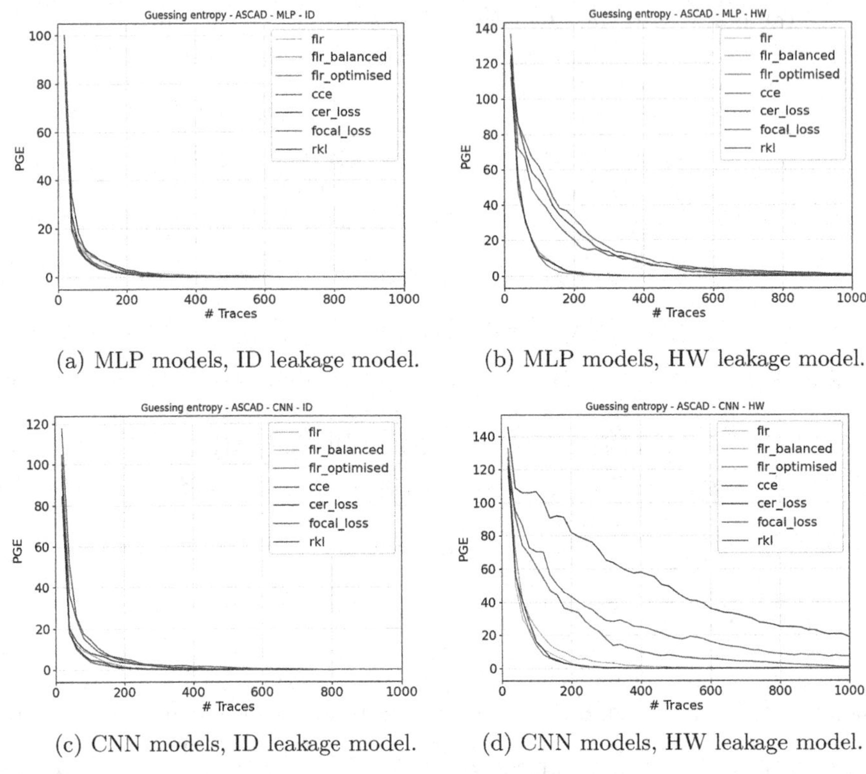

(a) MLP models, ID leakage model.

(b) MLP models, HW leakage model.

(c) CNN models, ID leakage model.

(d) CNN models, HW leakage model.

Fig. 2. Guessing entropy of the optimized models for the ASCAD_fixed dataset.

Table 4. Median $\overline{N}_{T_{GE}}$ for the ASCAD_fixed dataset. The lowest $\overline{N}_{T_{GE}}$ for each scenario is marked blue.

	L_{focal}	CCE	CER loss	RKL	FLR	FLR_balanced	FLR_optimized
MLP ID	580	860	570	900	810	540	680
MLP HW	1480	1560	560	1620	460	570	510
CNN ID	1250	1360	600	1760	610	850	550
CNN HW	1840	>2000	540	>2000	570	790	560

5.3 ASCAD_variable

Next, loss functions are tested on the ASCAD_variable dataset. The guessing entropy for each loss function is presented in Fig. 4. For the ID leakage model, neither the MLPs nor CNNs reach a GE of 1 with less than 3 000 traces. Still, the CER loss and FLR perform the best: the CER loss reaches a GE of 1.7 with MLP and 3.13 with CNN, while the models with FLR reach 2.11 and 1.18. When the HW leakage model is considered, as shown in Table 5, the secret key

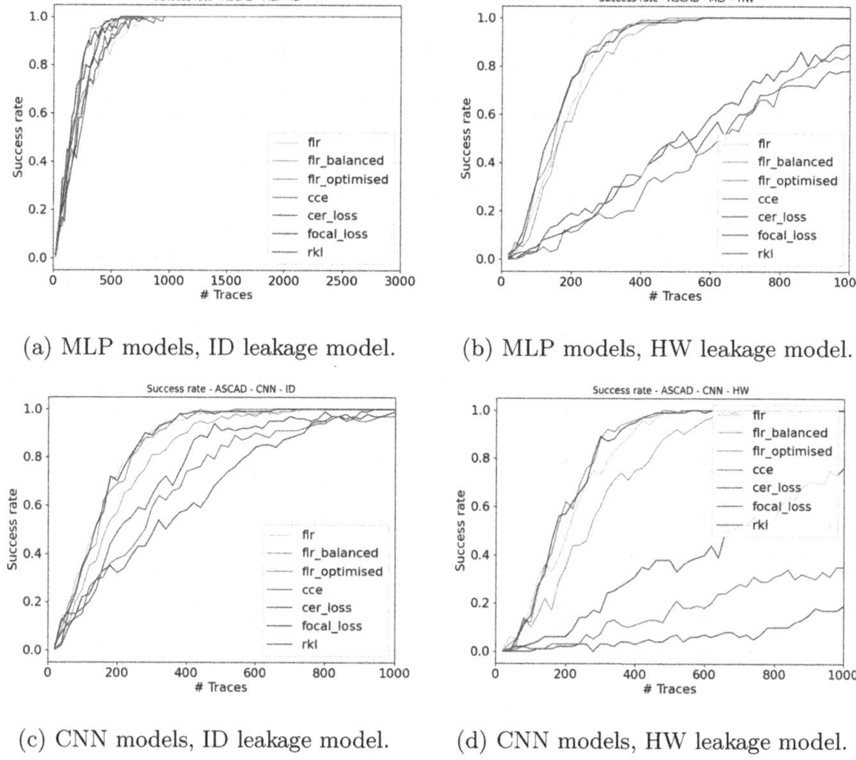

(a) MLP models, ID leakage model. (b) MLP models, HW leakage model.

(c) CNN models, ID leakage model. (d) CNN models, HW leakage model.

Fig. 3. Success rate of the optimized models for the ASCAD_fixed dataset.

can be retrieved successfully with all considered loss functions. For MLP, FLR loss performs slightly worse than CER ($\overline{N}_{T_{GE}} = 1\,800$ versus $\overline{N}_{T_{GE}} = 1\,340$). For CNN, FLR outperforms CER ($\overline{N}_{T_{GE}} = 800$ versus $\overline{N}_{T_{GE}} = 950$). Ranking loss, unfortunately, performs the worst in most of the test scenarios.

Table 5. Median $\overline{N}_{T_{GE}}$ for the ASCAD_variable dataset. The lowest $\overline{N}_{T_{GE}}$ for each scenario is marked blue.

	L_{focal}	CCE	CER loss	RKL	FLR	FLR_balanced	FLR_optimized
MLP ID	>3 000	>3 000	>3 000	>3 000	>3 000	>3 000	>3 000
MLP HW	1 940	2 600	1 340	2 910	2 180	2 460	1 800
CNN ID	>3 000	>3 000	>3 000	>3 000	>3 000	>3 000	>3 000
CNN HW	>3 000	2 840	950	>3 000	880	1 670	1 020

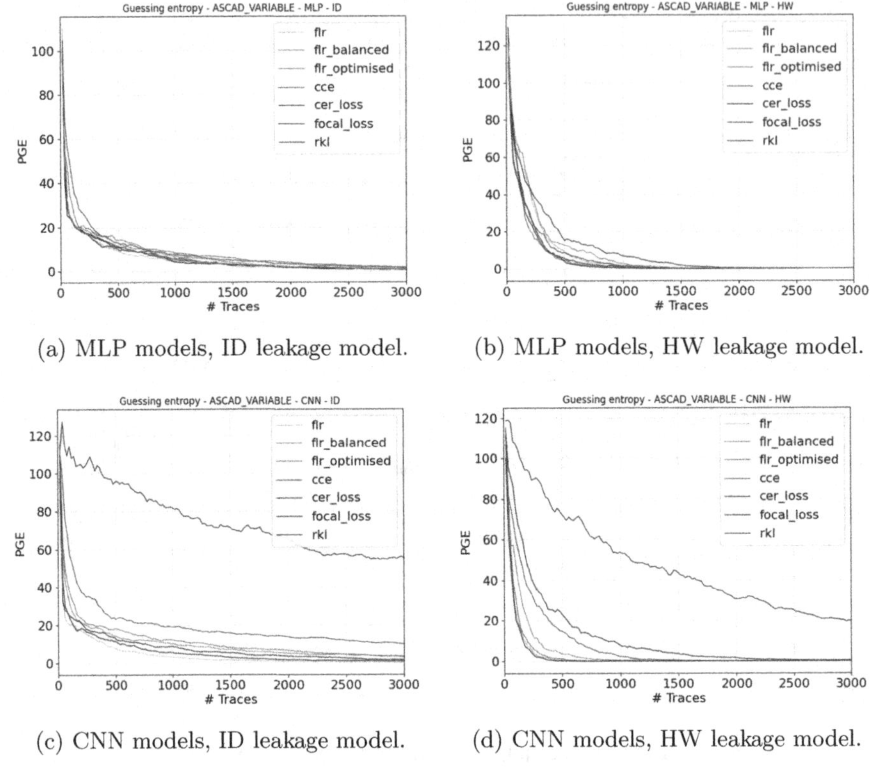

(a) MLP models, ID leakage model.

(b) MLP models, HW leakage model.

(c) CNN models, ID leakage model.

(d) CNN models, HW leakage model.

Fig. 4. Guessing entropy of the optimized models for the ASCAD_variable dataset.

Next, the success rates (SR) of each loss function are shown in Fig. 5. Interestingly, the FLR (default version) equipped model reaches a higher SR slightly faster than the other loss functions with the ID leakage model. The FLR and CER loss perform equally well for the HW leakage scenarios. Note that the performance of FLR can fluctuate with different hyperparameter tuning strategies. For the ASCAD_variable dataset, however, FLR with default values ($\alpha = 0.25$, $\gamma = 2.0$) would be a good choice.

5.4 CHES_CTF

In this section, we discuss the results for the CHES_CTF dataset. Figure 6 shows the guessing entropy in the different scenarios.

For all considered loss functions, 3 000 attack traces are not sufficient to obtain the correct key for the ID leakage model. Still, from the results, we see a significant performance improvement with the MLP models and the ID leakage when using FLR_balanced. Such an improvement is also visible in some of the CNN models with FLR. However, these models turned out to be less consistent in terms of performance when changing the attack settings. For instance, the

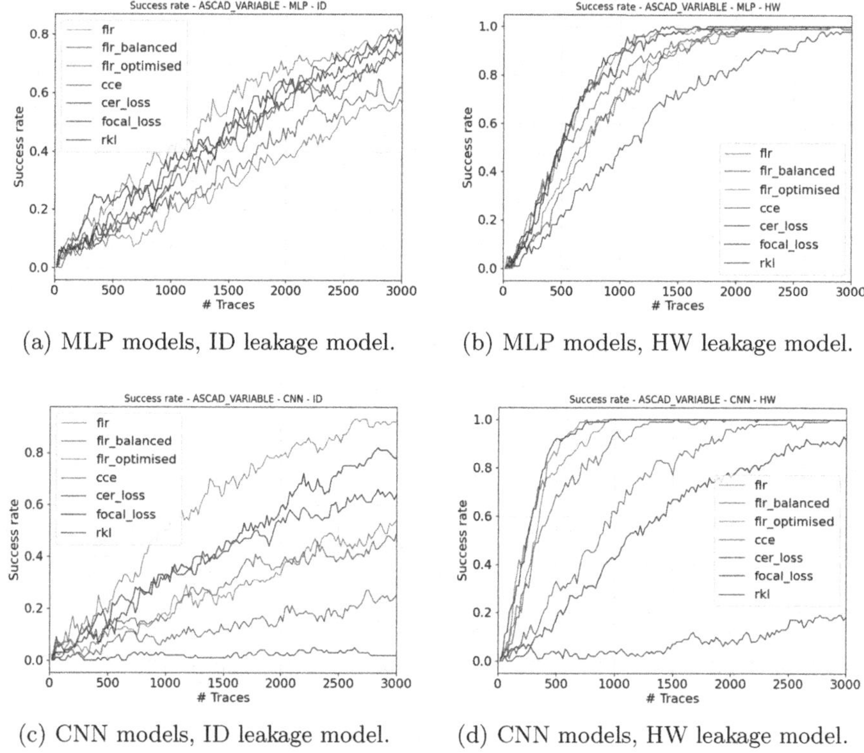

(a) MLP models, ID leakage model.

(b) MLP models, HW leakage model.

(c) CNN models, ID leakage model.

(d) CNN models, HW leakage model.

Fig. 5. Success rate of the optimized models for the ASCAD_variable dataset.

FLR_balanced performs the best with MLP, but it performs mediocre with CNN. Similar behavior is also visible for the FLR_optimized.

When the HW leakage model is considered, we again see a significant increase in the performance when a CNN is used. As shown in Table 6, the models with FLR and FLR_optimized were the only ones that successfully retrieved the correct key. The median of 10 models with FLR and FLR_optimized were successful with a $\overline{N}_{T_{GE}}$ of 2 740 and 2 000, respectively. When MLPs are used, there is no significant increase in $\overline{N}_{T_{GE}}$, and the performance is approximately equal to the CER loss.

6 Discussion

FLR loss performs well in various test scenarios, while the only downside to using FLR as a loss function is the introduction of the α and γ parameters. We used three different strategies: 1) fixed value: $\alpha = 0.25$ and $\gamma = 2.0$; 2) optimized via random search; 3) determined by the frequency of each class.

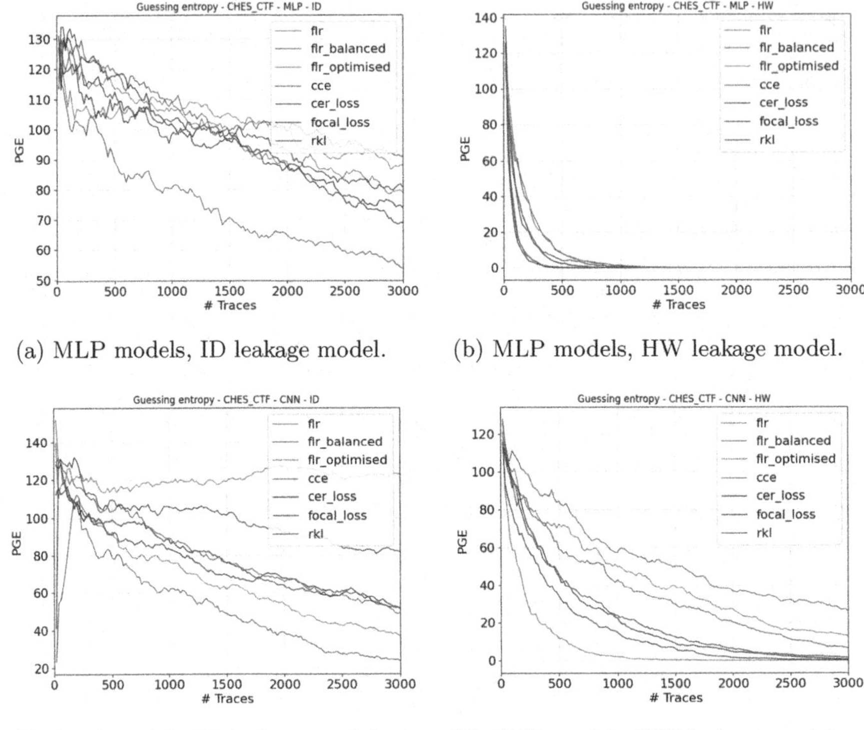

(a) MLP models, ID leakage model.

(b) MLP models, HW leakage model.

(c) CNN models, ID leakage model.

(d) CNN models, HW leakage model.

Fig. 6. Guessing entropy of the optimized models for the CHES_CTF dataset.

Table 6. Median $\overline{N}_{T_{GE}}$ for the CHES_CTF dataset. The lowest $\overline{N}_{T_{GE}}$ for each scenario is marked blue.

	L_{focal}	CCE	CER loss	RKL	FLR	FLR_balanced	FLR_optimized
MLP ID	>3 000	>3 000	>3 000	>3 000	>3 000	>3 000	>3 000
MLP HW	1 220	630	480	1 860	1 080	2 030	2 450
CNN ID	>3 000	>3 000	>3 000	>3 000	>3 000	>3 000	>3 000
CNN HW	>3 000	>3 000	>3 000	>3 000	2 740	>3 000	2 000

Throughout the experiments, there was not a single strategy that worked best for every scenario. Still, the best performing FLR variants have the fixed α values for every class in almost all cases. In some of the scenarios with the ID leakage model, the class re-balance strategy improves the performance. However, using class balancing with the ID leakage model results in almost constant and low values of α. This leads us to conclude that the best strategy is the variant where α is the same for every class and the α and γ parameters are optimized. Optimization via random search can be performed to set the α and γ values. In combination with an increased range of the possible values, e.g., the addition of lower α values, FLR_optimized should outperform the other variants. From Sect. 4.2, one should note that with lower α, the samples that trigger high loss value are the ones misclassified with high confidence (probability).

Compared with other loss functions that require models to be confident about predicting, this FLR configuration softens the restriction for the predictions: only (very) hard negative will be penalized, while the others that are correctly classified, or even misclassified but with low confidence would have limited loss contributions. From the learning perspective, loss functions forcing the model to reach high accuracy/low loss would normally lead to the learning from the major classes/overfitting. FLR with low α allows the models to make mistakes, increasing the model's generality and helping to learn from the imbalanced data.

We performed an additional set of experiments on ASCAD_fixed and ASCAD_variable datasets to test our hypothesis. The search space for α is now extended to $0.005, 0.01, 0.05, 0.1, 0.25, 0.5, 0.75$, and 0.9. We use FLR as the loss function for each test scenario and again optimize hyperparameters via random search. The results of these experiments are listed in Tables 7 and 8.

Table 7. Median $\overline{N}_{TGE}$ for the ASCAD_fixed dataset. The lowest $\overline{N}_{TGE}$ for each scenario is marked blue.

	L_{focal}	CCE	CER loss	RKL	FLR
MLP ID	580	860	570	900	640
MLP HW	1 480	1 560	560	1 630	490
CNN ID	1 250	1 360	600	1 760	520
CNN HW	1 840	>2 000	540	>2 000	500

Table 8. Median $\overline{N}_{TGE}$ for the ASCAD_variable dataset. The lowest $\overline{N}_{TGE}$ for each scenario is marked blue.

	L_{focal}	CCE	CER loss	RKL	FLR
MLP ID	>3 000	>3 000	>3 000	>3 000	>3 000
MLP HW	1 940	2 600	1 340	2 910	1 340
CNN ID	>3 000	>3 000	>3 000	>3 000	>3 000
CNN HW	>3 000	2 840	950	>3 000	800

From the results, in the scenarios in which the class balanced FLR was previously best, such as the ASCAD_fixed scenarios, the FLR with our new strategy still performs very well. For instance, when attacking ASCAD_fixed with MLP and the ID leakage model, the best performing model uses a fixed α that equals 0.005. Although it did not perform as well as the CER loss or FLR_balanced in this case, it did perform better than the other strategies. We also see results similar to the previous experiments when using the HW leakage model on the

ASCAD_variable dataset. FLR outperforms the CER loss in most cases. The benefit, however, is that a single strategy can be used for each scenario, namely the same optimized value for α for each class.

7 Conclusions and Future Work

In this paper, we proposed a novel loss function optimized for deep learning-based side-channel analysis. More precisely, we started by discussing the advantages and drawbacks of several loss functions in the context of SCA. Using those characteristics, we constructed a new loss function for deep learning-based SCA denoted as the Focal Loss Ratio (FLR).

We confirmed FLR's outstanding performance by testing it on combinations of datasets, leakage models, and neural network architectures. Finally, we showed that neural network models using FLR work with different parameter optimization strategies and that FLR outperforms the CER loss and other loss functions like the categorical cross-entropy in most of the considered scenarios. We plan to explore the hyperparameter selection for FLR loss when considering datasets with more complex countermeasures for future work.

Acknowledgements. This work was supported in part by the Netherlands Organization for Scientific Research NWO project DISTANT (CS.019) and project PROACT (NWA.1215.18.014).

References

1. Benadjila, R., Prouff, E., Strullu, R., Cagli, E., Dumas, C.: Deep learning for side-channel analysis and introduction to ASCAD database. J. Cryptogr. Eng. **10**(2), 163–188 (2019). https://doi.org/10.1007/s13389-019-00220-8
2. Cagli, E., Dumas, C., Prouff, E.: Convolutional neural networks with data augmentation against jitter-based countermeasures. In: Fischer, W., Homma, N. (eds.) CHES 2017. LNCS, vol. 10529, pp. 45–68. Springer, Cham (2017). https://doi.org/10.1007/978-3-319-66787-4_3
3. Cui, Y., Jia, M., Lin, T.Y., Song, Y., Belongie, S.J.: Class-Balanced Loss Based on Effective Number of Samples. CoRR abs/1901.05555 (2019). http://arxiv.org/abs/1901.05555
4. Goodfellow, I.J., Bengio, Y., Courville, A.: Deep Learning. MIT Press, Cambridge (2016). http://www.deeplearningbook.org
5. He, K., Zhang, X., Ren, S., Sun, J.: Deep Residual Learning for Image Recognition (2015)
6. Kerkhof, M., Wu, L., Perin, G., Picek, S.: No (good) loss no gain: systematic evaluation of loss functions in deep learning-based side-channel analysis. Cryptology ePrint Archive, Report 2021/1091 (2021). https://ia.cr/2021/1091
7. Kim, J., Picek, S., Heuser, A., Bhasin, S., Hanjalic, A.: Make some noise unleashing the power of convolutional neural networks for profiled side-channel analysis. IACR Trans. Cryptogr. Hardware Embed. Syst. **2019**(3), 148–179 (2019). https://doi.org/10.13154/tches.v2019.i3.148-179. ISSN 2569-2925

8. Kussul, N., Lavreniuk, M., Skakun, S., Shelestov, A.: Deep learning classification of land cover and crop types using remote sensing data. IEEE Geosci. Remote Sens. Lett. **14**(5), 778–782 (2017). https://doi.org/10.1109/LGRS.2017.2681128
9. Lin, T.Y., Goyal, P., Girshick, R.B., He, K., Dollár, P.: Focal Loss for Dense Object Detection. CoRR abs/1708.02002 (2017). http://arxiv.org/abs/1708.02002
10. Maghrebi, H., Portigliatti, T., Prouff, E.: Breaking cryptographic implementations using deep learning techniques. In: Carlet, C., Hasan, M.A., Saraswat, V. (eds.) SPACE 2016. LNCS, vol. 10076, pp. 3–26. Springer, Cham (2016). https://doi.org/10.1007/978-3-319-49445-6_1
11. Mangard, S., Oswald, E., Popp, T.: Power Analysis Attacks: Revealing the Secrets of Smart Cards. Springer, Cham (2006). http://www.dpabook.org/. ISBN 0-387-30857-1
12. Masure, L., Dumas, C., Prouff, E.: A Comprehensive Study of Deep Learning for Side-Channel Analysis (2019)
13. Moos, T., Wegener, F., Moradi, A.: DL-LA: deep learning leakage assessment: a modern roadmap for SCA evaluations. IACR Trans. Cryptogr. Hardware Embed. Syst. **2021**(3), 552–598 (2021). https://doi.org/10.46586/tches.v2021.i3.552-598. https://tches.iacr.org/index.php/TCHES/article/view/8986
14. Perin, G., Buhan, I., Picek, S.: Learning when to stop: a mutual information approach to fight overfitting in profiled side-channel analysis. Cryptology ePrint Archive, Report 2020/058 (2020). https://ia.cr/2020/058
15. Perin, G., Chmielewski, L., Picek, S.: Strength in numbers: improving generalization with ensembles in machine learning-based profiled side-channel analysis. IACR Trans. Cryptogr. Hardware Embed. Syst. **2020**(4), 337–364 (2020). https://doi.org/10.13154/tches.v2020.i4.337-364. https://tches.iacr.org/index.php/TCHES/article/view/8686
16. Picek, S., Heuser, A., Jovic, A., Bhasin, S., Regazzoni, F.: The curse of class imbalance and conflicting metrics with machine learning for side-channel evaluations. IACR Trans. Cryptogr. Hardware Embed. Syst. **2019**(1), 209–237 (2018). https://doi.org/10.13154/tches.v2019.i1.209-237. https://tches.iacr.org/index.php/TCHES/article/view/7339
17. Picek, S., Samiotis, I.P., Kim, J., Heuser, A., Bhasin, S., Legay, A.: On the performance of convolutional neural networks for side-channel analysis. In: Chattopadhyay, A., Rebeiro, C., Yarom, Y. (eds.) SPACE 2018. LNCS, vol. 11348, pp. 157–176. Springer, Cham (2018). https://doi.org/10.1007/978-3-030-05072-6_10
18. Rijsdijk, J., Wu, L., Perin, G., Picek, S.: Reinforcement learning for hyperparameter tuning in deep learning-based side-channel analysis. IACR Trans. Cryptogr. Hardware Embed. Syst. **2021**(3), 677–707 (2021). https://doi.org/10.46586/tches.v2021.i3.677-707. https://tches.iacr.org/index.php/TCHES/article/view/8989
19. Robissout, D., Zaid, G., Colombier, B., Bossuet, L., Habrard, A.: Online performance evaluation of deep learning networks for profiled side-channel analysis. In: Bertoni, G.M., Regazzoni, F. (eds.) COSADE 2020. LNCS, vol. 12244, pp. 200–218. Springer, Cham (2021). https://doi.org/10.1007/978-3-030-68773-1_10
20. Schroff, F., Kalenichenko, D., Philbin, J.: Facenet: a unified embedding for face recognition and clustering. In: Proceedings of the IEEE Conference on Computer Vision and Pattern Recognition, pp. 815–823 (2015)
21. Standaert, F.-X., Malkin, T.G., Yung, M.: A unified framework for the analysis of side-channel key recovery attacks. In: Joux, A. (ed.) EUROCRYPT 2009. LNCS, vol. 5479, pp. 443–461. Springer, Heidelberg (2009). https://doi.org/10.1007/978-3-642-01001-9_26

22. Chari, S., Rao, J.R., Rohatgi, P.: Template attacks. In: Kaliski, B.S., Koç, K., Paar, C. (eds.) CHES 2002. LNCS, vol. 2523, pp. 13–28. Springer, Heidelberg (2003). https://doi.org/10.1007/3-540-36400-5_3
23. Timon, B.: Non-profiled deep learning-based side-channel attacks with sensitivity analysis. IACR Trans. Cryptogr. Hardware Embed. Syst. **2019**(2), 107–131 (2019). https://doi.org/10.13154/tches.v2019.i2.107-131. https://tches.iacr.org/index.php/TCHES/article/view/7387
24. Wouters, L., Arribas, V., Gierlichs, B., Preneel, B.: Revisiting a methodology for efficient CNN architectures in profiling attacks. IACR Trans. Cryptogr. Hardware Embed. Syst. **2020**(3), 147–168 (2020). https://doi.org/10.13154/tches.v2020.i3.147-168. https://github.com/KULeuven-COSIC/TCHES20V3_CNN_SCA
25. Wu, L., Picek, S.: Remove some noise: on pre-processing of side-channel measurements with autoencoders. IACR Trans. Cryptogr. Hardware Embed. Syst. 389–415 (2020)
26. Wu, L., Won, Y., Jap, D., Perin, G., Bhasin, S., Picek, S.: Explain some noise: ablation analysis for deep learning-based physical side-channel analysis. IACR Cryptol. ePrint Arch. 717 (2021). https://eprint.iacr.org/2021/717
27. Yuan, B., Wang, J., Liu, D., Guo, W., Wu, P., Bao, X.: Byte-level malware classification based on Markov images and deep learning. Comput. Secur. **92**, 101740 (2020). https://doi.org/10.1016/j.cose.2020.101740. https://www.sciencedirect.com/science/article/pii/S0167404820300262
28. Zaid, G., Bossuet, L., Dassance, F., Habrard, A., Venelli, A.: Ranking loss: maximizing the success rate in deep learning side-channel analysis. IACR Trans. Cryptogr. Hardware Embed. Syst. **2021**(1), 25–55 (2020). https://doi.org/10.46586/tches.v2021.i1.25-55. https://tches.iacr.org/index.php/TCHES/article/view/8726
29. Zaid, G., Bossuet, L., Habrard, A., Venelli, A.: Methodology for efficient CNN architectures in profiling attacks. IACR Trans. Cryptogr. Hardware Embed. Syst. **2020**(1), 1–36 (2019). https://doi.org/10.13154/tches.v2020.i1.1-36. https://tches.iacr.org/index.php/TCHES/article/view/8391
30. Zhang, J., Zheng, M., Nan, J., Hu, H., Yu, N.: A novel evaluation metric for deep learning-based side channel analysis and its extended application to imbalanced data. IACR Trans. Cryptogr. Hardware Embed. Syst. 73–96 (2020)
31. Zhu, D., Yao, H., Jiang, B., Yu, P.: Negative Log Likelihood Ratio Loss for Deep Neural Network Classification (2018). http://arxiv.org/abs/1804.10690

On the Evaluation of Deep Learning-Based Side-Channel Analysis

Lichao Wu[1], Guilherme Perin[1], and Stjepan Picek[1,2(✉)]

[1] Delft University of Technology, Delft, The Netherlands
[2] Radboud University, Nijmegen, The Netherlands
stjepan@computer.org

Abstract. Deep learning-based side-channel analysis is rapidly positioning itself as a de-facto standard for the most powerful profiling side-channel analysis.The results from the last few years show that deep learning techniques can efficiently break targets that are even protected with countermeasures. While there are constant improvements in making the deep learning-based attacks more powerful, little is done on evaluating the attacks' performance. Indeed, how the evaluation process is done today is not different from what was done more than a decade ago from the perspective of evaluation metrics.

This paper considers how to evaluate deep learning-based side-channel analysis and whether the commonly used approaches give the best results. To that end, we consider different summary statistics and the influence of algorithmic randomness on the stability of profiling models. Our results show that besides commonly used metrics like guessing entropy, one should also show the standard deviation results to assess the attack performance properly. Even more importantly, using the arithmetic mean for guessing entropy does not yield the best results, and instead, a median value should be used.

Keywords: Side-channel Analysis · Deep Learning · Guessing Entropy · Median

1 Introduction

Side-channel analysis (SCA) encompasses techniques aiming at exploiting weaknesses of algorithms' implementations [11]. One standard division of SCA is into direct attacks and profiling attacks. Profiling attacks (two-stage attacks) are more powerful but require a stronger attacker who can access a copy of a device to be attacked. The attacker uses that copy to build a model of a device to be used to attack another similar (identical) device. In the last few years, the most explored profiling attacks have been based on machine learning (especially deep learning). Such attacks are very powerful as they can break targets protected with countermeasures [3,6] but are also somewhat "easier" to deploy as they do not necessarily require pre-processing/feature engineering stages [9,15]. Still, many open questions are usually connected with how to find machine learning architectures that

J. Balasch and C. O'Flynn (Eds.): COSADE 2022, LNCS 13211, pp. 49–71, 2022.
https://doi.org/10.1007/978-3-030-99766-3_3

perform well [27,30]. Unfortunately, this is just one side of the problem. A perspective that cannot be neglected is how to assess the performance of such a profiling model. While the state-of-the-art in deep learning SCA progressed tremendously in the last few years, no results consider how to evaluate the performance of such attacks and if commonly used techniques are the most appropriate ones.

It is common to use metrics like key rank, success rate, and guessing entropy to evaluate the attack performance in SCA [1,6,27,30]. While the first metric requires one experiment run, the latter two are run multiple times to counteract the effect of dataset/measurements selection. For direct attacks or simpler profiling attacks like the template attack, this repetition is sufficient as the algorithms are deterministic, so running them multiple times gives the same results (if the measurements and selected features do not change). On the other hand, deep learning techniques (i.e., artificial neural networks) have multiple sources of randomness (due to the initialization, regularization, and optimization procedure), making those algorithms stochastic. The randomly initialized weights and biases with selected initialization methods make the models perform differently before training, which may lead to performance variation after training as well. Regularization techniques like dropout randomly 'switch-off' some neurons, leading to unpredictable model behaviors. Optimization algorithms, such as stochastic gradient descent (SGD) and Limited-memory Broyden-Fletcher-Goldfarb-Shanno algorithm (L-BFGS), can lead to significant performance variation as well due to their different working principles. Thus, it is intuitive to expect different results when training deep learning models (and including the above-mentioned random sources multiple times), making the evaluation of the attack performance not straightforward. This problem becomes even more challenging when considering the differences among various neural network architectures.

To the best of our knowledge, there are not many works assessing the evaluation performance of side-channel attacks. For instance, Martin et al. investigated how to estimate key rank distribution for SCA [12]. Whitnall and Oswald considered robust profiling setting [26], which can also be connected with the stability of a profiling model, as intuitively, a more robust profiling model provides more stability. Picek et al. considered the robustness through the expectation estimation problem and provided theoretical foundations to assess the robustness of deep learning-based SCA [20]. The authors concluded that deep learning algorithms are robust, but they did not consider improving the evaluation process.

This paper investigates how to evaluate the attack performance of deep learning-based SCA. Our main contributions are:

- We investigate the influence of algorithmic randomness on the attack performance. More precisely, we use the standard deviation to showcase that running experiments multiple times can result in a significantly different assessment of the attack performance. This difference in the attack performance is confirmed for scenarios that use 1) different random models, and 2) the same profiling model and train it independently several times (where the randomness comes from the algorithmic settings).

- We investigate the most appropriate summary statistic for evaluating the attack performance. We consider the arithmetic mean, geometric mean, and median and show that the median works the best (fastest convergence). Our results indicate that deep learning-based SCA often results in skewed distributions of the attack performance, so the arithmetic mean is not appropriate statistics, which is relevant as it is commonly used in the SCA domain.
- We investigate how a different number of independent experiments (key rank evaluations) in the attack phase influences attack performance. Our results show that this value does not significantly influence the results, so much smaller values can be safely used.

We conduct an extensive experimental evaluation including three datasets, two leakage models, and different types of neural networks (multilayer perceptrons and convolutional neural networks) to confirm our observations.

2 Machine Learning-Based Side-Channel Analysis

We concentrate on supervised machine learning and the multi-class classification task (with c classes), as commonly done in related works (see Sect. 3). Supervised machine (deep) learning classification represents the task of learning a function f that maps an input to the discrete output ($f : \mathcal{X} \rightarrow Y$)) based on examples of input-output pairs. The function f is parameterized by n parameters learned in the profiling model: $\boldsymbol{\theta} \in \mathbb{R}^n$.

Hyperparameters are the variables determining the network structure (e.g., the number of neurons and layers) and the variables determining how the network is trained (e.g., learning rate). The parameters are the coefficients chosen through learning (e.g., weights).

Training. In the training phase, the goal is that the algorithm learns the parameters $\boldsymbol{\theta}$ minimizing the empirical risk represented by a loss function on a training dataset of size N.

Validation. When training a profiling model, it should generalize well to previously unseen data, i.e., the profiling model shows stability. To this end, it is common to use cross-validation techniques. Cross-validation is a statistical validation technique used to assess the performance of a machine learning model. Two commonly employed cross-validation techniques in the machine learning-based SCA are 1) validation and 2) k-fold cross-validation.

With the validation technique, we divide the dataset into training (size N), validation (size V), and test dataset (size Q) and use the validation dataset to assess the performance of a model trained on the training dataset. Finally, we use the best-obtained model to attack the test dataset. This technique is commonly used with deep learning-based SCA (due to computational simplicity) [22,28,30].

In the k-fold cross-validation, a dataset is divided into k parts. Then, a model is built on $k-1$ folds and evaluated on the k-th fold. This process is repeated until each fold serves as the k-th fold (every combination of $k-1$ folds serves to train the model). This technique is commonly used with computationally simpler machine learning techniques [20].

Test. In the test phase, the goal is to predict classes (or probabilities that a specific class would be predicted) y based on the previously unseen traces $\mathbf{x}$ (the number of traces equals Q), and the trained model f.

Evaluating the Attack Performance. The outcome of predicting with a model f on the attack set is a two-dimensional matrix P with dimensions equal to $Q \times c$. The cumulative sum $S(k)$ for any key byte candidate k is a valid SCA distinguisher, where it is common to use the maximum log-likelihood distinguisher $S(k) = \sum_{i=1}^{Q} \log(\mathbf{p}_{i,y})$. The value $\mathbf{p}_{i,y}$ denotes the probability that for a key k and a specific input, we obtain the class y (derived from the key and input through a cryptographic function and a leakage model).

It is common to estimate the effort to obtain the correct key k^* with metrics like success rate (SR) and guessing entropy (GE) [25].

With Q traces in the attack phase, an attack outputs a key guessing vector $\mathbf{g} = [g_1, g_2, \ldots, g_{|\mathcal{K}|}]$ in decreasing order of probability where g_1 denotes the most likely and $g_{|\mathcal{K}|}$ the least likely key candidate. Then, guessing entropy is the average position of the correct key in $\mathbf{g}$[1]. The success rate of order o is the average empirical probability that the correct key k^* is located within the first o elements of the key guessing vector $\mathbf{g}$.

Sources of Randomness in Deep Learning-Based SCA. When considering deep learning, several common sources of randomness will influence the obtained results. Informally, the random sources are connected with the dataset (dataset randomness) and the machine learning algorithm (algorithmic randomness). Dataset randomness is caused by the random selection of the traces included in the training/attack dataset. Averaging multiple results is a common way to reduce the effect of any specific traces. While the choice of traces can significantly influence the results, we consider it out of scope for this paper, as it influences any side-channel attack and not only the deep learning ones. For more results about attack performance when selecting different traces, see [29].

In terms of algorithmic randomness, we can obtain different results even if training/evaluating a neural network on the same set of traces (for experiments, see Sect. 5.2, Fig. 1). Indeed, the setting of the random seeds introduces randomness to the machine learning algorithm, where the common sources are:

- Initialization of weights and biases. Initialization of weights provides the first model that is then improved with the backpropagation algorithm. If the weights are chosen poorly (e.g., all the weights are the same value), the training process will not be efficient. The initialization of weight analysis in the context of SCA is done in [8].

[1] Averaging is commonly done over 100 independent experiments (attacks) to obtain statistically significant results.

- Regularization techniques, such as dropout. Regularization represents techniques used to reduce the error by fitting a function f appropriately on the training set. Regularization is used to prevent overfitting (when the model does not generalize to previously unseen data). Dropout is a regularization technique where during the training, some layer outputs are randomly ignored ("dropped out"). Dropout is used to approximate training many neural networks with different architectures in parallel.
- Optimization techniques used to minimize the loss function. Optimizers change the parameters (e.g., weights) of machine learning algorithms (e.g., neural networks) to reduce the loss. They can also change the hyperparameters like learning rate. The analysis of various optimization algorithms and their behavior in SCA is done in [14].

3 Related Works

The variety of techniques and choices one could take when using machine learning (even more deep learning) brought the need for much more detailed analyses, resulting in an abundance of results and papers. Indeed, since 2016, more than 120 papers have examined deep learning and SCA [21].

The first profiling SCA techniques like template attack [4] or stochastic models [23] have no tunable hyperparameters[2], making the analysis simpler and deterministic. Then, running the experiments multiple times results in the same solutions, provided that the same measurements are used. However, the data randomness is introduced by traces and feature selection and will affect the final attack performance. Note that the feature selection/engineering step is also a common one for simpler machine learning techniques[3].

Afterward, machine learning techniques like support vector machines [19], random forest [7], or Naive Bayes [5,17] started to attract more attention in the SCA community as the results were in general favorable compared to the template attack. Those techniques have different hyperparameters (except Naive Bayes, which has no hyperparameters) one needs to tune to reach their full potential. Still, the evaluation of the attack performance did not account for the algorithmic sources of randomness, and the SCA community continued to report the results in the same fashion as for the template attack (e.g., the average key rank for a specific number of attack traces).

Finally, in the last few years, we notice a general direction of using deep learning for profiling SCA. The first significant step was done by Maghrebi et al. as they showed that convolutional neural networks (CNNs) could efficiently break different targets [10]. Additionally, they showed that deep learning works well with raw traces, removing (or, at least reducing) the need for various feature selection techniques [16]. Cagli et al. demonstrated that deep learning could also break implementations protected with jitter countermeasures and introduced

[2] Besides the selection of features (points of interest).

[3] Even deep learning techniques are commonly used with a pre-selected window of features.

the concept of data augmentation in the profiling SCA [3]. Picek et al. evaluated several machine learning metrics and showed a discrepancy between those and the side-channel metrics [18]. The authors showed that the metrics problems also happen for deep learning techniques. Kim et al. designed a deep learning architecture capable of achieving excellent results on several datasets and regularized input with Gaussian noise to further improve the attack performance [6].

Benadjila et al. provided the first more detailed investigation into the importance of hyperparameter tuning [1]. Zaid et al. proposed the first methodology to select hyperparameters related to the size (number of learnable parameters, i.e., weights and biases) of layers in CNNs [30]. Wouters et al. [27] improved upon the work from Zaid et al. [30] where they showed how to reach similar attack performance with significantly smaller neural network architectures. Perin et al. investigated deep learning model generalization and showed that output class probabilities represent a strong SCA metric [13]. Wu et al. introduced Bayesian optimization for hyperparameter tuning [28]. With this approach, the authors managed to find small neural network architectures that perform well (surpassing the architectures' performance obtained by the previous methodologies). Rijsdijk et al. used reinforcement learning to find small convolutional neural networks surpassing the previous state-of-the-art results [22]. Unfortunately, these works showed the importance of hyperparameter tuning but did not consider the influence of algorithmic randomness. What is more, the ever-increasing number of hyperparameters to test resulted in a simpler (faster) validation process but also a larger variance in the results. Li et al. investigated the influence of randomness caused by the weight initialization for multilayer perceptron and convolutional neural network architectures and showed that, depending on the choice of the weight initialization method, SCA attack performance could vary significantly [8]. Perin and Picek explored the impact of the optimizer choice for deep learning-based SCA [14]. Their results indicated that some commonly used optimizers could easily overfit, requiring more effort during the training process.

4 Summary Statistics

Once we obtained the information about key rank from z independent experiments over space $\mathcal{S}$, we need to find the most appropriate estimator for the expected value of $\mathcal{S}$. A common way to do this is to use the **arithmetic mean**, where the arithmetic mean of z examples equals $\overline{x} = \frac{1}{z}\sum_{i=1}^{z} x_i$. While a common way to calculate guessing entropy, arithmetic mean has a drawback as it is dominated by numbers on a larger scale. This happens due to a simple additive relationship between numbers where scales do not play a role.

An alternative to arithmetic mean that takes into account the proportions is the **geometric mean** $\breve{x} = (\prod_{i=1}^{z} x_i)^{\frac{1}{z}}$.

We can also consider the middle value of the dataset, which is called **median** $\tilde{x} = \frac{x_{\frac{z}{2}} + x_{\frac{z}{2}+1}}{2}$. The median is less affected by outliers and skewed data than the arithmetic mean.

The **standard deviation** is a measure of the amount of variation or dispersion of a set of values $\sigma_x = \sqrt{\frac{1}{z}\sum_{i=1}^{z}(x_i - \overline{x})^2}$. In the SCA context, a large standard deviation means that the adversary will have a high probability to be "lucky" (or "unlucky") in the choice of traces or hyperparameters.

5 Experimental Evaluation

5.1 Settings

We investigate two scenarios in our experiments: random profiling models and state-of-the-art profiling models from related works. We experiment with multilayer perceptron (MLP) and convolutional neural networks (CNNs) in the Hamming weight (HW) and Identity (ID) leakage models. Finally, we consider the ASCAD fixed key (ASCAD_F), ASCAD random keys (ASCAD_R)[4], and CHES 2018 Capture-The-Flag (CHES_CTF) datasets)[5]. For both ASCAD versions, we attack key byte 3 (the first masked key byte) and use 50 000 traces for profiling and 5 000 traces for the attack. For CHES_CTF, we use 45 000 traces with 2 200 features each for profiling and 5 000 traces for the attack, and we attack the first key byte. We opted for these settings to make our experiments aligned with related works. Additionally, it is common to attack only one key byte as it is expected that the attack difficulty should be similar for the other key bytes, see, e.g., [22,27,30].

The machine learning model was implemented in python version 3.6, using TensorFlow library version 2.0. The model training algorithms were run on a cluster of Nvidia GTX 1080 and GTX 2080 graphics processing units (GPUs), managed by Slurm workload manager version 19.05.4. The number of random profiling models is set to 100 for all experiments. We set the maximum sizes (in terms of the number of training parameters) for architectures for the random model generation to the ones from the ASCAD paper [1], which we denote as 'MLP_best' and 'CNN_best'. Since more recent state-of-the-art models are even smaller, we can assume we do not need bigger models for the dataset under investigation. The detailed model implementations are listed in Table 1. Aligned with the settings provided by the ASCAD paper [1], we use RMSProb as the optimizer with a learning rate of 1e–5. The number of training epochs is set to 75. To generate the random models from the baseline models (MLP_best and CNN_best), for CNN models, we randomized the kernel size of the convolution layer and the number of neurons in the dense layer. The latter one is also randomized for MLP models. Specifically, the range is from the $half$ of the original parameter to the original parameter. For instance, the kernel values of the first convolution layer in the CNN model range from 32 to 64. For MLP, the range of the neurons is from 100 to 200. We use diverse architectures to provide general conclusions, but they should still perform relatively well (break the target) since they are based on well-performing architectures that we do not change radically.

[4] https://github.com/ANSSI-FR/ASCAD/tree/master/ATMEGA_AES_v1.

[5] http://aisylabdatasets.ewi.tudelft.nl/ches_ctf.h5.

Table 1. Baseline MLP and CNN architectures used in the experiments.

Test models	Convolution (filter_number, size)	Pooling (size, stride)	Dense layer	Activation
MLP_best	-	-	200*5	ReLU
CNN_best	Conv (64, 128, 256, 512, 512)	avg(2,2)*5	4096*2	ReLU

In terms of attacks with the state-of-the-art models, we used the MLP models obtained through the Bayesian Optimization [28]. The CNN models we used are developed with the reinforcement learning approach [22]. The details about the architectures are listed in Tables 2 and 3. All of the training hyperparameters are aligned with the original papers [22,28]. Specifically, CNNs use He uniform as the kernel initializer, and the corresponding learning rate is handled by OneCycleLR policy [24] with the maximum learning rate (LR) of 5e–3. For MLPs, Glorot uniform is used as the kernel initializer. Both MLPs and CNNs apply categorical crossentropy as the loss function and mini-batch as the optimization method. While there are other state-of-the-art models we could use (e.g., from [27,30]), we opted for these as the related works did not run experiments for the HW leakage model but only the ID leakage model. We used the selected state-of-the-art models as the authors provided the code for their architectures, making the risk of wrongly interpreting and implementing an architecture impossible. The training effort of each model (i.e., the number of epochs) is set based on the related works [1,22,28]. Specifically, MLP_best and CNN_best are trained with 75 epochs, while the other models are trained with 50 epochs.

Table 2. MLP architectures used in the experiments [28].

Test models	Dense layer	Activation	Learning rate
$ASCAD\_F_{HW}$	1024, 1024, 760, 8, 704, 1016, 560	ReLU	1e–5
$ASCAD\_F_{ID}$	480,480	ELU	5e–3
$ASCAD\_R_{HW}$	448, 448, 512, 168	ELU	5e–4
$ASCAD\_R_{ID}$	664, 664, 624, 816, 624	ELU	5e–4
$CHES\_CTF_{HW}$	192, 192, 616, 248, 440	ELU	1e–3

In all the experiments, we conduct the following steps to obtain the results:

1. To evaluate the general performance of different averaging methods and training settings, we perform multiple independent training phases for state-of-the-art and random models. Based on the preliminary experiments, 20 independent models (thus, independent training phases of a model) are sufficient to assess the performance of the state-of-the-art models, while to evaluate the performance variation of random architectures, we increase the number of the tested models to 100.

Table 3. CNN architectures used in the experiments [22].

Test models	Convolution (filter_number, size)	Pooling (size, stride)	Dense layer	Activation
$ASCAD\_F_{HW}$	Conv(16,100)	avg(25,25)	15+4+4	selu
$ASCAD\_F_{ID}$	Conv(128,25)	avg(25,25)	20+15	selu
$ASCAD\_R_{HW}$	Conv(4, 50)	avg(25, 25)	30+30+30	selu
$ASCAD\_R_{ID}$	Conv(128, 3)	avg(75, 75)	30+2	selu
$CHES\_CTF_{HW}$	Conv(4, 100)	avg(4, 4)	15+10+10	selu

2. For each independent training, we calculate summary statistics (arithmetic mean, geometric mean, and median) for the evaluation metrics (GE, SR) over a number of attacks. Note that an attack represents an individual key rank experiment. For instance, having 100 attacks means running 100 key rank evaluations and providing summary statistics using the evaluation metrics.
3. The arithmetic average and standard deviation of the attack performance metric are plotted. Since the attack performance is averaged over profiling models, the influence of algorithmic randomness is present but not dataset randomness (in that case, we should show standard deviation over different selections of the attack traces).
4. As all of the models effectively retrieve the key or converge to close to zero guessing entropy, we use T_{GE0} (i.e., the number of attack traces to reach GE of zero) to evaluate the attack result. Note that this is still GE metric, but now, with an adjusted number of traces required for a successful attack instead of the fixed number of traces.
5. To conclude which summary statistics is the best, we consider two aspects: the metric that converges to the best value (e.g., GE of 0) and the metric that converges the fastest (with the minimum number of attack traces) to the best value. Since for most experiments provided here, we obtain the best possible value (GE of 0), the main objective is to reach the GE of 0 with the lowest number of attack traces.

Naturally, one could argue that the best metric is the one that gives the worst results as it approximates the worst-case security evaluation. However, we believe this somewhat negates the idea of using the most powerful attack approach, which is a common setup for deep learning-based SCA.

We also investigated the success rate but observed that it commonly does not change regardless of the averaging methods and thus offers limited information. Therefore, we omit these results and only present the success rate results that contain more information. We postulate this happens as success rate considers only the most likely key guess (first-order success rate). At the same time, guessing entropy uses the information from the whole key guessing vector. Thus, if the attack is more difficult, i.e., the probability differences among the best guesses are less pronounced, it will affect the guessing entropy metric more. For success rate, algorithmic randomness is less likely to cause such significant differences in the profiling models so that the most likely guess will change. To conclude, the success rate metric can help avoid the influence of outliers, but that comes with a price of less information about the attack performance.

In the next section, most of the results are plotted with the number of attacks on x-axis (for GE calculation) and T_{GE0} on y-axis. The solid lines represent the average of the T_{GE0} metric (i.e., arithmetic mean, geometric mean, or median of several independent key rank experiments), while the dashed lines of the same color indicate the upper and lower bound of the standard deviation ($\pm\ \sigma$). The spaces between of upper and lower bound are filled with the corresponding but lighter color.

5.2 Results

A Demonstration of Algorithmic Randomness Influence. We showcase the effects of algorithmic randomness in Fig. 1 for the ASCAD fixed key dataset. We select two models from a random hyperparameter tuning: one performs well (GE converges to zero), and the other performs poorly (GE does not converge). For every value of the solid line, we train 100 random models, and for each of those random models, we run the number of attacks as denoted on the x-axis. The influence of the random weight initialization on the poor-performing model is greater than on the well-performing model over 100 independent training experiments. This behavior indicates that a better model suffers less from the random weight initialization, but there will still be differences in performance (recall, finding a model with optimal weights is difficult, and there is no methodology allowing that in the general case). The influence of the dropout layer is limited in this example (cf. Fig. 1a), but still, we can observe slight differences caused by dropout randomization. Finally, two optimization techniques, SGD and L-BFGS, are tested with the same (well-performing) models. In both cases, the attack performance varies more significantly than the original mini-batch optimization method, confirming the impact of the optimizer's randomness on the attack performance. Interestingly, L-BFGS does not reach GE of zero, making a model that performed well into a model that performs poorly.

Since most deep learning-based SCAs use random search to find good hyperparameters, from Fig. 1, we can expect (radically) different evaluation results based on the used architectures. While there are already results showing that these sources of randomness introduce instability in deep learning-based SCA (as discussed in Sect. 3), there is no discussion on how to resolve such issues or at least report the results in a more meaningful way. On the other hand, the algorithm randomness is also beneficial as it gives the model a better chance to converge when training networks. For example, stochastic gradient descent uses randomness to give the model the best chance to jump out of local minima and converge to the global minimum for a convex loss function. Correspondingly, algorithm randomness should cause better model convergence and lower standard deviation under the correct settings. This assumes that the training and test data have similar distributions, and optimal hyperparameters are chosen.

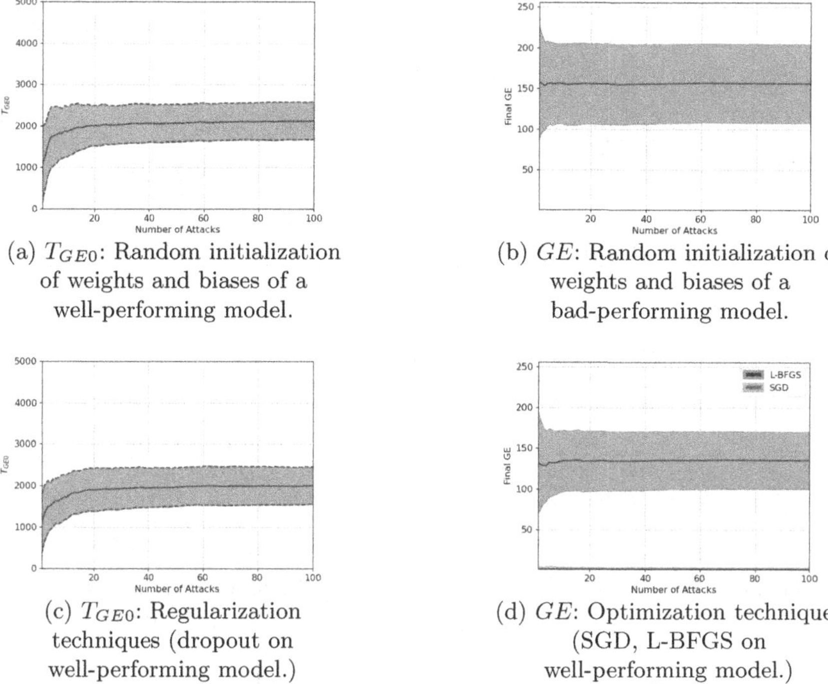

(a) T_{GE0}: Random initialization of weights and biases of a well-performing model.

(b) GE: Random initialization of weights and biases of a bad-performing model.

(c) T_{GE0}: Regularization techniques (dropout on well-performing model.)

(d) GE: Optimization techniques (SGD, L-BFGS on well-performing model.)

Fig. 1. A demonstration of the algorithm randomness for the Hamming weight (HW) leakage model and the arithmetic mean as summary statistics.

Since those two constraints are not easy to fulfill [2,30], algorithmic randomness can (and will) also have a negative influence on the attack performance.

Results for the ASCAD_F Dataset. The results for random models are shown in Fig. 2. All the results indicate relatively stable behavior: when attacking with 100 random models, the median is a statistic indicating the best attack performance while the worst is the arithmetic mean. Interestingly, we can observe that the upper deviation value for the median gives similar results as the lower deviation value for the arithmetic mean, indicating that the median is a significantly better evaluation statistic. The differences in the number of attack traces are also significant: from around 700 to 2 000 attack traces. We analyzed the key rank histogram for all attacks, and outliers (failed attacks) have a significant influence on the arithmetic mean (and to a smaller extent, geometric mean), as they consider all attack results. On the other hand, the median mean is equivalent to the attack performance of a medium-performing model, thus can reliably represent the attack performance. To demonstrate this, Fig. 3 shows the GE histogram of 100 trained models with the smallest and largest averaging performance differences (see Figs. 2b and 2d). Clearly, GE calculated with the arithmetic mean tends to have larger values.

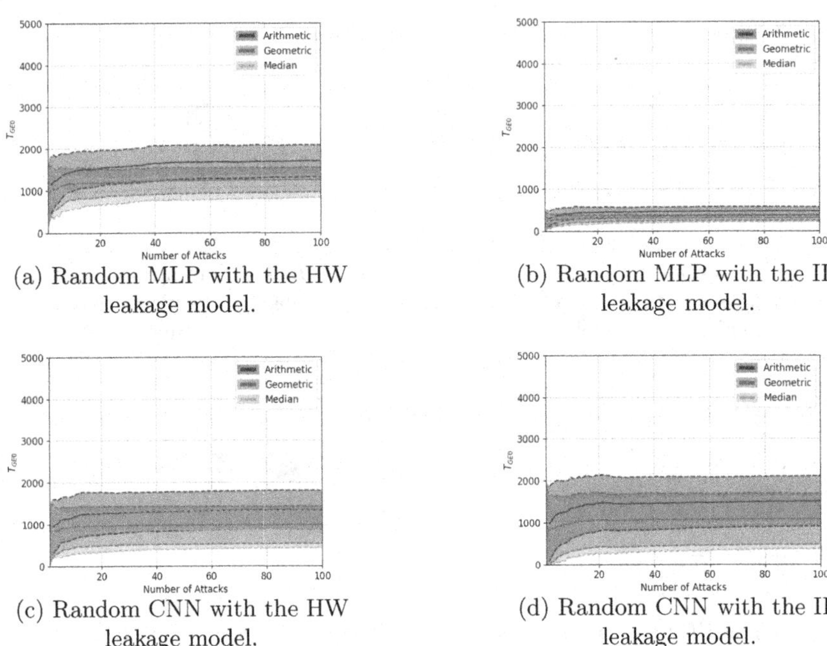

(a) Random MLP with the HW leakage model.

(b) Random MLP with the ID leakage model.

(c) Random CNN with the HW leakage model.

(d) Random CNN with the ID leakage model.

Fig. 2. T_{GE0}: attack on ASCAD_F with random MLP and CNN models.

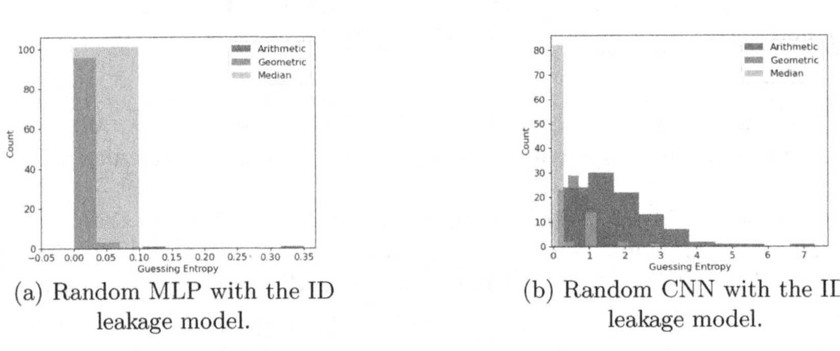

(a) Random MLP with the ID leakage model.

(b) Random CNN with the ID leakage model.

Fig. 3. Histograms of guessing entropy.

The behavior for a different number of attacks remains stable with no differences when using more than 40 attacks. This result indicates that instead of averaging 100 times as commonly done in the literature [13,22], the dataset randomness can be sufficiently countered with less computation effort. Notice how the arithmetic mean can lead to comparable or even better attack performance than its counterparts with a small number of attacks. We hypothesize this happens due to the random shuffling of attack traces and insufficient number of experiments to assess the average behavior properly. Indeed, with more attacks being performed, the increasing number of outliers introduced by data randomness can degrade the attack performance, resulting in less favorable results for the arithmetic mean. With a larger number of attacks, the standard deviation results are comparable regardless of the number of attacks, again confirming that outliers are the main contributors to the reduced attack performance for the arithmetic mean and geometric mean. From a different perspective, this indicates that random models perform well for this dataset and that more elaborate tuning mechanisms are not needed [28]. MLP for the ID leakage model shows the best results and smallest standard deviation. We postulate that this happens as the model's capacity is well aligned with the characteristic of the dataset, so most of the experiments end up with a rather similar attack performance.

We also show averaged success rate results in Fig. 4. Arithmetic mean shares the same tendency with the geometric mean, so the lines are overlapping. The rest of the results are omitted as the success rate results are the same for the three averaging methods. Compared with T_{GE0}, the success rate metric is less sensitive to the variation of the averaging methods since it uses information about the best guess only. We see a drop for both geometric and arithmetic mean with more attack results averaged, while the median remains stable. This behavior indicates that the influence of outliers when considering more attacks becomes more significant, as it skews the distribution.

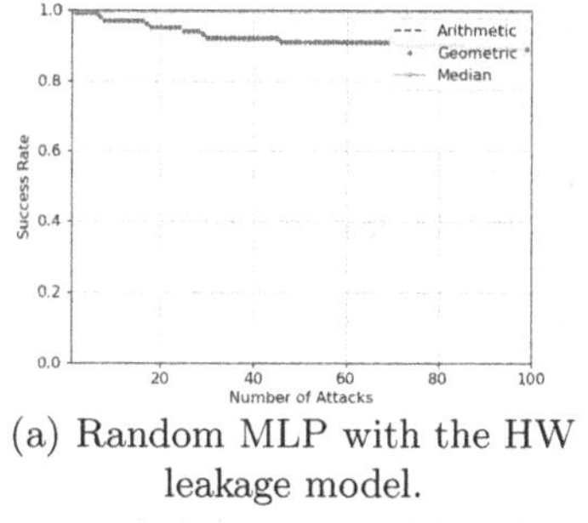

(a) Random MLP with the HW leakage model.

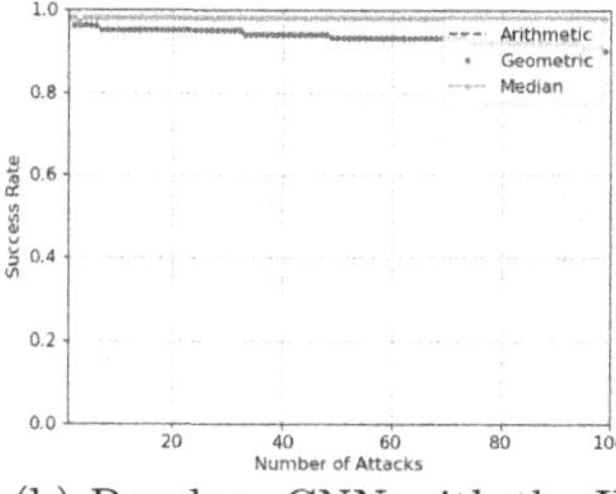

(b) Random CNN with the ID leakage model.

Fig. 4. Success Rate: attack on ASCAD_F with random MLP and CNN models.

Next, we investigate the performance of four state-of-the-art models. The results are shown in Fig. 5. The green dashed line represents the attack performance reported in the original papers [22,28]. For MLP, the median gives the best results, while the arithmetic mean indicates significantly worse behavior (around twice as many traces required to reach GE of zero). Aligned with previous experiments, the increased number of attacks (i.e., larger than 50) has a limited effect on the performance of each averaging method. In terms of the attack performance of each model, the results reported in related works are better than the averaged performance from multiple models, meaning that obtaining the results on the level of those reported in related works requires a significant number of experiments (until the appropriate weights of a model are found). Large standard deviation values confirm this as many of the found models do not even approach the reported performance. Therefore, we argue that averaging with multiple models initialized with random weights should be mandatory to report their performance reliably.

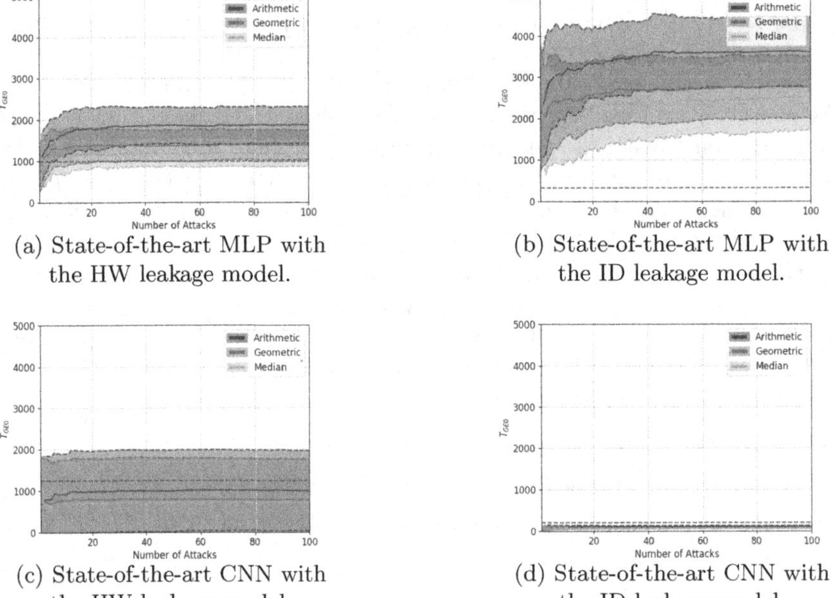

(a) State-of-the-art MLP with the HW leakage model.

(b) State-of-the-art MLP with the ID leakage model.

(c) State-of-the-art CNN with the HW leakage model.

(d) State-of-the-art CNN with the ID leakage model.

Fig. 5. T_{GE0}: attack on state-of-the-art MLP and CNN models with the ASCAD_F dataset.

The median performs the best for CNN results, aligned with the previous results. The number of attacks shows only a marginal influence, and the deviation is large for the HW leakage model while small for the ID leakage model. We hypothesize this happens as with fewer classes scenario (as it is for the HW leakage model), the profiling model has more capacity (recall that these optimized models are already quite small from the perspective of the number of trainable parameters) and more choice to end up with different performing architectures. The model capacity seems better aligned with the task for the ID leakage model, so most of the experiments end up with similar attack performance. Interestingly, we can reach an even better performance than reported in related works. We believe this happens as we (in essence) show results for ensembles of classifiers (recall, we train a single architecture but with different parameters), which is reported to work better than a single classifier [13].

In general, there is a significant deviation even when using a single optimized model, indicating that reporting the attack performance for a single setup can be misleading. On the other hand, our results suggest that the standard deviation correlates with the model's fitness to the dataset. For example, in Fig. 5b, the models had high standard deviation, and the performance was significantly worse than the literature's performance in the green curve. Meanwhile, when looking at Fig. 5d, the standard deviation was very small, and the performance was better than the performance presented in the literature.

Results for the ASCAD_R Dataset. Recall that the profiling traces for this dataset contain random keys while the attack set contains a fixed but unknown key. This setting is closer to the real attack scenario as it increases the difficulty of retrieving the correct key from the attack set. Figure 6 presents the attack results for 100 random models. Compared with ASCAD_F, we see performance degradation, especially when attacking in the ID leakage model. For instance, when attacking with random MLP for the ID leakage model, 74% of the models failed to converge GE to zero within 5 000 attack traces. Still, even in the worst attack cases, the median reliably represents the attack result and requires the smallest number of attack traces to obtain the correct key. Aligned with the previous results, there is a limited influence of the number of attacks, while standard deviation is large for all cases except one (MLP with the ID leakage model). This result indicates that several randomly selected models perform poorly and need to be optimized.

Aligned with the previous experiment, in Fig. 7, we observe a drop in success rate for the arithmetic and geometric means when the number of attacks increases, indicating the influence of outliers. The median reaches the highest success rate of all tested averaging methods in all scenarios. We also observe a slight increase in SR for the ID leakage model with the increase in the number of attacks, suggesting significant differences among specific attacks and requiring more experiments to stabilize them. We omit other results for SR as they are similar to the presented ones.

Moving to the results for the state-of-the-art models (Fig. 8), the attack performance is significantly improved compared to the previous result on random models. This means that using random models will not suffice to reach the top attack performance due to a more difficult dataset. Again, the median performs the best, consistently indicating the superiority of this averaging method. When comparing our results with the one reported in the original papers [22,28] (green dashed line), we again see a slight mismatch between them. Specifically, the reported results for CNN with the HW leakage model act as an outlier in Fig. 8c, again emphasizing the influence of the random weight initialization and the need to provide averaged results over a number of profiling models.

The number of attacks has a small influence, but there is no reason to use more than 50 attacks in the experiments. We see a very large standard deviation for the CNN architecture and the ID leakage model, indicating that the profiling model is not stable, so multiple experiments should be done to assess the attack performance properly. Finally, for CNNs, there is the synergistic effect of using

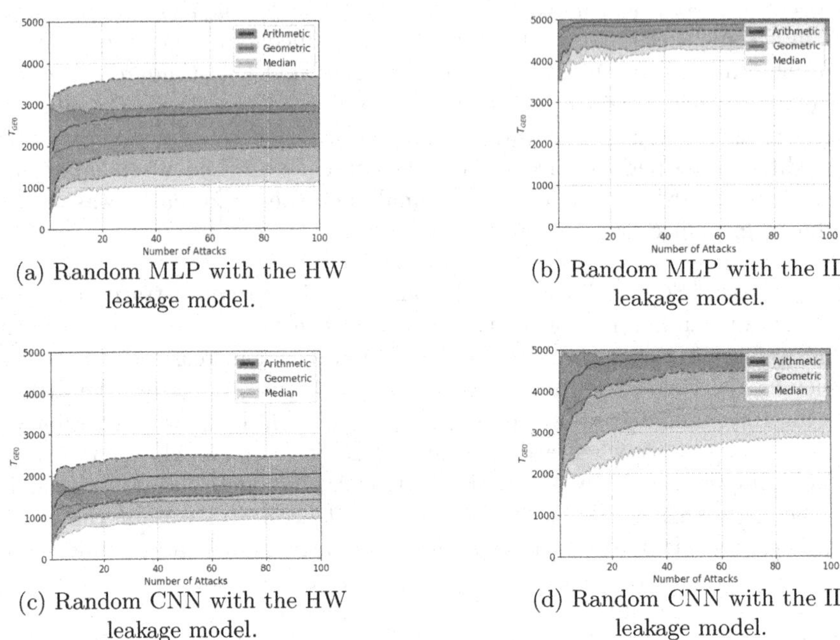

(a) Random MLP with the HW leakage model.

(b) Random MLP with the ID leakage model.

(c) Random CNN with the HW leakage model.

(d) Random CNN with the ID leakage model.

Fig. 6. T_{GE0}: attack on ASCAD_R with random MLP and CNN models.

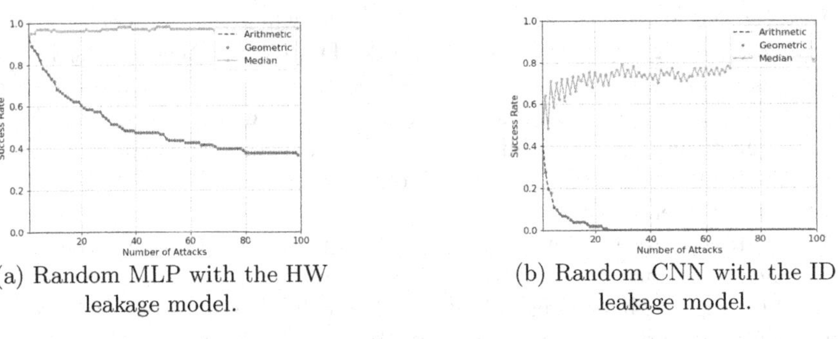

(a) Random MLP with the HW leakage model.

(b) Random CNN with the ID leakage model.

Fig. 7. Success Rate: attack on ASCAD_R with random MLP and CNN models.

multiple profiling models as we effectively develop an ensemble. An interesting perspective is that we can improve state-of-the-art architectures' results by making ensembles of the same architectures with different trainable parameters. We consider this relevant as it allows easy constructions of ensembles based on the available architectures from the literature.

Results for the CHES_CTF Dataset. Note that CHES_CTF with the ID leakage model results in attack failure according to [22,28], so we consider only the HW

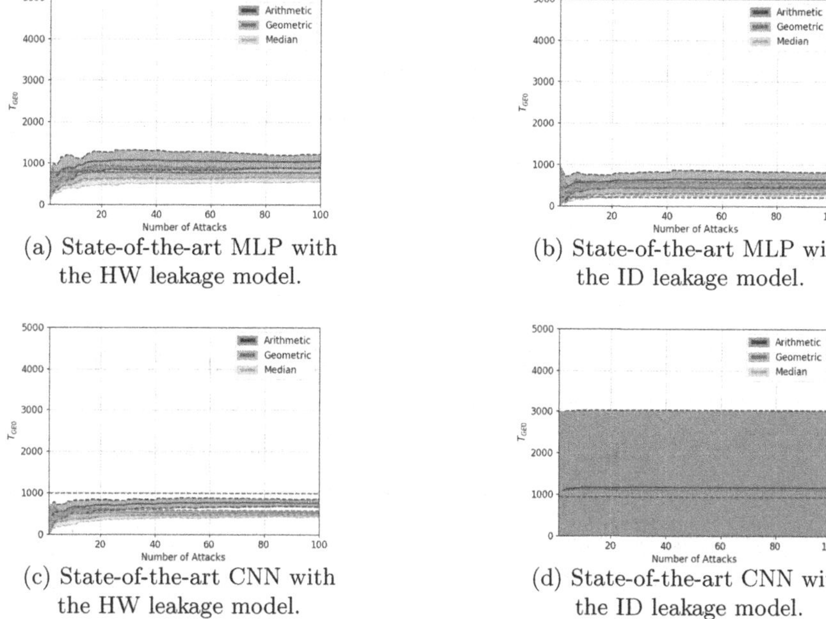

(a) State-of-the-art MLP with the HW leakage model.

(b) State-of-the-art MLP with the ID leakage model.

(c) State-of-the-art CNN with the HW leakage model.

(d) State-of-the-art CNN with the ID leakage model.

Fig. 8. T_{GE0}: attack on state-of-the-art MLP and CNN models with the ASCAD_R dataset.

leakage model. The results from random model attacks are shown in Fig. 9. The performance of the median and the geometric mean is similar, and both of them outperform the arithmetic mean that is commonly used by researchers and evaluators. The random CNNs show unsuccessful attacks, which means that the random selection of profiling architectures is not appropriate for this dataset. The number of attacks does not show a difference if using more than 40 attacks, and the deviation for MLP is large, as many profiling models do not succeed in breaking the target.

When attacking with state-of-the-art profiling models, the attack efficiency is dramatically improved. As shown in Fig. 10, for both MLP and CNN, the median performs better than the geometric and arithmetic means. Therefore, we can conclude that the median should be the preferred way of calculating GE. Comparing our results and [22,28] (green dashed line), the latter performs significantly better. As mentioned before, since 20-model averaging compensates for the effect of the random weight initialization, we believe that our results reflect the real performance compared to the results reported in related works. A large deviation value additionally confirms those observations. Aligned with all previous cases, we do not see a significant impact of the number of attacks.

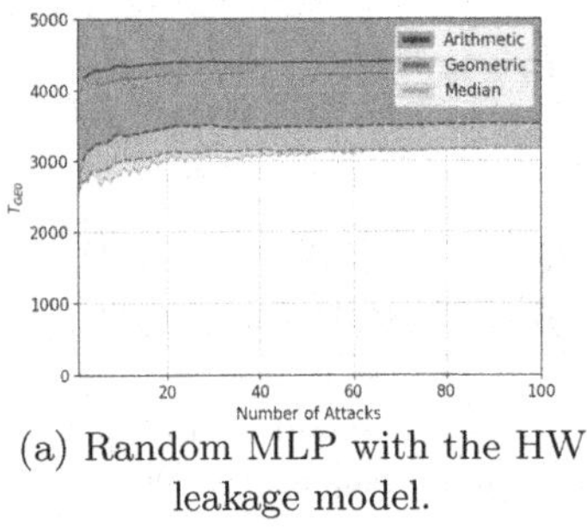

(a) Random MLP with the HW leakage model.

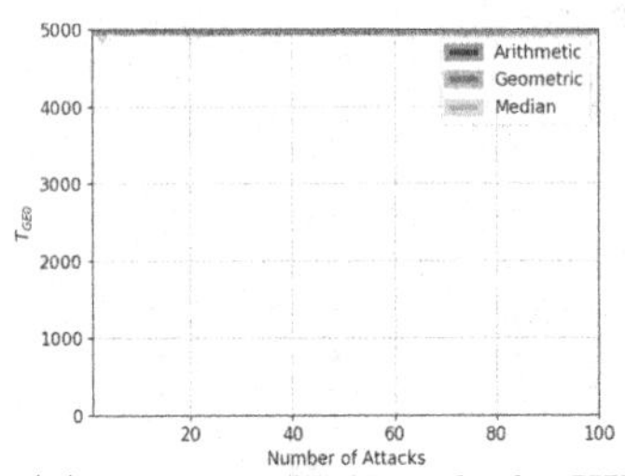

(b) Random CNN with the HW leakage model (most of the attacks failed to converge).

Fig. 9. T_{GE0}: attack on CHES_CTF with random MLP and CNN models.

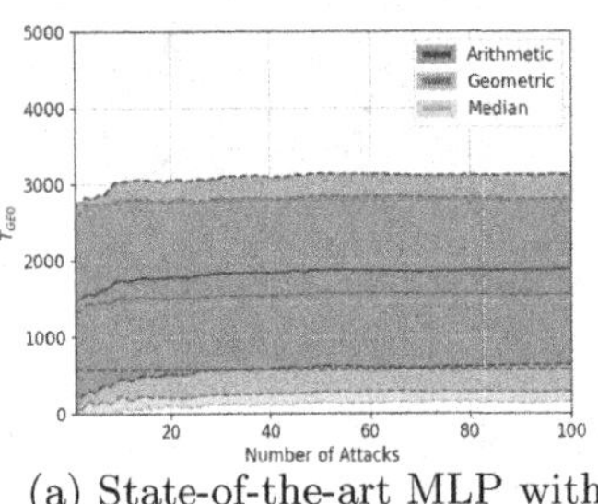

(a) State-of-the-art MLP with the HW leakage model.

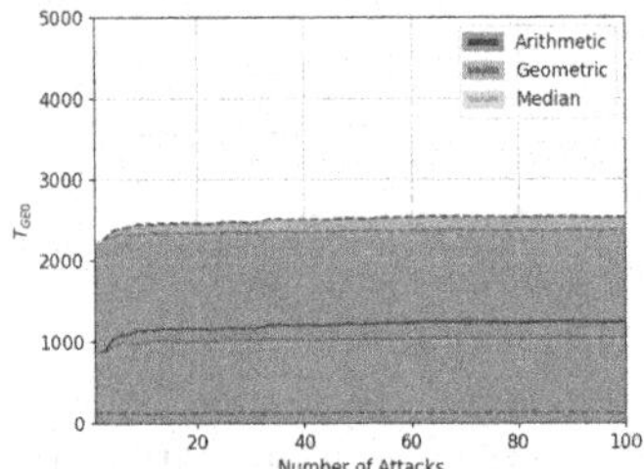

(b) State-of-the-art CNN with the HW leakage model.

Fig. 10. T_{GE0}: attack on state-of-the-art MLP and CNN models with the CHES_CTF dataset.

5.3 Discussion

Based on the experimental results, we provide several general observations:

1. Deep learning-based SCA can show different attack results due to algorithmic randomness and skewed distribution of attack results. This, in turn, makes the proper attack assessment potentially difficult, requiring the usage of summary statistics when reporting the attack performance. Naturally, if the number of models that do not converge is significantly larger than the number of converging models, even the median will indicate poor attack performance. Still, we do not consider this a problem as in such cases, the attack is difficult, and the attack performance is generally poor.
2. Arithmetic mean should not be used as the average attack performance estimate as it suffers from a skewed distribution. Our experiments show that the median is the best choice since it is not affected by outliers and thus represents a resistant measure of a center.

3. Large number of independent experiments to average the attack performance does not increase the stability of results, indicating this as a simple option to speed up the evaluation process. According to our results, the averaged results from already 40 attacks are stable and representative in all cases.
4. Large standard deviation with random models is expected as we use (radically) different profiling models. For state-of-the-art models, a large standard deviation indicates the low stability of the model. Thus, the performance of such models could be questionable when facing challenges from the real-world such as devices' portability [2].
5. In many research works, the attack performance is presented for an optimized model (regardless of the technique to achieve it) with specific hyperparameters. However, even for a fixed model, we emphasize the necessity of reporting the averaged performance over a number of profiling models with different weight initialization so that the actual attack performance can be reliably estimated.
6. It is possible to build strong attacks by using ensembles where we use different profiling models (as done in related works) and by using a single model trained a number of times (thus, having different trainable parameters).

We note that the median is well-known to be the preferable metric if a dataset contains outliers or the underlying distribution is skewed. Thus, it could be stated that the results are not surprising. While we agree, we emphasize that related works do not commonly consider or report the media or standard deviation results. Additionally, since the results show that algorithmic randomness plays a significant role, extending the discussion outside of metrics and including appropriate representations is possible. For instance, instead of showing line plots as commonly done in the SCA community, a better option could be to use boxplots. A boxplot provides the minimum, the maximum, the sample median, and the first and third quartiles, allowing better representation for spread and skewness. At the same time, with boxplots, it would be less straightforward to provide results for many values on the x-axis. As a demonstration, we attack ASCAD_F with the HW and ID leakage models 20 times and compare the boxplot of three averaging methods with different numbers of attack traces. As shown in Fig. 11, median averaging performs the best compared to other averaging methods. For Fig. 11b, the results that are not visible indicate the attack reached GE of 0, and there is no variance.

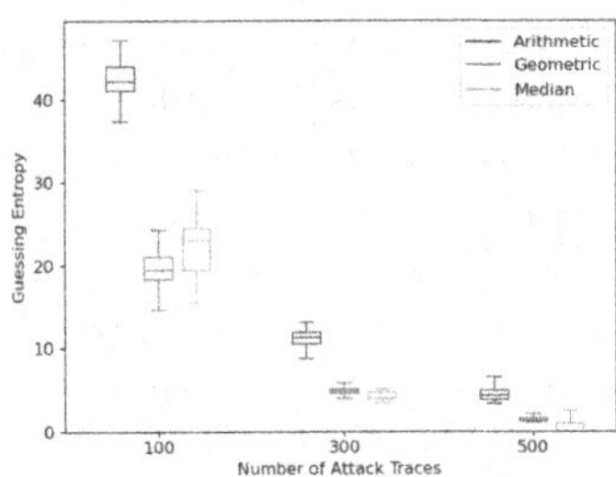

(a) State-of-the-art CNN with the HW leakage model.

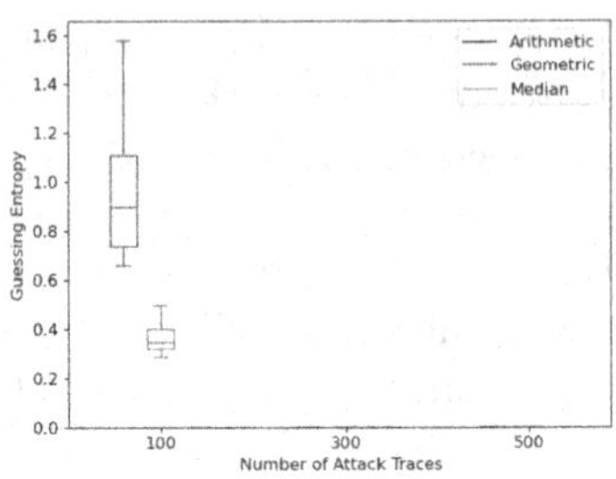

(b) State-of-the-art CNN with the ID leakage model.

Fig. 11. Guessing entropy in a boxplot representation: attack on state-of-the-art CNN models with the ASCAD_F dataset.

6 Conclusions and Future Work

This paper investigates the difficulty of assessing the attack performance for deep learning-based side-channel analysis. By doing so, we also provide a way to assess if selected random hyperparameters are well-selected (i.e., they result in models where GE converges). We experimentally show that the most appropriate summary statistics for evaluating deep learning-based SCA is the median and not the arithmetic mean as commonly used. We show that the number of attacks (independent experiments) plays only a marginal role where it is enough to use a small number of attacks (e.g., around 40 independent attacks) to assess the attack performance properly. Naturally, this holds under the assumption that the ranges for random search are optimized. Next, we demonstrate that algorithmic randomness has a significant effect on the results, and to properly assess them, it is necessary to show averaged results and not only a single one (as commonly done). Thus, while it is common to run multiple experiments to account the data randomness (e.g., averaging with guessing entropy), algorithmic randomness also plays an important role (possibly, even being more important), and the results should be reported in such a way to account for it, e.g., using the median over a number of independent training phases.

This paper dealt only with algorithmic randomness. It would be relevant to consider dataset randomness and use more summary statistics. For instance, while reporting average results over multiple experiments is common, no other summary statistics are reported. We consider reporting standard deviation a good option. Indeed, when comparing several deep learning algorithms, one can often see rather similar results. Nevertheless, the question is how stable those results are and if such additional information can help us judge what algorithm performs better. Finally, comparing the results for line plots (as commonly used) and boxplots when depicting the GE results would be interesting.

Acknowledgements. This work was supported in part by the Netherlands Organization for Scientific Research NWO project DISTANT (CS.019) and project PROACT

(NWA.1215.18.014). The authors thank our anonymous reviewers and our shepherd, Michael Pehl, for their valuable comments and suggestions.

References

1. Benadjila, R., Prouff, E., Strullu, R., Cagli, E., Dumas, C.: Deep learning for side-channel analysis and introduction to ASCAD database. J. Cryptograph. Eng. **10**(2), 163–188 (2020). 10.1007/s13389-019-00220-8, https://doi.org/10.1007/s13389-019-00220-8
2. Bhasin, S., Chattopadhyay, A., Heuser, A., Jap, D., Picek, S., Shrivastwa, R.R.: Mind the portability: a warriors guide through realistic profiled side-channel analysis. In: 27th Annual Network and Distributed System Security Symposium, NDSS 2020, San Diego, California, USA, 23–26 February 2020. The Internet Society (2020). https://www.ndss-symposium.org/ndss-paper/mind-the-portability-a-warriors-guide-through-realistic-profiled-side-channel-analysis/
3. Cagli, E., Dumas, C., Prouff, E.: Convolutional neural networks with data augmentation against jitter-based countermeasures. In: Fischer, W., Homma, N. (eds.) CHES 2017. LNCS, vol. 10529, pp. 45–68. Springer, Cham (2017). https://doi.org/10.1007/978-3-319-66787-4_3
4. Chari, S., Rao, J.R., Rohatgi, P.: Template attacks. In: Kaliski, B.S., Koç, K., Paar, C. (eds.) CHES 2002. LNCS, vol. 2523, pp. 13–28. Springer, Heidelberg (2003). https://doi.org/10.1007/3-540-36400-5_3
5. Heuser, A., Picek, S., Guilley, S., Mentens, N.: Side-channel analysis of lightweight ciphers: does lightweight equal easy? In: Hancke, G.P., Markantonakis, K. (eds.) Radio Frequency Identification and IoT Security - 12th International Workshop, RFIDSec 2016, Hong Kong, China, November 30–December 2, 2016, Revised Selected Papers, LNCS, vol. 10155, pp. 91–104. Springer, Berlin (2016). https://doi.org/10.1007/978-3-319-62024-4_7
6. Kim, J., Picek, S., Heuser, A., Bhasin, S., Hanjalic, A.: Make some noise. unleashing the power of convolutional neural networks for profiled side-channel analysis. In: IACR Trans. Cryptogr. Hardw. Embed. Syst. **2019**, 148–179 (2019)
7. Lerman, L., Medeiros, S.F., Bontempi, G., Markowitch, O.: A machine learning approach against a masked AES. In: CARDIS, LNCS, Springer, Berlin (2015). https://doi.org/10.1007/s13389-014-0089-3
8. Li, H., Krček, M., Perin, G.: A comparison of weight initializers in deep learning-based side-channel analysis. In: Zhou, I., et al. (eds.) Applied Cryptography and Network Security Workshops, pp. 126–143. Springer International Publishing, Cham (2020)
9. Lu, X., Zhang, C., Cao, P., Gu, D., Lu, H.: Pay attention to raw traces: a deep learning architecture for end-to-end profiling attacks. IACR Trans. Cryptogr. Hardw. Embed. Syst. **2021**(3), 235–274 (2021). 10.46586/tches.v2021.i3.235-274, https://tches.iacr.org/index.php/TCHES/article/view/8974
10. Maghrebi, H., Portigliatti, T., Prouff, E.: Breaking cryptographic implementations using deep learning techniques. In: Carlet, C., Hasan, M.A., Saraswat, V. (eds.) SPACE 2016. LNCS, vol. 10076, pp. 3–26. Springer, Cham (2016). https://doi.org/10.1007/978-3-319-49445-6_1
11. Mangard, S., Oswald, E., Popp, T.: Power Analysis Attacks: Revealing the Secrets of Smart Cards. Springer, Boston (December 2006). https://doi.org/10.1007/978-0-387-38162-6I, SBN 0-387-30857-1, http://www.dpabook.org/

12. Martin, D.P., Mather, L., Oswald, E., Stam, M.: Characterisation and estimation of the key rank distribution in the context of side channel evaluations. In: Cheon, J.H., Takagi, T. (eds.) ASIACRYPT 2016. LNCS, vol. 10031, pp. 548–572. Springer, Heidelberg (2016). https://doi.org/10.1007/978-3-662-53887-6_20
13. Perin, G., Chmielewski, L., Picek, S.: Strength in numbers: Improving generalization with ensembles in machine learning-based profiled side-channel analysis. IACR Trans. Cryptogr. Hardw. Embed. Syst. **2020**(4), 337–364 (2020). https://doi.org/10.13154/tches.v2020.i4.337-364, https://tches.iacr.org/index.php/TCHES/article/view/8686
14. Perin, G., Picek, S.: On the influence of optimizers in deep learning-based side-channel analysis. In: Dunkelman, O., Jacobson, Jr., M.J., O'Flynn, C. (eds.) SAC 2020. LNCS, vol. 12804, pp. 615–636. Springer, Cham (2021). https://doi.org/10.1007/978-3-030-81652-0_24
15. Perin, G., Wu, L., Picek, S.: Exploring feature selection scenarios for deep learning-based side-channel analysis. Cryptology ePrint Archive, Report 2021/1414 (2021). https://ia.cr/2021/1414
16. Picek, S., Heuser, A., Jovic, A., Batina, L.: A systematic evaluation of profiling through focused feature selection. IEEE Trans. Very Large Scale Integr. (VLSI) Syst. **27**(12), 2802–2815 (2019)
17. Picek, S., Heuser, A., Guilley, S.: Template attack versus bayes classifier. J. Cryptogr. Eng. **7**(4), 343–351 (2017). https://doi.org/10.1007/s13389-017-0172-7
18. Picek, S., Heuser, A., Jovic, A., Bhasin, S., Regazzoni, F.: The curse of class imbalance and conflicting metrics with machine learning for side-channel evaluations. IACR Trans. Cryptogr. Hardw. Embed. Syst. 2019(1), 209–237 (2018). https://doi.org/10.13154/tches.v2019.i1.209-237, https://tches.iacr.org/index.php/TCHES/article/view/7339
19. Picek, S., et al.: Side-channel analysis and machine learning: a practical perspective. In: 2017 International Joint Conference on Neural Networks, IJCNN 2017, Anchorage, AK, USA, 14–19 May 2017, pp. 4095–4102 (2017)
20. Picek, S., Heuser, A., Wu, L., Alippi, C., Regazzoni, F.: When theory meets practice: a framework for robust profiled side-channel analysis. Cryptology ePrint Archive, Report 2018/1123 (2018). https://eprint.iacr.org/2018/1123
21. Picek, S., Perin, G., Mariot, L., Wu, L., Batina, L.: Sok: Deep learning-based physical side-channel analysis. Cryptology ePrint Archive, Report 2021/1092 (2021). https://ia.cr/2021/1092
22. Rijsdijk, J., Wu, L., Perin, G., Picek, S.: Reinforcement learning for hyperparameter tuning in deep learning-based side-channel analysis. IACR Trans. Cryptogr. Hardw. Embed. Syst. **2021**(3), 677–707 (2021). https://doi.org/10.46586/tches.v2021.i3.677-707, https://tches.iacr.org/index.php/TCHES/article/view/8989
23. Schindler, W., Lemke, K., Paar, C.: A stochastic model for differential side channel cryptanalysis. In: Rao, J.R., Sunar, B. (eds.) CHES 2005. LNCS, vol. 3659, pp. 30–46. Springer, Heidelberg (2005). https://doi.org/10.1007/11545262_3
24. Smith, L.N.: Cyclical learning rates for training neural networks. In: 2017 IEEE Winter Conference on Applications of Computer Vision (WACV), pp. 464–472. IEEE (2017)
25. Standaert, F.-X., Malkin, T.G., Yung, M.: A unified framework for the analysis of side-channel key recovery attacks. In: Joux, A. (ed.) EUROCRYPT 2009. LNCS, vol. 5479, pp. 443–461. Springer, Heidelberg (2009). https://doi.org/10.1007/978-3-642-01001-9_26

26. Whitnall, C., Oswald, E.: Robust profiling for DPA-style attacks. In: Güneysu, T., Handschuh, H. (eds.) CHES 2015. LNCS, vol. 9293, pp. 3–21. Springer, Heidelberg (2015). https://doi.org/10.1007/978-3-662-48324-4_1
27. Wouters, L., Arribas, V., Gierlichs, B., Preneel, B.: Revisiting a methodology for efficient CNN architectures in profiling attacks. IACR Trans. Cryptogr. Hardw. Embed. Syst. 2020(3), 147–168 (2020). https://doi.org/10.13154/tches.v2020.i3.147-168, https://tches.iacr.org/index.php/TCHES/article/view/8586
28. Wu, L., Perin, G., Picek, S.: I choose you: automated hyperparameter tuning for deep learning-based side-channel analysis. IACR Cryptol. ePrint Arch. **2020**, 1293 (2020)
29. Wu, L., et al.: On the attack evaluation and the generalization ability in profiling side-channel analysis. Cryptology ePrint Archive, Report 2020/899 (2020). https://eprint.iacr.org/2020/899
30. Zaid, G., Bossuet, L., Habrard, A., Venelli, A.: Methodology for efficient CNN architectures in profiling attacks. IACR Trans. Cryptogr. Hardw. Embed. Syst. **2020**(1), 1–36 (2019). https://doi.org/10.13154/tches.v2020.i1.1-36, https://tches.iacr.org/index.php/TCHES/article/view/8391

Tools and References

A Second Look at the ASCAD Databases

Maximilian Egger[2], Thomas Schamberger[1(✉)], Lars Tebelmann[1], Florian Lippert[1], and Georg Sigl[1]

[1] TUM Department of Electrical and Computer Engineering, Chair of Security in Information Technology, Technical University Munich, Munich, Germany
{t.schamberger,lars.tebelmann,florian.lippert,sigl}@tum.de

[2] TUM Department of Electrical and Computer Engineering, Institute for Communications Engineering, Technical University Munich, Munich, Germany
maximilian.egger@tum.de

Abstract. The ASCAD databases marked the starting point for a large amount of research regarding deep learning-based (SCA). While most work focuses on the analysis of different architectures, little attention has been paid to the datasets used for training and evaluation. In this paper, we provide a detailed analysis of the ASCAD datasets that examines all 16 bytes of the targeted AES implementation and reveals leakage from intermediate values of interest for attribution of Machine Learning (ML)-based SCA. We show that some bytes exhibit first-order or univariate second-order leakage that is unexpected for a protected implementation. Subsequently, we investigate how training on the fixed key we provide a detailed analysis of the ASCAD database is an easier task for (CNNs) based on two different hyperparameter architectures. Our findings suggest that results based on the we provide a detailed analysis of the *ASCAD fix* dataset should be revisited and that the more recent *ASCAD variable* dataset with variable key training should be used in future work. Finally, we investigate the attack success for all bytes. Performance differences with the same network architecture for different bytes highlight that even traces of identical operations on the same dataset pose challenges to CNNs. This highlights the possibility to use different bytes of the ASCAD dataset in order to evaluate the robustness of ML approaches in future work.

Keywords: Side-Channel Analysis · ASCAD · Machine Learning · CNNs

1 Introduction

The publication of the ANSSI SCA Database (ASCAD) database[1] in June 2018 [2,17] initiated a large amount of research in the domain of deep learning-based Side-Channel Analysis (SCA) as it provides a reference dataset such that different approaches can be compared. The ASCAD fixed key (*ASCAD fix*) database

[1] https://github.com/ANSSI-FR/ASCAD, accessed 29.04.2021.

J. Balasch and C. O'Flynn (Eds.): COSADE 2022, LNCS 13211, pp. 75–99, 2022.
https://doi.org/10.1007/978-3-030-99766-3_4

contains measurements of a first-order protected (AES) implementation written in assembly on an ATMega8515. A fixed key is used for all measurements, i.e., for Machine Learning (ML)-based SCA settings the same key is used during training and attack. In order to cope with this shortcoming, the ASCAD variable key (*ASCAD variable*) dataset was released in August 2019 containing measurements with random keys intended for training and with a fixed key as attack set[2]. Along with the measurements, the implementation details of the attacked AES algorithm are made available, allowing researchers to analyze the leakage behavior, which enables an understanding of important features for ML models.

Understandably, most research related to the ASCAD databases has tried to propose, improve, and compare deep learning approaches in the SCA realm, and consequently little attention has been paid to the details of the underlying datasets so far. The analysis of the leakage behavior has been limited to a few intermediate values and a single key byte of the *ASCAD fix* dataset [2], i.e., the greater part has not yet been analyzed in detail. Furthermore, despite its availability for two years, only few publications [10,11,15,18,21] make use of the *ASCAD fix* dataset, i.e., most work is limited to training and attacking on the same key.

In this work we provide results from Correlation Point-of-Interest (CPOI) analysis [8], first-order, and uni- and multivariate second-order SCA results for *all key bytes* of the ASCAD AES implementation. Our findings show that research may benefit from using the different key bytes of the ASCAD databases to evaluate robustness under varying leakage conditions. Furthermore, we show that for the ASCAD databases learning and attacking on the same key is a substantially easier task for (CNNs) than learning on randomized keys and attacking on a fixed key. The findings highlight that the *ASCAD variable* dataset is to be preferred for ML-based SCA research, and raises the question if results based on the *ASCAD fix* dataset are similar if re-evaluated on *ASCAD variable*.

Related Work: The main body of research is devoted to the proposal and improvement of network architectures and little attention has been paid to analyzing the datasets by classical SCA techniques. Prouff et al. [17] and Benadjila et al.[3] [2] provide some analysis in terms of the Signal-to-Noise Ratios (SNRs) of intermediate values related to mask values of the round mask r_2 and the output mask r_{out}, but limit their analysis to the processing of key byte[4] k_2 only. They show further that there is no SNR related to the unmasked value of the S-box output of the first round $\mathrm{S}(ptxt_2 \oplus k_2^\star)$ for the correct key byte $k_2^\star$ and the respective plaintext byte $ptxt_2$. Furthermore, they note that key bytes k_0 and k_1 are unmasked. Other works that compute leakage behavior also use the *ASCAD fix* dataset and use the results for comparison with attribution techniques that are supposed to

[2] Recently, in May 2021, a database with traces from a 32-bit STM32F303 microcontroller was released as *ASCADv2* database. As most related work is based on the ATMega databases, the in-depth analysis of the new database is left as future work.

[3] Note that Benadjila et al. [2] is the peer-reviewed version of Prouff et al. [17] and is used in the remainder of the paper.

[4] Note that we use byte indices according to the AES standard in contrast to the indexing introduced with the ASCAD databases [17] starting with index 1.

highlight important features for the ML models: Masure et al. [13] show the SNR of r_{out} and $\mathrm{S}(k_2 \oplus ptxt_2) \oplus r_{out}$ to compare it to their results on gradient visualization. Timon [20] computes Correlation Power Analysis (CPA) results with known values for the round mask r_2 and the S-box value $\mathrm{S}(k_2 \oplus ptxt_2) \oplus r_2$ to evaluate his sensitivity analysis. As proposed by Benadjila et al. [2], in most research the third key byte k_2 is selected as target and the proposed Point-of-Interests (POIs) are used for training and attack. However, there are some exceptions: Wu and Picek [21] simulate shuffling of the masked bytes for *ASCAD fix*, but do not compare attacks for different bytes. Zhou and Standaert [23] compare rank results of all 16 S-boxes of the *ASCAD fix* dataset and the $\mathrm{CNN}_{\mathrm{best}}$ network from [2]. They show that unmasked bytes can be attacked using a single trace and observe that significantly more traces are needed for k_{10} compared to other bytes. However, there is no analysis of the similarities or differences of the leakage behavior between bytes to explain the performance differences. Lu et al. [11] introduce an architecture that takes the entire trace of *ASCAD fix* and *ASCAD variable* instead of the preselected POIs proposed by Benadjila et al. [2]. The analysis is limited to k_2, for which fewer traces are required for a successful attack when using the entire trace. Bronchain et al. [4] use the entire traces of *ASCAD variable* and derive an attack based on template matching with Linear Discriminant Analysis (LDA) preprocessing. They pass the results to a belief propagation algorithm to reduce the number of traces for an attack. The results from [4,11] suggest that learning benefits from leakage points outside the proposed POI range. Rijsdijk et al. [18] optimize network hyperparameter search to reduce the number of traces for a successful attack as well as the amount of trainable parameters and compare to similar approaches. They provide the number of traces to reach an average key rank of zero for *ASCAD fix* and *ASCAD variable* datasets datasets simultaneously. Results suggest that *ASCAD fix* requires fewer traces for ID labels, while for models using the HW label *ASCAD variable* can be at least as easily attacked. Regarding differences in the difficulty for training on fixed or variable key datasets, Hoang et al. [10] show that if *ASCAD fix* is used and the plaintext is added as input label to the S-box output, the model can learn the bijection of the S-box from the labels.

Contribution: With this work we provide detailed leakage analysis and classical SCA of the ASCAD datasets that allows for new insights beneficial for ML attribution techniques. A comparison of the impact of fixed-key vs. variable-key training shows that the *ASCAD variable* dataset should be used instead of the *ASCAD fix* dataset. Finally, attack results for different bytes highlight that depending on the hyperparameter architecture slightly differing leakage from operations are challenging for CNNs. In particular, the contributions are the following:

- We provide a detailed leakage analysis for all bytes of the ASCAD implementation that highlights leakage from additional intermediate values not considered by related work. In addition, this leakage also largely differs between individual bytes. The findings are important to better understand how networks learn from side-channel traces.

- We show first-order and second-order univariate vulnerabilities, that are unexpected for a masked implementation as the key byte can be recovered from a single sample. The first-order vulnerabilities occur only for up to two bytes when using the proposed trace segments of the ASCAD authors, while most (*ASCAD fix*) and all (*ASCAD variable*) bytes can be attacked using the entire traces. This highlights a direction for future work on understanding if ML-based SCA approaches actually implement multivariate higher-order attacks when using the whole sample ranges contained in the ASCAD databases.
- We show that training on the same fixed key as during the attack yields significantly better attack results than training on variable keys for both ASCAD datasets. This suggests that results on the *ASCAD fix* dataset overestimate the performance of networks and that the *ASCAD variable* dataset should be used in future work.
- Finally, we provide results for ML-based SCA for all key bytes of the *ASCAD variable* dataset that show that even traces of identical operations on the same dataset pose challenges to CNNs. The substantial variations for different bytes indicate that research in addition to evaluating different datasets benefits from using the entire ASCAD datasets to improve robustness of results.

2 Leakage Analysis of the ASCAD Implementation

The ASCAD databases contain side-channel measurements on an ATmega8515 of a first-order protected AES implementation written in assembly. The *ASCAD fix* database consists of 60000 measurements using a fixed key for all measurements. The *ASCAD variable* database contains 200000 measurements under random keys for training and 100000 measurements with the same fixed key as attack set. For the measurements in the ASCAD databases the first two S-box look-ups, corresponding to key bytes k_0 and k_1, are not masked. From the 14 masked S-boxes, the third key byte k_2 is usually selected as target as proposed by Benadjila et al. [2]. This section establishes results from classical SCA for the two datasets as well as for different bytes of the implementation. First, we recapitulate the underlying implementation in Sect. 2.1, followed by a leakage analysis using CPOIs in Sect. 2.2, where the implementation and POIs are mapped. Finally, in Sect. 2.3 we provide results for first- and second-order SCA, that show some unexpected vulnerabilities for several key bytes.

2.1 Implementation Details

The implementation used for the ASCAD databases employs a first-order boolean masking[5]. The masked implementation of the SubBytes operation of the first AES round commonly targeted by SCA is shown in Fig. 1.

[5] https://github.com/ANSSI-FR/secAES-ATmega8515, accessed 29.04.2021.

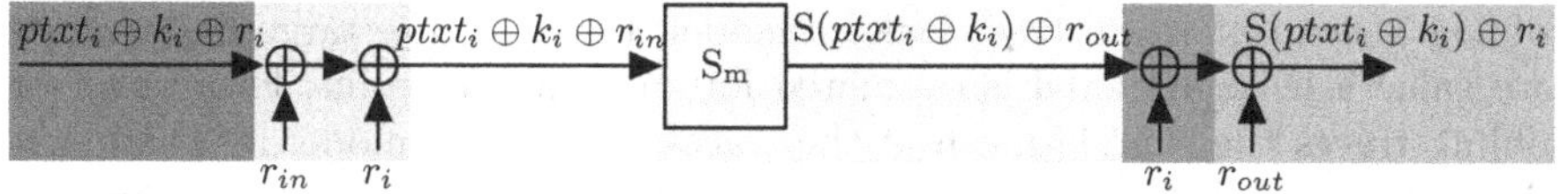

Fig. 1. Masked SubBytes operation of the ASCAD implementation.

Every key byte k_i is randomized using a mask byte r_i. In order to protect the S-box look-up a table recomputation method is used that determines for all possible entries $x \in \{0, \ldots, 255\}$ the masked S-box output values according to

$$\mathrm{S}_m(x) = \mathrm{S}(x \oplus r_{in}) \oplus r_{out}, \tag{1}$$

where r_{in} and r_{out} refer to the S-box input and output masks and are used for all bytes. In other words, a total of 18 random bytes is required to protect the Sub-Bytes operation. Note that for the measurements in the ASCAD databases the S-box look-ups corresponding to key bytes k_0 and k_1 are not masked. This is due to the fact that the implementation supports a shuffling countermeasure that determines the order of S-box accesses from the values of the mask bytes r_0 and r_1, which are set to 0x00 to switch off shuffling and facilitate the analysis. The sequence of the S-box accesses is therefore fixed to the following processing order of key bytes:

$$15 \rightarrow 12 \rightarrow 13 \rightarrow \mathbf{1} \rightarrow 8 \rightarrow 10 \rightarrow \mathbf{0} \rightarrow 3 \rightarrow 7 \rightarrow 6 \rightarrow 9 \rightarrow 5 \rightarrow 11 \rightarrow 2 \rightarrow 4 \rightarrow 14, \tag{2}$$

where the unmasked bytes are highlighted in bold. Note that the implementation makes use of additional operations that aim at clearing the value at a destination address/register or on the read/write bus in order to prevent Hamming distance (HD) leakage. An example of such an operation, which will be referred to as *security load*, is done as follows

$$\text{security load} = \mathrm{S}_m(\underbrace{\mathrm{S}(k_{\underline{i}-1} \oplus ptxt_{\underline{i}-1}) \oplus r_{\underline{i}-1}}_{:=\mathrm{S}_{prev}}) = \mathrm{S}(\mathrm{S}_{prev} \oplus r_{in}) \oplus r_{out}, \tag{3}$$

where $\underline{i}$ denotes the byte index of the shuffled order and $\underline{i}-1$ indicates the previous byte according to Eq. (2). Our leakage analysis shows that leakage correlating to this particular operation is present in the trace segment suggested by the ASCAD authors.

2.2 Correlation Point-of-Interest (CPOI) Analysis

We use known-value analysis of different intermediate values in the processing of the protected SubBytes operation from Sect. 2.1 to establish a link between the implementation[6] and points in time of the measurements. We leverage the CPOI method [8], which is a correlation-based leakage detection based on

[6] https://github.com/ANSSI-FR/secAES-ATmega8515/blob/master/src/Version1/maskedAES128enc.S.

profiling instead of an abstract leakage model. First, for the targeted intermediate value a leakage model is estimated for each sample point. From a set of profiling traces the sample mean of the traces derives the model for each possible value. Second, the correlation is computed between the modeled leakage and the measurements from a test set with known intermediates. Finally, k-fold cross-validation is applied, i.e., the correlation is repeated with k distinct test sets and results are averaged. In this paper, all CPOI results are calculated using a total of 20000 traces and a two-fold cross-validation ($k = 2$).

We start our CPOI evaluation with the trace segment proposed by the ASCAD authors, that contains the processing of key byte k_2. This analysis is subsequently extended to all key bytes, where we identify the respective trace segments corresponding to the same operations as for k_2. In a second step, we provide results for the whole masked SubBytes operation of key byte k_2. This is used to fit the different assembly instructions (with their corresponding line number in the source) to the best of our knowledge onto the CPOI plot, allowing further research about the origin of exploitable leakage used by ML models. Our results show that the proposed segments contain additional leakage that has not been considered in related work.

Before starting the analysis, we emphasize that both datasets differ in their measurement characteristics. The *ASCAD fix* and *ASCAD variable* datasets consist of measurements with 100000 and 250000 time samples taken at a sampling frequency of $f_s = 200\,\mathrm{MS/s}$[7] and $f_s = 500\,\mathrm{MS/s}$, respectively. The measurements correspond to the first round of an AES encryption software implementation running on an ATmega8515 at a clock frequency of $f_{clk} = 4\,\mathrm{MHz}$[8]. This leads to 50 and 125 samples per clock cycle, respectively.

Analysis of Proposed Trace Segments. In order to facilitate ML-based SCA, the ASCAD authors propose to use a subsegment of the traces that only contains some operations of the whole masked SubBytes operation: For key byte k_2 a range of 700 and 1400 samples for *ASCAD fix* and *ASCAD variable*, respectively[9]. The rationale for this selection is to include intermediate values $\mathrm{S}(k_2 \oplus ptxt_2) \oplus r_{out}$ and $\mathrm{S}(k_2 \oplus ptxt_2) \oplus r_2$ as well as the respective mask values r_{out} and r_2, allowing for a second-order SCA attack. The leakage of these intermediates has been evaluated in [2] by calculating SNR values for the *ASCAD fix* dataset.

Comparison of Datasets. In Figs. 2a and 2b the difference between both datasets is shown in terms of CPOI results for key byte k_2 for the limited ranges and the state-of-the-art intermediates from [2]. For comparison, we additionally provide an SNR evaluation in Figs. 2c and 2d, where in contrast to [2] the SNR is calculated in logarithmic scale. As both methods perform equally well, we use CPOI

[7] The sampling frequency is not $f_s = 2\,\mathrm{GS/s}$ as provided by [2] and generally adopted by related work. In this case the whole trace segment would only show 1.4 clock cycles, which is not consistent with the CPOI results.

[8] https://github.com/ANSSI-FR/ASCAD/issues/2, accessed 29.04.2021.

[9] https://github.com/ANSSI-FR/ASCAD, accessed 29.04.2021.

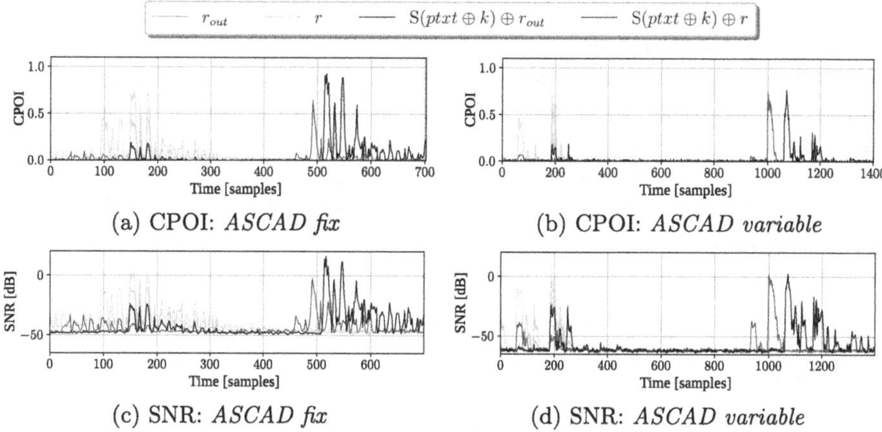

(a) CPOI: *ASCAD fix*

(b) CPOI: *ASCAD variable*

(c) SNR: *ASCAD fix*

(d) SNR: *ASCAD variable*

Fig. 2. Leakage analysis of k_2 for the ranges and state-of-the-art intermediates from [2] proposed for both ASCAD datasets.

for the remainder of this paper due to the more intuitive nature of correlation results, which are confined to the interval between 0 and 1. By a direct comparison of Fig. 2a and Fig. 2b the leakage from *ASCAD fix* measurements is present during the whole clock cycle and in addition spread among multiple clock cycles. In contrast, *ASCAD variable* shows a different very temporal confined leakage characteristic. We attribute these differences to changes in the measurement setup; see [14] for a detailed discussion of setup characteristics that can induce this behavior. A possible explanation is that the measurements in *ASCAD fix* are subject to low-pass filtering[10]. It can also be noted that both ranges do not correspond to the same time interval. Due to the factor of 2.5 between sampling rates (200 MS/s vs. 500 MS/s), the subtraces of 1400 samples for *ASCAD variable* correspond to a shorter time interval than the subtraces of 700 samples for *ASCAD fix*, i.e., the first 92 samples and the last 48 samples in Fig. 2a do not have a correspondence in Fig. 2b. Nevertheless, the important leakage features are contained in the proposed segments of both datasets.

We conclude that the leakages do not differ significantly between both datasets (except that leakage is spread over multiple clock cycles in the *ASCAD fix* case) as expected from the identical underlying implementation. In the following we only show results for the *ASCAD variable* measurements because the temporal confinement eases the match of the intermediate values from masked SubBytes operation (c.f. Fig. 1) and POIs.

Comparison of Key Bytes. To obtain comparable ML-based SCA results for all key bytes it is crucial to provide the network with input data that contains the

[10] The authors revised their claim that both datasets consist of EM measurements to them actually being power measurements in https://github.com/ANSSI-FR/ASCAD/issues/13, accessed 15.02.2022.

same operations among the different key bytes. We identify the leakage of the intermediate value $S(ptxt_i \oplus k_i) \oplus r_{out}$ as a suitable target for alignment, as its maximum is easily identified[11] for all key bytes. We align the sample index of this characteristic leakage in accordance to its location in the proposed range of key byte k_2. Consequently, in case of the *ASCAD fix* dataset, the maximum CPOI is fixed to sample index 492. In the *ASCAD variable* case the leakage is fixed to sample index 1000. The exact sample ranges for the different bytes are given in Appendix A.1.

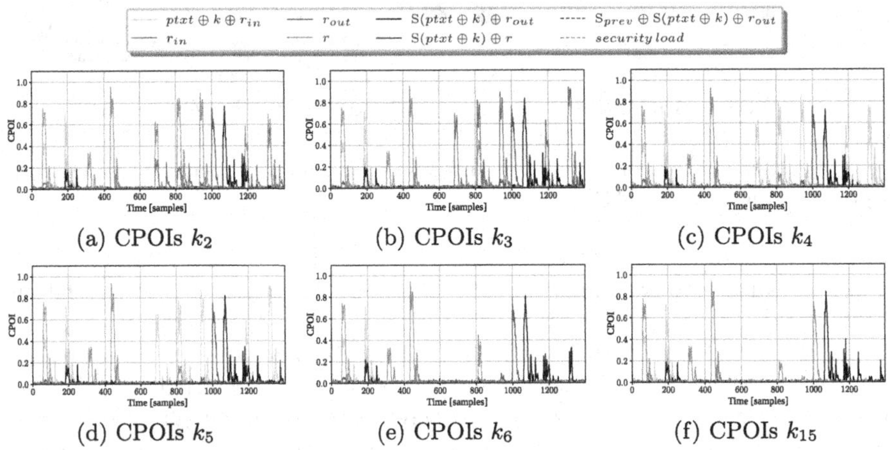

(a) CPOIs k_2 (b) CPOIs k_3 (c) CPOIs k_4

(d) CPOIs k_5 (e) CPOIs k_6 (f) CPOIs k_{15}

Fig. 3. CPOI analysis of the *ASCAD variable* dataset: key bytes k_2, k_3, k_4, k_5, k_6 (k_6 to k_{14} behave qualitatively similar among each other) and k_{15}.

The CPOI results for the remaining key bytes of *ASCAD variable* after alignment are shown in Fig. 3. To increase readability, we omit the byte index i in the legends of the plots, and the respective byte is given in the caption. In contrast to the leakage evaluated in the state-of-the-art and shown in Fig. 2, we identify additional leakage contained in the segments. A similarity between all bytes is the additional leakage of $ptxt \oplus k \oplus r_{in}$ from sample 300 to 500 (green color). It can also be seen that the CPOI plots of the individual bytes largely differ in two regions, namely from samples 600 to 1000 and 1100 to 1400. In these regions an additional leakage of either the security load (k_2; dashed gray), r_{in} (k_2, k_3; red), r_{out} (k_4; cyan), or r_i (k_5; yellow) is present. The remaining bytes do not show this leakage characteristic. For k_{15} an additional leakage of $S(k \oplus ptxt) \oplus r_{out}$ (blue) is visible in the beginning of the trace segment (around sample 70). A reason for this could be that k_{15} is the byte that is processed first (c.f. Eq. (2)) and therefore registers are still empty, which leads to additional leakage.

[11] Note that for key byte k_{15} of the *ASCAD variable* dataset there is one additional peak compared to the other bytes. We manually corrected the range such that the same operations/code lines are contained.

From the CPOI evaluation in Fig. 3 two conclusions can be drawn. First, there is a significant difference between the leakage observed for the individual key bytes. As most of the related work on the ASCAD databases has been conducted on k_2, the performance of ML-based SCA for other key bytes (with different leakage characteristics) might differ. We evaluate this assumption in Sect. 3.3. Second, in addition to the intermediate values r_i and r_{out} provided by related work, the results show that trace segments include additional leakage like the input mask r_{in} and $ptxt_i \oplus k_i \oplus r_{in}$ that might be utilized by the networks for the attack. In particular for key byte k_2, there is a significant leakage of these values that has not been considered by related work to the best of our knowledge. The presence of leakage resulting from additional intermediate values is of interest for attribution techniques to determine important features for ML-based SCA. The additional leakages we outline can lead to a better understanding of attribution difficulties for the ASCAD database of existing methods [9,13,20], which consider only the leakage evaluation by Benadjila et al. [2].

Analysis of the Entire Masked SubBytes Operation. In this section, we analyze the leakage behavior of the entire masked SubBytes operation for key byte k_2 of *ASCAD variable*. The resulting CPOI analysis is shown in Fig. 4. By analyzing the assembly code, the correlation peaks can be related to the respective parts of the masked SubBytes operation, which are denoted by the color bars on top of the figure in the same colors as for the parts of Fig. 1. The trace segment evaluated in the previous section is marked by a horizontal bar with the label *ASCAD*. The resulting sample range mainly covers the second part of the masked SubBytes operation depicted in Fig. 1, namely after the lookup of the masked S-box.

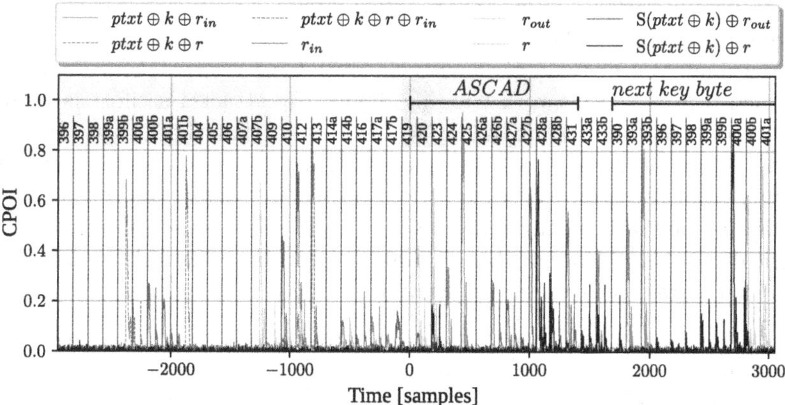

Fig. 4. CPOI analysis for the entire masked SubBytes operations for key byte 2 of *ASCAD variable* (samples 78000 to 84000). The indices are aligned such that samples 0-1399 correspond to trace segment proposed by ASCAD [2].

We further fitted the individual assembly instructions of the implementation onto the CPOI plot in Fig. 4 to ease the analysis of the leakage origins[12]. The different line numbers of the implementation are depicted by vertical lines. Code lines marked with a and b represent subcycles of assembler instructions which take more than one clock cycle to be executed. Despite a thorough analysis and study of the microcontroller architecture as well as the implementation, some correlation peaks and their corresponding code lines can not be easily explained. We attribute this to leakage behavior observable between all registers of AVR microcontrollers, as analyzed, e.g., in [19]. The processing of the next byte according to Eq. 2 is marked by another horizontal bar and a corresponding label in Fig. 4. Note that since several registers[13] do not get cleared after the calculations of each key byte, the intermediate value $\mathrm{S}(ptxt \oplus k) \oplus r$ is also visible during the processing of the following SubBytes operation, e.g., around samples 2500 to 2800.

As a summary the trace segment chosen by the ASCAD authors includes only a part of the whole masked SubBytes operation. This is clearly due to the fact that the authors chose atrade-off between the size of the sample range, and therefore the input size of the network, which has an influence on the required training time, and the contained information. Nevertheless, the narrow selection of samples omits additional information and leakages that could further be used to improve training and attacks of CNNs.

2.3 Classical Side-Channel Analysis

One of the main benefits of ML-based SCA is that it reduces the attacker's effort to perform higher-order side-channel attacks. In a classical higher-order CPA the leakage of the individual shares, e.g., $\mathrm{S}(k_i \oplus ptxt_i) \oplus r_i$ and r_i, has to be combined. The individual leakage points are not known in a masked implementation and therefore all combinations of a chosen sample range have to be evaluated. For large numbers of sample points this requires large computational resources and may even be infeasible. Therefore, a lot of effort and expertise is needed to find a promising small sample range for an attack. With CNNs the correct combinations are learned during the network training, hence the attacker's effort is reduced. In order to claim this benefit, it has to be verified that there is no first-order or second-order univariate leakage contained in the traces. This could be an easier target for the network, since it does not need to learn the correct sample combinations but rather learns directly on this leakage. In addition, the results of classical SCA are also valuable to interpret ML-based attack results for the different key bytes and to perform attribution of learned features by a network.

[12] We map the beginning of a correlation peak to the rising edge of a clock cycle, as the highest current change is reflected by a high leakage. We build our mapping on load and store operations that normally exhibit higher leakage for microcontrollers as the data transfer over the bus consumes more power than normal ALU operations. The first operation, namely the load of r_i in line 407, is mapped to the corresponding first correlation peak. The second operation is the store of the final S-Box result $\mathrm{S}(k_i \oplus ptxt_i) \oplus r_i$ in line 428.

[13] Namely `r3`, `r24`, `r26` and `r27`, for details please refer to the assembly implementation.

We therefore evaluate both databases regarding first-order and univariate/multivariate second-order CPA. For all evaluations we use the Hamming weight (HW) power model and target the intermediate $S(ptxt \oplus k)$, which corresponds to the intermediate used as ML training label. In case of the second-order attacks we use the normalized (mean-free) product as a preprocessing function to combine the respective samples and perform a CPA on the preprocessed traces. This preprocessing has been shown to be optimal under the assumption of HW leakage [16]. For the first- and second-order univariate attacks we use all available traces in the datasets, while for the second-order multivariate attack we limit the amount of attack traces to 10000. This is due to the vastly increasing computational complexity for multivariate attacks, as all possible sample combinations have to be evaluated. The correlation is evaluated every 20 traces for all bytes except k_0 and k_1, where the correlation is updated every trace.

Table 1. First and second-order CPA results for both ASCAD databases. For each key byte the amount of traces after which a key rank of zero first occurs is given. For entries marked with "–" the correct key could not be found from the provided traces.

	Order	k_0	k_1	k_2	k_3	k_4	k_5	k_6	k_7	k_8	k_9	k_{10}	k_{11}	k_{12}	k_{13}	k_{14}	k_{15}
ASCAD fix	1st	19	12	–	–	–	1960	–	–	–	–	–	–	–	–	–	–
	2nd (uni.)	x	x	5440	2060	4900	3160	4880	9400	5180	2360	2940	5200	8580	7920	1980	2730
	2nd (mult.)	x	x	620	280	540	260	200	480	340	1340	400	460	620	460	240	300
ASCAD variable	1st	10	24	–	–	85700	1580	–	–	–	–	–	–	–	–	–	–
	2nd (uni.)	x	x	–	–	–	–	–	–	–	–	–	–	–	–	–	–
	2nd (mult.)	x	x	560	640	900	540	880	740	680	960	900	1220	1100	1380	520	660

Evaluation of Trace Segments. The attack results for the trace segments of the individual key bytes (c.f. Sect. 2.2) are shown in Table 1, where we provide the amount of attack traces after which a key rank of zero first occurs. There are successful first-order attacks for both datasets, which should be unexpected for a first-order secure implementation[14]. Namely, k_5 can be successfully attacked in both datasets and additionally k_4 is retrieved in *ASCAD variable*. In comparison to the unmasked key bytes k_0 and k_1 where at most 24 traces are sufficient, k_5 requires 1960 (*ASCAD fix*) and 1580 (*ASCAD variable*) traces for a successful attack. In contrast, k_4 of *ASCAD variable* can be attacked with 85700 traces, which is almost the whole attack set of the database. As *ASCAD fix* contains only 60000 measurements, it can be assumed that the CPA is not successful due to the lack of measurements. Note that masked software implementations

[14] Note that the possibility of a first-order leak has already been discussed in https://github.com/ANSSI-FR/ASCAD/issues/15, where a normalization step allows for a sort of second-order univariate attack if observing a certain sample (sample 188) independently. Nevertheless, this does not have an influence in practice, as in a masked setting an attacker can not perform leakage evaluation to identify this sample directly, but rather has to use the maximum correlation among all samples.

are known to exhibit security order reductions due to unexpected and therefore unconsidered transitional leakage of the target platform [1,7].

For the second-order univariate attack we show successful attacks on all masked key bytes in *ASCAD fix*, while for *ASCAD variable* no successful attack can be observed. A plausible explanation of this difference is that due to differences in the measurement setup or preprocessing of *ASCAD fix* (see Sect. 2.2) multivariate leakage is transformed to univariate [14]. The amount of required attack traces for a successful univariate second-order attack ranges from a minimum of 1980 (k_{14}) up to 9400 (k_7). In the case of a multivariate second-order attack the results in Table 1 show that the chosen amount of 10000 traces is more than sufficient for a successful attack on all key bytes. As this is expected behavior, we additionally provide an evaluation of the different sample combinations that lead to a successful attack for *ASCAD variable* in Appendix A.2.

Evaluation of the Whole Dataset. In this section we provide classical SCA results for the whole sample range of both datasets. From Table 2, all key bytes of *ASCAD variable* can successfully be retrieved with a first-order attack, while for *ASCAD fix* not all key bytes are attackable (k_8, k_{10}, k_{12}, k_{13}, k_{15} are not retrievable). Nevertheless, a univariate second-order attack is still only possible for *ASCAD fix*.

The possibility of a first-order leak using the whole trace set is worth noticing regarding the interpretation of attack results. Bronchain et al. [4] show a successful attack on all key bytes, that is constructed such that first-order leaks cannot be exploited (c.f. [5] for a detailed discussion). In contrast, the attack methodology of Lu et al. [11] includes a POI selection step consisting of an encoder before an attention network making it possible that this method indeed focuses on the first-order leakage. While we consider attribution methods such as gradient visualization [13] out of scope for this paper the example shows that a thorough understanding of the underlying dataset is important. In conclusion, the availability of first-order leakage has to be considered in future work in order to understand whether ML-based SCA actually implement multivariate higher-order attacks using the whole sample range of the ASCAD databases.

Table 2. First and second-order CPA results using all available samples. For each key byte the amount of traces after which a key rank of zero first occurs is given. For entries marked with "–" the correct key could not be found from the provided traces.

	Order	k_0	k_1	k_2	k_3	k_4	k_5	k_6	k_7	k_8	k_9	k_{10}	k_{11}	k_{12}	k_{13}	k_{14}	k_{15}
ASCAD fix	1st	14	14	12960	11220	11640	2280	15240	10220	–	6980	–	27580	–	–	34660	–
	2nd (uni.)	x	x	3960	4460	5160	3120	6540	15560	9820	10380	6780	6400	12000	9160	12840	3100
ASCAD variable	1st	14	16	17160	10900	14060	2260	7760	22220	11720	15480	13800	19360	6120	22200	12740	16520
	2nd (uni.)	x	x	–	–	–	–	–	–	–	–	–	–	–	–	–	–

3 ML-SCA on ASCAD: Impact of Training Scenarios and Varying Key Byte Leakage

In this section, we evaluate the ASCAD datasets regarding ML-based SCA results. First, we describe the networks CNN_{best} and $\text{CNN}_{\text{small}}$ used in our experiments in Sect. 3.1. Second, in Sect. 3.2 we evaluate the impact of training and attacking on the same fixed key compared to using variable keys during the training process and a fixed key for the attack set. The results show that the former scenario, provided by the *ASCAD fix* dataset, is an easier task for CNNs. As the latter scenario is more realistic, we provide results for all key bytes of the *ASCAD variable* dataset in Sect. 3.3. The results show that certain key bytes of the dataset are easier to learn than others. Furthermore, performance differences for different bytes highlight that even traces of identical operations on the same dataset pose challenges to CNNs.

3.1 Experimental Setup

In the following evaluations we focus on the difference of the ASCAD datasets regarding the difficulty of training depending on the provided learning data and the different bytes of the AES implementation. For a fair comparison of the datasets, we use two different CNNs models from the literature that differ in their complexity: The CNN_{best} network by Benadjila et al. [2] is a relatively large VGG-16-based architecture, whereas hyperparameter optimization based on reinforcement learning by Rijsdijk et al. [18] provides a smaller CNN denoted as $\text{CNN}_{\text{small}}$ in the following. For both models we perform a five-fold cross-validation for all results, i.e., each model is trained five times with a different split of training and attack set, reducing the effect of initial weights and data selection.

CNN_{best}: Hand-Crafted VGG-16 Network. We use the CNN_{best} network proposed by Benadjila et al. [2] with the 256 different values of the S-box output as labels. The network's hyperparameters have been optimized on key byte k_2 of the *ASCAD fix* dataset by manual search. As we are mainly interested in the different properties of the ASCAD datasets, for the attacks on the *ASCAD variable* dataset we change the input layer width from 700 to 1400, and keep the remaining architecture identical, i.e., we use the same number and sizes of convolutional, max-pooling, and fully connected layers. With the identical underlying implementation in both datasets, it can be assumed that the same hyperparameters work reasonably well. The training uses a batch size of 200 and is stopped after 100 epochs [2].

$\text{CNN}_{\text{small}}$: Optimized Hyperparameters Based on Reinforcement Learning. In addition, we use the optimized network from Rijsdijk et al. [18]. The hyperparameter selection is achieved by reinforcement learning resulting in a network with a considerably smaller number of parameters for training, which maintains a low number of required traces for a successful attack. The authors perform the hyperparameters search for key byte k_2. For the attacks, we use their best architecture of the identity (ID) model for *ASCAD variable* [18, Table 12][15] with 256 output classes. The training with a batch size of 400 is stopped after 50 epochs [18].

3.2 Fixed Key vs. Variable Key Training

A general question regarding ML-based SCA results is how well the models generalize. On the one hand, hyperparameters such as the number of epochs in the training process can have an effect on the results and the models may overfit, i.e., only learn the specific relation between features and labels in the training dataset. On the other hand, the generalization capabilities are inherently limited by the provided training data. The major drawback of the *ASCAD fix* dataset is that it uses the exact same key during the training and the attack phase. First, the scenario is unrealistic as an attacker does not know the correct key and can hence not train the model with the same key that is later used for the attack. Second, the question arises whether models benefit from the tailored training set, i.e., whether the results obtained from the *ASCAD fix* dataset overestimate the abilities of ML-based approaches.

To answer the question we compare two settings: A) training and attacking is done on traces that use the same key, and B) training is done on traces with variable key values and the attack is carried out on traces with the same key. Setting A corresponds to the use of the *ASCAD fix* dataset, which only contains traces with the same fixed key. Setting B is targeted by the *ASCAD variable* dataset, which contains traces with variable keys for training and a fixed key for the attack. In order to have a fair comparison for both settings on the same dataset, we additionally perform training on the fixed key traces from the *ASCAD variable* dataset.

Fixed Key Training on *ASCAD Fix*. To provide a baseline for the fixed key training with CNN_{best} on *ASCAD variable*, we perform training and attack on the *ASCAD fix* dataset. With this reference, we can later determine whether the CNN_{best} architecture performs better or worse on *ASCAD variable*, i.e., whether our assumption that the hyperparameters can stay unchanged is valid. For all training processes we use 48000 traces for training and validation with a validation split ratio of 1/8, i.e., 42000 training and 6000 validation traces. For the attack we use 12000 traces split into 12 subsets of 1000 traces, for which the attack is carried out separately. Hence, considering the five-fold cross-validation 60 attack sets are available. For $\text{CNN}_{\text{small}}$ there exists an optimized version for *ASCAD variable*, i.e., we do not need the baseline.

Fixed Key Training on *ASCAD Variable*. In order to emulate training and attacking on the same key, we use a part of the traces with a fixed key value in the *ASCAD variable* dataset for the training and validation. As the results are

[15] Interestingly, one main difference compared to the architecture for *ASCAD fix* [18, Table 10] is the kernel size of the convolutional layer, which is considerably smaller – a further indication that the information is concentrated on fewer samples.

generated on the *ASCAD variable* dataset, a fair comparison with the setting of a variable key training is possible.

For the CNN_{best} network, the training and validation uses 48000 traces and the attack set uses 12000 traces from the remaining 52000 traces. We restrict the numbers to be identical with the *ASCAD fix* setting for a fair comparison. Similarly, we use 1000 traces for the attack, resulting in 60 attack sets in total. For the $\text{CNN}_{\text{small}}$ network, we use 75000 traces for training and 5000 traces for validation, and 20000 attack traces resulting in 100 attack sets in total. We use more traces for training, as the model architecture has been evaluated with 100000 traces during the reinforcement learning, and therefore tends to produce worse results with fewer traces. Our fixed key scenario nevertheless imposes a total limit of 100000 traces including both training and attack set.

Variable Key Training on *ASCAD Vriable*. Finally, the training on variable keys for the *ASCAD variable* dataset is carried out to compare with the fixed key training. We use 48000 traces for training and validation, but this time with variable keys, and 12000 traces from the fixed key traces for the attack. The attack traces are split into subsets of 1000 traces, i.e., 60 sets in total can be compared. For the $\text{CNN}_{\text{small}}$ network, we use 75000 traces for training and 5000 traces for validation, and 20000 attack traces resulting in 100 attack sets in total. Although the training set size could be increased in this scenario, we use the same size as for the fixed key training to keep the results comparable.

Comparison of Results. The analysis is carried out on key byte k_2. We calculate the key rank for an increasing number of traces and monitor the evolution after each trace. The performance of the trained models is depicted in Fig. 5 where the median key rank from the available attack sets is plotted against the number of evaluated traces.

The results for the *ASCAD fix* dataset and CNN_{best} in Fig. 5a are in line with Benadjila et al. [2], where approximately 500 traces were needed to reach a key rank of zero using the same model. The median key rank reaches zero at 428 traces, i.e., rank zero is reached for half of the attack sets with less than 428 traces and for the other half with more than 428 traces. The quantiles from 0.25 to 0.75, which are visualized as filled area show that 50% of the attack sets reach a key rank of zero between 147 and around 812 traces. From the 60 attacks sets, 12 do not reach a median key rank of zero with the provided 1000 traces.

The fixed key training with CNN_{best} on *ASCAD variable* in Fig. 5b reaches a median key rank of zero with 200 traces in half of the cases and the majority of attacks succeeds with less than 341 traces. Comparing the results for the fixed key training in Figs. 5a and 5b, CNN_{best} requires fewer traces for a successful attack with the *ASCAD variable* dataset than with the *ASCAD fix* dataset. Hence, the question from Sect.3.1 whether the hyperparameters optimized on *ASCAD fix* can be used on *ASCAD variable* can be answered affirmatively, and we use CNN_{best} to compare the fixed key training against the variable key training on *ASCAD variable*. A dedicated hyperparameter search for the *ASCAD variable* dataset could yield even better results, but as we are mainly concerned with the

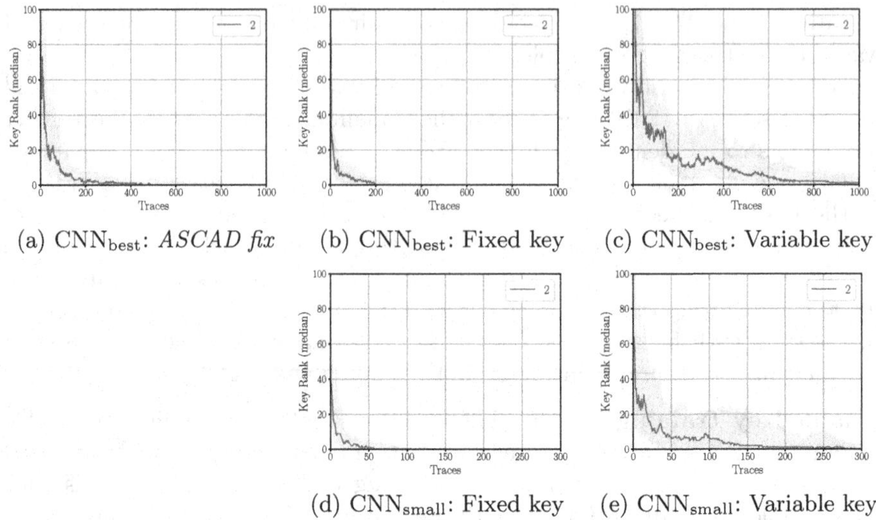

(a) CNN_{best}: *ASCAD fix* (b) CNN_{best}: Fixed key (c) CNN_{best}: Variable key

(d) $\text{CNN}_{\text{small}}$: Fixed key (e) $\text{CNN}_{\text{small}}$: Variable key

Fig. 5. Median key rank for different training scenarios for key byte k_2. (a) *ASCAD fix*, (b)–(e) *ASCAD variable*. The blue area fills between the 0.25 and 0.75 quantiles, i.e., it contains 50% of all results. (Color figure online)

comparison of the effect of training sets, this is beyond the scope of this work. The use of an optimized network is covered by the results from $\text{CNN}_{\text{small}}$.

Finally, in Fig. 5c, the training of CNN_{best} on variable keys does not achieve perfect key recovery for more than half of the attacks (37 out of 60) even after 1000 traces. Only a quarter of the attack sets, corresponding to the 0.25 quantile, can be attacked with less than 638 traces. Compared to the fixed key training in Fig. 5b more than five times as many traces are required for a successful attack.

The results for the different training conditions for the $\text{CNN}_{\text{small}}$ in Figs. 5d and 5e show similar results. While the optimized hyperparameter architecture achieves key recovery with fewer traces than CNN_{best}, the number of traces to reach a median key rank of zero is about four times higher with variable key training: The training on the same fixed key as during the attack in Fig. 5d requires 58 traces for a successful attack. On the other hand, the training on variable keys leads to a median key rank of zero after 239 traces, and for 20 out of 100 attack sets the key byte can not be recovered with 1000 traces.

Summary. We compared the results for fixed key and variable key training on the *ASCAD variable* dataset using two different network architectures. For both networks, successful attacks require at least four times as many traces when training on a variable key compared to training on the same fixed key as used during the attack. Our results suggest that the performance of networks based on a fixed key training is systematically overestimated, and the use of the variable key training is preferable to generate reliable results. Consequently, as the *ASCAD fix* dataset only contains measurements from a single key, future research should rely on the *ASCAD variable* dataset with variable training keys. Furthermore, results only obtained on the *ASCAD fix* dataset should be re-evaluated regarding their capabilities with variable key training on *ASCAD variable*. We emphasize that the results are valid for the ASCAD databases, and based on the available data we made the best effort to support our claim. Nevertheless, training on a random key may not be more difficult in every scenario, especially if the whole AES execution is considered. Measurements with a variable key could contain additional information on e.g., the key transfer and the key schedule that could be exploited by the models.

3.3 Training on Different Key Bytes

Following the differences in the side-channel leakage for different bytes revealed in Sect. 2, we evaluate how networks perform when training on different key bytes of the *ASCAD variable* dataset. The expectation that unmasked bytes k_0 and k_1 and bytes k_4 and k_5, which exhibit first-order leaks are easier targets leads to the following question: *1. Are certain key bytes easier to attack independent of the network architecture?* In Sect. 2 we showed that the leakage differs between bytes. Therefore, hyperparameter search may overfit on the leakage behavior of the byte used during the search, and the network may not be able to generalize to other bytes even from the same implementation, which leads to the question: *2. Do networks perform equally well on key bytes other than the one used for the hyperparameter search?* The first question addresses the properties of the dataset, while the second directs towards the generalization capabilities of networks.

As from Sect. 3.2 learning on variable keys provides the more realistic assessment of the capabilities of the ML models, we use the *ASCAD variable* dataset for the analysis. For training and validation we use 110000 traces with variable keys, with a validation split ratio of 1/11 resulting in 100000 training and 10000 validation traces. The two architectures CNN_{best} and $\text{CNN}_{\text{small}}$ are trained with traces from a key byte k_i and traces from the same key byte are used to evaluate the attacks. All 100000 traces with the fixed key are split up into subsets of 2000 traces, i.e., 50 attack sets are tested yielding a total of 250 attack sets taking into account the five-fold cross validation.

In Fig. 6 the median key rank of all 250 attacks is depicted for the different bytes and networks CNN_{best} and $\text{CNN}_{\text{small}}$. Table 3 provides further details in terms of the number of traces required to reach a median key rank of zero. For bytes that require more than 2000 traces to converge to zero, we repeated the attacks with 20 attack sets of 5000 attack traces to provide numbers for the comparison. Consequently, the median key ranks are based on a total of 100 attack sets instead of 250 attacks for other bytes.

Regarding the question whether certain key bytes are easier or harder to attack for both models, a part of the expectation is confirmed by Figs. 3 and 6a to 6d. The key bytes k_0, k_1, and k_5 reach a median key rank of zero with less than 30 traces compared to more than 100 ($\text{CNN}_{\text{small}}$) and more than 400 traces (CNN_{best}) for most other bytes. For the unmasked bytes k_0 and k_1 two traces

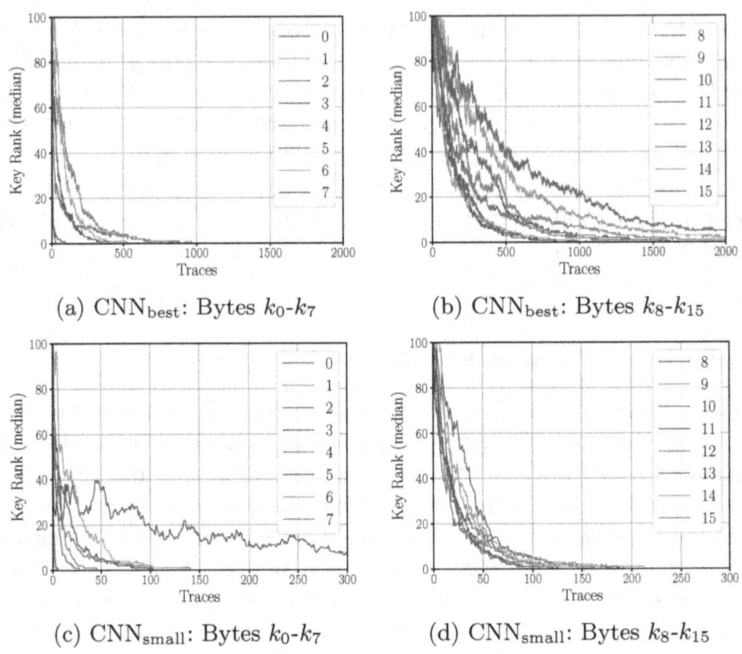

(a) CNN_{best}: Bytes k_0-k_7 (b) CNN_{best}: Bytes k_8-k_{15}

(c) $\text{CNN}_{\text{small}}$: Bytes k_0-k_7 (d) $\text{CNN}_{\text{small}}$: Bytes k_8-k_{15}

Fig. 6. Median key rank of 250 attacks for *ASCAD variable*.

Table 3. Traces to reach median key rank zero for all bytes of *ASCAD variable*.

	k_0	k_1	k_2	k_3	k_4	k_5	k_6	k_7	k_8	k_9	k_{10}	k_{11}	k_{12}	k_{13}	k_{14}	k_{15}
CNN_{best}	2	2	875	95	755	28	517	401	1598	2945*	1597	931	2265*	2966*	966	830
$\text{CNN}_{\text{small}}$	7	5	142	1210	47	29	135	104	163	214	127	118	148	176	151	108

* Results did not converge to zero with 2000 traces. Repetitions with 20 attack sets of 5000 traces results in median values obtained from 100 attacks compared to 250 attacks for other bytes.

suffice to recover the correct key with CNN_{best}, which is in line with previous work that reported similar findings on the *ASCAD fix* dataset [23]. The $\text{CNN}_{\text{small}}$ network is also able to break k_0 and k_1, but requires 7 and 5 traces respectively. The fact that k_5 is recovered with fewer traces than other bytes with both networks is explained by the first-order leak discussed in Sect. 2.3. Either the network directly exploits the first-order leakage or the leakage at least simplifies the classification task. In either case, as the CPA requires more traces for k_5 compared to the unmasked bytes k_0 and k_1, it is plausible that the network also requires more traces for a successful attack. Key bytes k_9 and k_{13} require more traces compared to the other bytes for both networks, CNN_{best} and $\text{CNN}_{\text{small}}$. Interestingly, both bytes are also among the bytes that require most traces for a second-order multivariate CPA in Table 1. However, the results for $\text{CNN}_{\text{small}}$

vary in a narrow range, i.e., establishing a link between CPA and ML requires further research.

With respect to the question whether the same network performs equally well among all bytes, it has to be noted that both networks are capable of retrieving all 16 key bytes. Apart from the bytes k_0, k_1, k_3 and k_5 that require less than 100 traces for CNN_{best}, three groups of bytes can be identified in the first row of Table 3 and Figs. 6a and 6b: k_9, k_{12}, k_{13} with more than 2000 traces, k_8 and k_{10} with about 1600 traces, and the remaining seven bytes with 400 to 970 traces. The second row of Table 3 and Figs. 6c and 6d shows leveled results among the different bytes for $\text{CNN}_{\text{small}}$: apart from k_0, k_1, k_4 and k_5 with less than 50 traces, most bytes require 100 to 150 traces. The existence of only a few moderate outliers (k_8, k_9, k_{13}) indicates that the network $\text{CNN}_{\text{small}}$ performs equally well for most key bytes. The only exception is k_3 that converges to a key rank of zero with more than 1200 traces. A possible explanation is that the hyperparameters of $\text{CNN}_{\text{small}}$ are highly optimized for the leakage pattern of k_2, which occurs in most bytes. Therefore, results for $\text{CNN}_{\text{small}}$ are constant across different bytes, except that the distinct leakage pattern of k_3 is not captured by the architecture.

Notably, for key byte k_4, which exhibits a first-order leak with more traces than k_5, $\text{CNN}_{\text{small}}$ requires fewer traces than for other bytes, while CNN_{best} does not show an improved performance on k_4. On the other hand, CNN_{best} seems to benefit from the different leakage pattern of k_3 shown in Fig. 3. A possible explanation is that CNN_{best} is oversized, i.e., its internal filters do not focus on single events such as the first-order leakage pattern from k_4. Rather information from multiple points is aggregated, but as the hyperparameters are not highly optimized (as for $\text{CNN}_{\text{small}}$), differing leakage as from r_{in} of k_3 can be exploited.

Summing up, k_3 and k_4 are not inherently easier to attack, but the network architecture used for the attacks plays an important role. This shows that the byte used for hyperparameter search exhibits an influence depending on the architecture.

Cross-byte Analysis. We conclude the training evaluation by performing attacks on key bytes different from the one the network is trained on. The aim of the *cross-byte analysis* is to establish the influence of the different leakage patterns from Fig. 3 on the training process. The 100000 traces with fixed keys from *ASCAD variable* are split into 20 attack sets of 5000 traces resulting into 100 attacks considering the five-fold cross-validation. The results of all possible training and attack combinations for both networks are shown in Fig. 7 in terms of the number of traces to reach a median key rank of zero. Combinations for which 5000 traces do not suffice to recover the key are depicted in white. Note that the diagonals consist of the required traces for training and attacking on the same byte from Table 3.

As expected, from the first two rows in Figs. 7a and 7b networks trained on trace segments of the unmasked bytes k_0 and k_1 are not able to successfully attack trace segments from the masked key bytes. Networks trained on bytes that show a different leakage characteristic compared to the majority of other

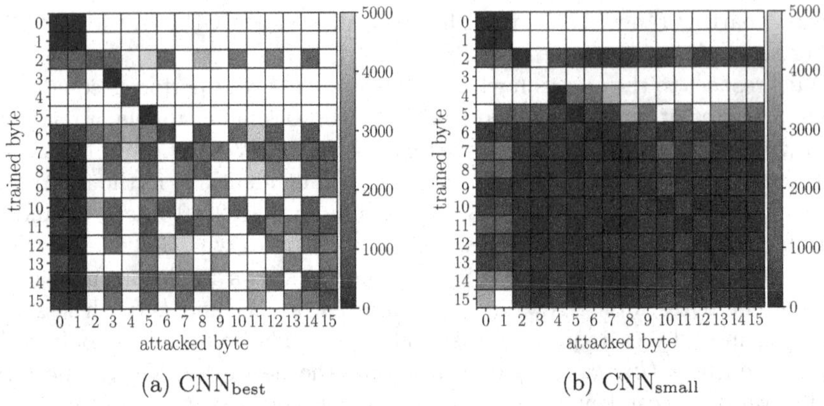

Fig. 7. Cross-byte analysis on *ASCAD variable* for $\mathrm{CNN_{best}}$ and $\mathrm{CNN_{small}}$. The color bar represents the traces required to reach a median key rank of zero. Results where 5000 traces do not suffice to recover the key are depicted in white.

bytes, namely k_3, k_4, k_5 (c.f. Fig. 3), tend to only perform well on attacking the byte they are trained for. This highlights that the different leakage characteristics (and possibly intermediate values) are targeted by the CNNs and that trained networks do not easily generalize for attacks on all bytes of the *ASCAD variable* database. Finally, for $\mathrm{CNN_{small}}$, the key bytes that show a similar leakage behavior in Fig. 3 (k_2, k_6-k_{14}) perform reasonably well among each other, while for $\mathrm{CNN_{best}}$ results vary.

To sum up, attack results vary between bytes and trained networks can not easily be used for attacks on all bytes of the *ASCAD variable* database. This implies that an attacker has to train a separate model for each leakage, i.e., results from a single byte may not be representative. This is not specific behavior of ML-based SCA but also observable in classical template attacks. Nevertheless, our results show the extent of this difference and, as most work is done on k_2, results on this byte might be implicitly expected for attacks on other bytes. Alternatively, in order to improve generalization, training on a mixture of leakages from different bytes, which has been shown to be effective for cross-device attacks [3], could be applied. Other more sophisticated methods used in cross-device learning like Domain Adaption [6] or Meta-Transfer Learning [22] should also be evaluated in this context. We conclude that cross-byte analysis can serve as a first step to assess the robustness of CNNs architectures on the same dataset.

Summary. We showed that results of ML-based SCA with CNNs differ for the distinct key bytes of the *ASCAD variable* dataset. For some bytes, the results are consistent for different networks, i.e., they are easier (k_0, k_1, k_5) or more difficult (k_9, k_{13}) to learn. Results coincide with classical SCA in Sect. 2, which highlights that an understanding of the datasets is beneficial to understand and compare ML-based SCA results. The performance differences with the same network architecture for different bytes highlight that even traces of identical operations on the same dataset pose challenges to CNNs. The highly optimized architecture $\text{CNN}_{\text{small}}$ shows constant results across different bytes, except for the distinct leakage pattern of k_3. With an oversized architecture such as CNN_{best} results vary across different bytes. Hence, we emphasize that in addition to results from different datasets, research can benefit from using the entire ASCAD dataset to test whether models are robust under varying leakage conditions.

4 Conclusion

In this work, we provided a second look at the ASCAD databases both in terms of classical SCA and regarding the difficulty of CNNs-based attacks. In contrast to most related work, we considered all bytes of the implementation. The CPOI analysis demonstrated a contribution of different intermediate values in the leakage, which has not been considered yet. Our CPA results revealed first-order and univariate second-order leakage for several key bytes that are unexpected for a masked implementation. These results along with the matching of implementation and SCA leakage can be useful tools for understanding the network's learning behavior.

Subsequently, we showed that training CNNs on the same fixed key as used for the attack yields significantly better results than training on variable keys for the ASCAD databases. Hence, the *ASCAD fix* dataset can be seen as the best case scenario from an attacker's point of view. In order to evaluate a more realistic attack, future work should be based on the *ASCAD variable* dataset and a variable key training. Finally, we compared CNNs attack results for all bytes of the *ASCAD variable* dataset, which showed that only slightly differing leakage poses challenges to CNNs depending on their hyperparameter architecture. In addition to comparing results on different datasets, the different key bytes of the *ASCAD variable* dataset can be leveraged by future work to improve robustness of results.

As a final remark we stress that the ASCAD databases provide a valuable contribution towards openly available datasets that are crucial for comparable ML-based SCA results. We emphasize that apart from the research on ML architectures a thorough analysis of the underlying datasets is required to interpret the results.

Acknowledgment. This work was supported by the German Federal Ministry of Education and Research in the project SIKRIN-KRYPTOV through grant number 16KIS1070. We also gratefully acknowledge the support of NVIDIA Corporation with the donation of the Titan V GPU used for this research. We would like to thank all reviewers for their valuable feedback during the review process.

A Appendix

A.1 Sample Ranges for Different Bytes

See Table 4.

Table 4. Sample indices for the alignment on CPOI values.

	ASCAD fix		ASCAD var.			*ASCAD fix*		ASCAD var.	
Byte	min	max	min	max	Byte	min	max	min	max
0	30824	31524	45943	47343	8	26660	27360	35942	37342
1	24577	25277	30942	32342	9	39154	39854	65944	67344
2	45400	46100	80945	82345	10	28742	29442	40942	42342
3	32906	33606	50943	52343	11	43318	44018	75945	77345
4	47482	48182	85946	87346	12	20413	21113	20941	22341
5	41235	41935	70945	72345	13	22495	23195	25941	27341
6	37071	37771	60944	62344	14	49565	50265	90946	92346
7	34989	35689	55943	57343	15	18330	19030	15940	17340

A.2 Multivariate Second-Order Attack - Sample Combinations

The resulting correlation results for all sample combinations are shown in Fig. 8. Note that for visualization, we used a convolution filter as due to the low amount of combination points they were barely visible. Furthermore, correlations of less than $4/\sqrt{10000}$ are depicted in white [12]. We limit our evaluation to key bytes with different leakage characteristics as shown in Fig. 3. For all these key bytes it can be concluded that samples corresponding to r_{out} (around 70) and r_i (200) can be combined with their corresponding masked S-Box value (1000 and 1100). For k_{15} the additional leakage of $\mathrm{S}(k_{15} \oplus ptxt_{15}) \oplus r_{out}$ allows for an additional combination with samples around index 200. Further, key bytes that are vulnerable against first-order CPA (k_4, k_5) show possible additional combinations.

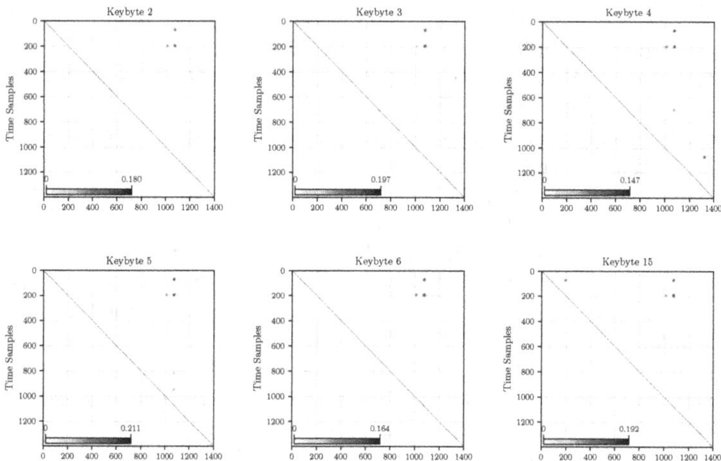

Fig. 8. Second-order attack results for k_2, k_3, k_4, k_5, k_6 and k_{15} of *ASCAD variable*. The resulting correlation value for the different sample combinations of the correct key hypothesis is shown.

References

1. Balasch, J., Gierlichs, B., Grosso, V., Reparaz, O., Standaert, F.-X.: On the cost of lazy engineering for masked software implementations. In: Joye, M., Moradi, A. (eds.) CARDIS 2014. LNCS, vol. 8968, pp. 64–81. Springer, Cham (2015). https://doi.org/10.1007/978-3-319-16763-3_5
2. Benadjila, R., Prouff, E., Strullu, R., Cagli, E., Dumas, C.: Deep learning for side-channel analysis and introduction to ASCAD database. J. Cryptogr. Eng. **10**, 163–188 (2019)
3. Bhasin, S., Chattopadhyay, A., Heuser, A., Jap, D., Picek, S., Shrivastwa, R.R.: Mind the portability: a warriors guide through realistic profiled side-channel analysis. Cryptology ePrint Archive, Report 2019/661, https://eprint.iacr.org/2019/661
4. Bronchain, O., Cassiers, G., Standaert, F.X.: Give me 5 minutes: attacking ASCAD with a single side-channel trace. Cryptology ePrint Archive, Report 2021/817 (2021). https://ia.cr/2021/817
5. Bronchain, O., Durvaux, F., Masure, L., Standaert, F.X.: Efficient profiled side-channel analysis of masked implementations, extended. IEEE Trans. Inf. Forensics Secur. **17**, 1–1 (2022)
6. Cao, P., Zhang, C., Lu, X., Gu, D.: Cross-device profiled side-channel attack with unsupervised domain adaptation. IACR Trans. Cryptogr. Hardw. Embed. Syst. **2021**(4), 27–56 (2021). https://doi.org/10.46586/tches.v2021.i4.27-56, https://tches.iacr.org/index.php/TCHES/article/view/9059
7. Corre, Y.L., Großschädl, J., Dinu, D.: Micro-architectural power simulator for leakage assessment of cryptographic software on ARM Cortex-M3 processors. In: Constructive Side-Channel Analysis and Secure Design, pp. 82–98. Springer, CHam (2018). https://doi.org/10.1007/978-3-319-21476-4

8. Durvaux, F., Standaert, F.-X.: From improved leakage detection to the detection of points of interests in leakage traces. In: Fischlin, M., Coron, J.-S. (eds.) EUROCRYPT 2016. LNCS, vol. 9665, pp. 240–262. Springer, Heidelberg (2016). https://doi.org/10.1007/978-3-662-49890-3_10
9. Hettwer, B., Gehrer, S., Güneysu, T.: Deep neural network attribution methods for leakage analysis and symmetric key recovery. In: Paterson, K.G., Stebila, D. (eds.) SAC 2019. LNCS, vol. 11959, pp. 645–666. Springer, Cham (2020). https://doi.org/10.1007/978-3-030-38471-5_26
10. Hoang, A.T., Hanley, N., O'Neill, M.: Plaintext: a missing feature for enhancing the power of deep learning in side-channel analysis? Breaking multiple layers of side-channel countermeasures. IACR Trans. Cryptogr. Hardw. Embed. Syst. **2020**(4), 49–85 (2020)
11. Lu, X., Zhang, C., Cao, P., Gu, D., Lu, H.: Pay attention to raw traces: a deep learning architecture for end-to-end profiling attacks. IACR Trans. Cryptogr. Hardw. Embed. Syst. **2021**(3), 235–274 (2021). https://doi.org/10.46586/tches.v2021.i3.235-274, https://tches.iacr.org/index.php/TCHES/article/view/8974
12. Mangard, S., Oswald, E., Popp, T.: Power Analysis Attacks: Revealing the Secrets of Smart Cards (Advances in Information Security). Springer, Boston (2007). https://doi.org/10.1007/978-0-387-38162-6
13. Masure, L., Dumas, C., Prouff, E.: Gradient visualization for general characterization in profiling attacks. In: Polian, I., Stöttinger, M. (eds.) Constructive Side-Channel Analysis and Secure Design, pp. 145–167. Springer International Publishing, Cham (2019)
14. Moradi, A., Mischke, O.: On the simplicity of converting leakages from multivariate to univariate. In: Bertoni, G., Coron, J.-S. (eds.) CHES 2013. LNCS, vol. 8086, pp. 1–20. Springer, Heidelberg (2013). https://doi.org/10.1007/978-3-642-40349-1_1
15. Perin, G., Chmielewski, L., Picek, S.: Strength in numbers: improving generalization with ensembles in machine learning-based profiled side-channel analysis. IACR Trans. Cryptogr. Hardw. Embed. Syst. **2020**(4), 337–364 (2020). https://doi.org/10.13154/tches.v2020.i4.337-364, https://tches.iacr.org/index.php/TCHES/article/view/8686
16. Prouff, E., Rivain, M., Bevan, R.: Statistical analysis of second order differential power analysis. IEEE Trans. Comput. **58**(6), 799–811 (2009)
17. Prouff, E., Strullu, R., Benadjila, R., Cagli, E., Dumas, C.: Study of deep learning techniques for side-channel analysis and introduction to ASCAD database. Cryptology ePrint Archive, Report 2018/053 (2018). https://eprint.iacr.org/2018/053
18. Rijsdijk, J., Wu, L., Perin, G., Picek, S.: Reinforcement learning for hyperparameter tuning in deep learning-based side-channel analysis. IACR Trans. Cryptogr. Hardw. Embed. Syst. **2021**(3), 677–707 (2021). https://doi.org/10.46586/tches.v2021.i3.677-707, https://tches.iacr.org/index.php/TCHES/article/view/8989
19. Seuschek, H., Rass, S.: Side-channel leakage models for RISC instruction set architectures from empirical data. Microprocess. Microsyst. **47**, 74–81 (2016)
20. Timon, B.: Non-profiled deep learning-based side-channel attacks with sensitivity analysis. IACR Trans. Cryptogr. Hardw. Embed. Syst. **2019**(2), 107–131 (2019)
21. Wu, L., Picek, S.: Remove some noise: on pre-processing of side-channel measurements with autoencoders. IACR Trans. Cryptogr. Hardw. Embed. Syst. **2020**(4), 389–415 (2020)

22. Yu, H., Shan, H., Panoff, M., Jin, Y.: Cross-device profiled side-channel attacks using meta-transfer learning. In: 2021 58th ACM/IEEE Design Automation Conference (DAC). IEEE, December 2021. https://doi.org/10.1109/dac18074.2021.9586100
23. Zhou, Y., Standaert, F.-X.: Deep learning mitigates but does not annihilate the need of aligned traces and a generalized ResNet model for side-channel attacks. J. Cryptogr. Eng. **10**(1), 85–95 (2019). https://doi.org/10.1007/s13389-019-00209-3

FIPAC: Thwarting Fault- and Software-Induced Control-Flow Attacks with ARM Pointer Authentication

Robert Schilling[1(✉)], Pascal Nasahl[1], and Stefan Mangard[1,2]

[1] Graz University of Technology, Graz, Austria
{robert.schilling,pascal.nasahl,stefan.mangard}@iaik.tugraz.at
[2] Lamarr Security Research, Graz, Austria

Abstract. With improvements in computing technology, more and more applications in the Internet-of-Things, mobile devices, or automotive area embed powerful ARM processors. These systems can be attacked by redirecting the control-flow to bypass critical pieces of code such as privilege checks or signature verifications or to perform other fault attacks on applications or security mechanisms like secure boot. Control-flow hijacks can be performed using classical software vulnerabilities, physical fault attacks, or software-induced faults. To cope with this threat and to protect the control-flow, dedicated countermeasures are needed.

Control-flow integrity (CFI) aims to be a generic solution to counteract control-flow hijacks. However, software-based CFI typically either protects against software or fault attacks, but not against both. While hardware-assisted CFI can mitigate both, they require hardware changes, which are unrealistic for existing architectures. Thus, a wide range of systems remains unprotected and vulnerable to control-flow attacks.

This work presents FIPAC, a software-based CFI scheme protecting the execution at basic block granularity against software *and* fault attacks. FIPAC exploits ARM pointer authentication of ARMv8.6-A to implement a cryptographically signed control-flow graph. We cryptographically link the correct sequence of executed basic blocks to enforce CFI at this level. We use a custom LLVM-based toolchain to automatically instrument programs. The evaluation on SPEC2017 with different security policies shows a geometric mean code overhead between 51–91% and a runtime overhead between 19–63%. For embedded benchmarks, we measured geometric mean runtime overheads between 49–168%. While these overheads are higher than for countermeasures against software attacks, FIPAC outperforms related work protecting the control-flow against faults. FIPAC is an efficient solution to protect software- *and* fault-based CFI attacks on basic block level on modern ARM devices.

1 Introduction

ARM-based systems are ubiquitous as billions of devices featuring such a processor are shipped, including mobile devices, the Internet-of-Things, or electronic

J. Balasch and C. O'Flynn (Eds.): COSADE 2022, LNCS 13211, pp. 100–124, 2022.
https://doi.org/10.1007/978-3-030-99766-3_5

control units. This growing trend continues, and ARM expects to embed up to a trillion cores over the next two decades [34]. However, those devices are attacked using control-flow hijacks, posing a severe threat. These attacks hijack the control-flow to further bypass safety- and security-critical checks, such as privilege or password verifications, but they also bypass additional countermeasures implemented in software. Multiple attack methodologies covering different attacker models have been developed, which can induce control-flow hijacks.

Classical control-flow hijacks are performed in software, exploiting a memory vulnerability to modify code-pointers or return addresses. This strategy allows an adversary to perform powerful Turing-complete attacks, such as ROP [49] or JOP [12]. These techniques have successfully been used to attack many devices, from embedded devices to secure enclaves [22,24,30].

When considering faults, the attack surface of control-flow hijacks increases. Faults can manipulate the control-flow at a much finer granularity. Direct branches or calls are a target of fault-based control-flow attacks, allowing an attacker to arbitrarily jump. Consequently, faults on the control-flow are used to bypass security defenses. Recent work [63] describes a NaCl sandbox exploit, where Rowhammer was used to manipulate the branch target of an indirect branch. In [52], remote code execution was crafted by inducing bitflips via the network on the program's global offset table. There are several exploits where faults are used to bypass secure boot [17,19,55] or escalate Linux privileges [54,57].

To counteract control-flow attacks, control-flow integrity (CFI) aims to protect the control-flow in different threat models. CFI addressing a software attacker [2,27,33,38] protect code-pointers enforcing coarse-grained CFI. They only protect indirect control-flow transfers, *i.e.*, indirect calls or returns, but they do not offer protection against faults. Fine-grained countermeasures [3,18,42] protect any control-flow transfer, *i.e.*, direct and indirect calls/branches or jumps and returns, to mitigate control-flow hijacks triggered by faults. Consequently, this comprehensive protection yields larger overheads when realized in software.

Although fine-grained CFI schemes are strong countermeasures against fault attacks, they do not consider software attackers in their threat model. While there exist countermeasures protecting against both threats, they presume intrusive hardware changes [13,59]. Those schemes require to implement a custom processor, which is unrealistic for large-scale deployment, especially on closed architectures. This leaves many applications exposed to software- or fault-based control-flow attacks. Hence, there is a need for new countermeasures that protect programs against both threats but without hardware changes.

Contribution

We present FIPAC, a software-based CFI scheme protecting the execution at basic block granularity of ARM devices against software *and* fault attacks. FIPAC's threat model considers an attacker hijacking the control-flow on basic block level, independent of the attack methodology. We address this threat model and protect the control-flow by implementing a basic block level CFI scheme, using a keyed state update resistant to memory bugs. FIPAC cryptographically links the sequence of basic blocks at compile-time and verifies the executed sequence at runtime. We exploit ARM pointer authentication of ARMv8.6-A for efficient linking and verification. We provide an LLVM-based toolchain to protect programs without user interaction. We validate the prototype using a simulator supporting ARMv8.6-A. To evaluate the runtime performance of FIPAC, we emulate the overheads of PA instructions and run SPEC2017 and other embedded benchmarks on existing hardware. Moreover, we provide a security evaluation and discuss different security policies. Summarized, our contributions are:

- We present an efficient basic block granular CFI protection scheme for ARM-based systems protecting the control-flow against fault *and* software attacks.
- We present a prototype implementation exploiting the ARM pointer authentication of the ARMv8.6-A.
- We provide a custom open-source[1] LLVM-based toolchain to automatically instrument and protect arbitrary programs.
- We perform a functional and performance evaluation based on SPEC2017 and other embedded benchmarks and discuss different security policies.

2 Background

This section introduces fault attacks control-flow attacks and discusses CFI.

2.1 Fault Attacks

In a fault attack, the attacker influences the device's operating conditions to manipulate an inner system state. Established fault attacks require physical access [6], but new methodologies, like Rowhammer [26], Plundervolt [40], or VoltJockey [45], allow an attacker to induce faults remotely in software, increasing the severity on commodity devices. Irrespective of the methodology, the fault model defines if the fault targets data or the control-flow. When targeting data, the induced fault is mainly used to break cryptographic primitives [8,10,45,51]. Counteracting these attacks requires data redundancy schemes [7,25] capable of detecting such faults. However, data protection schemes cannot prevent hijacks of the control-flow of a program using a fault. In this threat model [41,52,54,63], the adversary arbitrarily redirects the control-flow, e.g., to sensitive code blocks.

2.2 Control-Flow Attacks

In a control-flow attack, the adversary hijacks the program's control-flow to redirect it, by using software vulnerabilities or faults. In software-triggered control-flow attacks, the adversary exploits a memory bug and overwrites code- or data pointers, used for return addresses [49], jumps [12], or data-pointers [21].

[1] Available at https://github.com/Fipac/Fipac.

Although faults can be used to attack the same control-flow (return addresses, code- or data pointers), faults increase the attack surface. While in a software attack the adversary is limited by the exploitability of the underlying memory bug, faults allow to hijack the control-flow arbitrarily. Faults can corrupt [31] or skip instructions [9], change the program counter [41,54,55], or modify addresses used by indirect or direct calls in registers, memory, or the code segment [39, 56]. These attacks target the control-flow within (intra) or over (inter) a basic block, *i.e.*, consecutive instructions without control-flow. While intra basic block attacks allow the attacker to skip/manipulate individual instructions in a basic block, inter basic block attacks enable the attacker to redirect the control-flow to an arbitrary code position by corrupting addresses of branches/calls.

2.3 Control-Flow Integrity

To protect a program from intra/inter basic block control-flow attacks, enforcing control-flow integrity has shown to be an effective defense [2]. Existing software-based CFI schemes provide different enforcement granularities and either address a software *or* fault attacker but not both. Although there are schemes addressing both threats, they require hardware changes, which are not feasible for commodity systems.

Software CFI Schemes. Software CFI (SCFI) [2] protects the program from a software adversary performing control-flow hijacks. The coarse-grained CFI policy only protects indirect calls or returns. CPI [15] and CCFI [38] protect a broad range of forward- and backward-edges of the program by maintaining the integrity of code-pointers. PARTS [33] protects code-pointers by signing and verifying them using ARM pointer authentication before using them. If the verification fails, *i.e.*, the pointer authentication code (PAC) does not match the expected PAC, the application stops. PACStack [32] protects return addresses on the stack by utilizing PA to cryptographically link and verify them.

Fault CFI Schemes. Fault CFI schemes (FCFI) consider an attacker performing fault attacks, thus, operating on a finer granularity. FCFI schemes capable of *detecting* intra basic block control-flow hijacks, e.g., instruction skips, employ a global CFI state, which is updated with the execution of each instruction. Maintaining and checking a state at this granularity is expensive, so these schemes require hardware changes [13,50,59,60]. As this is not possible for commodity devices, software-based FCFI schemes provide a trade-off between security and performance by protecting all control-flow transitions between basic blocks, hence, providing inter basic block CFI. In CFCSS [42] and SWIFT [47], each basic block is assigned a signature to update a global CFI state.

Pseudocode 1 shows an XOR-based state update function, like in CFCSS [42], where a global CFI state S is XORed with the basic block signature Sig_{BB}. At certain program locations, checks are included, comparing the CFI state to the expected value to detect control-flow deviations. This approach of CFCSS yields a runtime overhead between 107–426% [18]. ACFC [58] reduces the performance

Pseudocode 1. CFI state update function.

```
function UPDATE(S, Sig_BB)
    r_1 ← Sig_BB
    S ← S ⊕ r_1
```

penalty down to 47% by decreasing the checking precision and thereby reducing the security guarantees. Other approaches [20,28] annotate the source code with counter increment and verification macros to detect control-flow deviations.

3 Threat Model and Attack Scenario

This section presents the threat model, shows how it bypasses existing SCFI and FCFI schemes, and then states the required properties for secure SCFI schemes.

3.1 Threat Model

FIPAC considers an attacker performing software and fault attacks. This attacker aims to hijack direct or indirect control-flow transfers, *i.e.*, the threat model of FIPAC covers all transfers between basic blocks of the program, *i.e.*, direct, indirect, and conditional branches, direct and indirect calls, and arbitrary jumps. We consider attacks on the control-flow independently of the methodology, *i.e.*, we cover physical or software-induced fault attacks or software attacks. We expect the CFI protection to detect control-flow deviations to avoid further exploitation. The detection rather than its prevention aligns with threat models of related FCFI schemes. The attacker has binary access and can read all instructions and data. This threat model includes software attackers using this information to exploit a memory bug to conduct a control-flow hijack, e.g., manipulating code-pointers. We assume ARM pointer authentication to be cryptographically secure and that its keys are isolated from user applications.

We only consider control-flow hijacks on the CFG's edges, so we exclude attacks within a basic block, e.g., instruction skips. However, our assumed threat model aligns with several real-world exploits [11,41,63] hijacking the control-flow at these edges. Nevertheless, as security-critical code can still require stronger protection, we discuss the usage of FIPAC at instruction granularity in Sect. 7. DOP or faults on the data or the computation are not in the scope, including data used during a conditional branch or data used in cryptographic algorithms. To protect them, it requires orthogonal defenses, e.g., data encoding or instruction replication. For a full fault protection, a combination of both the protection of data and processing and a control-flow protection like FIPAC is required.

3.2 Attack Scenario

Bypassing SCFI. Most software CFI schemes [2,15,32,33,53,64] do not consider a faults in their threat model. As the programs' code section is immutable, SCFI

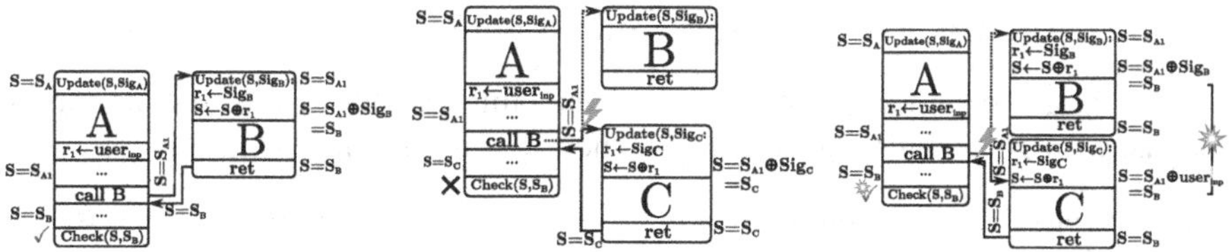

(a) Valid control-flow. **(b) Detectable attack.** **(c) Successful attack.**

Fig. 1. Attacker scenario to bypass FCFI.

schemes only protect indirect control-flow transfers but not direct calls and other branches. Hence, a targeted fault to the code segment of a program or directly within the execution, e.g., a fault on the program counter or the immediate value of a direct call, cannot be detected by SCFI.

Bypassing FCFI. The threat models of software-based FCFI schemes do not consider classical software attackers. Contrary to SCFI [2], where memory is considered to be vulnerable, typical FCFI schemes do not include this in their threat model. An attacker exploiting a memory bug can tamper the CFI state, which is maintained in software. As the state update function is known, an attacker-controlled CFI state can be crafted. Even a naïve combination of SCFI and FCFI, secure in their threat model, can be bypassed (Sect. 6.2) with a combined fault and software attack. To highlight the conceptional weaknesses of FCFI schemes, we demonstrate an attack bypassing FCFI with its state update function, shown in Pseudocode 1 and similarly used in many software-based FCFI schemes [42]. They compute their CFI states in software and load them into a register at some point. The goal is to exploit this instruction sequence of the state update to manipulate the CFI state to an attacker-defined value, *i.e.*, bypassing CFI.

Figure 1 shows the attacker scenario for a control-flow hijack. Without an attacker, Fig. 1a shows a valid control-flow transfer, where `A` calls `B`. When entering `B`, the state update function updates the global state S to the beginning state S_B by XORing Sig_B to S. After returning from `B`, a CFI check verifies that S equals the pre-computed state S_B. In Fig. 1b, we consider an attacker redirecting the control-flow of the call from `B` to `C`. At the beginning of `C`, the state update XORs the current state S with the signature `C`. As this state $S = S_C$ deviates from the pre-computed state S_B, the control-flow hijack can be detected in the final check. Figure 1c shows a successful attack on the control-flow, bypassing FCFI. The attacker controls register r_1, e.g., it is used to store user input, or it is modified due to a memory bug or fault. The adversary again redirects the control-flow from `B` to `C` but omits the signature load to r_1. Since r_1 is controlled by the attacker, who knows all states and signatures, the final state of `C` can be forged to match the end state of `B`. Eventually, the final CFI check in `A` cannot detect the control-flow hijack. Note, the control-flow redirect in Fig. 1b or 1c can either be performed with a software attack or by inducing faults.

3.3 CFI Against Software and Fault Attacks

To protect the system against software *and* fault attacks and to enable large-scale usage, CFI schemes need to fulfill the following requirements:

1. The defense needs to enforce the CFI at a fine granularity, *i.e.*, at least on basic block level, to protect from a fault attacker.
2. The proper selection of the CFI state update function is essential, as it directly influences the security of the CFI scheme. Choosing a weak state update function, e.g., an XOR, allows an attacker to bypass the protection. Furthermore, the state update function must be accumulating, meaning that the next CFI state depends on the value of the previous CFI state.
3. The protection should not require hardware changes and can be implemented in software to make the protection deployable for a wide range of devices.
4. To support legacy codebases and to enable easy deployment, the protection must be applied automatically, *i.e.*, during compilation, and must not require source code changes.

Previous fine-grained CFI protection with keyed update functions require expensive hardware changes and are not suitable for commodity devices. In [13,59], the program is encrypted at compile-time, and the instructions are decrypted at runtime using control-flow dependent information. However, both schemes require intrusive hardware changes in the processor and are therefore inapplicable for large-scale deployment. Hence, there is a need for efficient CFI schemes considering software and fault attacks, which do not require hardware changes.

4 FIPAC

This section presents FIPAC, an efficient software-based CFI solution for ARM-based devices, fulfilling the abovementioned requirements. We first show the state-based CFI concept based on the work of Wilken and Shen [61,62] and then discuss how indirect calls are protected. Finally, we discuss the selection of the state update function and the check placement in the program.

4.1 Signature-Based Control-Flow Integrity

FIPAC is a state-based CFI protection scheme, where every basic block in the program corresponds to a well-defined CFI state. This state is maintained globally through the program execution. The CFI state is checked to match the expected state at certain program locations, indicating that no control-flow error occurred. To consider the history of the execution-flow, the next CFI state is linked with the previous one, allowing FIPAC to enforce the CFG.

Programs do not have a linear control-flow but contain control-flow transfers, such as conditional branches, loops, or calls. Depending on which program path is executed, the CFI state for a certain basic block differs since it has more than one predecessor. When the control-flow merges, *i.e.*, for conditional branches,

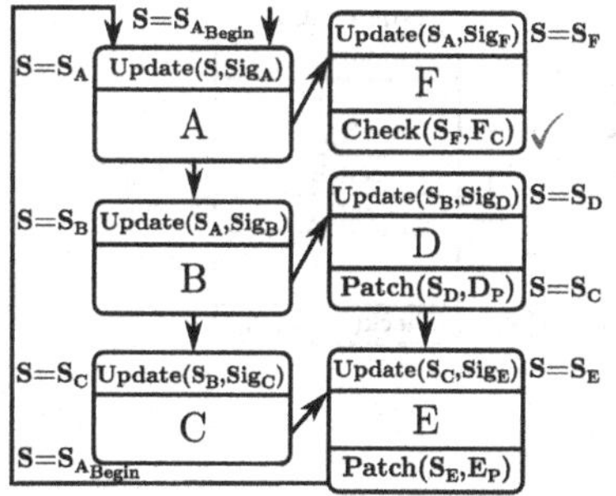

Fig. 2. Justifying signature for control-flow merges.

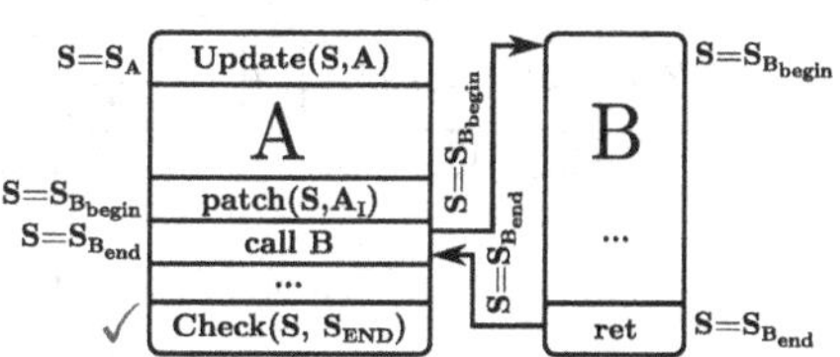

Fig. 3. CFI state patch for direct calls.

two different paths of CFI states merge and would turn into a state collision. To avoid that, we adopt generalized path signature analysis from Wilken and Shen and insert justifying signatures for correction. Figure 2 shows a conditional branch, where the control-flow merges in basic block `E` and a loop, which control-flow merges in `A`. At the end of `D`, there is a state patch with D_P, ensuring the CFI state at the beginning of `E` is the same, whether coming from `C` or `D`. Furthermore, `E` jumps back to `A`, forming a loop. Thus, a patch E_P is inserted at the end of `E`, correcting the CFI state to $S_{A_{Begin}}$. At the end in basic block `F`, a check compares the actual state with the expected value F_C.

Direct Calls. In Fig. 3, function `A` directly calls `B`. To support calling `B` from multiple call sites, the beginning state of `B` always needs to be the same. Thus, we apply a justifying signature at the call site before the direct call, transforming the call site's CFI state to the beginning state of function `B`. When returning, the CFI state continues with the end state of the called function, here $S_{B_{end}}$.

Indirect Calls. Indirect calls require special handling of signatures, not covered by the work of Wilken and Shen. Determining the exact function that is being called during the indirect call is not always possible at compile-time. The best that FIPAC can do is to determine a possibly over-approximated set of potential call targets and enforce that the indirect call can only call one of them. Figure 4 shows the patching for indirect calls and the interaction with direct calls.

To provide the CFI for indirect calls, FIPAC determines an intermediate CFI state S_I for every set of indirectly called functions. This can also lead to merging sets if the same function is called indirectly from different call sites. When performing an indirect call, the call site `A`, in ①, first patches its state S_A to an intermediate state $S_{I_{begin}}$, the same for all possible call targets of this indirect call. In ②, the indirect call is performed. At the beginning of the indirectly called function `B`, we transform the state, in ③, from the intermediate state $S_{I_{begin}}$ to the beginning state of $S_{B_{begin}}$. Furthermore, in ④, we set up the patch value used for the function return. We jump over the direct call entry in ⑤ and continue the execution of `B` until the return patch in ⑥. This patch transforms the end

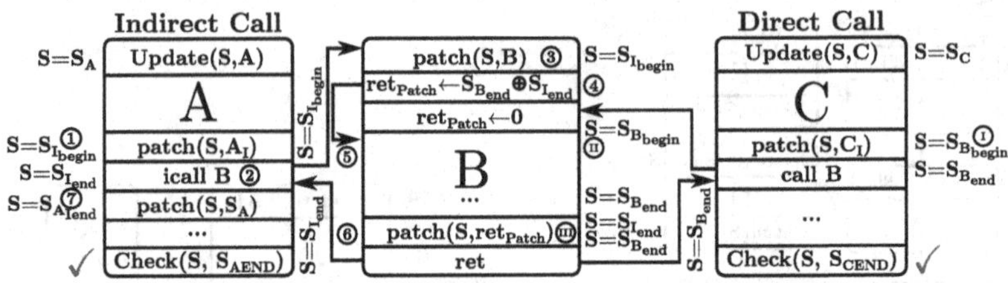

Fig. 4. CFI state patch for indirect calls.

state $S_{B_{End}}$ of B to the common intermediate return state $S_{I_{End}}$ followed by a return. The caller A uses the pre-call signature S_A, which was saved, for a state update in ⑦, to transform the intermediate return state to a unique state for A. Note, the call site could simply continue with the execution using the state $S_{I_{end}}$. However, this would introduce undetectable control-flow vulnerabilities between different indirect call sites of the same function. Therefore, the patch with S_A is necessary to avoid different call sites continuing with the same signature and ensure that the function was actually called. The call site continues with the execution using the state $S_{A_{I_{end}}} = S_{I_{end}} \oplus S_A$, different for every call site.

Since any function must be callable with direct or indirect calls, the handling of indirect and direct calls interacts. On the right of Fig. 4, we show how C calls B directly. In Ⓘ, a justifying signature is applied to transform C's CFI state to the beginning state $S_{B_{begin}}$ of B. The direct call does not jump to the beginning of B. Instead, it jumps to a dedicated entry point setting up the return patch ret_{Patch} to be zero ((II)), and continues with the execution of B. At the end of the function in (III), the return patch ret_{Patch} is applied. Since the patch value is zero, this statement does not affect the state, which remains $S_{B_{end}}$. After the return, the call site then continues with the execution using the state $S_{B_{end}}$.

4.2 State Updates with Pointer Authentication

As discussed in Sect. 3.3, the state must not be computable by the attacker and must depend on all previous CFI states. FIPAC uses a chained cryptographic message authentication code (MAC) for the state update function to solve this problem. Thereby, we bind the security of FIPAC to a secret cryptographic key, which is unknown to the attacker and isolated by the OS. To efficiently implement such a cryptographic function, we exploit ARM pointer authentication (PA), introduced in ARMv8.3-A and updated in ARMv8.6-A [35]. It is designed to cryptographically sign pointers with a pointer authentication code (PAC) and verify their integrity before using it [46]. The PAC is computed as the MAC over the pointer and a modifier using QARMA [4]. Although pointers are 64-bit values, the size of the virtual address space limits the actual size of the pointer values. In AArch64 Linux, the virtual address space is typically configured for 39 or 48-bit [37], leaving the upper bits unused. ARM PA uses them to store the PAC value in the unused upper bit, thus having no storage overhead.

To use pointer authentication, ARMv8.6-A was extended for computing and verifying a PAC. The instructions `PACI*` and `PACD*` use the destination register as input, the source register as a modifier, and XOR the PAC in the upper bits of the destination register. The PAC can be verified by using the `AUTI*` and `AUTD*` instructions. On a successful verification, the PAC is removed from the address, and the pointer can be used. If the verification fails, `AUT*` instructions trap (this is different from ARMv8.3-A, which only sets an error bit).

This work uses the PA mechanism of ARMv8.6-A to implement the state update function rather than sign pointers. This extension fulfills the requirements needed for the state update. It uses a keyed mechanism and brings in the accumulating functionality required to link subsequent states.

4.3 Placement of Checks

Although the CFI check placement is essential for the security of the CFI scheme, there is no general solution for the correct placement. However, at minimum, there needs to be one check at the end of the program. For programs that do not return, *i.e.*, server programs, at least one CFI check in the main event loop is needed. This strategy, however, has the longest detection latency and the worst detection probability. To reduce the detection latency and improve the detection probability of CFI errors, more CFI checks are required. However, the granularity is a trade-off between overheads and security. The more checks inserted, the more overhead but also better detection probability and lower latency. At worst, a check is placed at the end of every basic block, yielding the best security but worst runtime and code performance. In between, there exist arbitrary policies with different trade-offs. For example, a generic policy places a CFI check at the end of each function. Even fully custom strategies of placing checks are possible. With the help of dynamic runtime profiling, a compiler can place the checks more efficiently. e.g., a policy can place a check after every 100th basic block.

5 Implementation

FIPAC computes a rolling CFI state throughout the program's execution implemented in software on top of ARMv8.6-A without hardware changes. FIPAC exploits the PA instruction set extension to implement the cryptographic state update function. The `PACI*` and `PACD*` instructions cryptographically compute a MAC over a pointer and a modifier register and store the result in the upper bits of the pointer. In ARMv8.6-A, these instructions do not simply replace the upper bits of the pointer with the computed MAC but instead XOR them to the existing upper bits. Pseudocode 2 shows the simplified behavior of the `PACIA` instruction ignoring that the configuration bit 55 is excluded from the PAC.

Key Management. By utilizing `PACIA`, FIPAC uses the `APIAKey`, which is managed in the kernel (`EL1`) and not accessible from user mode (`EL0`) [46]. To provide CFI protection with FIPAC for the kernel, the key management can be delegated to a higher privilege level, e.g., `EL2`. As PA instructions do not differentiate privilege levels, these instructions can be used in `EL0` and `EL1`. To prevent cross-EL attacks [5], FIPAC protected user and kernel tasks can either use different keys for each privilege level (e.g., `APIAKey` for `EL0` and `APIBKey` for `EL1`), or the key manager in `EL2` could swap the keys on mode transitions. As the key needs to be known at compile-time, the prototype implementation of FIPAC statically configures the `APIAKey` in a kernel module in `EL1`. We discuss the dynamic configuration of the PA keys in Sect. 7.

Interrupts. FIPAC supports interrupts and OS interactions without any change. When an interrupt diverts the control-flow to the kernel, it saves all registers of the user application, including the current CFI state. The CFI state is restored after resuming from the interrupt, allowing the program to continue.

Pseudocode 2. Simplified behavior of `PACIA` in the 15-bit configuration.

```
function PACIA(Xd, Xm)
    PAC[63:0] ← ComputePAC(Xd[47:0], Xm, K)
    Xd[63:48] ← Xd[63:48] ⊕ PAC[63:48]
    Xd[47:0]  ← Xd[47:0]
```

```
adr    x2,   #4
pacia  x28,  x2
```

Listing 1.1. State update with `PACIA`.

```
mov   x2,  #patch
eor   x28, x28, x2
```

Listing 1.2. CFI state patch.

```
mov      x2, #const
eor      x2, x28, x2
autiza   x2
```

Listing 1.3. CFI check with `AUTIZA`.

5.1 CFI Primitives

We first discuss the CFI primitives and then show how they protect different control-flow instructions.

CFI State and Updates. Instead of signing a pointer with `PACIA`, we use it to compute the CFI state. The upper bits of a `PACIA` computation (the size depends on the virtual memory configuration, but we use a 15-bit configuration), the PAC bits, denote our CFI state. To accumulate the CFI state, the `PACIA` instruction is always executed on the same "pointer", in our case, the CFI state stored in `Xd`. The `PACIA, Xd, Xn` instruction computes a PAC of register `Xd` with `Xn` as a modifier and XORs it to the upper bits of `Xd`. For each basic block, a unique identifier, *i.e.*, the program counter (PC), is used as the modifier `Xm` for this instruction. By subsequently XORing the new CFI state to the previous one, we create a dependency link between succeeding basic blocks. We store the global CFI state in the exclusively reserved general-purpose register `x28`.

Listing 1.1 shows the CFI state update, placed at the beginning of each basic block. `ADR, x2, #4` first loads a unique constant for the basic block to a temporary register `x2`, in this case, the program counter. We use this constant to compute a new PAC, which gets XORed to the previous CFI state in `x28`.

State Patches. To inject a justifying signature needed for control-flow merges, we use the instruction sequence from Listing 1.2. We load an immediate constant to a temporary register in `x2`, which gets XORed to the CFI state in `x28`, thus correcting it to a target state. The computation of this immediate constant happens during the post-processing stage, as discussed in Sect. 5.3.

State Checks. A check compares the current CFI state with the expected state at this program location and executes an error handler on a mismatch. Such instruction sequences typically involve conditional branches, which slows down the program execution, as they impact the instruction pipeline. We also exploit the PA instructions for efficiently performing the necessary CFI checks. Similar to generating a PAC, ARM also provides `AUTI*` and `AUTD*` instructions to verify the integrity of PACs. In ARMv8.6-A, these instructions even trap on an invalid PAC verification. Since we use `PACIA` to compute a PAC, it is tempting to directly use `AUTIZA` for verification. However, the CFI state in `x28` is not a valid PAC value in the classical sense. Instead, it is an accumulated XOR-sum of many valid PAC values combined do not form a valid PAC anymore. Thus, we cannot directly use the `AUTIZA` instruction to verify the CFI state.

At every location in the program, we know the expected CFI state at compile-time. Thus, we can compute a differential constant, which is XORed the CFI state, transforming it to a valid PAC. By applying this constant to the CFI state, we receive a valid PAC that can be verified with `AUTIZA`. This constant is determined in the post-processing tool and explained in Sect. 5.3. In Listing 1.3, we show the corresponding assembly sequence. We first insert an instruction sequence that patches the current CFI state to a valid PAC value using a constant for this program location. Then, we use the `AUTIZA` instruction to verify the integrity of this PAC value. On a control-flow deviation, applying the constant to the incorrect CFI state in `x28` generates an invalid PAC, which the `AUTIZA` instruction detects. If the check fails, `AUTIZA` traps and stops the program.

CFI checks can be placed arbitrarily within the program. FIPAC supports three strategies: one check at the end of a program, a check at the end of every function, or a check at the end of every basic block. The check strategy directly impacts performance and security, which is discussed in Sect. 6.

5.2 Protection of Control-Flow Instructions

We now discuss how the CFI primitives are used to protect different control-flow instructions. At the beginning of each basic block, we insert a PA-based CFI state update sequence. This instruction sequence uniquely updates the CFI state for the current basic block based on the previous state value.

```
1    mov x1 , #I_PATCH       ; Indirect call entry point
2    eor x28 , x28 , x1      ; Patch to beginning state of function
3    mov x1 , #RET_PATCH     ; Load return patch
4    b #8
5    mov x1 , #0             ; Direct Call entry point
6    ...                     ; sets up zero patch
7    eor x28 , x28 , x1      ; Apply return patch
8    ret
```

Listing 1.4. Function entry points for indirect and direct calls.

Protection of Direct Branches, Jumps, and Conditional Branches. These control-flow instructions create control-flow merges, where state collisions occur. At control-flow merges, our compiler instruments those instructions and inserts the state patches for justifying signatures. Note, the final patch values are determined during the post-processing, as discussed in the next section. To identify the locations of patches, we compute the inverted maximum spanning tree over the edges of the CFG, defining the patch locations.

Direct Calls. Direct calls are instrumented with state patches at call site, transforming the state to the beginning state of the called function. When returning from a directly called function, the caller's CFI state continues with the callee's end state. Note, functions are instrumented to only have single return nodes.

Indirect Calls and Returns. At the call site, indirect calls are instrumented to stack the current CFI state and patch the state for the intermediate state for this set of indirect calls. When returning, the pre-call state saved on the stack is retrieved and XORed to the CFI state to provide a link over the indirect call.

Indirect calls require more complicated instrumentation besides the call site. As discussed in Sect. 4.1, the function header of an indirectly called function needs to set up the patch value used during the function's return. However, a function generally does not know how it was called and must support being called directly and indirectly. We solve this problem by adding a second function entry point, one for direct calls and the second one for indirect calls.

We add a custom function entry for indirect calls in the compiler, shown in Listing 1.4. This entry patches the intermediate state of the indirect call to the beginning state of the called function (Line 1–3). We then load the CFI update patch (Line 4), used during the function's return, and jump, in Line 5, over the direct call entry point. When the function is called directly, it jumps to the direct call function entry in Line 6, setting up a zero-patch for the return. During the function return, Line 8 uses the previously set up return patch. For direct calls, where the return patch is zero, this statement has no effect, but for indirect calls, it patches the end state to the intermediate return state. The compiler is unaware that the inserted instructions have control-flow and implement a second function entry. Thus, direct calls also use the second entry point, which is exclusively for indirect calls. We correct this during the post-processing, where all direct calls get rewritten to the second entry.

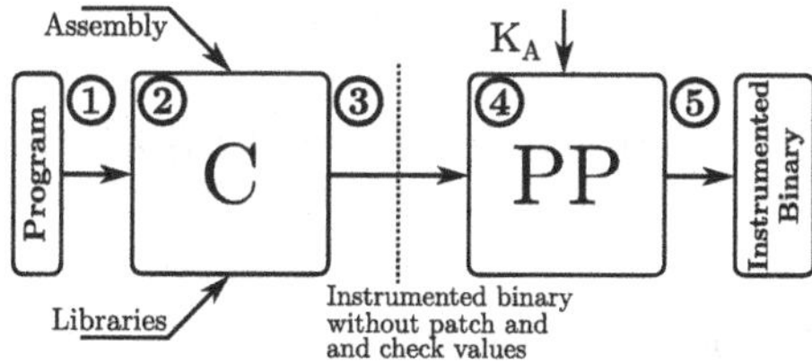

Fig. 5. Custom toolchain to build protected binaries.

5.3 Toolchain

Our prototype toolchain uses a combination of both approaches, shown in Fig. 5. We use a custom compiler ② based on the LLVM compiler framework [29], to insert all necessary state update and patch instructions using two backend passes during the compilation of a program ①. We extend the AArch64 backend and reserve the general-purpose register `x28`, which is exclusively used to store the CFI state, disable tail calls, and ensure that functions have only a single return point. The compiler emits an instrumented ELF binary ③, but the concrete state patches and check values are set to zero. In a second step, we use a post-processing tool (PP) ④, which has access to the compiled and linked binary to compute all expected states and insert the patch updates.

The toolchain supports instrumented or non-instrumented libraries, but only instrumented libraries have CFI. Instrumented libraries must be linked statically, such that the PP tool can replace the patch and check values in the binary. The toolchain also supports inline assembly and external assembler files. However, the programmer's responsibility is to insert the necessary state update and patch sequences into the assembly code. If the assembly code is not instrumented, the code is still fully functional but does not have CFI protection. The toolchain currently supports the instrumentation of programs written in C. However, extending the support to other languages supported by LLVM, e.g., C++ or Rust, only requires more engineering work but no changes to the design of FIPAC.

Post-processing Tool. The post-processing tool performs the call rewriting, the CFI state computation, the insertion of the patch values, and the computation of the CFI check values. It has access to the PA key and consumes the instrumented binary with zeroed patches and checks. The tool rewrites all direct calls to use the second function entry point (the first one is used for indirect calls). Next, it computes the CFI state for every location in the program. Every function is assigned a random start signature, which is propagated through all PAC-based state updates of the function. At a control-flow merge, the state values of both branches are known such that the tool can compute the justifying signature as the XOR-difference between both states and replaces the patch values `#patch`. The post-processing tool knows the CFI state at every location in the program; thus, it can also compute the XOR-differences to form a valid PAC. For `AUTIZA`-based check sequences, it replaces `#const` with the corresponding XOR-difference.

6 Evaluation

This section discusses the security guarantees of FIPAC and analyzes its overheads for different checking policies.

6.1 Security Evaluation

FIPAC considers a software and a fault attacker aiming to hijack control-flow transfers between basic blocks. To protect these control-flow transfers, FIPAC performs a state update of the global CFI state S at the beginning of every basic block allowing FIPAC to detect inter basic block manipulations.

Software Attacker Protection. A software attacker is able to hijack the control-flow by modifying indirect calls or returns by exploiting a memory bug. FIPAC mitigates these hijacks, *i.e.*, ROP or JOP, by ensuring that the executed control-flow follows the statically derived CFG. When entering a basic block, FIPAC derives a new state considering the execution history and a unique basic block identifier. On a control-flow hijack, the attacker redirects the control-flow to a basic block that is not in the set of valid targets. Hence, the state update derives a faulty state, which is detectable by the following check. If the attacker omits the update, e.g., by redirecting the control-flow to the middle of the basic block, the check before the return instruction detects the wrong state, mitigating ROP attacks. Suppose the attacker omits the state update, e.g., by redirecting the control-flow to the middle of the basic block. In that case, the check before the return detects the wrong state, mitigating ROP attacks.

Compared to other CFI schemes, which only consider a fault attacker, FIPAC uses a keyed state update to prevent a software or combined attacker from forging a CFI state. Equation 1 depicts the state update function ignoring the excluded bit 55 for simplification purposes. This function consists of the secret key K_A, the current state S, and a unique identifier Sig_{BB} for the basic block. The secret key K_A, inaccessible by the adversary, is initialized at boot time and ensures that the attacker cannot forge a specific state.

$$S = \text{Update}(S, Sig_{BB}, K_A) = S \oplus \text{MAC}_{K_A}(Sig_{BB})_{PAC_{Size}} \tag{1}$$

Fault Attacker Protection. While mitigating software-triggered control-flow attacks only requires protecting a subset of control-flow transfers, *i.e.*, returns and indirect calls, thwarting a fault attacker necessitates the protection of all control-flow transfers. Hence, in addition to SCFI schemes, FIPAC also updates the CFI state for direct calls and branches, detecting any faults on addresses stored in the memory, registers, or during the execution.

Detection of a Control-Flow Violation. FIPAC does not prevent a control-flow hijack; instead, it detects an attack after the control-flow violated the CFG at the next check. This is the best that software-based CFI can do, as they cannot verify branches or calls ahead of executing them. If an attacker skips the check

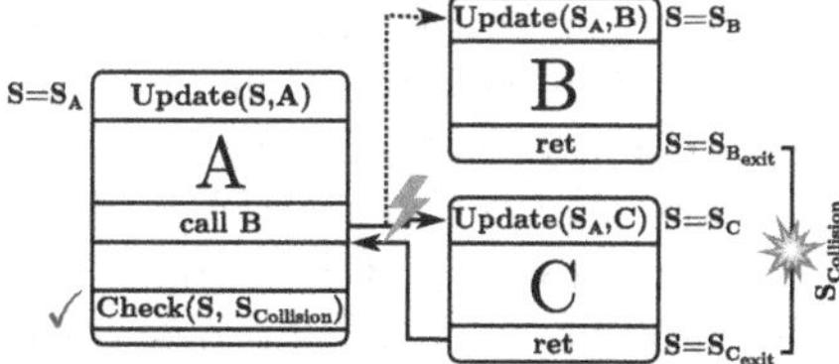

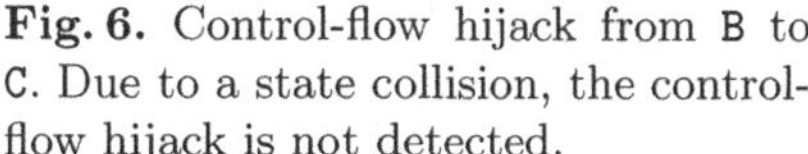

Fig. 6. Control-flow hijack from B to C. Due to a state collision, the control-flow hijack is not detected.

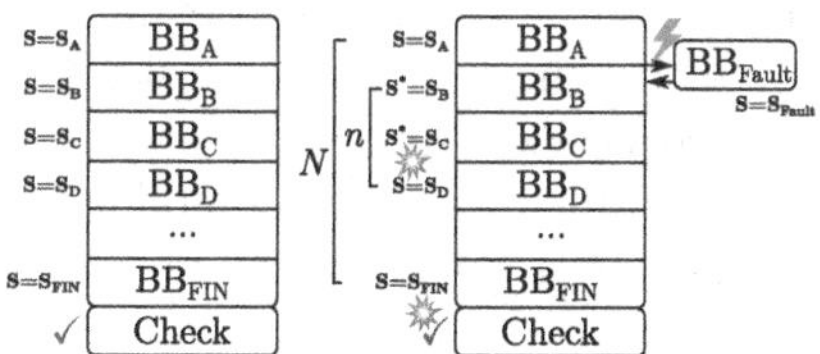

Fig. 7. A coarse-grained check policy. After n updates, a collision rectifies the faulty state.

at the end of the basic block/function, the hijack is not detected in the first place. However, depending on the checking policy, a new check occurs at the end of the next basic block or function. Since the CFI state is invalid at this point, it requires the attacker to skip all subsequent checks such that the control-flow attack is not detectable. Control-flow attacks, which redirect the execution to the program's end, are not detectable, as there is no check anymore.

CFI State Collision Probability. Due to the truncated MAC, state collisions are possible with a probability of $P_{Coll} = \frac{1}{2^{PAC\_SIZE}}$, which can lead to a bypass. Figure 6 illustrates a control-flow hijack, redirecting the call from B to C. When returning to the caller A, the state mismatch $S_{C_{exit}} \neq S_{B_{exit}}$ should be detected by the check of FIPAC. However, with probability P_{Coll}, a state collision $S_{C_{exit}} = S_{B_{exit}} = S_{Coll}$ occurs, and the control-flow attack remains undetected.

Checking Policy. To reliably detect state collisions, the sufficient placement of checks, *i.e.*, the checking policy, is crucial for the security of FIPAC. However, properly placing CFI checks is a challenging problem with no general solution. Figure 7 shows the problem of a too coarse-grained checking policy. Left, a valid control-flow from basic block BB_A to BB_{FIN} is shown. Right, the attacker manages to redirect the control-flow to BB_{Fault} and therefore alter all subsequent states to S^*. However, with a probability of P_{Coll}, a state collision occurs after each state update. In this example, after n updates, a collision occurs, and S^* becomes S_D. Thus, the state S is valid again, and the control-flow hijack cannot be detected in further CFI checks. To give a quantitative measure on the security of the check placement, we analyze the probability of undetectable state collisions between subsequent checks. $\mathrm{MP}_{Coll_N} = 1 - \left(1 - \frac{1}{2^{PAC\_SIZE}}\right)^N$ denotes the minimum probability that a state collision occurs in one of N state updates. After 50,000 state updates, the state collision probability reaches 78%, and after 250,000 updates almost 100% for a 15-bit PAC.

Selecting the checking policy is a trade-off between security and performance. Although a precise policy, *i.e.*, a check at each basic block, maximizes the detection probability of a control-flow hijack, the performance overhead also increases. While a loose checking policy, e.g., a check at the program's end, might be sufficient for small programs, programs with a high number of executed basic blocks might be vulnerable. Between these two policies, arbitrary checking strategies can be selected; for example, a check at the end of each function. A more advanced check strategy can incorporate additional information, e.g., runtime profiling. This allows the compiler to better decide where checks are needed to enforce a lower bound of the minimum detection probability of CFI errors.

A check at the end of a function is a good trade-off between runtime overhead and security. For example, SPEC2017 consists of 28391 functions. 12583 of these functions, or 44%, contain only a single basic block with a check at the end. Thus, calling such a function is equivalent to performing a CFI state check at the call site. For example, calling this function within a loop containing no explicit checks implicitly performs a state validation at each loop iteration.

We analyzed the number of basic blocks per function for SPEC2017. The number of functions with a small number of basic blocks is much larger than functions comprising a large number of basic blocks. Almost 75% of all functions consist of less than 13 basic blocks, which is in favor of our checking policy, since smaller functions perform a CFI check earlier than large ones. Thus, the detection probability of a state mismatch is higher. To summarize, we expect that a CFI check at the end of each function is a good trade-off for a static policy.

	SCFI		FCFI		FIPAC
	Prot.	Vuln.	Prot.	Vuln.	
Return Addr.	Software	Combined	Fault	Software	✔
Indirect Calls	Software	Combined	Fault	Software	✔
Indirect Br.	Software	Combined	Fault	Software	✔
Direct Calls		Fault	Fault	Combined	✔
Direct Br.		Fault	Fault	Combined	✔

✔ Full · Software · Fault · Combined

Fig. 8. Protection guarantees and vulnerabilities for SCFI and FCFI schemes compared to FIPAC.

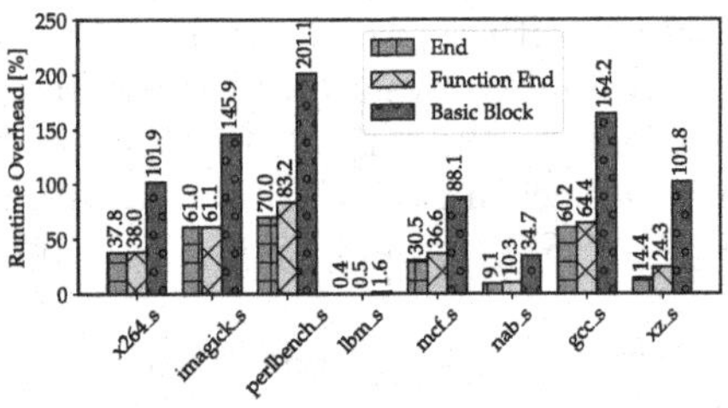

Fig. 9. Runtime overhead for SPECspeed 2017.

6.2 Security Comparison

Figure 8 compares CFI schemes addressing software [2,15,32,33,38,53,64] or fault [20,28,42,47,58] adversaries with FIPAC. Software CFI schemes, like PARTS [33] or CPI [15], enforce CFI at a coarse granularity by protecting a wide range of forward- and backward edges on function level. Although these approaches mitigate software attacks (Software) exploiting a memory vulnerability, they fail to protect against a fault attacker (Fault). FCFI schemes enforce CFI at a finer granularity to protect the control-flow from fault attacks, *i.e.*, on basic block or instruction level. In contrast to a software attacker exploiting memory bugs, a precise fault can tamper with direct and indirect control-flow transfers. While software-based FCFI schemes protect all control-flow transfers from faults (Fault), they fail to protect against software adversaries (Software). As the state update of these schemes are counters or predictable IDs, an adversary can use a memory bug to modify the state and prevent the detection of a control-flow hijack.

To protect against control-flow attacks from a fault and software attacker, it is tempting to naïvely combine existing schemes such as PARTS with FCFI, e.g., CFCSS. While these schemes are secure in their own threat model, a combined fault and software attack (💣) can bypass them. First, the adversary gains control over a register used for the FCFI state update. Then, it redirects the control-flow to a wrong function, e.g., with a fault. Finally, the tampered register is used for the state update, thus, can forge a valid CFI state.

To protect against fault and software attacks and to support a large-scale deployment, FIPAC fulfills the key requirements stated in Sect. 3.3. First, FIPAC comprehensively enforces CFI for transfers between basic blocks. Hence, our scheme operates on a much finer granularity than typical software CFI schemes. Second, FIPAC uses, in comparison to fault CFI schemes, a keyed state update function to mitigate attacks targeting to manipulate the global CFI state. FIPAC is implemented in software and is applied automatically during compilation.

6.3 Functional Evaluation

To evaluate the functional correctness of FIPAC, we compiled SPEC2017 [14] and Embench [43] with our LLVM-based toolchain. We executed these instrumented binaries on the QEMU 6.0 [44], which we modified to support PAC of ARMv8.6-A. In QEMU, we started the 5.4.58 Linux kernel and initialized the PA keys during the boot procedure before starting the benchmarks.

6.4 Performance Evaluation

To the best of our knowledge, there is currently no publicly available device supporting ARMv8.6-A. To conduct our performance evaluation on hardware, we use the Raspberry Pi 4 Model B [16]. Since the ARM Cortex-A72 CPU is based on ARMv8-A without PAC, we emulate the runtime overhead of the PA instructions in software by replacing them with their PA-analogue, *i.e.*, four consecutive XORs. PARTS [33] evaluated this sequence to model the timing of native PA instructions, which is also used in related work [32].

SPEC 2017. To measure the performance overhead of FIPAC, we compiled all C-based benchmarks with OpenMP support disabled of SPECspeed 2017 Integer. We enabled three different checking policies, from coarse-grained to fine-grained checks, to compare the performance penalty introduced by them. More concretely, we configured FIPAC to insert a CFI check at the end of the program, at the end of every function, or at each basic block. Verifying the CFI state at the end of every basic block has the largest geometric mean penalty in code size of 90.6% as it requires 3 additional instructions per basic block. Interestingly, placing a CFI check at the end of every function only has a geometric mean overhead of 52.5%, slightly higher than a single check at the program end with a geometric mean penalty of 50.6%. Due to this small increase in code size but

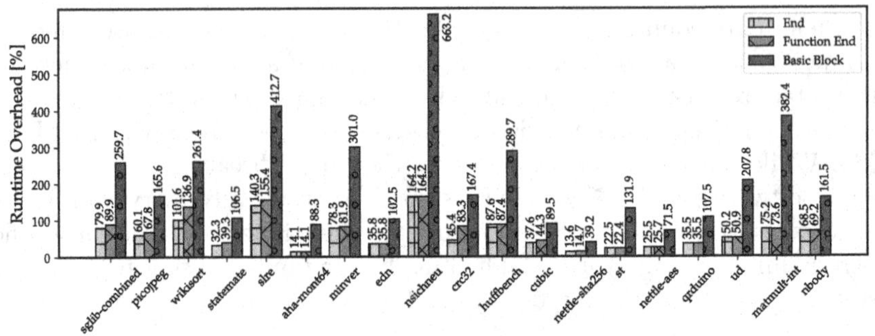

Fig. 10. Runtime overhead for Embench.

its stronger security guarantees, this policy is a good trade-off. Figure 9 shows the runtime overhead of FIPAC compared to the baseline without protection. The coarse-grained checking policy with a single check at the program end introduces the smallest geometric mean runtime overhead of 18.8%. The fine-grained checking policy with CFI checks at the end of every basic block has the largest geometric mean runtime penalty of 62.9%. Interestingly, the intermediate policy with a check at the end of each function introduces a geometric mean runtime overhead of 22.1%. This is only a small increase compared to a single check at the end, but it provides much better security. These runtime overheads are outperforming related work with overheads between 107–426% [18].

Embench. To evaluate FIPAC on embedded workloads, we use Embench. The geometric mean code overheads are between 55–95%, and the runtime overheads are between 49–168% (Fig. 10), depending on the checking policy. This increased overhead is due to Embench's small codebase with a larger number of control-flow transfers compared to application-grade benchmarks like SPEC.

7 Discussion

This section discusses the hardware requirements of FIPAC, how it can be implemented on other architectures, and future improvements.

FIPAC Hardware Requirements. FIPAC requires pointer authentication from ARMv8.6-A. Although it is not yet widely available in existing processors, ARM has already announced the successor ARMv9-A [36]. Hence, we expect new designs, e.g., Apple's new processors, to feature ARMv8.6-A or even ARMv9-A.

FIPAC on ARMv8.3-A. FIPAC can also be implemented on ARMv8.3-A with the following adaptions. ARMv8.3-A PA instructions only compute a new PAC without accumulation, which must be done manually using an additional `eor` instruction per state update. This increases the overhead of an update to 3 instructions and requires one more register. `autiza` in ARMv8.3-A cannot be used as a check as it does not trap. However, ARMv8.3-A features `blraa`, a branch with link operation with pointer authentication, which traps if the jump-target contains an invalid PAC. This instruction can be misused to perform a CFI check. First, we transform the known CFI state to a valid PAC with the address of the next instruction. When executing this branch, it first verifies the target address and, if valid, jumps to the next instruction. If the PAC, and therefore also the CFI state, is invalid, the verification traps. Both solutions increase code size and runtime overheads compared to the prototype of FIPAC.

Similar to ARMv8.6-A, there is currently no open hardware available for ARMv8.3-A yet. Although Apple offers cores, such as the M1 and A14 [23], they restrict the usage of this feature. iOS applications are not allowed to load kernel modules; thus, FIPAC cannot configure the PA keys. FIPAC may run on the Apple M1 core with PA of ARMv8.3-A. However, we currently do not have access to such a device, and it requires future research to clarify if PA key access is possible in the EL1 kernel mode or if Apple restricts it.

FIPAC on Other Architectures. The design of FIPAC is generic and could also be implemented on other architectures. It is tempting to implement FIPAC on x86 with the AES-NI [48], supporting partial encryption with one instruction. However, we see limitations with this approach. First, AES-NI operates on a 128-bit state, also requiring to embed 128-bit patches. Second, one AES-NI operation only computes one round, just providing scrambling and no cryptographic strength. Third, it requires the encryption keys to be held in general-purpose registers. Thus, there is no key isolation between the user and the kernel. Hence, we do not envision FIPAC to be implemented with AES-NI.

Dynamic Key Handling. FIPAC uses a static PA key configured by the OS. However, ARM pointer authentication supports up to five keys for different domains. By using different keys, FIPAC could isolate the control-flow of the kernel and user programs. For better isolation between applications, FIPAC could embed the PA key in the binary, allowing applications to use different keys. Existing key exchange algorithms are then used to protect the embedded PA key. The OS has access to a private key for the key exchange, can read the PA key, and configure the system before starting the binary. To dynamically change the PA key, the post-processing can be integrated into the OS. Before starting the application, the OS chooses a random key and performs the post-processing step, *i.e.*, the computation of the CFI states, patches, and check values. Thus, every invocation of the application is different in terms of FIPAC related patch and check values, which also hardens the attack surface.

Instruction Granular Protection. FIPAC does not protect the linear instruction sequence within a basic block as it only performs state updates at the beginning of a basic block. If a more fine granular protection is required, *i.e.*, intra basic block security, FIPAC supports the placement of state updates within security-critical basic blocks. For such pieces of code, the state update from Listing 1.1 is placed after every instruction to emulate instruction-granular CFI. Instruction granular CFI increases the overhead and adds two additional instructions per instruction to protect. Automatically identifying such critical pieces of code is a challenging task and not in the scope of this work. Instead, it requires the developer to manually place a check, e.g., via inline assembly.

Compatibilty. FIPAC uses the instruction address for the signature computation. When ASLR is enabled, it leads to randomized signatures not being compatible with the static computation. This problem can be solved by using static numbers to compute the signatures or by integrating dynamic key handling in the OS.

FIPAC is a software-based CFI protection scheme, and therefore, comes with certain degrees of flexibility compared to hardware-centric approaches. As FIPAC supports arbitrary checking policies on the same system, critical applications, e.g., running within a TEE or an enclave, can have a stronger checking policy than a non-critical application. FIPAC is backward compatible and supports non-instrumented applications.

8 Conclusion

We presented FIPAC, a fine-granular software-based CFI protection scheme for upcoming ARM-based hardware. FIPAC offers fine granular control-flow protection on basic block level for both fault and software attacks. The design exploits a cryptographically secure state update function, which cannot be recomputed without knowing a secret key. FIPAC utilizes ARM pointer authentication of ARMv8.6-A, to efficiently implement the keyed CFI state update and checking mechanism. We provide a toolchain to automatically instrument and protect applications. The evaluation of FIPAC with the SPEC2017 benchmark with different security policies shows a geometric mean runtime overhead between 19–63% and is slightly larger for small embedded benchmarks. FIPAC is a software-based CFI protection, requires no hardware changes, and outperforms related work.

Acknowledgments. This project has received funding from the European Research Council (ERC) under the European Union's Horizon 2020 research and innovation programme (grant agreement No 681402).

References

1. 26th USENIX Security Symposium, USENIX Security 2017, Vancouver, BC, Canada, 16–18 August 2017 (2017). https://www.usenix.org/conference/usenixsecurity17
2. Abadi, M., Budiu, M., Erlingsson, Ú., Ligatti, J.: Control-flow integrity. In: Conference on Computer and Communications Security - CCS 2005 (2005). https://doi.org/10.1145/1102120.1102165
3. Alkhalifa, Z., Nair, V.S.S., Krishnamurthy, N., Abraham, J.A.: Design and evaluation of system-level checks for on-line control flow error detection. IEEE Trans. Parallel Distrib. Syst. **10**(6), 627–641 (1999). https://doi.org/10.1109/71.774911

4. Avanzi, R.: The QARMA block cipher family. Almost MDS matrices over rings with zero divisors, nearly symmetric even-mansour constructions with non-involutory central rounds, and search heuristics for low-latency S-boxes. IACR Trans. Symmetric Cryptol. **2017**(1), 4–44 (2017). https://doi.org/10.13154/tosc.v2017.i1.4-44
5. Azad, B.: Examining Pointer Authentication on the iPhone XS (2019). https://googleprojectzero.blogspot.com/2019/02/examining-pointer-authentication-on.html. Accessed 10 Dec 2021
6. Bar-El, H., Choukri, H., Naccache, D., Tunstall, M., Whelan, C.: The sorcerer's apprentice guide to fault attacks. Proc. IEEE **94**(2), 370–382 (2006). https://doi.org/10.1109/JPROC.2005.862424
7. Bertoni, G., Breveglieri, L., Koren, I., Maistri, P., Piuri, V.: Error analysis and detection procedures for a hardware implementation of the advanced encryption standard. IEEE Trans. Comput. **52**(4), 492–505 (2003). https://doi.org/10.1109/TC.2003.1190590
8. Biham, E., Shamir, A.: Differential fault analysis of secret key cryptosystems. In: Kaliski, B.S. (ed.) CRYPTO 1997. LNCS, vol. 1294, pp. 513–525. Springer, Heidelberg (1997). https://doi.org/10.1007/BFb0052259
9. Blömer, J., da Silva, R.G., Günther, P., Krämer, J., Seifert, J.: A practical second-order fault attack against a real-world pairing implementation. In: Fault Diagnosis and Tolerance in Cryptography - FDTC 2014 (2014). https://doi.org/10.1109/FDTC.2014.22
10. Boneh, D., DeMillo, R.A., Lipton, R.J.: On the importance of checking cryptographic protocols for faults. In: Fumy, W. (ed.) EUROCRYPT 1997. LNCS, vol. 1233, pp. 37–51. Springer, Heidelberg (1997). https://doi.org/10.1007/3-540-69053-0_4
11. Carré, S., Desjardins, M., Facon, A., Guilley, S.: Exhaustive single bit fault analysis A use case against Mbedtls and OpenSSL's protection on ARM and Intel CPU. Microprocess. Microsyst. **71**, 102860 (2019). https://doi.org/10.1016/j.micpro.2019.102860
12. Checkoway, S., Davi, L., Dmitrienko, A., Sadeghi, A., Shacham, H., Winandy, M.: Return-oriented programming without returns. In: Conference on Computer and Communications Security - CCS 2010 (2010). https://doi.org/10.1145/1866307.1866370
13. de Clercq, R., Götzfried, J., Übler, D., Maene, P., Verbauwhede, I.: SOFIA: software and control flow integrity architecture. Comput. Secur. **68**, 16–35 (2017). https://doi.org/10.1016/j.cose.2017.03.013
14. Standard Performance Evaluation Corporation: SPEC CPU 2017 (2019). https://www.spec.org/cpu2017. Accessed 10 Dec 2021
15. Evans, I., et al.: Missing the Point(er): on the effectiveness of code pointer integrity. In: IEEE Symposium on Security and Privacy - S&P 2015 (2015). https://doi.org/10.1109/SP.2015.53
16. Raspberry Pi Foundation: Raspberry Pi 4 Model B (2020). https://www.raspberrypi.org/products/raspberry-pi-4-model-b. Accessed 10 Dec 2021
17. Free60.org: Reset Glitch Hack. https://free60.org/Reset_Glitch_Hack/. Accessed 10 Dec 2021
18. Goloubeva, O., Rebaudengo, M., Reorda, M.S., Violante, M.: Soft-error detection using control flow assertions. In: IEEE International Symposium on Defect and Fault Tolerance in VLSI and Nanotechnology - DFT 2003 (2003). https://doi.org/10.1109/DFTVS.2003.1250158

19. NCC Group: There's a Hole in Your SoC: Glitching the MediaTek BootROM. https://research.nccgroup.com/2020/10/15/theres-a-hole-in-your-soc-glitching-the-mediatek-bootrom. Accessed 10 Dec 2021
20. Heydemann, K., Lalande, J., Berthomé, P.: Formally verified software countermeasures for control-flow integrity of smart card C code. Comput. Secur. **85**, 202–224 (2019). https://doi.org/10.1016/j.cose.2019.05.004
21. Hu, H., Shinde, S., Adrian, S., Chua, Z.L., Saxena, P., Liang, Z.: Data-oriented programming: on the expressiveness of non-control data attacks. In: IEEE Symposium on Security and Privacy - S&P 2016 (2016). https://doi.org/10.1109/SP.2016.62
22. Hund, R., Holz, T., Freiling, F.C.: Return-oriented rootkits: bypassing kernel code integrity protection mechanisms. In: USENIX Security Symposium - USENIX 2009 (2009). http://www.usenix.org/events/sec09/tech/full_papers/hund.pdf
23. Apple Inc.: Apple SoC security. https://support.apple.com/guide/security/apple-soc-security-sec87716a080/web. Accessed 10 Dec 2021
24. Jaloyan, G., Markantonakis, K., Akram, R.N., Robin, D., Mayes, K., Naccache, D.: Return-oriented programming on RISC-V. In: Asia Conference on Computer and Communications Security - AsiaCCS 2020 (2020). https://doi.org/10.1145/3320269.3384738
25. Joshi, N., Wu, K., Karri, R.: Concurrent error detection schemes for involution ciphers. In: Joye, M., Quisquater, J.-J. (eds.) CHES 2004. LNCS, vol. 3156, pp. 400–412. Springer, Heidelberg (2004). https://doi.org/10.1007/978-3-540-28632-5_29
26. Kim, Y., et al.: Flipping bits in memory without accessing them: an experimental study of DRAM disturbance errors. In: International Symposium on Computer Architecture - ISCA 2014 (2014). https://doi.org/10.1109/ISCA.2014.6853210
27. Kuznetsov, V., Szekeres, L., Payer, M., Candea, G., Sekar, R., Song, D.: Code-pointer integrity. In: Operating Systems Design and Implementation - OSDI 2014 (2014). https://www.usenix.org/conference/osdi14/technical-sessions/presentation/kuznetsov
28. Lalande, J.-F., Heydemann, K., Berthomé, P.: Software countermeasures for control flow integrity of smart card C codes. In: Kutyłowski, M., Vaidya, J. (eds.) ESORICS 2014. LNCS, vol. 8713, pp. 200–218. Springer, Cham (2014). https://doi.org/10.1007/978-3-319-11212-1_12
29. Lattner, C., Adve, V.S.: LLVM: a compilation framework for lifelong program analysis & transformation. In: Symposium on Code Generation and Optimization - CGO 2004 (2004). https://doi.org/10.1109/CGO.2004.1281665
30. Lee, J., et al.: Hacking in darkness: return-oriented programming against secure enclaves. In: USENIX Security Symposium - USENIX 2017 [1]. https://www.usenix.org/conference/usenixsecurity17/technical-sessions/presentation/lee-jaehyuk
31. Liao, H., Gebotys, C.H.: Methodology for EM fault injection: charge-based fault model. In: Design, Automation & Test in Europe - DATE 2019 (2019). https://doi.org/10.23919/DATE.2019.8715150
32. Liljestrand, H., Nyman, T., Gunn, L.J., Ekberg, J., Asokan, N.: PACStack: an authenticated call stack. CoRR (2019). http://arxiv.org/abs/1905.10242
33. Liljestrand, H., Nyman, T., Wang, K., Perez, C.C., Ekberg, J., Asokan, N.: PAC it up: towards pointer integrity using ARM pointer authentication. In: USENIX Security Symposium - USENIX 2019 (2019). https://www.usenix.org/conference/usenixsecurity19/presentation/liljestrand

34. ARM Limited: Inside the numbers: 100 billion ARM-based chips. https://community.arm.com/developer/ip-products/processors/b/processors-ip-blog/posts/inside-the-numbers-100-billion-arm-based-chips-1345571105. Accessed 10 Dec 2021
35. ARM Limited: ARM architecture reference manual ARMv8, for ARMv8-a architecture profile (2020). https://documentation-service.arm.com/static/5fa3bd1eb209f547eebd4141. Accessed 10 Dec 2021
36. ARM Limited: ARM's solution to the future needs of AI, security and specialized computing is v9. https://www.arm.com/company/news/2021/03/arms-answer-to-the-future-of-ai-armv9-architecture. Accessed 10 Dec 2021
37. Marinas, C.: Memory Layout on AArch64 Linux (2020). https://www.kernel.org/doc/html/latest/arm64/memory.html. Accessed 10 Dec 2021
38. Mashtizadeh, A.J., Bittau, A., Boneh, D., Mazières, D.: CCFI: cryptographically enforced control flow integrity. In: Conference on Computer and Communications Security - CCS 2015 (2015). https://doi.org/10.1145/2810103.2813676
39. Moro, N., Dehbaoui, A., Heydemann, K., Robisson, B., Encrenaz, E.: Electromagnetic fault injection: towards a fault model on a 32-bit microcontroller. In: Fault Diagnosis and Tolerance in Cryptography - FDTC 2013 (2013). https://doi.org/10.1109/FDTC.2013.9
40. Murdock, K., Oswald, D.F., Garcia, F.D., Bulck, J.V., Gruss, D., Piessens, F.: Plundervolt: software-based fault injection attacks against Intel SGX. In: IEEE Symposium on Security and Privacy - S&P 2020 (2020). https://doi.org/10.1109/SP40000.2020.00057
41. Nasahl, P., Timmers, N.: Attacking AUTOSAR using software and hardware attacks. In: escar, USA (2019)
42. Oh, N., Shirvani, P.P., McCluskey, E.J.: Control-flow checking by software signatures. IEEE Trans. Reliab. **51**(1), 111–122 (2002). https://doi.org/10.1109/24.994926
43. Patterson, D., Bennett, J., Palmer Dabbelt, C.G., Madhusudan, G.S., Mudge, T.: Embench^{TM}: A Modern Embedded Benchmark Suite. https://www.embench.org. Accessed 10 Dec 2021
44. QEMU: QEMU the FAST! Processor Emulator (2020). https://www.qemu.org. Accessed 10 Dec 2021
45. Qiu, P., Wang, D., Lyu, Y., Qu, G.: VoltJockey: breaching TrustZone by software-controlled voltage manipulation over multi-core frequencies. In: Conference on Computer and Communications Security - CCS 2019 (2019). https://doi.org/10.1145/3319535.3354201
46. Qualcomm Technologies, Inc.: Pointer Authentication on ARMv8.3 (2017). https://www.qualcomm.com/media/documents/files/whitepaper-pointer-authentication-on-armv8-3.pdf. Accessed 10 Dec 2021
47. Reis, G.A., Chang, J., Vachharajani, N., Rangan, R., August, D.I.: SWIFT: software implemented fault tolerance. In: Symposium on Code Generation and Optimization - CGO 2005 (2005). https://doi.org/10.1109/CGO.2005.34
48. Rott, J.K.: Intel®Advanced Encryption Standard Instructions (AES-NI) (2012). https://software.intel.com/content/www/us/en/develop/articles/intel-advanced-encryption-standard-instructions-aes-ni.html. Accessed 10 Dec 2021
49. Shacham, H.: The geometry of innocent flesh on the bone: return-into-libc without function calls (on the x86). In: Conference on Computer and Communications Security - CCS 2007 (2007). https://doi.org/10.1145/1315245.1315313

50. Sugihara, M.: A dynamic continuous signature monitoring technique for reliable microprocessors. IEICE Trans. Electron. **94**(4), 477–486 (2011). https://doi.org/10.1587/transele.E94.C.477
51. Tang, A., Sethumadhavan, S., Stolfo, S.J.: CLKSCREW: exposing the perils of security-oblivious energy management. In: USENIX Security Symposium - USENIX 2017 [1]. https://www.usenix.org/conference/usenixsecurity17/technical-sessions/presentation/tang
52. Tatar, A., Konoth, R.K., Athanasopoulos, E., Giuffrida, C., Bos, H., Razavi, K.: Throwhammer: rowhammer attacks over the network and defenses. In: USENIX Annual Technical Conference - USENIX ATC 2018 (2018). https://www.usenix.org/conference/atc18/presentation/tatar
53. Tice, C., et al.: Enforcing forward-edge control-flow integrity in GCC & LLVM. In: USENIX Security Symposium - USENIX 2014 (2014). https://www.usenix.org/conference/usenixsecurity14/technical-sessions/presentation/tice
54. Timmers, N., Mune, C.: Escalating privileges in Linux using voltage fault injection. In: Fault Diagnosis and Tolerance in Cryptography - FDTC 2017 (2017). https://doi.org/10.1109/FDTC.2017.16
55. Timmers, N., Spruyt, A., Witteman, M.: Controlling PC on ARM using fault injection. In: Fault Diagnosis and Tolerance in Cryptography - FDTC 2016 (2016). https://doi.org/10.1109/FDTC.2016.18
56. Trouchkine, T., Bouffard, G., Clédière, J.: Fault injection characterization on modern CPUs. In: Laurent, M., Giannetsos, T. (eds.) WISTP 2019. LNCS, vol. 12024, pp. 123–138. Springer, Cham (2020). https://doi.org/10.1007/978-3-030-41702-4_8
57. van der Veen, V., et al.: Drammer: deterministic rowhammer attacks on mobile platforms. In: Conference on Computer and Communications Security - CCS 2016 (2016). https://doi.org/10.1145/2976749.2978406
58. Venkatasubramanian, R., Hayes, J.P., Murray, B.T.: Low-cost on-line fault detection using control flow assertions. In: International Symposium on On-Line Testing and Robust System Design - IOLTS 2003 (2003). https://doi.org/10.1109/OLT.2003.1214380
59. Werner, M., Unterluggauer, T., Schaffenrath, D., Mangard, S.: Sponge-based control-flow protection for IoT devices. In: IEEE European Symposium on Security and Privacy - EURO S&P 2018 (2018). https://doi.org/10.1109/EuroSP.2018.00023
60. Werner, M., Wenger, E., Mangard, S.: Protecting the control flow of embedded processors against fault attacks. In: Homma, N., Medwed, M. (eds.) CARDIS 2015. LNCS, vol. 9514, pp. 161–176. Springer, Cham (2016). https://doi.org/10.1007/978-3-319-31271-2_10
61. Wilken, K.D., Shen, J.P.: Continuous signature monitoring: efficient concurrent-detection of processor control errors. In: International Test Conference - ITC 1988 (1988). https://doi.org/10.1109/TEST.1988.207880
62. Wilken, K.D., Shen, J.P.: Continuous signature monitoring: low-cost concurrent detection of processor control errors. IEEE Trans. Comput. Aided Des. Integr. Circ. Syst. **9**(6), 629–641 (1990). https://doi.org/10.1109/43.55193
63. Google Project Zero: Exploiting the DRAM rowhammer bug to gain kernel privileges (2015). https://googleprojectzero.blogspot.com/2015/03/exploiting-dram-rowhammer-bug-to-gain.html. Accessed 10 Dec 2021
64. Zhang, M., Sekar, R.: Control flow integrity for COTS binaries. In: USENIX Security Symposium - USENIX 2013 (2013). https://www.usenix.org/conference/usenixsecurity13/technical-sessions/presentation/Zhang

Body Biasing Injection: To Thin or Not to Thin the Substrate?

G. Chancel(✉), J.-M. Galliere, and P. Maurine

University of Montpellier, LIRMM, 161 rue Ada, 34095 Montpellier CEDEX 5, France
gchancel@lirmm.fr

Abstract. Body Biasing Injection (BBI), compared to other injection techniques, is quite recent. It consists in applying a voltage pulse onto the backside surface of an integrated circuit with a needle. Despite its simplicity, and probably because of its recentness, there is very little knowledge on how faults occur, nor as on the characteristics of this injection technique. Within this context, this paper provides insights about the interest of thinning the substrate of ICs in order to enhance the efficiency of BBI as well as its spatial resolution. Those insights were obtained both by experiment and simulation. As a result, elements for simulating the propagation of a perturbation are provided.

Keywords: Integrated circuits · Body Biasing Injection · Fault Injection

1 Introduction

Nowadays, several fault injection techniques exist. Among them, one can find voltage glitch [1], electromagnetic fault injection (EMFI) [2,6] or laser fault injection (LFI) [10]. They allow inducing in integrated circuits (ICs), with a high reproducibility rate, transient or semi-permanent faults that can be exploited to carry out attacks or inhibit countermeasures.

In addition to these techniques, there is Body Biasing Injection (BBI) [7,11], a quite recent fault injection technique, which consists in applying a voltage pulse onto the backside of ICs. Probably because of its recentness, there is very little information available in the literature about it. Up to the best of our knowledge, only [3,7,8,11] are focused on this topic but mainly aim at demonstrating its efficiency. Indeed [7] and [11] both demonstrate that a Bellcore attack [1] can be performed on a modern micro-controller using BBI, while [3] evaluates the sensitivity of various circuits to this threat. Eventually, [8] introduces a very low cost BBI setup and demonstrates its efficiency to perform fault attacks on a hardware AES co-processor. Very interestingly, this paper also highlights that BBI is able to induce both transient and semi-permanent faults and can probably induce faults in flash memory at rest.

J. Balasch and C. O'Flynn (Eds.): COSADE 2022, LNCS 13211, pp. 125–139, 2022.
https://doi.org/10.1007/978-3-030-99766-3_6

Furthermore, with the different manufacturing processes, depending on the purpose for which the IC is developed for but also or the wafer size, it is possible to have different substrate thicknesses. While, for 300 mm diameter wafers, it is common to find 700 µm thickness, in some applications like in Smartcards or SoCs (where vertical stacking is used) this value can be smaller (200 µm or less). For Smartcards or ID cards, security constraints are high. It is thus interesting to tackle the interest of substrate thinning to evaluate and study the influence of this parameter on BBI fault injection or other fault injection techniques. This explains why this work focuses on BBI efficiency and not on the possible attacks around this injection method.

Within this context, because BBI is done in contact with the silicon substrate of ICs, and as there is currently no electrical model precise enough to take into account the substrate effects on BBI, the objective of this paper is threefold.

First, it tackles the interest of thinning the substrate of ICs in order to enhance BBI efficiency as well as its spatial resolution. Second, because this study was conducted both experimentally and through simulations, another objective is to introduce an improvement of an existing IC model for EMFI simulations. This improvement allows to take more precisely the substrate into account and above all to analyse the propagation of perturbations through it.

Finally, it reports experimental results validating this enhanced model and at providing insights on how BBI faults occur.

The main shortcomings of this work are diverse. First, the work was done using constant PVT (Process, Voltage, Temperature) conditions, in order to limit the number of parameters and to focus only around the injection parameters. Second, this work did not address any consideration concerning countermeasures, whether it was the already implemented ones or the potential new ones that could be designed.

The remainder of the paper is organized as follows: Sect. 2 describes the simulation methodology that has been set up for analyzing BBI effects on IC operation, which is an extension of the one introduced in [4] for simulating EMFI. This section also provides simulation results of use to understand how the applied voltage pulses propagate from the backside of ICs towards their front side and thus apprehends what is the spatial resolution of BBI. Then, Sect. 3 provides experimental results sustaining the correctness of the proposed simulation methodology but also demonstrates that thinning the substrate of ICs eases the injection of faults but does not change its spatial resolution. Eventually, Sect. 4 concludes this paper.

2 Modelling

Modelling and simulating fault injections or side channel attacks at chip level is a complex task. Especially if the considered attack involves spatial considerations such as the position of the laser spot above the IC surface or that of an EM probe. Tools like Voltus and Redhawk respectively from Cadence and ANSYS are helpful for this purpose [9,12]. However, their usage for simulating electromagnetic fault injections (EMFI) or body biasing fault injections is not straightforward. Indeed, concerning BBI, the role of the substrate in which the voltage spikes propagate is central and is not finely considered in standard Voltus or Redhawk simulations. It explains why the approach proposed in [4] has been preferred in order to model the impact of BBI on IC operation.

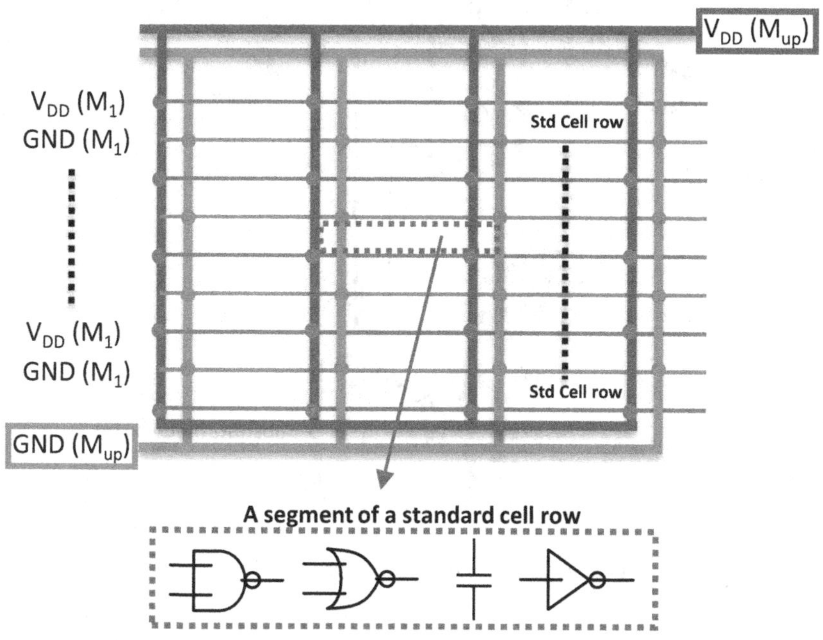

Fig. 1. IC floorplan split into a matrix of SC segments

In [4], a simulation flow for EMFI is proposed. In the latter, the surface of the IC is split in standard cell (SC) segments defined accordingly to the routing of the power and ground grids as illustrated in Fig. 1. Each SC segment (30 µm long and 5 µm high in the rest of the paper), delimited by the lower and upper levels of metal lines used to route perpendicularly the supply, contains about fifty of CMOS gates and some decoupling capacitors; it is important to note that at the level of abstraction of the work, logic gates functionality has no importance, thus only the electrical equivalent effect is considered by the model. Of course, they are connected to the power grids, the ground grids, and the substrate. The equivalent electrical transistor-less circuit of a SC segment proposed in [4] is depicted in Fig. 2.

The role of each element of this equivalent circuit is detailed in the related publication [4]: region ⓪ models the local power and ground grids delimiting and thus surrounding a SC segment, region ① represents the decoupling capacitors,

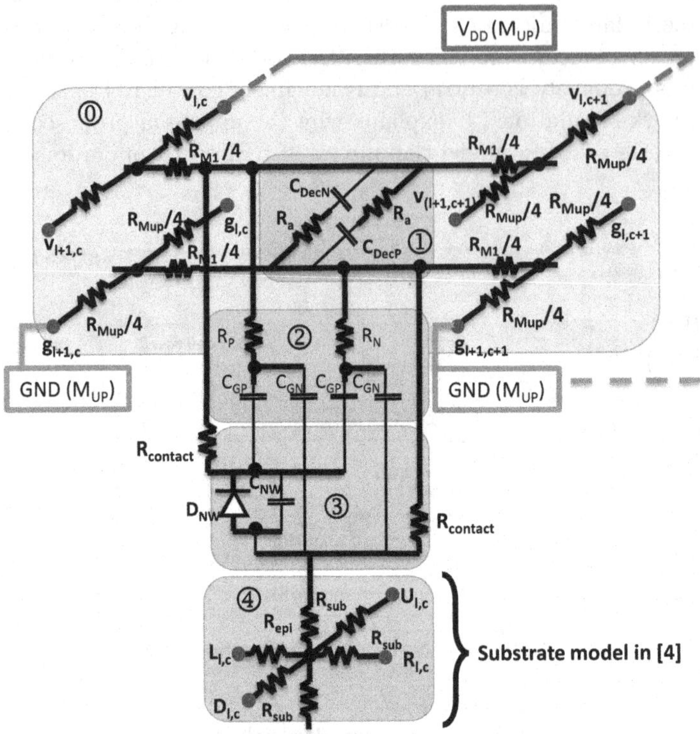

Fig. 2. Equivalent transistor-less circuit of a standard-cell segment

region ② the standard cell gates, region ③ the N-well and eventually region ④ the substrate below the SC segment.

One can observe the substrate in its whole is modelled by six resistors, which is not precise enough to study the propagation of voltage pulses across it. This model was, as a consequence, enhanced to be able to finely analyse the propagation of the perturbation through the substrate but also to respect its isotropy. This enhancement, illustrated in Fig. 3, consists in splitting the substrate below each SC segment in small cuboids of side length equal to the height of a SC segment in itself (see Fig. 1). This length is a good trade-off between accuracy and simulation time.

2.1 Simulation Results

With the previously described enhanced model, whose elementary blocks are written manually in a SPICE netlist, body biasing injections on a 1 mm × 1 mm die (which represents 200 × 35 of the described elementary blocks) with a substrate thickness of 240 µm, were simulated using HSPICE device level circuit simulator. The modelled probe needle was a square of 30 µm × 30 µm. It was thus connected to the substrate of six elementary blocks. The entire simulated

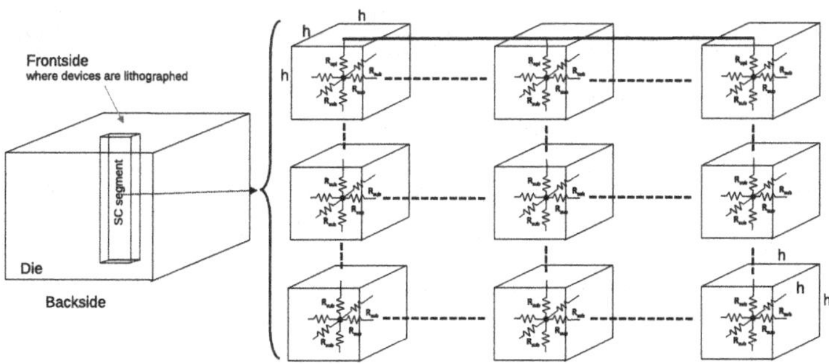

Fig. 3. Enhanced substrate lumped model of a SC segment

SPICE netlist was automatically generated using a custom Python script which connects the required blocks together: in our case, 7000 blocks.

The results of such simulations allow to get the evolution of the local supply voltages (V_{DD} and G_{ND}) with respect to time, as well as the one of the substrate, all over the IC surface and in the whole substrate volume. Such information can be used to run electrical simulations (similar to those performed to look for SCA leakages), allowing to analyze the behavior of the logic blocks and thus to perform fault occurrences and propagation analyses. None are reported in this paper which focuses on the potential benefit of thinning the substrate.

The time spent by our machine (460 GB of available memory, 48 cores and 96 threads CPU cadenced at 3 GHz) to perform a simulation is about three hours for a 1 mm × 1 mm × 240 µm circuit. The peak memory usage was around 170 GBytes and the number of used threads was of 10. There is thus still room to simulate larger surface.

Three different positions A, B and C of the needle tip end on the backside were considered to analyse how the injected voltage pulses propagate from the backside towards the front side. The voltage pulses delivered to the needle had an amplitude V_{Pu} of −230 V and a pulse width (PW) at half maximum equal to 6 ns.

Figure 4 shows the evolution of the bias through the substrate at the apex of the observed perturbation. As described in Fig. 1, V_{DD} and G_{ND} pads are respectively on the top and bottom of the die respectively. One can observe on this figure that the bias distribution around the contact point between the needle and the substrate is roughly a truncated half-sphere. The observed asymmetry with respect to this global trend are due to the relative position of the needle with respect to V_{DD} and G_{ND} pads.

2.2 Effect of the Substrate Thickness

From the latter simulation results, one can anticipate the effect of thinning the substrate on the BBI efficiency as well as on its spatial resolution. For this purpose, let us consider that one aims at injecting a fault at the point P of the

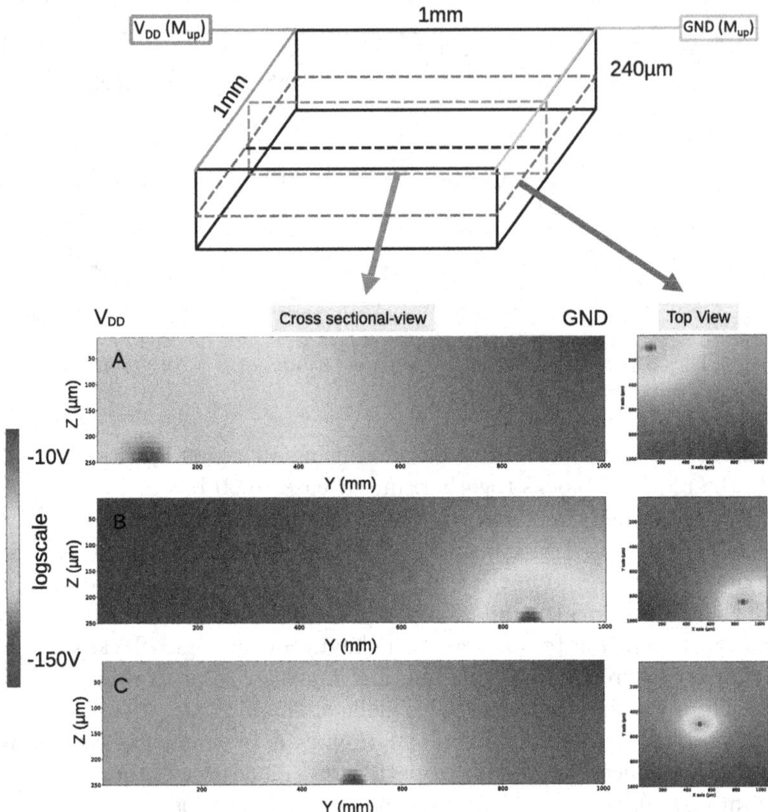

Fig. 4. Cross sectional and top views (at the back side level) of the bias across the substrate at the apex of body bias injections performed at three different points of the backside surface.

IC front side where devices and CMOS gates are lithographed as represented in Fig. 5. In this figure, two dies of the same device with two different substrate thicknesses are considered. Let us also assume that to induce a fault at this point P, the potential must reach V_F or an higher value (considering the absolute values). In such a situation, an attacker applying a voltage pulse inducing a substrate bias $V_{Pu} > V_F$ creates a truncated half sphere of radius:

$$r = \frac{V_{Pu} - V_F}{\rho_{sub} \cdot I_{gen}} \quad (1)$$

centered on the tip end of the needle in which the bias of the substrate is greater or equal to V_F. Hence, to induce a fault at P, the attacker has to place the tip end of the needle within a disc, on the IC backside, of diameter:

$$\phi = 2 \cdot \sqrt{r^2 - t_{sub}^2} \quad (2)$$

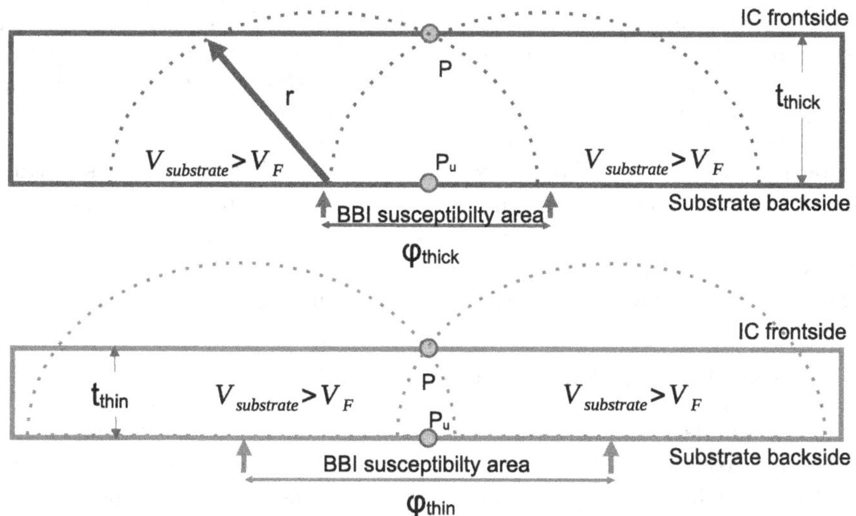

Fig. 5. BBI susceptibility area of a device without and with thinning of the substrate.

with t_{sub} the thickness of the substrate, ρ_{sub} its resistivity by unit length and I_{gen} the current delivered by the voltage pulse generator. The previously mentioned disc is denoted as the susceptibility area afterward.

As illustrated in Fig. 5, thinning the substrate from a thickness t_{thick} down to t_{thin} increases the BBI susceptibility area if the amplitude of the voltage pulse applied with the needle is kept constant and equal to V_{Pu}:

$$\frac{\phi_{thin}}{\phi_{thick}} = \sqrt{\frac{r^2 - t_{thin}^2}{r^2 - t_{thick}^2}} > 1 \tag{3}$$

In return, one can obtain the same susceptibility area after thinning the substrate by reducing the amplitude of the applied voltage pulse from V_{Pu} to V_{Pu}^* with:

$$V_{Pu}^* = \frac{t_{thin}}{t_{thick}} \cdot V_{Pu} + V_F \cdot (1 - \frac{t_{thin}}{t_{thick}}) \tag{4}$$

These theoretical results and expressions deduced from simulation and geometrical considerations indicate that:

- Outcome 1: thinning the substrate increases, while working at constant V_{Pu}, the susceptibility area of a device to BBI which could be of help to find hotspots, i.e. susceptibility areas.
- Outcome 2: thinning the substrate does not increase the spatial resolution of BBI, actually, the susceptibility area of a device to BBI does not depend solely on its substrate thickness but rather on the couple (t_{sub}, V_{Pu}). Therefore similar spatial resolution could be obtained for different substrate thickness by simply adjusting V_{Pu}.

- Outcome 3: thinning the substrate allows being more stealthy by reducing the minimal amplitude of the pulse required to induce a fault. It implies a reduction on the induced parasitic current flowing from the needle to the G_{ND} and V_{DD} pads.

As a result, there is potentially interest in simultaneously thinning the substrate and reducing the amplitude of the voltages pulse to bypass countermeasures like glitch detectors or BBI detectors [5,13,14]. However, up to this point, all these results are deduced from simulation. It is now mandatory to prove their soundness by experimental results. This is the goal of Sect. 3.

2.3 About the BBI Fault Model

During the simulations that have been performed to analyze how voltage pulses propagate across the substrate, the evolution of the electrical potential of several V_{DD} and G_{ND} lines were observed, similarly to what had been done in [4]. It has been observed that the most perturbed ones are located above the tip end of the needle (point P in Fig. 5).

Figures 6 and 7 show respectively for negative and positive pulses, the typical waveforms of V_{DD} and G_{ND} of the previously mentioned lines, but also those of the resulting swing $V_{DD} - G_{ND}$. One can observe that because of the Nwell diode D_{NW} (see Fig. 2), the response to a BBI injection of V_{DD} and G_{ND} lines to a negative pulse are different. Indeed, the perturbation hardly propagates towards V_{DD} lines through R_{sub}, R_{epi}, and C_{Nwell} and $R_{contact}$ while it more easily propagates towards G_{ND} lines directly through R_{sub}, R_{epi} and $R_{contact}$. Therefore, in that case, V_{DD} lines are capacitively coupled to the substrate through C_{NW} (the diode being turn off), while G_{ND} lines are directly connected to the substrate through the resistor $R_{sub} + R_{epi} + R_{contact}$.

In the case of positive pulses, the perturbation propagates towards G_{ND} lines similarly than for negative pulses. However, the propagation towards V_{DD} lines is different. Indeed, D_{NW} is now conducting. Thus, the perturbation propagates more easily towards V_{DD} lines through R_{sub}, R_{epi} and $R_{contact}$. As a result, the local supply voltage, $V_{DD} - G_{ND}$, of CMOS gates, is simply the difference of two RC responses with slightly different time constants. This is due to a slight difference in the length of the electrical paths followed by the perturbation through the supply and ground grids to reach the power and ground pads. Therefore, to obtain large variations of $V_{DD} - G_{ND}$ (as one can observe when comparing Figs. 6 and 7), positive voltage pulses with greater amplitudes are required. These different behaviours explain why negative pulses are more efficient than positive ones to induce faults.

Whatever the electrical phenomenon, one can also observe that these waveforms are surprisingly similar to those reported in [4] for EMFI. This observation is further sustained by Fig. 8 showing the probability to induce faults over several clock cycles for BBI and EMFI. Indeed, both appear to be periodical and highly reproducible, in a certain range of V_{Pu}, with a period equal to the clock period. Similarly to EMFI, below and above this V_{Pu} range the probability to induce a

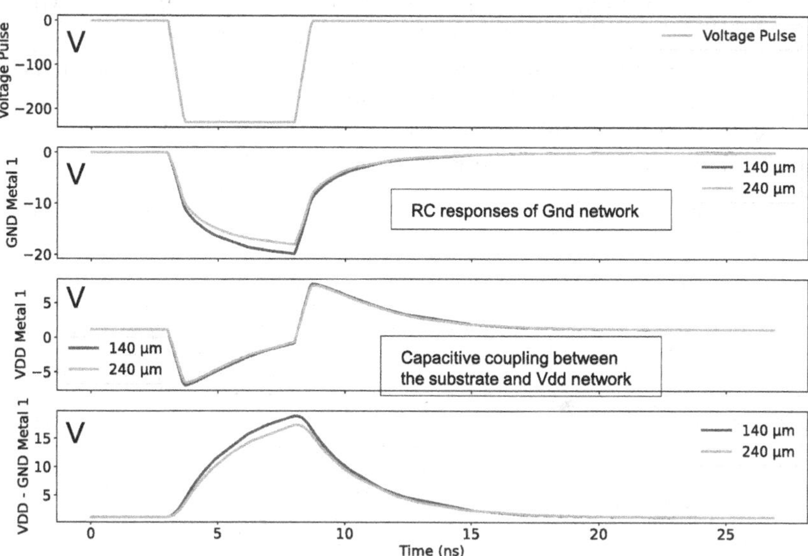

Fig. 6. $V_{DD}(t)$ and $GND(t)$ voltage waveforms at Metal 1 level (above the tip end needle) during a BBI (V_{Pu} = −230 V) for two substrate thicknesses: 140 µm and 240 µm.

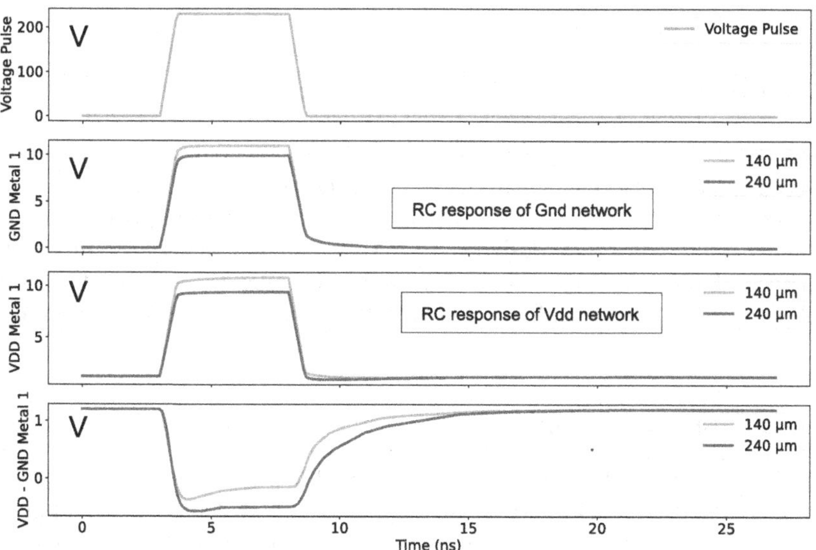

Fig. 7. $V_{DD}(t)$ and $GND(t)$ voltage waveforms at metal1 level (above the tip end needle) during a BBI (V_{Pu} = +230 V) for two substrate thicknesses: 140 µm and 240 µm.

fault is respectively equal to zero and one. Hence, it seems that the EMFI and BBI fault models could share many characteristics. However, this observation has to be confirmed by further works. Among considered work, it is planned to inject the results of such simulations, and more precisely the evolution of local V_{DD}, G_{ND}, and bias in gate netlists to analyze the effects of BBI on IC operation. It will also be necessary to compare the resulting faulty behaviors with experiments.

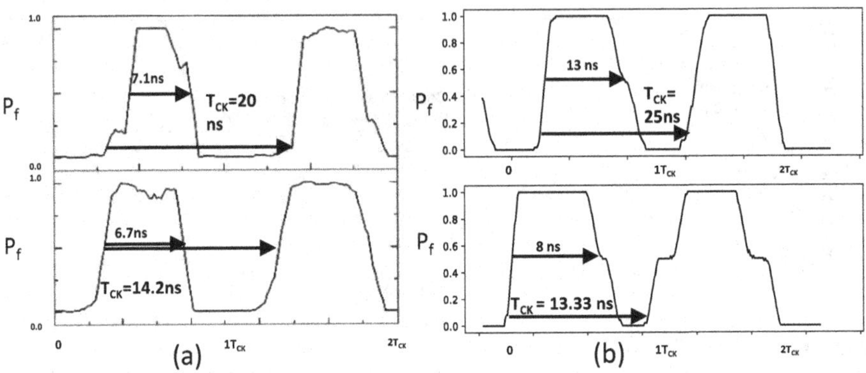

Fig. 8. Fault induction probability obtained with: (a) EMFI on a device running at 50 MHz (top) and 70 MHz (bottom) from [4], (b) BBI on a device running at 40 MHz (top) and 75 MHz (bottom). In both case the substrate thickness was equal to 140 µm.

3 Experiments

Several experiments were performed to verify the soundness of the outcomes derived from simulation which are listed at the end of Sect. 2. These experiments all aimed at analyzing the effect of (t_{sub}, V_{Pu}) on BBI susceptibility areas of a modern micro-controller designed in CMOS 90 nm technology in order to evaluate and understand the fault injection mechanisms, and not to perform any fault injection attacks afterwards. The die area of this device being roughly 5 mm × 6 mm.

3.1 Substrate Thinning

First of all, a brief introduction to substrate thinning is required. One of the main shortcomings of BBI is that almost every target has to be uncapped, in order to get a direct electrical access to the IC substrate, in addition to the potential thinning and polishing of the substrate. Thinning and polishing the substrate is usually achieved with solutions like ASAP System (https://www.ultratecusa.com/), which also allows to decapsulate and remove the eventual heatsink present inside the IC package. If the package can also be removed with chemical processes (etching), in our case, an ASAP was used for all the required operations: remove the package, thin the substrate and polish it.

3.2 BBI Platform

The BBI platform used during these experiments is organized around a voltage pulse generator from AVTECH (AVRK-4-B-PN). The amplitude V_{Pu} and the pulse width at half maximum of the generated pulses can be set respectively between ±50 V to ±750 V and between 6 ns to 20 ns. BBI probes were fabricated using a 3D printer and ATE test probes with gold finishing and the ability to convey 3 A. As shown in Fig. 9, spring-loaded pins (RS PRO Test Pin 3A: 542–4990), with a tip-end diameter equal to ~2 × 20 µm, were chosen to avoid scratching too much the backside of the device or the device itself when thinned down to 50 µm, but also to maintain a good electrical contact.

3.3 Device Under Fault Injection

The device under fault injection is a modern micro controller featuring a cortex M4 core and various co-processors. Among them the hardware AES co-processor was chosen as the target of the injections. The package of several of these devices was first removed and their substrate thinned to have thicknesses equal to 200 µm, 140 µm and 50 µm.

A board was specifically designed to control and limit the current that can be supplied to the device. During all experiments the supply source current was limited to 150 mA. The typical current consumption of the device being 40 mA. It should be taken into account that setting a greater limit for the current would allow injecting faults with lower amplitude pulses than those reported afterward but at the risk of damaging the device faster. Whatever the adopted value, this limit is definitely a control parameter of the BBI efficiency as well as of the risk to damage target devices.

Concerning the risk of damaging the devices, we observed that applying positive pulses to the substrate is far more dangerous than applying negative ones, and in addition to that, is less efficient. The most plausible reason is the presence of the N-Well diode that limits the current crossing the device when a negative pulse is applied and imposes a different response of both power grids; differences that seem to ease the induction of faults. This explains why only negative pulses are considered in the rest of the paper.

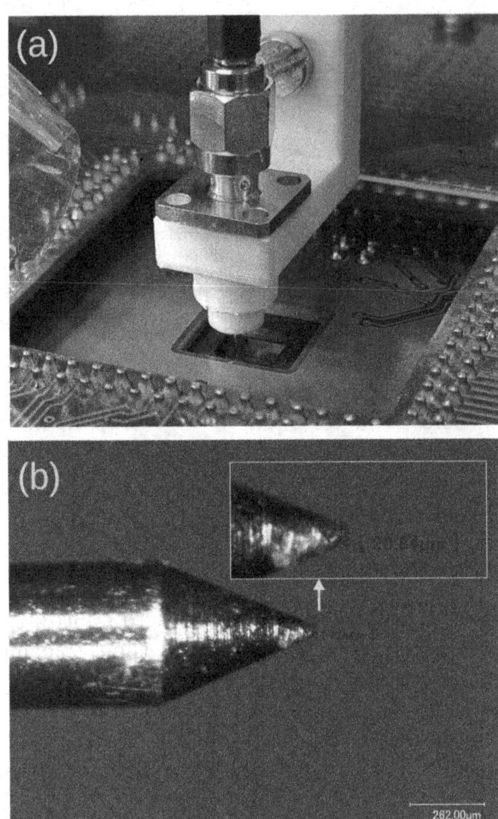

Fig. 9. (a) Overview of BBI probes fabricated around spring-loaded pins. (b) Tip-end radius measurement of the probe (b).

3.4 Experimental Results

Among the different experiments that have been performed, one of them had aimed at measuring the minimal amplitude V_{Pu}^{min} of the pulse required to induce a fault at different positions of the needle on the backside. For this purpose, a scan of a surface enclosing the AES was performed with a displacement step of the needle of 40 μm. The search for V_{Pu}^{min} was limited to the voltage range [30 V; 280 V] by step of 5 V while PW was set to 6 ns. Scans were performed with the same settings for devices with substrate thicknesses of 200 μm, 140 μm and 50 μm. The scanned surface has an area of around 1.7 mm × 1.7 mm.

Figure 10 shows the V_{Pu}^{min} maps, with the exact same color scale, for the three considered circuits. One can observe that, as expected from simulation, thinning the substrate allows inducing faults at lower values of V_{Pu} values. Indeed, the average value of V_{Pu}^{min} are respectively 136 V, 180 V and 220 V for the three presented maps in Fig. 10. This experimental result sustains the outcome 3 of Sect. 2 that has been deduced from simulation.

Figure 11 shows the positions of the needle at which faults are obtained for $|V_P| \leq 180\,\text{V}$ for the three considered substrate thicknesses. The spreading of the BBI susceptibility area (performed at constant V_{Pu}) is clearly visible. These results sustain the outcome 1 drawn from simulation in Sect. 2.

To sustain outcome 2 stating that similar fault maps could be obtained for different couples (t_{sub}, V_{Pu}), we looked for such couples with the help of (4). We found that couples ($t_{sub} = 200$ µm, $V_{Pu} = -170$ V), ($t_{sub} = 140$ µm, $V_{Pu} = -145$ V) and ($t_{sub} = 50$ µm, $V_{Pu} = -85$ V), as shown in Fig. 12, provide not identical, but similar susceptibility areas. Consequently, outcome 2 seems sound, especially if one considers that several parameters were not perfectly controlled during experiments. Among them, one can find the variation of environmental conditions during such long experiments (about 10 h are required to draw a map), the pressure of the needle on the IC backside, the imperfect silicon surface of the IC backside, the too much coarse voltage step and finally the difference in the I_{gen} values when the generator is set to a different V_{Pu}. Eventually, we did observe that the power consumption of the devices changes significantly with the substrate thickness. We do not have any explanation for this at the moment.

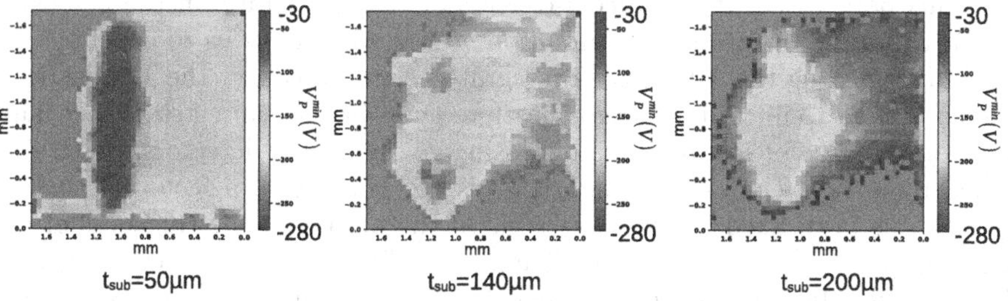

Fig. 10. V_{Pu}^{min} for different substrate thicknesses

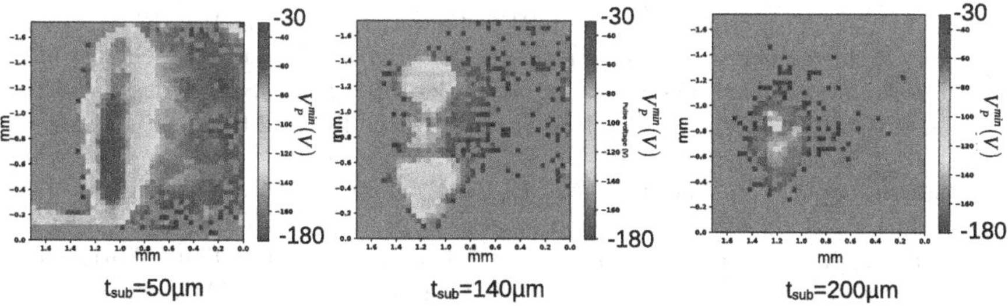

Fig. 11. Spreading of the BBI susceptibility area with the thinning of the substrate.

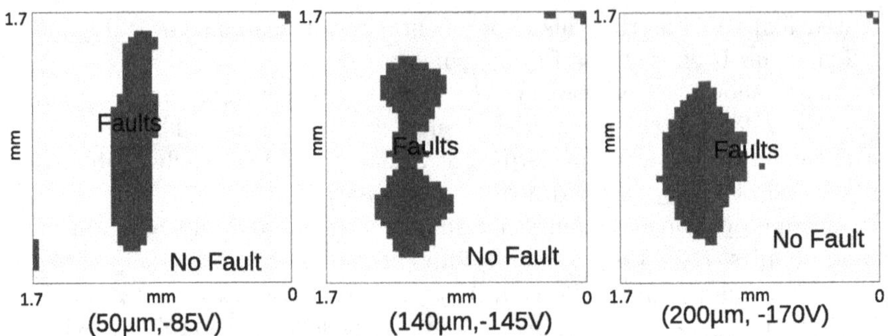

Fig. 12. BBI fault maps for couples ($t_{sub} = 200\,\mu\text{m}, V_{Pu} = -185\,\text{V}$), ($t_{sub} = 140\ \mu\text{m}$, $V_{Pu} = -160$ V) and ($t_{sub} = 50\ \mu\text{m}, V_{Pu} = -115$ V)

4 Conclusion

Body bias injection is a quite recent fault injection technique consisting in injecting voltage pulses directly onto the substrate of the target device with a needle. Despite the fact that its efficiency had been demonstrated in former works, there is very little knowledge about this technique in the literature. Within this context, this paper studied the effects of thinning the substrate on the efficiency of BBI as well as on its spatial resolution. Our results allow us to conclude the following: thinning the substrate of integrated circuits reduces the amplitude of pulses required to inject faults and therefore helps in performing stealthier fault injection attacks, for instance, via bypassing voltage glitch detectors. Regarding spatial resolution, thinning the substrate is not beneficial, in fact, BBI spatial resolution is both fixed by the amplitude of the pulse and the thickness of the substrate. It means that similar fault maps can be obtained with different couples of values. In addition to these conclusions regarding the practice of BBI, the paper provides elements to simulate it.

References

1. Aumueller, C., Bier, P., Fischer, W., Hofreiter, P., Seifert, J.-P.: Concrete results and practical countermeasures. In: CHES, Fault attacks on RSA with CRT (2002)
2. Bayon, P., et al.: Contactless electromagnetic active attack on ring oscillator based true random number generator. In: Schindler, W., Huss, S.A. (eds.) COSADE 2012. LNCS, vol. 7275, pp. 151–166. Springer, Heidelberg (2012). https://doi.org/10.1007/978-3-642-29912-4_12
3. Beringuier-Boher, N., Lacruche, M., El-Baze, D., Dutertre, J.-M., Rigaud, J.-B., Maurine, P.: Body biasing injection attacks in practice. In: Palkovic, M., Agosta, G., Barenghi, A., Koren, I., elosi, G., (eds.), Proceedings of the Third Workshop on Cryptography and Security in Computing Systems, CS2@HiPEAC, Prague, Czech Republic, 20 January 2016, pp. 49–54. ACM (2016)
4. Dumont, M., Lisart, M., Maurine, P.: Modeling and simulating electromagnetic fault injection. IEEE Trans. Comput. Aided Des. Integr. Circuits Syst. **40**(4), 680–693 (2021)

5. El-Baze, D., Rigaud, J.-B., Maurine, P.: An embedded digital sensor against EM and BB fault injection. In: 2016 Workshop on Fault Diagnosis and Tolerance in Cryptography, FDTC 2016, Santa Barbara, CA, USA, August 16, 2016, pp. 78–86. IEEE Computer Society (2016)
6. Maurine, P.: Techniques for EM fault injection: equipments and experimental results. In: Bertoni, G., Gierlichs, B., (eds.) 2012 Workshop on Fault Diagnosis and Tolerance in Cryptography, Leuven, Belgium, 9 September 2012, pp. 3–4. IEEE Computer Society (2012)
7. Maurine, P., Tobich, K., Ordas, T., Liardet, P.Y.: Yet another fault injection technique : by forward body biasing injection. In: YACC 2012: Yet Another Conference on Cryptography, Porquerolles Island, France, September 2012
8. O'Flynn, C.: Low-cost body biasing injection (BBI) attacks on WLCSP devices. In: Liardet, P.-Y., Mentens, N. (eds.) CARDIS 2020. LNCS, vol. 12609, pp. 166–180. Springer, Cham (2021). https://doi.org/10.1007/978-3-030-68487-7_11
9. Poggi, D., Ordas, T., Sarafianos, A., Maurine, P.: Checking robustness against EM side-channel attacks prior to manufacturing. IEEE Trans. Comput. Aided Des. Integr. Circuits Syst. 1 (2021)
10. Skorobogatov, S.P., Anderson, R.J.: Optical fault induction attacks. In: Kaliski, B.S., Koç, K., Paar, C. (eds.) CHES 2002. LNCS, vol. 2523, pp. 2–12. Springer, Heidelberg (2003). https://doi.org/10.1007/3-540-36400-5_2
11. Tobich, K., Maurine, P., Liardet, P.-Y., Lisart, M., Ordas, T.: Voltage spikes on the substrate to obtain timing faults. In: 2013 Euromicro Conference on Digital System Design, DSD 2013, Los Alamitos, CA, USA, 4–6 September 2013, pp. 483–486. IEEE Computer Society (2013)
12. Viera, R.A.C., Maurine, P., Dutertre, J.-M., Bastos, R.P.: Simulation and experimental demonstration of the importance of IR-drops during laser fault injection. IEEE. Trans. Comput. Aided Des. Integr. Circuits Syst. **39**(6), 1231–1244 (2020)
13. Yanci, A.G., Pickles, S., Arslan, T.: Detecting voltage glitch attacks on secure devices. In: 2008 Bio-Inspired, Learning and Intelligent Systems for Security, pp. 75–80. IEEE (2008)
14. Zussa, L., et al.: Efficiency of a glitch detector against electromagnetic fault injection. In: 2014 Design, Automation Test in Europe Conference Exhibition (DATE), pp. 1–6 (2014)

Attacks

On the Susceptibility of Texas Instruments SimpleLink Platform Microcontrollers to Non-invasive Physical Attacks

Lennert Wouters(✉), Benedikt Gierlichs, and Bart Preneel

imec-COSIC, KU Leuven, Kasteelpark Arenberg 10, 3001 Heverlee, Belgium
{lennert.wouters,benedikt.gierlichs,bart.preneel}@esat.kuleuven.be

Abstract. We investigate the susceptibility of the Texas Instruments SimpleLink platform microcontrollers to non-invasive physical attacks. We extracted the ROM bootloader of these microcontrollers and then analysed it using static analysis augmented with information obtained through emulation. We demonstrate a voltage fault injection attack targeting the ROM bootloader that allows to enable debug access on a previously locked microcontroller within seconds. Information provided by Texas Instruments reveals that one of our voltage fault injection attacks abuses functionality that is left over from the integrated circuit manufacturing process. The demonstrated physical attack allows an adversary to extract the firmware (i.e. intellectual property) and to bypass secure boot. Additionally, we mount side-channel attacks and differential fault analysis attacks on the hardware AES co-processor. To demonstrate the practical applicability of these attacks we extract the firmware from a Tesla Model 3 key fob.

This paper describes a case study covering Texas Instruments SimpleLink microcontrollers. Similar attack techniques can be, and have been, applied to microcontrollers from other manufacturers. The goal of our work is to document our analysis methodology and to ensure that system designers are aware of these vulnerabilities. They will then be able to take these into account during the product design phase. All identified vulnerabilities were responsibly disclosed.

Keywords: SimpleLink · Firmware recovery · Fault injection · Side-channel analysis

1 Introduction

Embedded devices are often interconnected using a broad variety of wireless technologies. Texas Instruments (TI) offers the SimpleLink microcontroller platform to enable the development of such connected embedded devices. The platform offers code portability, enabling the reuse of the same code (i.e. Intellectual Property (IP)) on a variety of microcontrollers with different functionalities. The microcontroller lineup includes Bluetooth Low Energy (BLE) and Wi-Fi enabled

J. Balasch and C. O'Flynn (Eds.): COSADE 2022, LNCS 13211, pp. 143–163, 2022.
https://doi.org/10.1007/978-3-030-99766-3_7

microcontrollers but also sub-1 GHz and multi-protocol enabled microcontrollers. According to TI these microcontrollers are suitable for a wide variety of applications ranging from home automation to automotive and medical applications as well as critical infrastructure applications [56].

TI advertises the SimpleLink microcontrollers to implement secure boot and other security features that allow protection of user data and IP [52,53]. While TI does not claim any resistance to physical attacks for the SimpleLink platform microcontrollers, it is clear that many of the products designed using these microcontrollers will be deployed in an open and possibly hostile environment.

This hostile environment may comprise physical attackers who want to extract IP or compromise the secure boot chain. Extracting the IP or firmware also enables remote attackers to more easily identify application specific software vulnerabilities [17,48,58]. Therefore, performing a physical attack on a single device can lead to remote attacks that scale without having to perform the physical attack on each device [25,45,59].

In this paper we take on the role of the physical attacker and use non-invasive physical attacks. We use Voltage Fault Injection (VFI) to extract the contents of non-volatile memory of SimpleLink microcontrollers that have all debug functionalities disabled. Additionally, we demonstrate secret key extraction by targeting the Advanced Encryption Standard (AES) hardware accelerator using Side-Channel Analysis (SCA) and Differential Fault Analysis (DFA).

While the physical attacker is outside of the attacker model used by TI it is still valuable to assess the physical security of these products. Furthermore, we argue that the purpose of debug security features is to protect from an attacker who has physical access to the device, as those debug features are only available to someone who already has physical access. The analysis presented in this work allows device manufacturers to make better informed decisions during their initial threat modeling phase.

1.1 Related Work

Embedded systems have been the subject of physical attacks for over 20 years [2,3,27,29]. Nevertheless, those same physical attack techniques can still be used today to extract secret information from many embedded systems.

The passive physical attacker has physical access to the device and observes its normal operation. For example, when performing a physical side-channel attack an adversary will observe one or multiple physical properties of the device. These physical properties, or side-channels, can be analysed to extract secret information from the device under attack [27]. Over the years researchers have shown that side-channels such as instantaneous power consumption [27,29], ElectroMagnetic (EM) emanations [16,43], execution time [26], temperature and photonic emissions [14] can all be used to recover secret information from a target device. In most cases statistical analysis is used to extract secret information from the side-channel measurements. Among the most widely used techniques are Differential Power Analyis (DPA) [27], Correlation Power Analysis (CPA) [6], Template Attacks [8] and more recently machine learning techniques [23].

The active physical attacker tries to transiently or permanently disrupt the device's normal operation. The most common non-invasive techniques for fault injection include Voltage Fault Injection (VFI) [29], clock glitching [1,29] and EM Fault Injection (EMFI) [10,29]. However, for some modern chip packaging standards (e.g. Wafer Level Chip Scale Package (WLCSP) and Flip Chip Ball Grid Array (FCBGA)) the list of non-invasive techniques can be extended with techniques that used to be considered semi-invasive such as optical fault injection [50] and body bias injection [33,40].

Both passive and active physical attacks have been demonstrated to be applicable in real world scenarios. Embedded microcontrollers are frequently the target of attacks, as they can contain proprietary code and hardcoded secrets. Consequently, it is not uncommon that a physical attack mounted on a single device leads to a system-wide compromise, these are also known as break-once run everywhere (BORE) attacks.

Goodspeed demonstrated a practical timing side-channel attack targeting the TI MSP430 microcontroller's BootStrap Loader (BSL), allowing to recover the BSL password [20,21]. Meriac extracted firmware from a Microchip PIC18F microcontroller by erasing a single block of program memory and loading it with a program to dump the remaining blocks [34]. Similarly, the popular STMicroelectronics STM32 series of microcontrollers has been the subject of multiple physical attacks that aim to bypass code readout protection features [37,38,47].

Practical side-channel attacks against Microchip's KeeLoq cipher, used in vehicle immobilisers and remote keyless entry products, were demonstrated on software and hardware implementations [13,25]. In some cases these side-channel attacks allowed to recover the master key, effectively compromising all devices of the same manufacturer by mounting a single side-channel attack [25]. Wouters et al. performed several practical attacks on DST80-based immobiliser systems [59]. The authors demonstrated fault injection attacks to bypass debug security features in automotive microcontrollers, and mounted both unprofiled and profiled side-channel attacks that allowed to extract cryptographic keys. For some DST80-based deployments the authors were able to compromise every immobiliser after carrying out physical attacks on a single device. Van den Herrewegen et al. demonstrated practical attacks targeting embedded bootloaders of several commercially available microcontrolllers [22]. Additionally, they provide a list of anti-patterns that can help guide the design of secure implementations.

Countless additional examples of physical attacks are available online [18,31,32] and in the academic literature [4,5,9,35,44], unfortunately we cannot cover all of them here. Interested readers can find more examples of physical attacks performed on embedded devices in the review paper by Shepherd et al. [49].

1.2 Contributions

The contributions of this paper can be summarised as follows:

- **ROM Bootloader Analysis.** We extracted and analysed the ROM bootloader of two SimpleLink microcontrollers. Our analysis includes emulating

the ROM bootloader to augment static analysis, and revealed two potential avenues for fault injection to bypass code readout protection. One of these code paths is, under normal circumstances, only used during the integrated circuit manufacturing process.
- **Voltage Fault Injection to Enable Debug Features.** We perform two voltage fault injection attacks allowing to enable debugging features on a previously locked down microcontroller. These physical attacks allow to bypass all IP protection functionality and secure boot features provided by the manufacturer. We perform both attacks on two distinct development boards with different microcontrollers of the SimpleLink series and demonstrate firmware recovery on a commercial product.
- **Side-Channel Analysis and Differential Fault Analysis on Hardware AES.** We mount a successful correlation power analysis attack on the hardware AES implementation included in these microcontrollers. Additionally, we successfully perform differential fault analysis on the hardware AES co-processor.
- **Open-source Implementations.** We provide open-source Python notebooks that can be used to reproduce and extend the experiments covered in this paper[1].

2 Experimental Setup

In Sect. 1 we introduced the SimpleLink platform and noted the similarity between the microcontrollers, and the portability of IP. Given these similarities it is likely that there are also similarities in the underlying hardware of the SimpleLink microcontrollers. While we cannot evaluate all 137 parts that are offered as part of the SimpleLink platform, it is likely that the physical attacks documented in this work can be adapted to work on most SimpleLink parts.

Nevertheless, the experiments documented in this work were performed on two distinct microcontrollers that are representative for the entire CC13xx and CC26xx lineup [55]. The first target is a CC2640R2F BLE microcontroller, the main application firmware is executed by an ARM Cortex-M3 CPU. Later, in Sect. 4.4 we also extract the firmware from the automotive variant, the CC2640R2F-Q1. The second target is a CC2652R1F multiprotocol wireless microcontroller using an ARM Cortex-M4F CPU to execute the main application firmware. By default both microcontrollers run at a clock frequency of 48 MHz generated by an internal RC oscillator or derived from an external crystal oscillator. Both microcontrollers use the internal RC oscillator during the execution of the ROM bootloader. Note that both targets include a secondary ARM Cortex-M0 CPU that is responsible for the lower level RF communications.

All of the physical attacks covered in this work were evaluated on commercially available development kits of the target microcontrollers. Throughout this work we use the NewAE ChipWhisperer Husky platform to acquire side-channel traces and to perform voltage fault injection. Similar results were obtained using the open-source NewAE ChipWhisperer-Lite [41].

[1] https://github.com/KULeuven-COSIC/SimpleLink-FI.

2.1 Target Modifications

All microcontrollers in the CC13xx and CC26xx lineup use a similar power supply configuration [55]. Most notably, an internal low-dropout regulator is used to generate the 1.28 V supply for the ARM Cortex CPU core. This internal core voltage rail is exposed on the `DCOUPL` pin of the package to add an external decoupling capacitor.

The availability of the internal CPU core voltage on an external pin of the microcontroller is convenient for the non-invasive physical attacker. As a result we choose to focus on voltage fault injection attacks and power side-channel analysis, but similar results are likely achievable using other techniques. To perform voltage fault injection we can momentarily short the core voltage supply to ground; this is also known as a crowbar voltage glitch [39]. Similarly, we can use an external power supply to supply our own voltage (larger than 1.28 V): this will disable the internal regulator and will allow us to measure the instantaneous power consumption over a shunt resistor.

For the experiments covered in this paper we modified two development boards, namely a LAUNCHXL-CC26x2R1 and LAUNCHXL-CC2640R2. Figure 1 shows the modified development boards. In both cases we removed the capacitor connected to the reset pin (C20) and the decoupling capacitor connected to the `DCOUPL` pin (C19). We also added a 10 Ω shunt resistor and an SMA connector to the `DCOUPL` pin. The SMA connector can be connected to the ChipWhisperer for both fault injection and side-channel analysis.

Side-channel measurements were acquired using a sample rate of 240 Megasamples Per Second (MSPS) while supplying 1.45 V to the `DCOUPL` pin using an external power supply. All fault injection experiments were performed with the ChipWhisperer configured to use a 200 MHz clock, resulting in a glitch offset and glitch width resolution of 5 ns. The targets were connected to the ChipWhisperer using a 50 cm SMA cable; note that the length of this cable can influence the glitch parameters.

3 The ROM Bootloader

The SimpleLink microcontrollers include a bootloader that is stored in Read-Only Memory (ROM). This bootloader is executed after an initial power-up or reset of the microcontroller. The ROM bootloader is responsible for initialising the microcontroller and enables or disables certain features based on settings stored in the Customer Configuration (CCFG) page, the Factory Configuration (FCFG) page and eFuses. As their names suggest, the CCFG can be programmed by the customer or device manufacturer, the FCFG is programmed by TI and cannot be modified by the customer. Both of these configuration pages are stored in the internal and non-volatile flash memory of the microcontroller. Similarly, eFuses are blown by Texas Instruments during chip manufacturing, but their state can be read by customers. The ROM code additionally implements a serial bootloader interface that allows to perform basic operations such as reading and writing memory. The serial interface is only started when no valid firmware

Fig. 1. The LAUNCHXL-CC2640R2 (left) and LAUNCHXL-CC26x2R1 (right) development boards modified for side-channel analysis and voltage fault injection. Both boards have C20 and C19 removed, indicated by A and B respectively. The SMA connector indicated by C allows to capture the voltage drop over the 10 Ω shunt resistor inserted at B. We supply 1.45 V through connection D while acquiring side-channel measurements, which disables the internal regulator. SMA connector E is optional and allows for differential measurements. Finally, we removed the crystal oscillator on the LAUNCHXL-CC2640R2 (left), which allows us to supply our own clock for synchronous sampling; this modification is optional and is indicated by F. The SMA connectors are grounded on the bottom side of the boards.

image is present in flash memory, or when the bootloader backdoor functionality is enabled and used [54].

Many of the security features implemented by the SimpleLink microcontrollers rely on an unaltered behaviour of the ROM bootloader. Debug security features allow a developer to disable access to the serial bootloader interface and to disable the Debug Access Port (DAP); these settings are stored in the CCFG and are parsed by the ROM bootloader. Disabling these debug features is paramount for the IP protection and secure boot features [53]. Texas Instruments recommends disabling the bootloader serial interface and the DAP in the CCFG of production hardware [54].

3.1 Extracting and Analysing the ROM Bootloader

As indicated earlier, the ROM bootloader is responsible for disabling debugging features. The ability to analyse this code is helpful to gain a better understanding of how certain features are enabled or disabled, and to identify potential vulnerabilities. However, we have to obtain a copy of the ROM bootloader code before we can analyse it.

We implemented a basic Python module that allows communication with the bootloader's serial interface over UART. Using this bootloader interface it is possible to read memory, including the ROM that stores the bootloader itself. We dumped the ROM bootloader from both of our target microcontrollers on development boards over which we had full control. In both cases the ROM could be extracted by reading data starting at address `0x10000000`.

We used the free and open-source Ghidra software reverse engineering tool to statically analyse the ROM code. We used the SVD-loader plugin [46] to automatically populate the Ghidra memory map for our target, including all documented peripheral registers. Afterwards we were able to identify the code responsible for disabling debug interfaces, by searching for references to the `CCFG:TAP_DAP_x` fields.

This initial analysis revealed that, in the case of the CC2640R2F, the `AON_WUC:JTAGCFG` register is used to enable or disable the Joint Test Action Group (JTAG) interface. The equivalent register for the CC2652R1F is referred to as `AON_PMCTL:JTAGCFG`. In the remainder of this paper we will refer to both registers by `JTAGCFG`. According to the publicly available documentation the least significant byte of the `JTAGCFG` is reserved. By reading the value of this register when JTAG is disabled and when JTAG is enabled, it is clear that these lower bits are used to enable or disable specific TAPs and DAPs. This observation will later help us to speed up initial fault injection campaigns in Sect. 4.2.

3.2 ROM Bootloader Emulation

To further extend the available information during static analysis we also emulated the ROM bootloader using Unicorn engine's Python bindings. We parsed a System View Description (SVD) file for our target to automatically generate the correct memory mappings; this is similar to what the SVD-loader plugin does in Ghidra. Additionally we have to manually guide the emulation the first time, as the bootloader may get stuck waiting for (non-emulated) peripherals or interrupts. Once these hurdles are identified they can be overcome by registering simple callback functions or patching the bootloader code. To ensure that all debug security related features were emulated correctly we also loaded valid CCFG and FCFG flash regions in the emulator. Additionally, we read the eFuse memory of our target using the SDK functions provided by TI and emulated the peripheral.

Execution coverage traces of the emulated bootloader can be exported and visualised in Ghidra using plugins such as Dragon Dance [24] or Emerald [36]. This visualization highlights parts of the code executed during normal operation and makes it easier to understand the execution flow of the bootloader. This visualization helped us to identify a, normally unused, code path which writes `0x6f` to the `JTAGCFG` register.

Figure 2 summarises our analysis of the bootloader and depicts the security-related actions performed by the bootloader. The first decision made by the ROM bootloader is based on the value of the ninth eFuse row. In commercially available chips the most significant fuse bit in this fuse row will be blown (i.e. set to 1). This results in the `JTAGCFG` register being set to zero, disabling all TAPs/DAPs. The alternative execution path writes 0x6F to the `JTAGCFG` register and sets a GPIO pin high. Information provided by TI indicates that this functionality is used during the integrated circuit manufacturing process. Note that subsequent updates of the `JTAGCFG` do not clear any bits that are already set. Afterwards, the FCFG and CCFG are parsed, and a TAP or DAP will only be enabled if it is enabled in both configurations.

The emulated bootloader can be further expanded to simulate fault injection or to fuzz the serial command interface using e.g. AFL++ in Unicorn mode [15]. Additionally, a side-channel trace can be emulated and compared to real side-channel measurements to determine approximate offsets in time for glitch attempts [30].

As part of the paper's artifacts we provide example code to communicate with the ROM bootloader's serial interface. Additionally, we provide information on how to load an extracted ROM bootloader in Ghidra and how to emulate the bootloader using the Unicorn engine.

4 Bypassing Debug Security

We will assume an attack scenario in which the target device is in the most locked down state possible. In other words the target is configured to disable the serial bootloader interface and all JTAG access is disabled. An attack that is able to compromise a device in this state will also work for a device using a less secure configuration. In this scenario our goal as the adversary is to disable the debug security features, as this allows us to completely compromise the device. On the one hand such an attack allows us to obtain a copy of the firmware stored in flash (i.e. the IP). This enables device cloning, vulnerability research and can expose device secrets. On the other hand, such an attack also compromises the secure boot functionality and any security feature relying on secure boot (e.g. remote attestation) [53].

Section 3, and in particular Fig. 2, reveal two potential avenues for enabling JTAG access using fault injection. We can try to inject a glitch during the first decision in the flowchart or during parsing of the CCFG JTAG configuration.

In the remainder of this section we will determine a suitable range of glitch parameters. Afterwards we evaluate voltage fault injection as a means to bypass debug security by targeting the CCFG parsing and the debug security eFuse check.

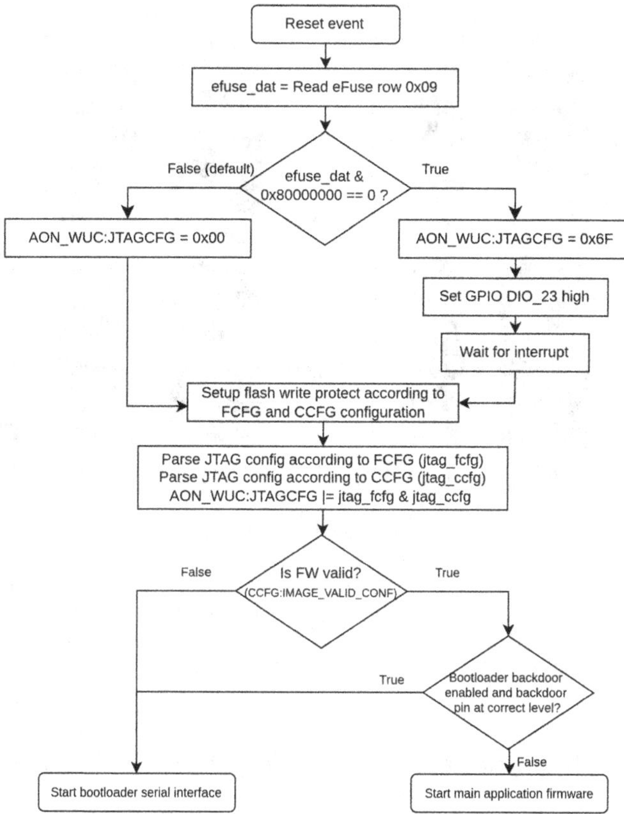

Fig. 2. Simplified ROM bootloader execution flowchart. This flowchart is based on the ROM bootloader extracted from a CC2640R2F chip. Note that the bootloader will additionally check if the bootloader serial interface option is enabled in the `CCFG:BL_CONFIG` register before executing incoming commands.

4.1 Determining a Suitable Glitch Width

A crowbar voltage glitch is characterised by two main parameters: the glitch width and and the glitch offset [39]. The glitch width is the amount of time the glitch MOSFET is enabled. The glitch offset is the offset in time from a reference signal.

We initially used a development board over which we have full control to determine a suitable range for the glitch width. We used a common fault injection target program consisting of two nested for loops that increment a counter value [7,39,40]. Figure 3 shows the results when targeting this dummy program. The most promising glitch width was selected as the one resulting in most faults overall (i.e. incorrect counter output), and is used as an initial value in the remaining experiments. Enabling the glitch MOSFET for 100 ns resulted in the most faulted counter outputs on the CC2640R2F using our setup. For the

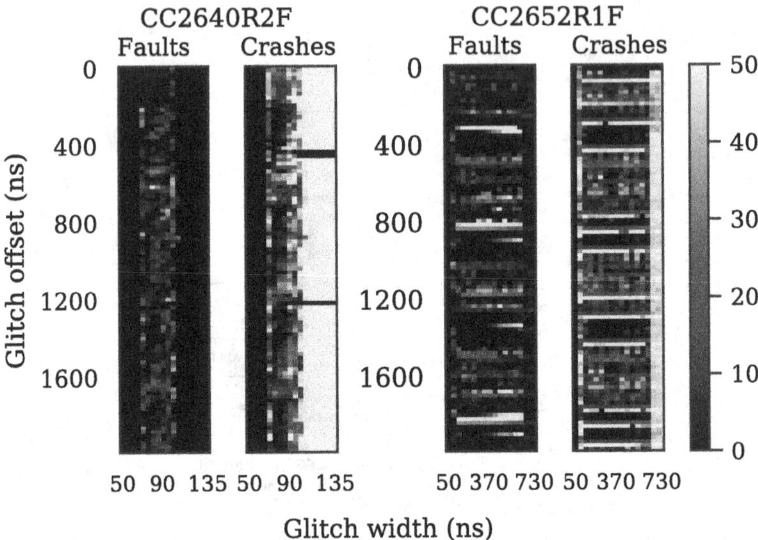

Fig. 3. Number of faulty counter outputs and crashes per combination of glitch offset and glitch width. We performed 50 attempts for each combination of glitch parameters, for a total of 90 k attempts per device. Note that the range of glitch widths (x-axis) is not the same for both targets.

CC2652R1F we determined that a 610 ns glitch width resulted in most faulted outputs.

Note from Fig. 3 that for the CC2640R2F a narrow range (approximately 70 ns to 110 ns) of glitch widths is applicable; a smaller width will not produce a faulty output and a longer glitch will always crash the device. The CC2652R1F produces faulty counter outputs over a glitch width range of approximately 90 ns to 730 ns. Presumably these differences are related to the different underlying micro-architectures (Cortex-M3 versus Cortex-M4F).

4.2 Debug Security Bypass: CCFG Configuration Parsing

From our analysis of the ROM bootloader we know that the JTAG configuration is read from the CCFG. Depending on the values stored in the `CCFG:CCFG_TAP_DAP_x` registers certain parts of the JTAG interface are enabled or disabled. As the adversary we will attempt to inject transient faults by momentarily shorting the core supply to ground while the ROM bootloader is parsing the CCFG.

We used side-channel analysis to determine the approximate offset in time from the reset signal when the ROM bootloader would be parsing the CCFG JTAG configuration. Figure 4 depicts two power traces from each of our targets that cover the execution of the ROM bootloader after the microcontroller has been reset. A noticeable difference can be observed between the black power

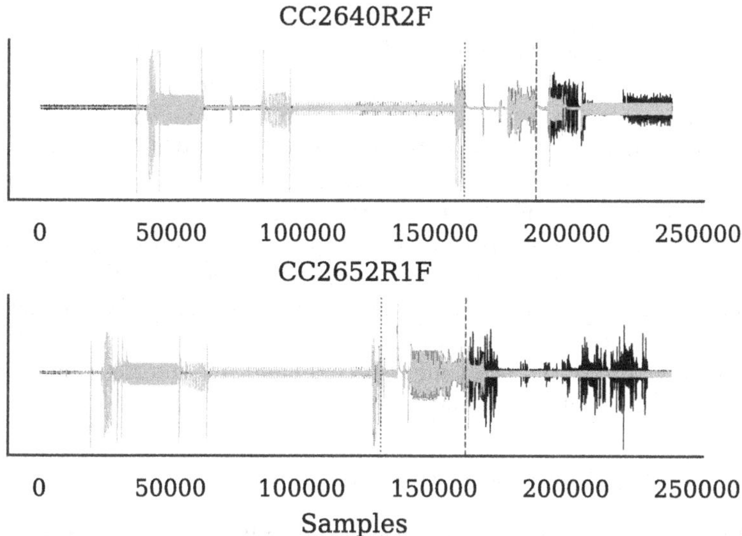

Fig. 4. Power traces covering the ROM bootloader execution of a CC2640R2F (top) and CC2652R1F (bottom) microcontroller. In gray the power trace when the flash memory is empty (i.e. invalid firmware), in black the power trace when a valid firmware image is present in flash. The vertical dotted lines indicate the offset in time when the debug security eFuse is checked. The vertical dashed lines indicate parsing of the CCFG debug security settings; note that this line is close to when the power traces start deviating. The power traces in this figure were acquired at 200 MSPS.

traces, corresponding to the execution of the ROM bootloader when a valid firmware image is present in flash, and the gray power traces corresponding to the execution of the ROM bootloader when the flash is erased (i.e. invalid firmware).

Recall from Fig. 2 that an erased microcontroller will start the serial bootloader interface and will be waiting for incoming commands over a UART or SPI interface. The configuration of the `JTAGCFG` register based on the CCFG and FCFG is performed right before the serial interface is started. When enumerating the glitch offset we thus work our way back from the point where the two traces deviate.

In a realistic setting an adversary would have to reset the target microcontroller, inject a glitch and attempt to connect to the target using a JTAG debugger to verify whether the glitch was successful. Connecting to the target using JTAG is relatively slow, and limits the rate at which attempts can be made. To speed up the initial glitch parameter enumeration we used a custom firmware image that sends the contents of the `JTAGCFG` register over UART to a control PC. In this way we can determine the state of the JTAG peripheral without having to connect using a JTAG debugger. Recall from our analysis of the ROM bootloader that parts of the JTAG peripheral are enabled if the ROM bootloader writes a non-zero value to the `JTAGCFG` register.

After basic glitch parameter enumeration we identified that glitching the CC2640R2F between 188,300 and 188,400 cycles (of the 200 MHz ChipWhisperer clock) after the reset signal goes high is likely to result in enabling JTAG access. We were able to obtain a success rate of approximately 5%. For the CC2652R1F we determined this offset to be between 161,700 and 162,000 cycles. On this target we achieved a success rate of approximately 1%. The glitch offsets are visualised in the side-channel traces shown in Fig. 4.

Using the aforementioned trick to speed up glitch attempts we could perform 10 glitch attempts per second on both targets. In a more realistic scenario in which the adversary tries to connect to the chip using a JTAG debugger the rate is reduced. When using the XDS110 debugger available on the development board in combination with the UniFlash command line interface we were able to perform one glitch attempt every 2.5 s.

4.3 Debug Security Bypass: eFuse Readout

Figure 2 reveals a more interesting avenue for fault injection, namely the first decision. Recall from Sect. 3.2 that in a normal scenario the false branch is taken, setting `JTAGCFG` to 0. Our goal is to use voltage fault injection to divert the ROM bootloader execution into the true branch, enabling access to all JTAG TAPs and DAPs. Conveniently the ROM bootloader will signal that our fault injection attempt was successful by pulling GPIO pin 23 high. This means that, even in a realistic scenario, we can inject glitches at a much higher rate. In our experiments we were able to perform up to 100 glitch attempts per second.

By enumerating glitch parameters we found that the CC2640R2F can be forced to take the alternative execution path by injecting a glitch between 161,100 and 161,200 cycles after releasing the microcontroller from reset. We found that slightly increasing the glitch width to 115 ns resulted in a success rate of 10%. With the ability to inject 100 glitches per second and a success rate of 10% it should not take more than a second to successfully enable all debugging features.

The same experiment was also performed on the CC2652R1F target, and successfull glitches were injected at offsets between 129,800 and 129,900 clock cycles. Similar to the previous experiments the glitch width did not seem to have a big impact on the success rate for the CC2652R1F target. Additionally we observed a success rate of approximately 0.1%. Even though this success rate is significantly lower, it would not take more than a few seconds to enable all debugging features.

4.4 Extracting Firmware from the Tesla Model 3 Key Fob

We extracted the firmware from a Tesla Model 3 key fob to evaluate the practical applicability of our attack. The key fob uses the CC2640R2F-Q1 chip, the automotive variant of the chip we targeted before. All debugging features were disabled, so simply reading the firmware using a debugger was not possible.

While it may be possible to perform our debug security bypass attack in-circuit, we chose to desolder the chip from a target key fob. We also removed the CC2640R2F from our LAUNCHXL-CC2640R2 development board and replaced it with the CC2640R2F-Q1 from the key fob. Using this setup and our previously gained knowledge about the target chip it was straightforward to enable the debug functionality. This allowed us to recover the proprietary firmware stored in the key fob.

Recovering this firmware enables vulnerability research that may result in a practical attack [58]. In the context of this work we performed some basic static analysis of the firmware in Ghidra, and identified an AES key stored in flash memory. Further analysis is required to determine the purpose of this key, but it may be used to protect the confidentiality of firmware updates. We note that the key fob firmware appears to also verify the authenticity of incoming firmware updates, and that a separate secure element is likely responsible for performing cryptographic operations related to unlocking or starting the car.

5 The Hardware AES Co-processor

The SimpleLink microcontrollers come with a hardware AES co-processor. According to the technical reference manual one AES operation takes $2 + 3 \cdot r$ clock cycles, where r denotes the number of rounds [54]. One AES-128 operation thus takes 32 clock cycles to complete, and the implementation operates on the full 128-bit state.

In this section we perform side-channel analysis and differential fault analysis of the hardware AES co-processor. In both scenarios we target AES-128 in a simple evaluation program that allows us to transmit the key and plaintext for one block operation to the target over UART. We modified the standard library code to insert a GPIO trigger signal as close to the AES operation as possible. The main reason for this modification is to ensure that our glitches are inserted during the actual AES operation instead of during the hardware accelerator setup.

5.1 Side-Channel Analysis

We used known-key analysis to determine the leakage model of the target implementation [28]. To that end we acquired a set of 100 k side-channel traces with random, but known, plaintexts and keys. For each of these traces we generated all intermediate states and performed CPA with the full state Hamming weight. Additionally, we perform CPA with the Hamming distance between all possible combinations of intermediate states.

The known-key analysis reveals Hamming weight leakage of the plaintext and ciphertext, marking the start and end of the encryption operation respectively. Within each round we observe Hamming distance between the `SubBytes` operation output and the `ShiftRows output`. Additionally, we observe Hamming distance leakage between round r `AddRoundKey` output and round $r + 1$

`AddRoundKey` output. Finally, we observe Hamming distance leakage between the `AddRoundKey` operation output in round 9 and the ciphertext, a common leakage model in unprotected hardware implementations that is easily exploitable [42].

During the initial known-key analysis we noticed that the captured traces could be divided into two distinct sets. Traces from the same set can be easily aligned using a sum of absolute difference alignment. However, traces that do not belong to the same set do not align well. To resolve this issue we first split the traces into the two sets and align them; afterwards each set is standardized (zero mean, unit variance scaling). Finally both sets are combined again and used during the attack phase. This preprocessing pipeline was automated in Python and reused for all further attacks.

We mounted CPA attacks targeting the Hamming distance between the ciphertext and the `AddRoundKey` operation output in round 9. Figure 5 shows the average guessing entropy of all 16 subkey bytes, averaged over 50 attacks with a random key for each microcontroller. In total we carried out 100 attacks, using 100 k traces per attack for a total of 10 M traces. Using the segmented memory feature of the ChipWhisperer Husky we were are able to acquire 100 k traces in approximately 1.5 min. The traces captured from the CC2640R2F were acquired synchronously by supplying a 12 MHz clock from the ChipWhisperer to the target, internally this clock is divided to a CPU operating frequency of 24 MHz. The CC2652R1F target was running at 48 MHz and traces were acquired asynchronously.

From Fig. 5 it is clear that some key bytes (e.g. byte 10 for the CC2640R2F) can be recovered consistently with a small number of traces. Other key bytes (e.g. byte 12 for both targets) cannot be consistently recovered, so there will be some key enumeration remaining. This also indicates that the Hamming distance model is not optimal in this scenario. The attack performance can likely be further improved using linear regression [11] or (non-)profiled deep learning approaches [57]. Alternatively one could attack multiple key bytes simultaneously, this should reduce the amount of algorithmic noise (recall that the implementation operates on the full state) at the cost of increased computational complexity.

5.2 Differential Fault Analysis

Side-channel analysis revealed Hamming distance leakage between the `SubBytes` operation output and the `ShiftRows output`. This indicates that it may be relatively straightforward to inject a fault before the last `MixColumns` operation. Such faults can be exploited using DFA to recover the cryptographic key [12,19]. A single byte fault before the last round `MixColumns` operation will result in four faulted bytes in the ciphertext. A valid ciphertext and two such faults for each column are then sufficient to recover the cryptographic key.

We perform voltage fault injection to determine the susceptibility of the hadware AES implementation to such an attack. While injecting faults we can record one valid ciphertext output and all faulted outputs; these faulted outputs were then split based on the number of faulted bytes and their positions within

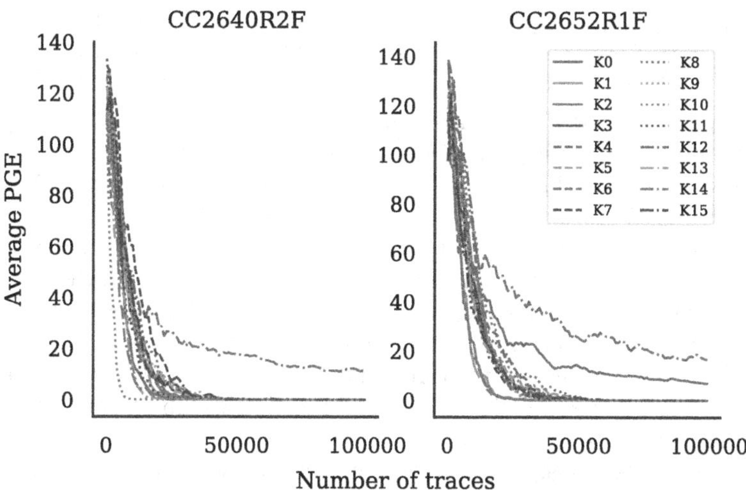

Fig. 5. Partial guessing entropy for all subkey bytes when targeting the hardware AES implementation of the CC2640R2F (left) and for the CC2652R1F (right). In both plots the partial guessing entropy is averaged over 50 experiments. Note that some key bytes are consistently easy to recover with a small number of traces (e.g. key byte 10 for the CC2640R2F). Other key bytes can not be consistently recovered (e.g. key byte 12 in both cases).

the ciphertext. We used the open source phoenixAES implementation that is part of the SideChannelMarvels project to recover the key from these faulted ciphertexts [51]. Open-source tools such as these demonstrate that an attacker does not necessarily need to understand the underlying key recovery mechanisms. The attack was determined to be successful on both targets and a demonstration Python notebook is provided in the repository.

We note that injecting a glitch before or after the AES operation would often result in the implementation outputting 96 bytes of data, even though our implementation is meant to output only 16 ciphertext bytes. This longer output often contained the full key that was being used for the AES operation. We did not investigate this behaviour further, as we were targeting a rather artificial implementation in which the key was hardcoded within the same function.

6 Conclusion

Physical attacks can be a realistic threat for embedded systems. In many cases these physical attacks can be carried out using commercially available and low-cost equipment. In this work we investigate the susceptibility of Texas Instruments SimpleLink microcontrollers to low-cost non-invasive physical attacks. We extracted the ROM bootloader of these microcontrollers and then analysed it using a combination of static analysis and emulation. Our analysis reveals two potential avenues for a physical attacker to circumvent debug security features.

To demonstrate our findings we perform two voltage fault injection attacks that disrupt the normal execution flow of the ROM bootloader. First, we show that code parsing the debug security settings is susceptible to fault injection. Secondly, we identified an execution path that, according to TI, is only used during the integrated circuit manufacturing process under normal circumstances. We demonstrate that this code can be reached using voltage fault injection, enabling all JTAG test access ports and debug access ports.

In summary, we demonstrate practical voltage fault injection attacks that allow a physical attacker to gain full debugging access on a previously locked down microcontroller. The attacks have a relatively high success rate and can in some cases be executed in a few seconds. They allow to extract the device's firmware, to bypass secure boot features and any other security features building on those. We apply our attacks to a Tesla Model 3 key fob to demonstrate the practical applicability.

Additionally, we investigate the susceptibility of the included hardware AES accelerator to physical attacks. First, we successfully mount a correlation power analysis based side-channel attack on the hardware AES accelerator. Secondly, we demonstrate key recovery by using voltage fault injection to introduce faults that are exploitable using differential fault analysis.

Basic non-invasive physical attacks have become more accessible in recent years, in no small part due to the availability of low cost open-source tooling and training material [41]. Unfortunately the large majority of general purpose microcontrollers lack countermeasures against such physical attacks. The classical threat model in which an adversary who has physical access is able to connect a JTAG debugger, but is not able to perform basic non-invasive physical attacks, may no longer be suitable today.

Similarly, it is important to remember that an adversary will attempt to identify the weakest link when attacking a device. For example, software countermeasures against side-channel attacks can be implemented on a device. A real world adversary may decide to circumvent code readout protection features, allowing to recover the cryptographic key from the firmware. This allows to extract the secret key without having to defeat side-channel countermeasures.

6.1 Responsible Disclosure

We first contacted the Texas Instruments Product Security Incident Response Team (PSIRT) on November 6th 2021[2]. The PSIRT indicated that they would be unable to resolve the issues that bypass debug security features as the ROM is immutable, and noted that these products were not designed to withstand physical attacks. As a result of our reports Texas Instruments released a general security advisory to inform customers on the possibility of physical attacks.[3].

[2] Instructions to report security vulnerabilities can be found at https://www.ti.com/security.

[3] The advisory can be found online at https://www.ti.com/lit/pdf/swra739.

We also contacted Tesla on November 6th 2021[4]. We recovered an AES key from the extracted firmware, but this by itself was not deemed a security issue. The recovered key may be used to protect the confidentiality (but not the authenticity) of firmware updates. The key fob also uses an additional secure element that is likely used when unlocking and starting the car.

Acknowledgements. We want to thank the Texas Instruments and Tesla product security incident response teams for their responsiveness. This work was supported in part by CyberSecurity Research Flanders with reference number VR20192203. In part by the Research Council KU Leuven C1 on Security and Privacy for Cyber-Physical Systems and the Internet of Things with contract number C16/15/058. In addition, this work was supported by the European Commission through the Horizon 2020 research and innovation programme under grant agreement Cathedral ERC Advanced Grant 695305, under grant agreement H2020-FETFLAG-2018-03-820405 QRANGE and under grant agreement H2020-DS-LEIT-2017-780108 FENTEC.

References

1. Agoyan, M., Dutertre, J.-M., Naccache, D., Robisson, B., Tria, A.: When clocks fail: on critical paths and clock faults. In: Gollmann, D., Lanet, J.-L., Iguchi-Cartigny, J. (eds.) CARDIS 2010. LNCS, vol. 6035, pp. 182–193. Springer, Heidelberg (2010). https://doi.org/10.1007/978-3-642-12510-2_13
2. Anderson, R., Kuhn, M.: Tamper resistance-a cautionary note. In: Proceedings of the Second USENIX Workshop on Electronic Commerce, vol. 2, pp. 1–11 (1996)
3. Anderson, R., Kuhn, M.: Low cost attacks on tamper resistant devices. In: Christianson, B., Crispo, B., Lomas, M., Roe, M. (eds.) Security Protocols 1997. LNCS, vol. 1361, pp. 125–136. Springer, Heidelberg (1998). https://doi.org/10.1007/BFb0028165
4. Balasch, J., Gierlichs, B., Verdult, R., Batina, L., Verbauwhede, I.: Power analysis of Atmel CryptoMemory – recovering keys from secure EEPROMs. In: Dunkelman, O. (ed.) CT-RSA 2012. LNCS, vol. 7178, pp. 19–34. Springer, Heidelberg (2012). https://doi.org/10.1007/978-3-642-27954-6_2
5. Bozzato, C., Focardi, R., Palmarini, F.: Shaping the glitch: optimizing voltage fault injection attacks. IACR Trans. Cryptogr. Hardw. Embed. Syst.**2019**(2), 199–224 (2019). https://doi.org/10.13154/tches.v2019.i2.199-224
6. Brier, E., Clavier, C., Olivier, F.: Correlation power analysis with a leakage model. In: Joye, M., Quisquater, J.-J. (eds.) CHES 2004. LNCS, vol. 3156, pp. 16–29. Springer, Heidelberg (2004). https://doi.org/10.1007/978-3-540-28632-5_2
7. Carpi, R.B., Picek, S., Batina, L., Menarini, F., Jakobovic, D., Golub, M.: Glitch it if you can: parameter search strategies for successful fault injection. In: Francillon, A., Rohatgi, P. (eds.) CARDIS 2013. LNCS, vol. 8419, pp. 236–252. Springer, Cham (2014). https://doi.org/10.1007/978-3-319-08302-5_16
8. Chari, S., Rao, J.R., Rohatgi, P.: Template attacks. In: Kaliski, B.S., Koç, K., Paar, C. (eds.) CHES 2002. LNCS, vol. 2523, pp. 13–28. Springer, Heidelberg (2003). https://doi.org/10.1007/3-540-36400-5_3

[4] Instructions to report security vulnerabilities can be found at https://www.tesla.com/legal/security?redirect=no.

9. Cui, A., Housley, R.: BADFET: defeating modern secure boot using second-order pulsed electromagnetic fault injection. In: Enck, W., Mulliner, C. (eds.) 11th USENIX Workshop on Offensive Technologies, WOOT 2017, Vancouver, BC, Canada, August 14–15, 2017. USENIX Association (2017). https://www.usenix.org/conference/woot17/workshop-program/presentation/cui
10. Dehbaoui, A., Dutertre, J., Robisson, B., Tria, A.: Electromagnetic transient faults injection on a hardware and a software implementations of AES. In: Bertoni, G., Gierlichs, B. (eds.) 2012 Workshop on Fault Diagnosis and Tolerance in Cryptography, Leuven, Belgium, September 9, 2012. pp. 7–15. IEEE Computer Society (2012). https://doi.org/10.1109/FDTC.2012.15
11. Doget, J., Prouff, E., Rivain, M., Standaert, F.: Univariate side channel attacks and leakage modeling. J. Cryptogr. Eng. **1**(2), 123–144 (2011)
12. Dusart, P., Letourneux, G., Vivolo, O.: Differential fault analysis on A.E.S. In: Zhou, J., Yung, M., Han, Y. (eds.) ACNS 2003. LNCS, vol. 2846, pp. 293–306. Springer, Heidelberg (2003). https://doi.org/10.1007/978-3-540-45203-4_23
13. Eisenbarth, T., Kasper, T., Moradi, A., Paar, C., Salmasizadeh, M., Shalmani, M.T.M.: On the power of power analysis in the real world: a complete break of the KeeLoq code hopping scheme. In: Wagner, D. (ed.) CRYPTO 2008. LNCS, vol. 5157, pp. 203–220. Springer, Heidelberg (2008). https://doi.org/10.1007/978-3-540-85174-5_12
14. Ferrigno, J., Hlavác, M.: When AES blinks: introducing optical side channel. IET Inf. Secur. **2**(3), 94–98 (2008)
15. Fioraldi, A., Maier, D., Eißfeldt, H., Heuse, M.: AFL++ : Combining incremental steps of fuzzing research. In: Yarom, Y., Zennou, S. (eds.) 14th USENIX Workshop on Offensive Technologies, WOOT 2020, August 11, 2020. USENIX Association (2020), https://www.usenix.org/conference/woot20/presentation/fioraldi
16. Gandolfi, K., Mourtel, C., Olivier, F.: Electromagnetic analysis: concrete results. In: Koç, Ç.K., Naccache, D., Paar, C. (eds.) CHES 2001. LNCS, vol. 2162, pp. 251–261. Springer, Heidelberg (2001). https://doi.org/10.1007/3-540-44709-1_21
17. Garbelini, M.E., Wang, C., Chattopadhyay, S., Sun, S., Kurniawan, E.: SweynTooth: unleashing mayhem over bluetooth low energy. In: Gavrilovska, A., Zadok, E. (eds.) 2020 USENIX Annual Technical Conference, USENIX ATC 2020, July 15–17, 2020. pp. 911–925. USENIX Association (2020). https://www.usenix.org/conference/atc20/presentation/garbelini
18. Gerlinksy, C.: Breaking code read protection on the NXP LPC-family microcontrollers. In: RECON, Brussels, Belgium (2017)
19. Giraud, C.: DFA on AES. In: Dobbertin, H., Rijmen, V., Sowa, A. (eds.) AES 2004. LNCS, vol. 3373, pp. 27–41. Springer, Heidelberg (2005). https://doi.org/10.1007/11506447_4
20. Goodspeed, T.: Practical attacks against the MSP430 BSL. In: Twenty-Fifth Chaos Communications Congress. Berlin, Germany (2008)
21. Goodspeed, T.: A side-channel timing attack of the MSP430 BSL. Black Hat USA (2008)
22. den Herrewegen, J.V., Oswald, D.F., Garcia, F.D., Temeiza, Q.: Fill your boots: enhanced embedded bootloader exploits via fault injection and binary analysis. IACR Trans. Cryptogr. Hardw. Embed. Syst. **2021**(1), 56–81 (2021). https://doi.org/10.46586/tches.v2021.i1.56-81
23. Hospodar, G., Gierlichs, B., Mulder, E.D., Verbauwhede, I., Vandewalle, J.: Machine learning in side-channel analysis: a first study. J. Cryptogr. Eng. **1**(4), 293–302 (2011)

24. Kartal, O.: Dragon Dance (2020). https://github.com/0ffffffffh/dragondance
25. Kasper, M., Kasper, T., Moradi, A., Paar, C.: Breaking KeeLoq in a flash: on extracting keys at lightning speed. In: Preneel, B. (ed.) AFRICACRYPT 2009. LNCS, vol. 5580, pp. 403–420. Springer, Heidelberg (2009). https://doi.org/10.1007/978-3-642-02384-2_25
26. Kocher, P.C.: Timing attacks on implementations of Diffie-Hellman, RSA, DSS, and other systems. In: Koblitz, N. (ed.) CRYPTO 1996. LNCS, vol. 1109, pp. 104–113. Springer, Heidelberg (1996). https://doi.org/10.1007/3-540-68697-5_9
27. Kocher, P., Jaffe, J., Jun, B.: Differential power analysis. In: Wiener, M. (ed.) CRYPTO 1999. LNCS, vol. 1666, pp. 388–397. Springer, Heidelberg (1999). https://doi.org/10.1007/3-540-48405-1_25
28. Kocher, P.C., Jaffe, J., Jun, B., Rohatgi, P.: Introduction to differential power analysis. J. Cryptogr. Eng. **1**(1), 5–27 (2011)
29. Kömmerling, O., Kuhn, M.G.: Design principles for tamper-resistant smartcard processors. In: Guthery, S.B., Honeyman, P. (eds.) Proceedings of the 1st Workshop on Smartcard Technology, Smartcard 1999, Chicago, Illinois, USA, May 10–11, 1999. USENIX Association (1999). https://www.usenix.org/conference/usenix-workshop-smartcard-technology/design-principles-tamper-resistant-smartcard
30. Ledger-Donjon: Rainbow (2021). https://github.com/Ledger-Donjon/rainbow
31. LimitedResults: nRF52 Debug Resurrection (APPROTECT Bypass) (2020). https://limitedresults.com/2020/06/nrf52-debug-resurrection-approtect-bypass/ Accessed 9 Dec 2021
32. Lu, Y.: Attacking Hardware AES with DFA (2019). https://yifan.lu/2019/02/22/attacking-hardware-aes-with-dfa/ Accessed 9 Dec 2021
33. Maurine, P.: Techniques for EM fault injection: Equipments and experimental results. In: Bertoni, G., Gierlichs, B. (eds.) 2012 Workshop on Fault Diagnosis and Tolerance in Cryptography, Leuven, Belgium, September 9, 2012. pp. 3–4. IEEE Computer Society (2012). https://doi.org/10.1109/FDTC.2012.21
34. Meriac, M.: Heart of darkness-exploring the uncharted backwaters of hid iclass (tm) security. In: 24th Chaos Communication Congress (2010)
35. Moradi, A., Schneider, T.: Improved side-channel analysis attacks on xilinx bitstream encryption of 5, 6, and 7 series. In: Standaert, F.-X., Oswald, E. (eds.) COSADE 2016. LNCS, vol. 9689, pp. 71–87. Springer, Cham (2016). https://doi.org/10.1007/978-3-319-43283-0_5
36. Moustafa, M.: Emerald (2021). https://github.com/reb311ion/emerald
37. Obermaier, J., Schink, M., Moczek, K.: One exploit to rule them all? on the security of drop-in replacement and counterfeit microcontrollers. In: Yarom, Y., Zennou, S. (eds.) 14th USENIX Workshop on Offensive Technologies, WOOT 2020, August 11, 2020. USENIX Association (2020). https://www.usenix.org/conference/woot20/presentation/obermaier
38. Obermaier, J., Tatschner, S.: Shedding too much light on a microcontroller's firmware protection. In: 11th USENIX Workshop on Offensive Technologies (WOOT 17). USENIX Association, Vancouver, BC (Aug 2017). https://www.usenix.org/conference/woot17/workshop-program/presentation/obermaier
39. O'Flynn, C.: Fault injection using crowbars on embedded systems. IACR Cryptol. ePrint Arch. p. 810 (2016). http://eprint.iacr.org/2016/810
40. O'Flynn, C.: Low-cost body biasing injection (BBI) attacks on WLCSP devices. In: Liardet, P.-Y., Mentens, N. (eds.) CARDIS 2020. LNCS, vol. 12609, pp. 166–180. Springer, Cham (2021). https://doi.org/10.1007/978-3-030-68487-7_11

41. O'Flynn, C., Chen, Z.D.: Chipwhisperer: an open-source platform for hardware embedded security research. In: Constructive Side-Channel Analysis and Secure Design - 5th International Workshop, COSADE 2014, Paris, France, April 13–15, 2014. Revised Selected Papers. pp. 243–260 (2014). https://doi.org/10.1007/978-3-319-10175-0_17
42. O'Flynn, C.: d'Eon Greg: I, for One. Welcome Our New Power Analysis Overlords - An Introduction to ChipWhisperer-Lint, Black Hat USA (2018)
43. Quisquater, J.-J., Samyde, D.: ElectroMagnetic analysis (EMA): measures and counter-measures for smart cards. In: Attali, I., Jensen, T. (eds.) E-smart 2001. LNCS, vol. 2140, pp. 200–210. Springer, Heidelberg (2001). https://doi.org/10.1007/3-540-45418-7_17
44. Roche, T., Lomné, V., Mutschler, C., Imbert, L.: A Side Journey To Titan. In: Bailey, M., Greenstadt, R. (eds.) 30th USENIX Security Symposium, USENIX Security 2021, August 11–13, 2021. pp. 231–248. USENIX Association (2021). https://www.usenix.org/conference/usenixsecurity21/presentation/roche
45. Ronen, E., Shamir, A., Weingarten, A., O'Flynn, C.: IoT goes nuclear: creating a ZigBee chain reaction. In: 2017 IEEE Symposium on Security and Privacy, SP 2017, San Jose, CA, USA, May 22–26, 2017. pp. 195–212. IEEE Computer Society (2017). https://doi.org/10.1109/SP.2017.14
46. Roth, T.: SVD-Loader for Ghidra (2019). https://github.com/leveldown-security/SVD-Loader-Ghidra
47. Roth, T., Nedospasov, D., Josh, D.: wallet.fail - hacking the most popular cryptocurrency hardware wallets. In: Thirty-Fifth Chaos Communications Congress. Berlin, Germany (2018)
48. Seri, B., Vishnepolsky, G., Zusman, D.: BLEEDINGBIT: The Hidden Attack Surface Within BLE Chips (2018). https://info.armis.com/rs/645-PDC-047/images/Armis-BLEEDINGBIT-Technical-White-Paper-WP.pdf. Accessed 12 Apr 2021
49. Shepherd, C., Markantonakis, K., van Heijningen, N., Aboulkassimi, D., Gaine, C., Heckmann, T., Naccache, D.: Physical fault injection and side-channel attacks on mobile devices: a comprehensive survey. CoRR abs/2105.04454 https://arxiv.org/abs/2105.04454 (2021)
50. Skorobogatov, S.P., Anderson, R.J.: Optical fault induction attacks. In: Kaliski, B.S., Koç, K., Paar, C. (eds.) CHES 2002. LNCS, vol. 2523, pp. 2–12. Springer, Heidelberg (2003). https://doi.org/10.1007/3-540-36400-5_2
51. Teuwen, P.: SideChannelMarvels - PhoenixAES (2021). https://github.com/SideChannelMarvels/JeanGrey
52. Texas Instruments: understanding security features for SimpleLink™Bluetooth® low energy CC2640R2F MCUs (2017). https://www.ti.com/lit/ml/swpb016a/swpb016a.pdf. Accessed 9 Dec 2021
53. Texas Instruments: Secure Boot in SimpleLink™CC13x2/CC26x2 Wireless MCUs (2019). https://www.ti.com/lit/an/swra651/swra651.pdf. Accessed 9 Dec 2021
54. Texas Instruments: CC13x0, CC26x0 SimpleLink™Wireless MCU Technical Reference Manual (2020). https://www.ti.com/lit/ug/swcu117i/swcu117i.pdf. Accessed 9 Dec 2021
55. Texas Instruments: CC13xx/CC26xx Hardware Configuration and PCB Design Considerations (2020). https://www.ti.com/lit/an/swra640e/swra640e.pdf. Accessed 9 Dec 2021
56. Texas Instruments: Applications for the SimpleLink™platform (2021). https://www.ti.com/wireless-connectivity/applications.html. Accessed 9 Dec 2021

57. Timon, B.: Non-profiled deep learning-based side-channel attacks with sensitivity analysis. IACR Trans. Cryptogr. Hardw. Embed. Syst. **2019**(2), 107–131 (2019). https://doi.org/10.13154/tches.v2019.i2.107-131
58. Wouters, L., Gierlichs, B., Preneel, B.: My other car is your car: compromising the Tesla Model X keyless entry system. IACR Trans. Cryptogr. Hardw. Embed. Syst. **2021**(4), 149–172 (2021). https://doi.org/10.46586/tches.v2021.i4.149-172
59. Wouters, L., den Herrewegen, J.V., Garcia, F.D., Oswald, D.F., Gierlichs, B., Preneel, B.: Dismantling DST80-based immobiliser systems. IACR Trans. Cryptogr. Hardw. Embed. Syst. **2020**(2), 99–127 (2020). https://doi.org/10.13154/tches.v2020.i2.99-127

Single-Trace Clustering Power Analysis of the Point-Swapping Procedure in the Three Point Ladder of Cortex-M4 SIKE

Aymeric Genêt[1,2(✉)] and Novak Kaluđerović[1]

[1] École Polytechnique Fédérale de Lausanne, Ecublens, Switzerland
{aymeric.genet,novak.kaluderovic}@epfl.ch
[2] Kudelski Group, Cheseaux-sur-Lausanne, Switzerland
aymeric.genet@nagra.com

Abstract. In this paper, the recommended implementation of the post-quantum key exchange SIKE for Cortex-M4 is attacked through power analysis with a single trace by clustering with the k-means algorithm the power samples of all the invocations of the elliptic curve point swapping function in the constant-time coordinate-randomized three point ladder. Because each sample depends on whether two consecutive bits of the private key are the same or not, a successful clustering (with $k = 2$) leads to the recovery of the entire private key. The attack is naturally improved with better strategies, such as clustering the samples in the frequency domain or processing the traces with a wavelet transform, using a simpler clustering algorithm based on thresholding, and using metrics to prioritize certain keys for key validation. The attack and the proposed improvements were experimentally verified using the ChipWhisperer framework. Splitting the swapping mask into multiple shares is suggested as an effective countermeasure.

Keywords: SIKE · Side-channel analysis · Power analysis · k-means clustering · Single-trace attack · Post-quantum key exchange · Isogeny-based cryptography · ARM Cortex-M4

1 Introduction

The cryptographic world as we know it will be coming to an end once a big enough quantum computer is stabilized. Such a prophecy was foretold due to the quantum capability of Shor's algorithm [49] to factor large numbers in polynomial time. As a result, cryptographers are currently developing substitutes for cryptographic primitives that resist quantum computation based attacks (known as *post-quantum cryptography*).

To further address the risk, the NIST (National Institute of Standards and Technology) supervises a standardization process for post-quantum cryptography [19]. The project aims to standardize the solutions that were submitted by

J. Balasch and C. O'Flynn (Eds.): COSADE 2022, LNCS 13211, pp. 164–192, 2022.
https://doi.org/10.1007/978-3-030-99766-3_8

cryptographers in a round-based competition-like process. Currently, the process reached its third round which comprises finalists (four key exchange schemes and three digital signature schemes), as well as alternate candidates that are retained but currently lack the sufficient scrutiny to advance further in the process [20].

Among the schemes that reached the third round, SIKE [31] (Supersingular Isogeny Key Exchange) is listed as an alternate candidate. SIKE is a key exchange mechanism which bases its security on the difficulty to compute isogenies between two elliptic curves. The key exchange works in a Diffie–Hellman fashion, where two parties (Alice and Bob) walk in a supersingular isogeny graph and exchange concealed information to reach a common curve. While SIKE is a relatively novel cryptosystem, the scheme still operates with methods from classical Elliptic Curve Cryptography (ECC), such as the scalar multiplication of elliptic curve points using a variant of the Montgomery ladder with three points (the *three point ladder*).

SIKE is, even though quantum-resistant, still a classical cryptosystem running on classical electronic devices. As these devices are subject to additional vectors of attacks, such as *side-channel attacks* in which secret information is recovered by measuring physical variables, SIKE can still be vulnerable when implemented in practice.

Power consumption is an example of such a leaking physical variable; leading thus to *side-channel power analysis* [32]. This analysis considers an adversary who typically has physical access to the targeted device and is therefore able to measure *power traces*; a collection of instantaneous samples of power consumption related to the executions of the cryptographic algorithms. The adversary's goal is to exploit the link between power consumption and data processed to infer information about the secrets concealed within the device from the measured power traces.

There exist many different ways of taking advantage of power consumption measurements in a side-channel power analysis. The most straightforward is to identify secret-dependent patterns in a power trace; an example of a Simple Power Analysis (SPA) [32,33]. Others, more complex, attempt to model the power consumption in order to apply statistical techniques, such as Correlation Power Analysis (CPA) [9]. Machine learning algorithms [28,35] can be trained to retrieve the secret values from the power consumption but usually necessitate a programmable device that is identical to the target device. This is avoided with unsupervised learning algorithms—in particular, clustering algorithms [43]—that are able to learn about secret values without creating a profile of the cryptographic device. Recently, deep learning algorithms have been used on top of unsupervised clustering to significantly increase the success of the power analysis [42].

1.1 Related Work

The first paper to ever consider clustering algorithms in side-channel analysis is due to Heyszl et al. [29] who used the k-means clustering algorithm to recover the private-key bits of an elliptic curve scalar multiplication, but on power samples from simultaneous electromagnetic probes positioned on different locations on a chip to boost the independent recovery of bits. Perin et al. extended this approach to a single-probe in [43] by combining the classification of multiple private-key bits in a fully-unsupervised process which was experimentally verified on a protected implementation of RSA. The attack was then further improved by Specht et al. in [52] by pre-processing the traces with a principal component analysis and by using expectation-maximization as a clustering algorithm. Then, Perin and Chmielewski proposed a semi-parametric framework that uses non-profiled learning both as a leakage assessment tool and as a private-key bits recovery tool in [41]. A practical unsupervised attack against ECC was mounted on the protected library of μNaCl in [39]. Recently, several other libraries were attacked with clustering power analysis on smartphones with low-cost equipment in [2]. Independent studies which also investigated clustering power analysis but on different parts of the Montgomery ladder obtained similar results in [48,50]. Finally, in [42], Perin et al. established the current state of the art in clustering power analysis by using deep learning methods on the traces and the output clusters to predict and correct wrong labelings.

Single-trace attacks against ECC are not limited to clustering power analysis. Horizontal correlation power analysis [12,44], for instance, can sequentially recover bits of a private key by correlating hypothesized intermediate values on the power traces. Other notable single-trace analyses are horizontal collision attacks [16,57] (also known as "Big Mac" attacks) which work by comparing a portion of the power trace with another to distinguish whether the processed data were similar or dissimilar. Template attacks [10,17,38,40] recover noisy information about specific secret values by operating in two phases: a profile of the power consumption that corresponds to (known) secret values is first created, and then applied to the power consumption of a target device. Online template attacks [3,6,21] propose an adaptative model in which profiles of the power consumption are created *after* receiving the target power trace. Templates of many different intermediate values can also be combined with belief propagation [4,56] to improve the recovery of said values.

Regarding the scrutiny of side-channel analysis on isogeny-based cryptography, the first concerns date back to 2017 [34], but the first practical side-channel attacks on SIKE were carried out in 2020 by Zhang et al. in [58] where the authors apply a multiple-trace differential power analysis; requiring thus one of the two parties key to be fixed. This study was extended to a single-trace horizontal correlation power analysis in [27] where the key pairs of both parties can be ephemeral. In parallel, isogeny-based cryptography was investigated with fault injections with a loop-abort attack in [26], and a corruption of the auxiliary points in [54]. The latter was verified experimentally in [53].

1.2 Contributions

This paper presents a side-channel clustering power analysis against the SIKE implementation of [47] which is recommended for the ARM Cortex-M4 microcontroller on the official SIKE website [31].

The attack works by clustering combined power samples of the calls to the `swap_points` function in the coordinate-randomized three point ladder involved in key exchange. Since the function swaps multiple values only when two consecutive private bits are different, the samples are expected to follow two distinct distributions (i.e., the values were swapped or not). If these sample distributions are distinct enough, the labeling of the provided measurements will directly lead to the bits of the private key thus compromising the confidentiality guarantees of the key exchange. Note that the attack is not limited to SIKE nor to the three point ladder, but to all swapping procedures based on masking values.

The most important feature of the attack is that a *single* execution of the key exchange is sufficient, and that only samples from the power domain of the microcontroller are necessary. More specifically, neither electromagnetic sampling, nor profiling, nor previous knowledge of the target device is required. The key recovery is completely *non*-supervised (i.e., no template is ever built) and can be performed without the need for public keys (which are still required to verify whether the key was successfully extracted).

As a result, since the attack exploits power consumption rather than localized electromagnetic radiations, the attack does not target specific registers and is expected to defeat countermeasures based on randomizing the physical locations of the registers, as initially studied by Heyszl et al. in [30] and recommended as an effective countermeasure in [39]. Moreover, in comparison with the approach of Nascimento and Chmielewski from [39], the attack is shown to successfully extract the key without, in particular, requiring leakage assessment, even though their approach is still expected to fully work on the same target.

In addition to the previous improvements, the paper exhibits the following contributions:

- Clustering the samples is shown to be also possible in the frequency domain, i.e., by first processing the power traces with a Fourier transform. As a result, the attack becomes tolerant to cases where traces are slightly misaligned due to, e.g., bad segmentation.
- Alternatively, the clustering power analysis can be improved by processing the traces with a wavelet transform to compress the power traces by filtering out high frequencies. Such a transform is shown to be relevant in practice because the compression reduces the number of timing locations to visit.
- A clustering method based on thresholding the distribution of sorted power samples is shown to be sufficient to successfully recover the key. This result shows that the clustering algorithm does not require to be sophisticated, and can be far less complex than the methods proposed so far.
- Finally, a countermeasure based on splitting the masking value into multiple random shares during the swapping procedure is shown to effectively protect against the attack described in the paper.

1.3 Outline

Section 2 briefly recalls SIKE and the k-means clustering algorithm. The clustering power analysis is then presented in Sect. 3, which is followed by further enhancements to improve the efficiency of the attack in Sect. 4. The experimental verification of the attack and improvements are explained in Sect. 5. Then, in Sect. 6, the suggested countermeasure is described and validated so that the paper can finally conclude with Sect. 7.

2 Background

2.1 Supersingular Isogeny Key Encapsulation (SIKE)

The following sub-section gives a brief overview of the SIKE protocol with the emphasis being put on the three point ladder. A reader interested in a full description of SIKE is advised to read [24,31].

Alice		Bob
		$sk_B \leftarrow_{\$} [0, 3^{e_B})$
		$s \leftarrow_{\$} \{0,1\}^{\tau}$
		$R_B \leftarrow P_B + [sk_B]Q_B$
		Let $\phi_B : E_0 \rightarrow E_B$ be s.t. $\ker(\phi_B) = \langle R_B \rangle$
	$\xleftarrow{pk_B}$	$pk_B = (E_B, \phi_B(P_A), \phi_B(Q_A))$
$m \leftarrow_{\$} \{0,1\}^{\tau}$		
$sk_A \leftarrow G(m \| pk_B) \bmod 2^{e_A}$		
$R_A \leftarrow P_A + [sk_A]Q_A$		
Let $\phi_A : E_0 \rightarrow E_A$ be s.t. $\ker(\phi_A) = \langle R_A \rangle$		
$R'_A \leftarrow \phi_B(P_A) + [sk_A]\phi_B(Q_A)$		
Let $\phi'_A : E_B \rightarrow E_{AB}$ be s.t. $\ker(\phi'_A) = \langle R_A \rangle$		
$c_0 = (E_A, \phi_A(P_B), \phi_A(Q_B))$		
$c_1 = F(j(E_{AB})) \oplus m$		
$K = H(m \| c_0 \| c_1)$		
	$\xrightarrow{(c_0 \| c_1)}$	$R'_B \leftarrow \phi_A(P_B) + [sk_B]\phi_A(Q_B)$
		Let $\phi_B : E_B \rightarrow E'_{AB}$ be s.t. $\ker(\phi_B) = \langle R_B \rangle$
		$m' \leftarrow F(j(E'_{AB})) \oplus c_1$
		$sk'_A \leftarrow G(m' \| pk_B) \bmod 2^{e_A}$
		$R' \leftarrow P_A + [sk'_A]Q_A$
		Let $\phi' : E_0 \rightarrow E'_A$ be s.t. $\ker(\phi') = \langle R' \rangle$
		if $(E'_A, \phi'(P_B), \phi'(Q_B)) = c_0$
		$\quad K = H(m' \| c_0 \| c_1)$
		else
		$\quad K = H(s \| c_0 \| c_1)$

Fig. 1. The SIKE protocol.

Protocol Summary. SIKE [31] is an isogeny-based key exchange mechanism which extends SIDH [24] with the Fujisaki–Okamoto transform [25].

The public parameters of the protocol include a length $\tau > 0$, a prime $p = 2^{e_A}3^{e_B} - 1$ (s.t. $2^{e_A} \approx 3^{e_B}$), a starting elliptic curve: $E_0 = \{(x, y) \in \mathbf{F}_{p^2} : y^2 = x^3 + 6x^2 + x\}$, two basis points (P_A, Q_A) of the 2^{e_A}-torsion, two basis points (P_B, Q_B) of the 3^{e_B}-torsion, and three cryptographic hash functions F, G, and H.

The protocol works as shown in Fig. 1. The isogenies ϕ_A, ϕ_B can be computed using Vélu's formula [55]. The function $j(E)$ returns the j-invariant of the elliptic curve E.

Three Point Ladder. SIKE makes use of the *three point ladder* [23] to compute a secret point that is then used to generate the kernel of a party's secret isogeny. More specifically, the three point ladder is an optimized computation of the elliptic curve operation of $P + [sk]Q$ for a scalar sk of n bits, by using only the X (and Z) coordinates of the points Q, P, and $Q - P$ on a Montgomery curve.

Concretely, the three point ladder uses three variables: `R0`, `R`, and `R2`, whose values respectively start with both the X and Z coordinates of Q, P, and $Q - P$. Then, the bits of the private scalar sk are scanned from the least to the most significant bit. For each bit, `R0` is either added to `R` if the bit is one, or to `R2` if the bit is zero. The point `R0` is always doubled at the end of each iteration.

Implementation. The implementation of the three point ladder under consideration is the one from [47] (shown in Appendix A, Listing 1.1). The main feature of this implementation is that the point `R` is swapped with `R2` depending on the difference between the current and the previous private bits, so `R0` can always be added to `R2`.

Swapping Procedure. To perform the conditional swapping of points, a function `swap_points` (also shown in Appendix A, Listing 1.2) takes `R` and `R2` as parameters, as well as a mask that expands the value of the private bit difference on a whole word. Given two consecutive private-key bits sk_{i-1}, sk_i (for $0 \leq i < n$ with $sk_{-1} = sk_n = 0$), with 32-bit words, such a mask corresponds to:

$$\texttt{mask} = \begin{cases} \texttt{0x00000000} & \text{if } sk_{i-1} \oplus sk_i = 0, \\ \texttt{0xFFFFFFFF} & \text{if } sk_{i-1} \oplus sk_i = 1. \end{cases}$$

Then, each word of the two elliptic curve points (resp. a and b) are processed according to this formula:

$$\begin{aligned} \texttt{tmp} &= \texttt{mask} \mathbin{\&} (a \oplus b), \\ a &= \texttt{tmp} \oplus a, \\ b &= \texttt{tmp} \oplus b, \end{aligned}$$

where & corresponds to the bitwise "and" operator. Such a procedure is known to achieve constancy in timing and execution (see [15]).

Coordinate Randomization. To prevent an adversary from exploiting the values of the points in a power analysis, a random non-zero field element r can be uniformly drawn and multiplied into the X and Z coordinates [13]. This is based on the observation that, in projective coordinates, an elliptic curve point $(X : Y : Z)$ is equivalent to $(rX : rY : rZ)$ (for $r \neq 0$). This countermeasure requires $3 \times \log_2(p^2) \approx 12e_A$ bits of entropy and six additional field multiplications per iteration.

2.2 Clustering

k-Means. The *k-means algorithm* [36] is an unsupervised clustering algorithm that partitions a population of n samples[1] into k sets solely based on the values of the samples.

Informally, the algorithm starts with k groups of means μ_j $(0 \leq j < k)$, and reassigns the samples to the group with the closest mean. As doing so may change the means of the groups, the process is repeated until convergence. The procedure is shown in pseudocode in Algorithm 1.

Algorithm 1. The k-means algorithm.

Require: $\{s_i \in \mathbf{R}\}_{0 \leq i < n}$: Collection of n samples.

```
Assign each s_i to a cluster j at random (0 ≤ i < n, 0 ≤ j < k).
repeat
    Compute each μ_j as the mean of each cluster (0 ≤ j < k).
    Assign each s_i to the cluster j = argmin|s_i − μ_j| (0 ≤ i < n).
until no μ_j change (for all 0 ≤ j < k).
return the final cluster assignments of all s_i (0 ≤ i < n).
```

3 Clustering Power Analysis of SIKE

This section describes the attack which recovers a party's private key by classifying the power samples (in Volts) of a single execution of the three point ladder in SIKE.

Target. The attack targets the three point ladder of n bits as described in Sect. 2.1. As a result, the attack can be applied at every stage of the protocol. For the sake of simplicity, the paper assumes that the attack targets the three point ladder invoked in the key decapsulation.

Threat Model. The attack assumes a passive adversary able to monitor the messages exchanged in the SIKE protocol, and the power consumption of the attacked device.

Traces Collection. In the premise of the attack, the power consumption of the entire three point ladder is measured with a fixed and fast enough sampling rate. The power samples are then segmented into multiple power traces synchronized at the beginning of each step of the three point ladder. Moreover, only

[1] In the scope of this paper, the population is one-dimensional.

Algorithm 2. Clustering power analysis.

Require: $\{s_i\}_{0 \le i < n}$: Collection of all the power samples at a same t.

1: Run the k-means clustering on $\{s_i\}_{0 \le i < n}$ (with $k = 2$).
2: Let $sk_{-1} = 0$.
3: Let $l_i = \begin{cases} 0 \text{ if } s_i \in \text{first cluster,} \\ 1 \text{ if } s_i \in \text{second cluster,} \end{cases} \quad (i \le 0 < n)$.
4: Let $sk_i = l_i \oplus sk_{i-1}$ $(i \le 0 < n)$.
5: **return** $sk = (sk_0, sk_1, sk_2, \ldots, sk_{n-2}, sk_{n-1})$.

the segments corresponding to the execution of the `swap_points` functions are considered, each of them ultimately consisting of M samples (typically, a few thousands).

Rationale. Because `swap_points` masks values with either `0x00000000` or `0xFFFFFFFF` depending on the difference between two consecutive secret bits, the attack attempts to distinguish for each iteration whether the swap occurred or not by gathering the samples at a same location in *all* iterations and clustering them with k-means. Since a difference of bits can only be zero (identical) or one (different), only two clusters are considered (i.e., $k = 2$). The private key can be entirely reconstructed from the labels at the end of the clustering.

Attack Procedure. Given the n segmented power traces T_i of M power samples each, the procedure consists of three steps:

1. Select a sample location $0 \le t < M$ in the power traces.
2. Cluster with k-means the n power samples at location t throughout the traces T_i (for $0 \le i < n$), and reconstruct the key from the labels.
3. Verify the key obtained.

Algorithm 2 shows the second step of the attack in more details. The samples s_i must all correspond to the samples at a same time throughout the n segmented power traces. Since Algorithm 2 considers samples from a single timing location in the power traces, the procedure can be repeated with all different positions until a returned key (or its bitwise inverse) successfully decrypts a ciphertext. As a result, the overall attack has a complexity of precisely M executions of k-means and key tryouts.

4 Attack Enhancements

In a full attack as described in Sect. 3, the adversary needs to pass through all sample locations in the traces and use k-means to recover a deterministic key candidate that eventually needs to be verified. Adopting a better strategy for any of these steps can lead to both faster and more successful results.

This section lists enhancements to speed up the eventual recovery of the key. These can sometimes be combined to improve even further the overall attack.

4.1 Enhancing Sample Selection

The original attack exploits the raw power consumption which requires visiting *all* sample locations. Applying a transform to the power consumption before the clustering step can reduce the number of samples and therefore speed up the attack. Moreover, relating the power consumption to a different domain can exhibit leakage points which may lead to improved results.

Fourier Transform. A (discrete) *Fourier transform* is a decomposition of a (discrete) signal into a representation that exhibits information about the frequency components of the signal. The representation is obtained by projecting the signal s_i $(0 \leq i < M)$ onto the (discrete) orthogonal Fourier basis $\{e^{I2\pi if/M}\}_{0\leq f<M} \in \mathbf{C}^M$ (where $I = \sqrt{-1}$ is the imaginary unit):

$$\hat{s}_f = \sum_{i=0}^{M-1} s_i e^{-I2\pi if/M} \qquad (0 \leq f < M).$$

In power analysis, the signal corresponds to the power consumption, and the frequency coefficients are associated to the samples from operations being performed at fixed intervals. Exploiting the power leakages in the frequency domain is a well-studied process (see [1]).

In the attack, because the power trace captures the operations that periodically swap words in a regular for-loop, some of the frequency coefficients are also expected to follow two distinct distributions. As a result, processing the power consumption with a Fourier transform prior to running the clustering algorithm is expected to give a similar success rate.

Clustering in the Fourier domain exhibits many advantages over clustering in the time domain:

- Due to the Hermitian symmetry ($\hat{s}_f = \hat{s}^*_{-f}$), the upper half of the coefficients is identical to the lower half. Accordingly, the number of locations visited by the clustering algorithm can be divided by two. Moreover, this number can be reduced by only considering a range of reasonable frequencies (such as all the frequencies below the clock speed of the targeted device).
- As the Fourier analysis treats the frequency components of the signal, the processed signal is tolerant to timing misalignments. Such misalignments are particularly common when monitoring the power consumption for a long time, or when segmenting a long power trace.
- The frequencies of interest (i.e., frequencies at which the information leakage is significant) are expected to be unique to a single device and can therefore be re-used in a subsequent analysis (resulting in an educated but still unsupervised attack).

Wavelet Transform. A (discrete) *wavelet transform* is a multi-level filter bank parameterized by a wavelet function $\psi(t)$ which decomposes a (discrete) signal into frequency bands. As opposed to the Fourier transform, the wavelet transform gathers information both from the frequency and the timing contents by iteratively correlating the signal with $\{1/\sqrt{2^j}\psi((t-2^j i)/2^j)\}_{(i,j)\in\mathbf{Z}^2}$.

A single step of the filter bank separates an input signal s_i $(0 \leq i < M)$ into two sub-signals of respectively low and high frequencies:

1) the *approximations*: $a_i = \sum_{k=-\infty}^{\infty} s_f L_{2i-k}$

2) the *details*: $d_i = \sum_{k=-\infty}^{\infty} s_f H_{2i-k}$

where L_i and H_i are respectively low-pass and high-pass filters obtained from the wavelet function $\psi(t)$ (see [37] for the technical details). The filter bank consists of recursing the above formulas with a_i with different scales (i.e., with 2^j for $j \geq 0$).

An example of a generic three-level wavelet transform is shown on Fig. 2. Given f the frequency of s_i and $\ell \geq 0$, $a_i^{(\ell)}$ corresponds to the sub-signal of frequencies $[0, f/2^{\ell+1}]$ and is re-injected into the filters H_i and L_i to ultimately output $a_i^{(2)}$, while $d_i^{(\ell)}$ corresponds to the sub-signals of frequencies $[f/2^{\ell+1}, f/2^{\ell}]$. Note that $d_i^{(0)}$, $d_i^{(1)}$, $d_i^{(2)}$, and $a_i^{(2)}$ cover the entire spectrum of $[0, f]$.

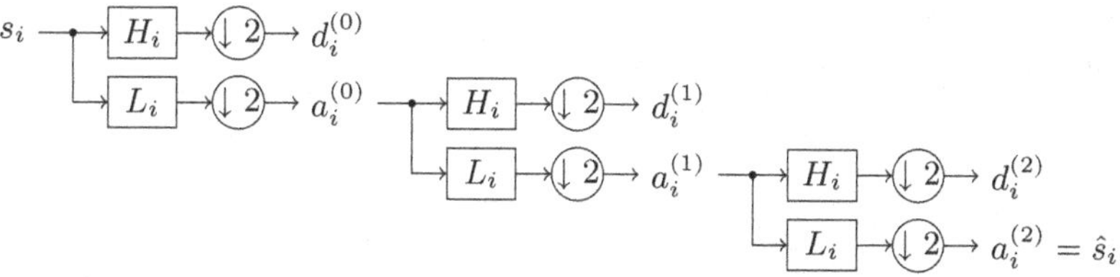

Fig. 2. A three-level wavelet transform.

In power analysis, the wavelet transform is recognized to refine the quality of the power traces acquired (see [11,51]). In clustering power analysis, two advantages are mainly capitalized upon:

- The wavelet transform downsamples the signal at each level while keeping the lower frequency bands. This process halves the length of a power trace each time and therefore results in fewer timing locations to check in the attack.
- By filtering out higher frequencies, the wavelet transform acts as a post-processing de-noiser. Cleaner signals are therefore expected to be output, which anticipates better results.

Other Transforms. In addition to the Fourier and the wavelet transforms, other transforms that compress the power traces can reduce their number of samples. For instance, principal component analysis [8] is a technique that reduces the dimensionality of the power traces. Such a transform was also reported to obtain better results in [52] by selecting the significant principal components.

4.2 Enhancing Power Samples Clustering

Since the overall attack needs to run a clustering algorithm several times, an algorithm that clusters the power samples more efficiently leads to faster results.

Thresholding. While Algorithm 1 already involves low-complexity computations, the clustering algorithm does not needs to be generic and can therefore be tailored to a one-dimensional two-population problem by splitting the distributions with an appropriate middle point.

Many solutions exist to find a suitable middle point, such as computing the overall mean of all the samples, or finding the biggest gap between two neighboring power sample. Algorithm 3 proposes a clustering which calculates the literal middle point of the distribution by finding the maximum and minimum. Such a solution runs in $\mathcal{O}(n)$, but can be tweaked to present other advantages that are described in the next subsection.

Algorithm 3. Thresholding clustering algorithm.

Require: $\{s_i \in \mathbf{R}\}_{0 \leq i < n}$: Set of n samples at a same time t.
1: Compute $d = (\min(\{s_i\}_{0 \leq i < n}) + \max(\{s_i\}_{0 \leq i < n}))/2$.
2: Let $l_i = \begin{cases} 0 \text{ if } s_i < d, \\ 1 \text{ otherwise}, \end{cases} \quad (0 \leq i < n)$.
3: **return** $(l_i)_{0 \leq i < n}$.

Other Clustering Methods. In a noisy environment, rigid clustering methods such as k-means, thresholding, and even expectation-maximization (as used in [52]) are inadequate due to the two clusters overlapping with each other. Relaxed clustering techniques, such as fuzzy c-means [22], have been reported to successfully overcome these limitations in [39,43].

4.3 Enhancing Key Verification

The attack achieves a better performance by reducing the number of key candidates to verify, or by correcting plausible clustering mistakes.

Majority Rule. As noted by [43], a same labeling re-occurring throughout many different locations is likely to be correct. Two majority rules are therefore proposed:

1. A *vertical* majority in which a candidate key occurring multiple times across the timing locations is verified in priority.

2. A *horizontal* majority in which individual key bits are labeled given their majority throughout the clusterings at all timing locations.

In a horizontal majority rule, a threshold can be selected to filter all the bits for which the clusterings give the same results, while the remaining bits can simply be guessed.

Educated Thresholding. In the clustering power analysis against the three point ladder of SIKE, two observations can be made:

1. A clustering is successful only when the two sub-distributions are distinct.
2. The number of swaps must always be even.

The first observation stems from the fact that two samples of identical value should always be assigned to the same cluster. Hence, a successful clustering can only be found by splitting the overall distribution in two in between two sample values.

The second observation is due to the fact that the three point ladder requires the points to always be "unswapped" at the end of the procedure. This means that the sizes of the two clusters are always even which can therefore be used to validate the key found.

As a result, one can design a thresholding algorithm similar to Algorithm 3 that first sorts the power samples and then separates the distribution in two, each call at a different threshold starting from a middle point. The threshold can move depending on the distance between the current threshold and the two cluster centers (similarly as in k-means). By iteratively calling such an algorithm, the labels that are more likely to be erroneous can be marked and subsequently flipped in a way that make sure that the Hamming weight of the labeling bitstring is even. The complexity of this new method is $\mathcal{O}(n \log n)$.

Other Post-processing. In case the sample location is known to correspond to a leakage point but the environment is too noisy to perfectly separate the clusters in two (see [39,43] for context), methods based on deep learning can still successfully extract the key, as reported by Perin et al. in [42].

5 Experimental Verification

This section reports a proof of concept for the clustering power analysis described in Sect. 3, in addition to an evaluation of the efficiency of the enhancements proposed in Sect. 4.

5.1 Setup

Hardware. The following equipment was used:

- A common laptop running Linux 5.13.5-arch1-1.

- The ChipWhisperer-Lite Level 2 Starter Kit:
  - A programmable STM32F3 (with a Cortex-M4 clocked at 7.37 MHz).
  - A ChipWhisperer-Lite.
  - A ChipWhisperer's "UFO" board.
  - A 20 dB Low-Noise Amplifier (LNA).
- A digital oscilloscope with the following characteristics:
  - A resolution of 10 bits.
  - A bandwidth of 20 MHz.
  - A sampling rate of 250 samples per µs.
  - A memory of 25,000 samples.

The laptop communicates to the toolkit through a micro-USB cable connected to the ChipWhisperer-Lite, which is itself linked to the "UFO" board through a 20-pin cable. The "UFO" board is connected via its `SHUNTL` port[2] to the oscilloscope through the LNA with optical fibers. The STM32F3 is plugged onto the "UFO" as a shield.

Note also that the sampling rate was intentionally made high to showcase the efficiency of the preprocessing transforms.

Software. The software considered is the SIKE implementation for Cortex-M4 of [47] which needs to be used in a certain way that enables power trace collection. In particular, the program that runs on the STM32F3 waits for the laptop to send the three byte-encoded elliptic curve points (i.e., Alice's public key) through a serial communication with the ChipWhisperer-Lite. Such a transfer prepares the STM32F3 to run the three point ladder with a pre-programmed private key which can be triggered anytime.

Coordinate Randomization. As the three point ladder from [47] does not originally offer protections against power analysis, coordinate randomization was only simulated. In this simulation, three multiplicative field elements are pseudo-randomly generated from a pre-programmed seed at the beginning of each iteration. Since only a cheap pseudo-random number generator was required, ChaCha8 [7] was chosen for this purpose. These pseudo-random elements are respectively multiplied (in $\mathbf{F}_{p^2}$) to the X and Z coordinates of the three points.

Note that while this simulation sufficiently protects the three point ladder from correlation attacks based on the values of the elliptic points (see, e.g., [27, 58]), the resulting code is not claimed to be secure in a real-life scenario. This implementation is evidently not what was considered by the attack, and the overhead was therefore not measured.

Further Modifications. Since the acquisition of power traces is not the main focus of the paper, the software was further modified to make the experiment easier. Particularly, the software allows an iteration-by-iteration execution of the three point ladder which toggles a GPIO pin at the beginning of the `swap_points`

[2] The mentioned port can be found in the official datasheet for the ChipWhisperer's "UFO" board: http://media.newae.com/datasheets/NAE-CW308-datasheet.pdf.

function. When switched on, the GPIO notifies the oscilloscope to start the collection of power measurements.

Though these modifications create an unrealistic attack scenario, the experiment is *still* practical on unmodified software but requires additional effort of marginal complexity. In a real-world scenario, the adversary first requires to observe the power consumption of the target device by measuring the current through a shunt resistor in series between the microcontroller and the ground (or the voltage collector). The collection of power samples can then be synchronized on communication which requires an oscilloscope with a buffer of a few hundred million samples to capture the consumption of the entire three point ladder. Finally, the parts which correspond to `swap_points` need to be identified in the collected trace, and then carefully segmented. A reader interested in such a process is advised to read [21].

Source Code. The final software on which power traces were acquired can be found here: https://github.com/AymericGenet/SIKE-clusterswap-2021.

5.2 Traces Collection

To collect power traces corresponding to `swap_points` executions, a simulation of an ephemeral SIKE key exchange was conducted:

(1) Program the STM32F3 with a random key and seed.
(2) Generate and send three valid points Q, P, and $Q - P$.
(3) Repeat the following n times:
  (a) Make the STM32F3 execute the next loop iteration.
  (b) Save the power trace from the oscilloscope.

The above was repeated 1,000 times (each time with a different key and seed) for SIKEp434 (hence $n = 218$). An example of a power trace along with its frequency components for SIKEp434 is shown in Fig. 3. Note that most of the frequency components are zero due to the limiting analog bandwidth of the oscilloscope (20 MHz).

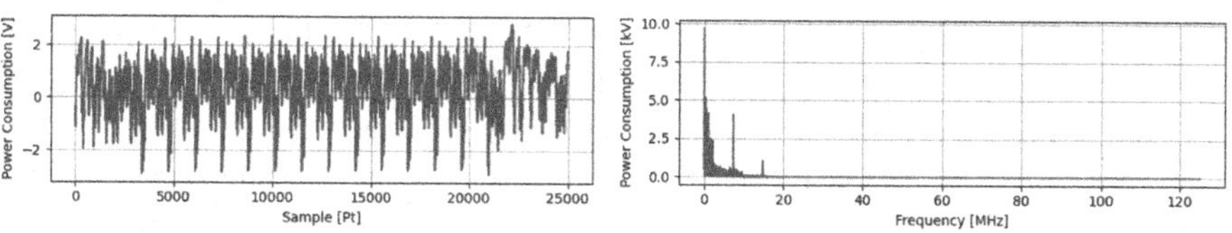

Fig. 3. Example of one of the n power traces corresponding to `swap_points` in a single iteration of the loop (left) along with its Fourier representation (right).

5.3 Clustering Power Analysis

In the next step of the experiment, the n collected traces of each experiment are exploited to attempt a key recovery as explained in Sect. 3 (cf. Algorithm 2).

(1) Process (for $0 \leq i < n$):
  (a) T_i with an ℓ-level *wavelet transform* ($\hat{T}_i$ of length $\hat{M} = M/2^\ell$),
  (b) $\hat{T}_i$ with a *Fourier transform* ($\hat{F}_i$).
(2) Run the attack on both $\hat{T}_i$ and $\hat{F}_i$:
  (a) Go to the next sample location $0 \leq t < \hat{M}$ (resp. $0 \leq f < \hat{M}/2$).
  (b) Run clustering on $\{\hat{T}_i[t]\}_{0 \leq i < n}$ (resp. on $\{\hat{F}_i[f]\}_{0 \leq i < n}$).
  (c) Record the sk_t returned for time t (resp. sk_f).

The above was repeated with $0 \leq \ell < 8$ levels of wavelet with a Symlet wavelet of filter length 8 (i.e., `sym4`) to further show the efficiency of the processing transforms. The success rate is calculated through all the timing positions and frequencies over the 1,000 sets of measured traces by comparing the recovered key with the correct key.

5.4 Results

Out of the 1,000 experiments, across all the levels $0 \leq \ell < 8$, the correct key is *always* found in the set of recovered keys sk_t or sk_f. Table 1 and Table 2 report various metrics about how often the correct key appears in the two sets of recovered keys. The independent success rates of each timing position and frequency are reported in Fig. 4. Finally, examples of samples distribution successfully clustered is shown in Fig. 5 both in timing and frequency.

Table 1. Statistics on the total number of timing locations which yield the correct key across the N = 1,000 experiments.

	k-means				Thresholding				
ℓ	min.	max.	$\mathbf{E}(\#t)$	SD($\#t$)	min.	max.	$\mathbf{E}(\#t)$	SD($\#t$)	$\hat{M}$
0	154	341	251.704	30.056	115	289	196.668	29.366	25000
1	72	172	125.611	15.153	58	144	97.923	14.764	12503
2	37	85	62.329	7.646	28	71	48.469	7.582	6255
3	15	44	29.425	4.171	11	36	22.958	3.971	3131
4	8	27	15.494	2.723	5	21	12.127	2.502	1569
5	6	21	13.445	2.371	4	18	10.531	2.195	788
6	2	12	6.036	1.615	1	9	4.033	1.408	397
7	0	5	1.645	0.941	0	5	0.853	0.878	202

Table 2. Statistics on the total number of frequencies which yield the correct key across the $N = 1{,}000$ experiments.

	k-means				Thresholding				
ℓ	min.	max.	$\mathbf{E}(\#f)$	SD$(\#f)$	min.	max.	$\mathbf{E}(\#f)$	SD$(\#f)$	$\hat{M}/2$
0	18	29	23.625	1.774	17	28	21.965	1.659	12500
1	16	26	20.704	1.630	15	24	19.382	1.584	6251
2	18	27	21.900	1.460	16	27	20.901	1.515	3127
3	15	30	22.641	2.288	13	26	19.993	2.239	1565
4	11	20	15.001	1.429	9	18	13.815	1.488	784
5	6	11	8.611	0.908	5	10	8.063	0.895	394
6	3	7	4.467	0.791	2	7	4.162	0.749	198
7	2	6	4.023	0.800	2	7	3.777	0.747	101

5.5 Discussion

The above experiment proves that the recommended Cortex-M4 implementation of SIKE from [47] is vulnerable to low-effort power analyses, even in the case when the implementation is protected with coordinate randomization. As a result, the main objective of the experiment is achieved.

The rest of the discussion focuses on the efficiency of the improvements.

Wavelet Efficiency. Contrary to expectations, processing the power traces with the wavelet transform does not improve the success rate (cf. Fig. 4). While the wavelet transform features noise filtering, information is still lost during the operation as the convolution involved in the transform combines significant power samples with insignificant ones. Nevertheless, the quality of the compression is fitting as the correct key still occurs on average more than once throughout the timing locations, even after several levels of filtering. Therefore, the number of samples to visit can be reduced by a significant factor using this transform.

As the power trace corresponds to the execution of the `swap_points` function, the sample locations reported in Fig. 4 correspond to specific instructions of the attacked implementation (shown in Appendix A, Listing 1.3) In particular, the very first spike in the figure correspond to the mask computation which expands a secret bit. The regular spikes in the middle correspond to the swap formula performed on each of the 32-bit words of the points. Finally, the last two spikes at the end of the graph correspond to exiting the function. These spikes show all the aspects of the implementation that need protection.

Note that the choice of the wavelet function (`sym4`) was guided by an experimental exploration and that similar results are expected by using a different family or a different filter length.

Fourier Efficiency. The Fourier analysis shows remarkable efficiency across all levels of wavelet transforms. Performing a clustering power analysis with

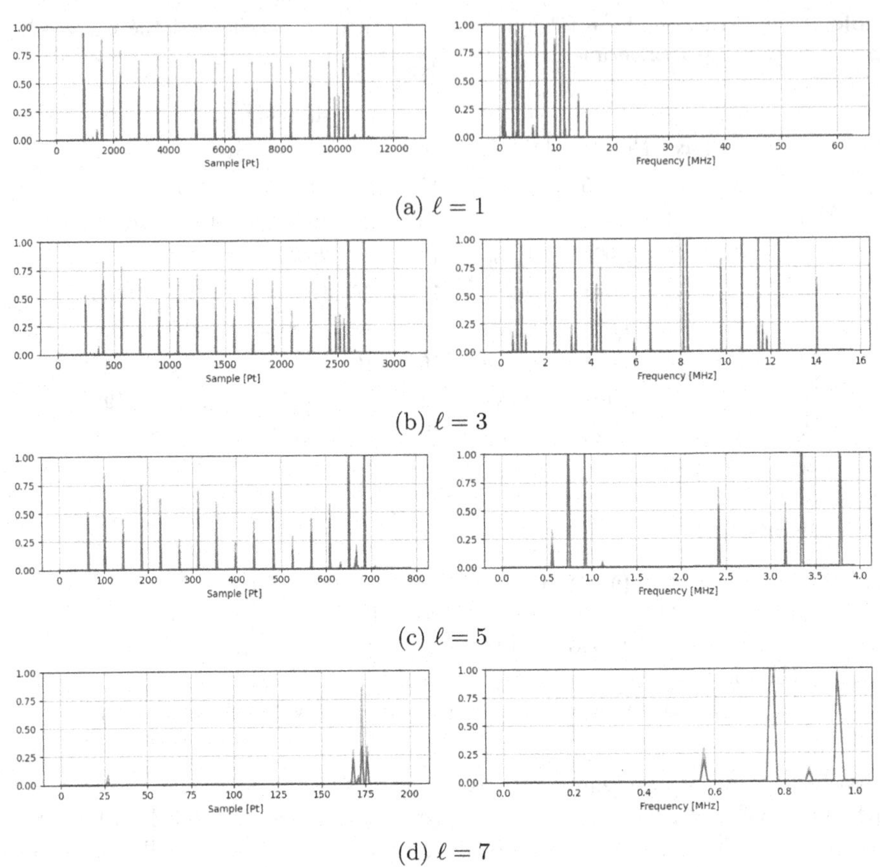

Fig. 4. Success rate of the clustering power analysis (thresholding in opaque vs. k-means in transparent) at each timing locations (left) and frequencies (right) across different levels of wavelet transforms.

frequency components rather than power samples is shown to have a resounding success rate across all experiments. Furthermore, such a success rate is kept throughout the wavelet levels, as the leakage happens at low frequencies which are preserved by the wavelet transform. The most notable observation to make is that clustering in the frequency domain is successful even at the last wavelet level where the same analysis in timing is shown to be inefficient. This proves that even though clustering power samples independently happens to be ineffective, their combination in the frequency domain may be sufficient to perform a successful analysis.

There may be many reasons why low frequencies leak most of the information in the current case. The frequencies of interest are suspected to be subharmonics of the clock speed. For instance, the spikes at 0.92 MHz likely correspond to the pattern of eight instructions in the `swap_points` function (see Listing 1.3). The same can be said for the spikes at 0.73 MHz and 0.74 MHz, as such frequencies also happen to be a tenth of the clock speed. These frequencies, as well as the other significant ones, may also be due to the consumption of sub-systems in the hardware (e.g., memory) that function at different paces.

Thresholding Efficiency. In addition to demonstrating the efficiency of the pre-processing phase, the experiments show that the thresholding proposed in Algorithm 3 is almost as successful as k-means. While k-means still obtains better results (cf. Fig. 4), our experiment with k-means took 29 h to be performed, while the same analysis with thresholding took only 6.5 h.

Majority Rule Efficiency. The extremely high occurrence of the correct key in Table 1 and Table 2 confirms that the vertical majority rule explained in Sect. 4 helps validating the key. In all experiments, the most recorded candidate was always observed to be the correct key. As a result, the correct key is expected to be recovered within the first try-outs as the other candidates were all observed to be either random or close to the correct key.

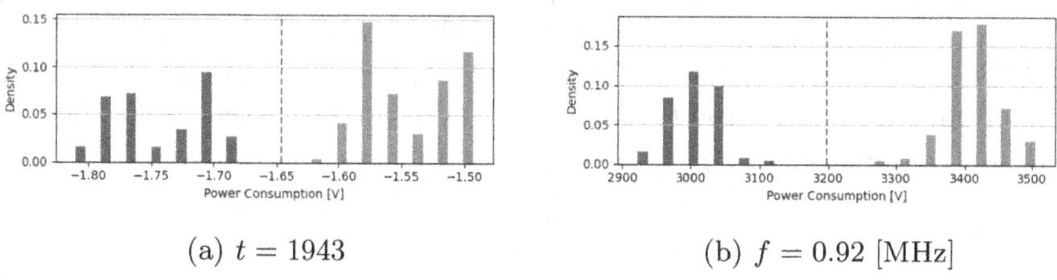

(a) $t = 1943$

(b) $f = 0.92$ [MHz]

Fig. 5. Example of a power sample distributions ($\ell = 0$). The threshold (in red) was found by Algorithm 3. (Color figure online)

5.6 Other SIKE Instances

Note that the success of the clustering is closely connected to the relatively big number of samples available. As more samples are obtained, the distinction between the two clusters becomes easier. However, depending on the noise, additional samples may undermine the success of the overall clustering.

Still, similar results (if not better) have been obtained by running the same experiment with the bigger instances of SIKE. The experiments were executed with fewer runs, a fixed wavelet level, and only using the thresholding algorithm. The results are reported in Table 3 and prove that the attack is not limited to SIKEp434.

Table 3. Statistics on the total number of timing locations and total number of frequencies which yield the correct key across the $N = 10$ experiments with the other instances of SIKE ($\ell = 5$).

		Timing				Frequency			
p	n	min.	max.	$\mathbf{E}(\#t)$	SD($\#t$)	min.	max.	$\mathbf{E}(\#f)$	SD($\#f$)
503	252	8	14	10.5	2.5	9	11	9.7	0.7
610	304	16	31	22.1	5.3	10	14	11.7	1.3
751	378	17	25	22.2	2.7	9	13	10.6	1.5

6 Countermeasure

Protecting the point-swapping procedure against clustering power analysis is not obvious, as the attack defeats classical countermeasures of [13] which include coordinate randomization, exponent randomization, point blinding, and even shuffling the for-loop. Moreover, due to the recent study which relies on deep learning [42], even the tiniest bias in the power consumption may lead to a full recovery.

To make the task even more challenging, the target CPU of the Cortex-M4 is known to be hard to protect (see [5]). As the Cortex-M4 appears to leak in the Hamming distance of the pipeline registers (see [14]), the countermeasures need not only to consider the Hamming weight of the processed values, but also the Hamming distance between the values used by two consecutive instructions.

In this section, a countermeasure based on thresholding the swapping mask is suggested.

6.1 Description

The proposed countermeasure revises the original swapping procedure from Sect. 2 in the following sense; instead of computing the value `mask` & $(a \oplus b)$ all at once, the idea is to split this quantity into two shares and add each share separately in a two-stage process (to both a and b). Such a procedure avoids computing values of extreme Hamming distances.

To this end, the swapping mask is replaced by two 32-bit masks: `m1` and `m2` such that their bitwise "xor" is equal to `mask`. In other words, given two consecutive private-key bits sk_{i-1}, and sk_i (for $0 \leq i < n$ with $sk_{-1} = sk_n = 0$):

$$\mathtt{m1} \oplus \mathtt{m2} = \begin{cases} \mathtt{0x00000000} & \text{if } sk_{i-1} \oplus sk_i = 0, \\ \mathtt{0xFFFFFFFF} & \text{if } sk_{i-1} \oplus sk_i = 1. \end{cases}$$

Given the two masks `m1` and `m2`, the new procedure works as follows:

$$\begin{aligned} \mathtt{tmp1} &= \mathtt{m1} \ \& \ (a \oplus b), \\ \mathtt{tmp2} &= \mathtt{m2} \ \& \ (a \oplus b), \\ a &= (\mathtt{tmp1} \oplus a) \oplus \mathtt{tmp2}, \\ b &= (\mathtt{tmp1} \oplus b) \oplus \mathtt{tmp2}. \end{aligned}$$

Because of the property of $\mathtt{m1} \oplus \mathtt{m2}$, the above procedure swaps a and b in the same sense as the method in Sect. 2.

6.2 Implementation

The results from Sect. 5 provide insight on the critical points of the procedure that require particular care. Mainly three leaking points were identified:

1. The generation of the masks.
2. The instructions used to perform the swapping operation.
3. Exiting the function.

The third point can be avoided by incorporating the procedure to the code without calling a function, so only the first two points are addressed.

Masks Generation. Let swap refer to the secret difference of private-key bits (i.e., $\mathtt{swap} = sk_{i-1} \oplus sk_i$). The suggested countermeasure involves generating two random masks m1 and m2 that are either equal or bit-wise complement depending on swap. To achieve this, given a random m1, the second mask m2 is derived with the following formula: $\mathtt{m2} = (1 - 2 \cdot \mathtt{swap})(\mathtt{m1} + \mathtt{swap})$. This makes m2 become the bitwise complement of m1 through the representation of negative numbers in the CPU with the two's complement (i.e., $\mathtt{m2} = -(\mathtt{m1} + 1)$ if $\mathtt{swap} = 1$).

Performance. Safely generating these two quantities requires sampling additional randomness. In particular, the multiplication of $(\mathtt{m1} + \mathtt{swap})$ by $(1 - 2 \cdot \mathtt{swap})$ is computed as $u_1(\mathtt{m1}+\mathtt{swap}) - u_2(\mathtt{m1}+\mathtt{swap})$ where $u_1 - u_2 = 1 - 2 \cdot \mathtt{swap}$. In total the mask generation requires at least 8 bytes of entropy (29 bits of which are effective) and introduces an overhead of at least 12 additional instructions when compared to the original mask computation. The code is given in Listing 1.4.

The Swapping Operation. Because of the Cortex-M4 leakage model, the order of the operations and of the operands play a critical role in the countermeasure. Particular care has to be taken with store and load instructions, as the power consumption of these procedures leaks sensitive values. As a result, given the two masks m1 and m2 generated as before, the implementation of the countermeasure must follow a special order given in Listing 1.5.

Performance. As opposed to the original pattern of 8 instructions, such a solution requires 14 instructions per iteration and doubles the numbers of loads and stores which introduces further delay.

Benchmarks. We compare the runtimes of our countermeasure against the runtimes of the unprotected version of SIKE. About 62% of the overhead stems from acquiring randomness for mask generation. As we generate a new mask for each swap (so for each word), we use a cheap pseudorandom number generator to limit the impact on performance; namely, the Tiny Mersenne Twister pseudorandom number generator [45] seeded with a 64-bit value obtained from a source of true randomness.

The protected `swap_points` is about 5.7 times slower than the unprotected swap. Within the three point ladder function, the overhead adds up to about 70,000 additional cycles which takes up to 5% of the total computing time of the three point ladder. When considered as a part of a full execution of SIKE, the overhead due to protecting the swap boils down from about 1% in the key generation and decapsulation to 0.7% in the encapsulation procedure (Table 4).

Table 4. Runtimes (in cycles) of the SIKEp434 implementation with and without the countermeasure on an Intel i9-8950HK CPU @ 2.90 GHz with Turbo boost turned off.

Operation	Unprotected	Protected
Mask generation	1	251
Swapping operation	71	148
Three point ladder	1,172,432	1,241,721
Key generation	6,083,645	6,153,241
Encapsulation	9,893,673	9,962,113
Decapsulation	10,625,881	10,747,176

6.3 Experimental Validation

The proposed countermeasure was validated by conducting Welch's t-test [46]. Such a test gives a degree of confidence that two classes of power samples are statistically indistinguishable. In the present case, the two classes respectively correspond to whether the points were swapped during the collection of the power traces, or not.

The t values are computed with the following formula:

$$t = \frac{\mu_0 - \mu_1}{\sqrt{\sigma_0^2/n_0 + \sigma_1^2/n_1}}$$

where μ_0, μ_1 correspond to the means of the two classes, σ_0^2, σ_1^2 to their variances, and n_0, n_1 to their cardinality (here, $n_0, n_1 \approx 1000$). A threshold of 4.5 for the t values is set to reject the null hypothesis (see [18]). In other words, a t value greater than the threshold gives evidence that the two distributions are not indistinguishable.

The results are shown in Fig. 6. Even though significantly large t values appear in the plots, the attack is still unsuccessful when re-run against the countermeasure as the histograms corresponding to the power samples from the two classes overlap with each other at all points in time and frequency. Fig. 7 illustrates this by showing the histograms at the highest peaks of the t-test plots from Fig. 6. As one can notice, both histograms exhibit a significant variance, which prevents the attack to fully recover the private key. The histograms at all other points showed a similar overlapping.

While such a discrepancy of distributions prevents a successful clustering with the techniques described in this paper, more sophisticated attacks (such as [42,43]) may still prevail. These attacks may therefore require additional efforts to withstand.

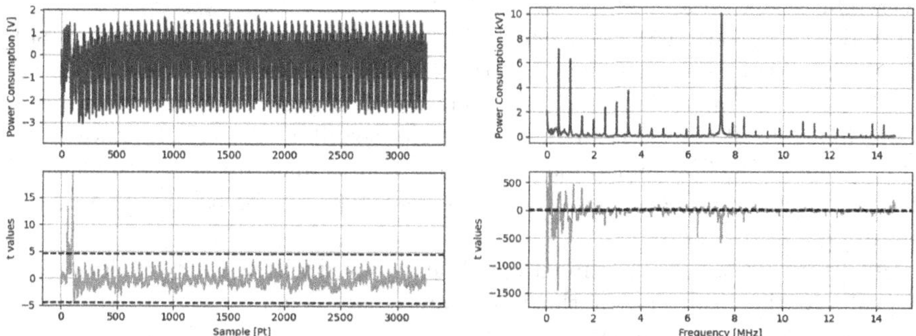

Fig. 6. t-test of the countermeasure both in timing and frequency. The horizontal lines in red show the threshold above which the null hypothesis is rejected. (Color figure online)

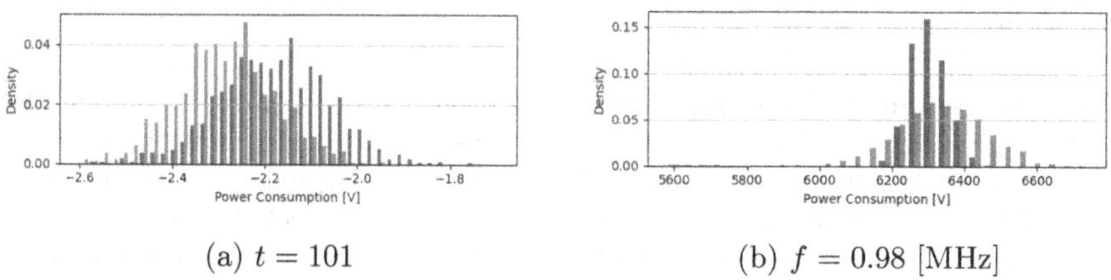

(a) $t = 101$

(b) $f = 0.98$ [MHz]

Fig. 7. Power sample distributions at the locations which produced the highest value in both t-tests.

6.4 Other Countermeasures

In addition to the countermeasure proposed, other techniques are likely to prevent a clustering power analysis of the swapping procedure. Desynchronizing the clock of the target device results in unaligned power traces with different random frequencies, so the attack is expected to be unsuccessful in neither domains. Such a countermeasure might be implemented by interleaving dummy `nop` instructions with the actual instructions of the regular `swap_points` function. Alternatively, swapping pointer addresses rather than values may be effective in the power domain but is shown to succumb to the same attack using electromagnetic radiations in [39].

7 Conclusion and Future Work

The paper described a plain clustering power analysis able to recover the entire private key in a single execution of the three point ladder in the implementation of SIKE for Cortex-M4. In particular, the paper demonstrated that processing the traces with a wavelet transform efficiently reduces the number of timing locations to visit, and that clustering frequency components may succeed even where clustering power samples is inefficient.

While the attack has been experimentally shown to be always successful, the reader must keep in mind that the experiment was performed using the ChipWhisperer framework on a chip that was deliberately made vulnerable to power analysis. However, the countermeasure described completely thwarts the attack even on such a vulnerable chip. If the countermeasure is safe under such defenseless circumstances, then the implementation can be assumed to be safe in a more realistic scenario.

As future work, the experiment could be repeated with a different clock speed to evaluate the evolution of the frequency components. Other improvements using, e.g., multiple samples of a single iteration in a multivariate clustering analysis may also be investigated. The proposed countermeasure requires to be evaluated against other side-channel attacks and improved both in performance and security. Finally, an evaluation of other sensitive operations in SIKE—such as the isogeny computation—can be conducted, as there are still many other points that have not been evaluated yet that may also leak secret information through power consumption.

Acknowledgements. We would like to thank Arjen K. Lenstra and Thorsten Kleinjung for the weekly discussions held on this paper. We are also grateful to Nicolas Oberli, Sylvain Pelissier, Hervé Pelletier, Kopiga Rasiah, Mathilde Raynal, and Karine Villegas for their precious help in the realization of this project. Finally, we want to express our gratitude to the reviewers of COSADE 2022 for their valuable comments.

A Attacked Code

```
for (i = 0; i < nbits; i++) {
  bit = (sk[i>>LOG2RADIX] >> (i&(RADIX-1))) & 1;
  swap = bit ^ prevbit;
  prevbit = bit;
  mask = 0 - (digit_t)swap;

  swap_points(R, R2, mask);
  xDBLADD(R0, R2, R->X, A24);
  randomize_coordinates(R0, R, R2);
}
swap = 0 ^ prevbit;
mask = 0 - (digit_t)swap;
swap_points(R, R2, mask);

return R2;
```

Listing 1.1. Attacked source code of the three point ladder in C (simplified).

```
for (i = 0; i < NWORDS_FIELD; i++) {
  temp = mask & (R->X[0][i] ^ R2->X[0][i]);
  R->X[0][i] = temp ^ R->X[0][i];
  R2->X[0][i] = temp ^ R2->X[0][i];
  temp = mask & (R->Z[0][i] ^ R2->Z[0][i]);
  R->Z[0][i] = temp ^ R->Z[0][i];
  R2->Z[0][i] = temp ^ R2->Z[0][i];
  temp = mask & (R->X[1][i] ^ R2->X[1][i]);
  R->X[1][i] = temp ^ R->X[1][i];
  R2->X[1][i] = temp ^ R2->X[1][i];
  temp = mask & (R->Z[1][i] ^ R2->Z[1][i]);
  R->Z[1][i] = temp ^ R->Z[1][i];
  R2->Z[1][i] = temp ^ R2->Z[1][i];
}
```

Listing 1.2. Attacked source code of `swap_points` in C (simplified).

```
rsb    r8, r6, #0     /* mask = (0 - swap) */
add.w r2, r4, #92     /* R->X  */
add.w r3, r4, #540    /* R2->X */
mov.w ip, #0          /* i = 0 */
<loop>:
ldr    r7, [r2, #0]
ldr    r1, [r3, #0]
eor.w r0, r7, r1      /* mask & (R->X[0][i] ^ R2->X[0][i]) */
and.w r0, r0, r8
eors   r7, r0         /* R->X[0][i] = temp ^ R->X[0][i] */
eors   r1, r0         /* R2->X[0][i] = temp ^ R2->X[0][i] */
str.w r7, [r2], #4
str.w r1, [r3], #4

...                   /* repeat above (with different offsets) */

add.w ip, ip, #1      /* i++ */
cmp.w ip, #14         /* i < NWORDS_FIELD */
bne.n <loop>
```

Listing 1.3. Compiled `swap_points` function with annotations (SIKEp434).

```
and.w %[u1], %[u1], #0xFFFFFFFD   /* u1 = randombytes(4) & 0xFFFFFFFD */
and.w %[m1], %[u2], #0xFFFFFFFE   /* m1 = randombytes(4) & 0xFFFFFFFE */
add.w %[u2], %[u1], %[swap]       /* u2 = u1 + swap */
add.w %[m2], %[m1], %[swap]       /* r  = m1 + swap */
add.w %[u1], %[u1], #1            /* u1 = u1 + 1 */
mul.w %[u1], %[u1], %[m2]         /* u1 = u1*r */
add.w %[u2], %[u2], %[swap]       /* u2 = u2 + swap */
mul.w %[u2], %[u2], %[m2]         /* u2 = u2*r */
sub.w %[m2], %[u1], %[u2]         /* m2 = u1 - u2 */
```

Listing 1.4. Source code of the secure masks generation in assembly.

```
ldr.w %[a], [%[R]]                /* a = R[i]  */
ldr.w %[b], [%[R2]]               /* b = R2[i] */
eor.w %[tmp1], %[a], %[b]         /* tmp1 = a ^ b */
and.w %[tmp1], %[m1]              /* tmp1 = tmp1 & m1 */
eor.w %[b], %[b], %[tmp1]         /* a = a ^ tmp1 */
eor.w %[a], %[a], %[tmp1]         /* b = b ^ tmp1 */
eor.w %[tmp2], %[a], %[b]         /* tmp2 = a ^ b */
str.w %[b], [%[R2]]               /* R2[i] = b */
and.w %[tmp2], %[m2]              /* tmp2 = tmp2 & m2 */
str.w %[a], [%[R]]                /* R[i]  = a */
eor.w %[b], %[b], %[tmp2]         /* b = b ^ tmp2 */
eor.w %[a], %[a], %[tmp2]         /* a = a ^ tmp2 */
str.w %[a], [%[R]], #4            /* R[i]  = a */
str.w %[b], [%[R2]], #4           /* R2[i] = b */

...                               /* repeat above */
```

Listing 1.5. Source code of the secure swapping operation in assembly.

References

1. Agrawal, D., Archambeault, B., Rao, J.R., Rohatgi, P.: The EM side—channel(s). In: Kaliski, B.S., Koç, K., Paar, C. (eds.) CHES 2002. LNCS, vol. 2523, pp. 29–45. Springer, Heidelberg (2003). https://doi.org/10.1007/3-540-36400-5_4
2. Alam, M., et al.: Nonce@Once: a single-trace EM side channel attack on several constant-time elliptic curve implementations in mobile platforms. In: 6th IEEE European Symposium on Security and Privacy, EuroS&P 2021, 6–10 September 2021. IEEE (2021). https://cs.adelaide.edu.au/~yval/pdfs/AlamYWSZGYP21.pdf
3. Aldaya, A.C., Brumley, B.B.: Online template attacks: revisited. IACR Trans. Cryptogr. Hardw. Embed. Syst. **2021**(3), 28–59 (2021). https://doi.org/10.46586/tches.v2021.i3.28-59
4. Azouaoui, M., Durvaux, F., Poussier, R., Standaert, F.-X., Papagiannopoulos, K., Verneuil, V.: On the worst-case side-channel security of ECC point randomization in embedded devices. In: Bhargavan, K., Oswald, E., Prabhakaran, M. (eds.) INDOCRYPT 2020. LNCS, vol. 12578, pp. 205–227. Springer, Cham (2020). https://doi.org/10.1007/978-3-030-65277-7_9
5. Batina, L., Chmielewski, Ł., Haase, B., Samwel, N., Schwabe, P.: SCA-secure ECC in software - mission impossible? IACR Cryptology ePrint Archive, p. 1003 (2021). https://eprint.iacr.org/2021/1003
6. Batina, L., Chmielewski, Ł, Papachristodoulou, L., Schwabe, P., Tunstall, M.: Online template attacks. In: Meier, W., Mukhopadhyay, D. (eds.) INDOCRYPT 2014. LNCS, vol. 8885, pp. 21–36. Springer, Cham (2014). https://doi.org/10.1007/978-3-319-13039-2_2
7. Bernstein, D.J.: The ChaCha family of stream ciphers (2008). https://cr.yp.to/chacha.html
8. Bohy, L., Neve, M., Samyde, D., Quisquater, J.: Principal and independent component analysis for crypto-systems with hardware unmasked units. In: Proceedings of e-Smart 2003 (2003)

9. Brier, E., Clavier, C., Olivier, F.: Correlation power analysis with a leakage model. In: Joye, M., Quisquater, J.-J. (eds.) CHES 2004. LNCS, vol. 3156, pp. 16–29. Springer, Heidelberg (2004). https://doi.org/10.1007/978-3-540-28632-5_2
10. Chari, S., Rao, J.R., Rohatgi, P.: Template attacks. In: Kaliski, B.S., Koç, K., Paar, C. (eds.) CHES 2002. LNCS, vol. 2523, pp. 13–28. Springer, Heidelberg (2003). https://doi.org/10.1007/3-540-36400-5_3
11. Charvet, X., Pelletier, H.: Improving the DPA attack using wavelet transform. In: NIST Physical Security Testing Workshop, vol. 46 (2005)
12. Clavier, C., Feix, B., Gagnerot, G., Roussellet, M., Verneuil, V.: Horizontal correlation analysis on exponentiation. In: Soriano, M., Qing, S., López, J. (eds.) ICICS 2010. LNCS, vol. 6476, pp. 46–61. Springer, Heidelberg (2010). https://doi.org/10.1007/978-3-642-17650-0_5
13. Coron, J.-S.: Resistance against differential power analysis for elliptic curve cryptosystems. In: Koç, Ç.K., Paar, C. (eds.) CHES 1999. LNCS, vol. 1717, pp. 292–302. Springer, Heidelberg (1999). https://doi.org/10.1007/3-540-48059-5_25
14. Le Corre, Y., Großschädl, J., Dinu, D.: Micro-architectural power simulator for leakage assessment of cryptographic software on ARM cortex-M3 processors. In: Fan, J., Gierlichs, B. (eds.) COSADE 2018. LNCS, vol. 10815, pp. 82–98. Springer, Cham (2018). https://doi.org/10.1007/978-3-319-89641-0_5
15. Costello, C., Smith, B.: Montgomery curves and their arithmetic - the case of large characteristic fields. J. Cryptogr. Eng. **8**(3), 227–240 (2018). https://doi.org/10.1007/s13389-017-0157-6
16. Danger, J.-L., Guilley, S., Hoogvorst, P., Murdica, C., Naccache, D.: Improving the big mac attack on elliptic curve cryptography. In: Ryan, P.Y.A., Naccache, D., Quisquater, J.-J. (eds.) The New Codebreakers. LNCS, vol. 9100, pp. 374–386. Springer, Heidelberg (2016). https://doi.org/10.1007/978-3-662-49301-4_23
17. De Mulder, E., et al.: Electromagnetic analysis attack on an FPGA implementation of an elliptic curve cryptosystem. In: EUROCON 2005 - The International Conference on "Computer as a Tool", vol. 2, pp. 1879–1882 (2005). https://doi.org/10.1109/EURCON.2005.1630348
18. Ding, A.A., Zhang, L., Durvaux, F., Standaert, F.-X., Fei, Y.: Towards sound and optimal leakage detection procedure. In: Eisenbarth, T., Teglia, Y. (eds.) CARDIS 2017. LNCS, vol. 10728, pp. 105–122. Springer, Cham (2018). https://doi.org/10.1007/978-3-319-75208-2_7
19. NIST Computer Security Division: Post-quantum cryptography standardization (2016). https://csrc.nist.gov/Projects/Post-Quantum-Cryptography
20. NIST Computer Security Division: Post-quantum cryptography standardization - round 3 submissions (2021). https://csrc.nist.gov/Projects/post-quantum-cryptography/round-3-submissions
21. Dugardin, M., Papachristodoulou, L., Najm, Z., Batina, L., Danger, J.-L., Guilley, S.: Dismantling real-world ECC with horizontal and vertical template attacks. In: Standaert, F.-X., Oswald, E. (eds.) COSADE 2016. LNCS, vol. 9689, pp. 88–108. Springer, Cham (2016). https://doi.org/10.1007/978-3-319-43283-0_6
22. Dunn, J.C.: A fuzzy relative of the ISODATA process and its use in detecting compact well-separated clusters. J. Cybern. **3**(3), 32–57 (1973). https://doi.org/10.1080/01969727308546046
23. Faz-Hernández, A., López-Hernández, J.C., Ochoa-Jiménez, E., Rodríguez-Henríquez, F.: A faster software implementation of the supersingular isogeny Diffie-Hellman key exchange protocol. IEEE Trans. Comput. **67**(11), 1622–1636 (2018). https://doi.org/10.1109/TC.2017.2771535

24. Feo, L.D., Jao, D., Plût, J.: Towards quantum-resistant cryptosystems from supersingular elliptic curve isogenies. J. Math. Cryptol. **8**(3), 209–247 (2014). https://doi.org/10.1515/jmc-2012-0015
25. Fujisaki, E., Okamoto, T.: Secure integration of asymmetric and symmetric encryption schemes. J. Cryptol. **26**(1), 80–101 (2013). https://doi.org/10.1007/s00145-011-9114-1
26. Gélin, A., Wesolowski, B.: Loop-abort faults on supersingular isogeny cryptosystems. In: Lange, T., Takagi, T. (eds.) PQCrypto 2017. LNCS, vol. 10346, pp. 93–106. Springer, Cham (2017). https://doi.org/10.1007/978-3-319-59879-6_6
27. Genêt, A., de Guertechin, N.L., Kaluđerović, N.: Full key recovery side-channel attack against ephemeral SIKE on the Cortex-M4. In: Bhasin, S., De Santis, F. (eds.) COSADE 2021. LNCS, vol. 12910, pp. 228–254. Springer, Cham (2021). https://doi.org/10.1007/978-3-030-89915-8_11
28. Heuser, A., Zohner, M.: Intelligent machine homicide. In: Schindler, W., Huss, S.A. (eds.) COSADE 2012. LNCS, vol. 7275, pp. 249–264. Springer, Heidelberg (2012). https://doi.org/10.1007/978-3-642-29912-4_18
29. Heyszl, J., Ibing, A., Mangard, S., De Santis, F., Sigl, G.: Clustering algorithms for non-profiled single-execution attacks on exponentiations. In: Francillon, A., Rohatgi, P. (eds.) CARDIS 2013. LNCS, vol. 8419, pp. 79–93. Springer, Cham (2014). https://doi.org/10.1007/978-3-319-08302-5_6
30. Heyszl, J., Mangard, S., Heinz, B., Stumpf, F., Sigl, G.: Localized electromagnetic analysis of cryptographic implementations. In: Dunkelman, O. (ed.) CT-RSA 2012. LNCS, vol. 7178, pp. 231–244. Springer, Heidelberg (2012). https://doi.org/10.1007/978-3-642-27954-6_15
31. Jao, D., et al.: SIKE - supersingular isogeny key exchange (2017). https://sike.org/
32. Kocher, P., Jaffe, J., Jun, B.: Differential power analysis. In: Wiener, M. (ed.) CRYPTO 1999. LNCS, vol. 1666, pp. 388–397. Springer, Heidelberg (1999). https://doi.org/10.1007/3-540-48405-1_25
33. Kocher, P.C., Jaffe, J., Jun, B., Rohatgi, P.: Introduction to differential power analysis. J. Cryptogr. Eng. **1**(1), 5–27 (2011). https://doi.org/10.1007/s13389-011-0006-y
34. Koziel, B., Azarderakhsh, R., Jao, D.: Side-channel attacks on quantum-resistant supersingular isogeny Diffie-Hellman. In: Adams, C., Camenisch, J. (eds.) SAC 2017. LNCS, vol. 10719, pp. 64–81. Springer, Cham (2018). https://doi.org/10.1007/978-3-319-72565-9_4
35. Lerman, L., Bontempi, G., Markowitch, O.: Power analysis attack: an approach based on machine learning. Int. J. Appl. Cryptogr. **3**(2), 97–115 (2014). https://doi.org/10.1504/IJACT.2014.062722
36. MacQueen, J.: Some methods for classification and analysis of multivariate observations. In: Proceedings of the Fifth Berkeley Symposium on Mathematical Statistics and Probability, Oakland, CA, USA, vol. 1, pp. 281–297 (1967)
37. Mallat, S.: A Wavelet Tour of Signal Processing: The Sparse Way, 3rd edn. Academic Press Inc. (2008)
38. Medwed, M., Oswald, E.: Template attacks on ECDSA. In: Chung, K.-I., Sohn, K., Yung, M. (eds.) WISA 2008. LNCS, vol. 5379, pp. 14–27. Springer, Heidelberg (2009). https://doi.org/10.1007/978-3-642-00306-6_2
39. Nascimento, E., Chmielewski, Ł: Applying horizontal clustering side-channel attacks on embedded ECC implementations. In: Eisenbarth, T., Teglia, Y. (eds.) CARDIS 2017. LNCS, vol. 10728, pp. 213–231. Springer, Cham (2018). https://doi.org/10.1007/978-3-319-75208-2_13

40. Nascimento, E., Chmielewski, Ł, Oswald, D., Schwabe, P.: Attacking embedded ECC implementations through cmov side channels. In: Avanzi, R., Heys, H. (eds.) SAC 2016. LNCS, vol. 10532, pp. 99–119. Springer, Cham (2017). https://doi.org/10.1007/978-3-319-69453-5_6
41. Perin, G., Chmielewski, Ł: A semi-parametric approach for side-channel attacks on protected RSA implementations. In: Homma, N., Medwed, M. (eds.) CARDIS 2015. LNCS, vol. 9514, pp. 34–53. Springer, Cham (2016). https://doi.org/10.1007/978-3-319-31271-2_3
42. Perin, G., Chmielewski, Ł, Batina, L., Picek, S.: Keep it unsupervised: horizontal attacks meet deep learning. IACR Trans. Cryptogr. Hardw. Embed. Syst. **2021**(1), 343–372 (2021). https://doi.org/10.46586/tches.v2021.i1.343-372
43. Perin, G., Imbert, L., Torres, L., Maurine, P.: Attacking randomized exponentiations using unsupervised learning. In: Prouff, E. (ed.) COSADE 2014. LNCS, vol. 8622, pp. 144–160. Springer, Cham (2014). https://doi.org/10.1007/978-3-319-10175-0_11
44. Poussier, R., Zhou, Y., Standaert, F.-X.: A systematic approach to the side-channel analysis of ECC implementations with worst-case horizontal attacks. In: Fischer, W., Homma, N. (eds.) CHES 2017. LNCS, vol. 10529, pp. 534–554. Springer, Cham (2017). https://doi.org/10.1007/978-3-319-66787-4_26
45. Saito, M., Matsumoto, M.: Tiny Mersenne Twister pseudo-random number generator (2011). https://github.com/MersenneTwister-Lab/TinyMT
46. Schneider, T., Moradi, A.: Leakage assessment methodology - extended version. J. Cryptogr. Eng. **6**(2), 85–99 (2016). https://doi.org/10.1007/s13389-016-0120-y
47. Seo, H., Anastasova, M., Jalali, A., Azarderakhsh, R.: Supersingular isogeny key encapsulation (SIKE) round 2 on ARM Cortex-M4. Cryptology ePrint Archive, Report 2020/410 (2020). https://eprint.iacr.org/2020/410
48. Shi, F., Wei, J., Sun, D., Wei, G.: A systematic approach to horizontal clustering analysis on embedded RSA implementation. In: 25th IEEE International Conference on Parallel and Distributed Systems, ICPADS 2019, Tianjin, China, 4–6 December 2019, pp. 901–906. IEEE (2019). https://doi.org/10.1109/ICPADS47876.2019.00132
49. Shor, P.W.: Algorithms for quantum computation: discrete logarithms and factoring. In: 35th Annual Symposium on Foundations of Computer Science, Santa Fe, New Mexico, USA, 20–22 November 1994, pp. 124–134. IEEE Computer Society (1994). https://doi.org/10.1109/SFCS.1994.365700
50. Sim, B.-Y., Han, D.-G.: Key bit-dependent attack on protected PKC using a single trace. In: Liu, J.K., Samarati, P. (eds.) ISPEC 2017. LNCS, vol. 10701, pp. 168–185. Springer, Cham (2017). https://doi.org/10.1007/978-3-319-72359-4_10
51. Souissi, Y., Aabid, M.A.E., Debande, N., Guilley, S., Danger, J.L.: Novel applications of wavelet transforms based side-channel analysis. In: Non-Invasive Attack Testing Workshop, November 2021
52. Specht, R., Heyszl, J., Kleinsteuber, M., Sigl, G.: Improving non-profiled attacks on exponentiations based on clustering and extracting leakage from multi-channel high-resolution EM measurements. In: Mangard, S., Poschmann, A.Y. (eds.) COSADE 2014. LNCS, vol. 9064, pp. 3–19. Springer, Cham (2015). https://doi.org/10.1007/978-3-319-21476-4_1
53. Tasso, É., De Feo, L., El Mrabet, N., Pontié, S.: Resistance of isogeny-based cryptographic implementations to a fault attack. In: Bhasin, S., De Santis, F. (eds.) COSADE 2021. LNCS, vol. 12910, pp. 255–276. Springer, Cham (2021). https://doi.org/10.1007/978-3-030-89915-8_12

54. Ti, Y.B.: Fault attack on supersingular isogeny cryptosystems. In: Lange, T., Takagi, T. (eds.) PQCrypto 2017. LNCS, vol. 10346, pp. 107–122. Springer, Cham (2017). https://doi.org/10.1007/978-3-319-59879-6_7
55. Vélu, J.: Isogénies entre courbes elliptiques. Comptes-Rendus de l'Académie des Sciences, Série I **273**, 238–241 (1971)
56. Veyrat-Charvillon, N., Gérard, B., Standaert, F.-X.: Soft analytical side-channel attacks. In: Sarkar, P., Iwata, T. (eds.) ASIACRYPT 2014. LNCS, vol. 8873, pp. 282–296. Springer, Heidelberg (2014). https://doi.org/10.1007/978-3-662-45611-8_15
57. Walter, C.D.: Sliding windows succumbs to big mac attack. In: Koç, Ç.K., Naccache, D., Paar, C. (eds.) CHES 2001. LNCS, vol. 2162, pp. 286–299. Springer, Heidelberg (2001). https://doi.org/10.1007/3-540-44709-1_24
58. Zhang, F., et al.: Side-channel analysis and countermeasure design on ARM-based quantum-resistant SIKE. IEEE Trans. Comput. **69**(11), 1681–1693 (2020). https://doi.org/10.1109/TC.2020.3020407

Canonical DPA Attack on HMAC-SHA1/SHA2

Frank Schuhmacher(✉)

Segrids GmbH, 53127 Bonn, Germany
Frank.Schuhmacher@Segrids.com
http://www.segrids.com

Abstract. We present a new DPA attack on the secret initial state in the "outer" hash of HMAC-SHA1/SHA2. This attack only requires a suitable leakage of the SHA1/SHA2 working variables a and e. Due to the fact that each value of a working variable a or e is used as an input to copy, add, shift, and logical operations in multiple successive SHA1/SHA2 rounds, they are the primary potential sources of side channel leakage. Our attack is different but equivalent in this aspect to a known attack [9] on the secret initial state in the "inner" hash of HMAC-SHA1/SHA2. The combination of the two attacks provides the first full-fledged attack on HMAC-SHA1/SHA2 that does not depend on leakage assumptions on any ephemeral intermediates. As a proof-of-concept, we present a full key disclosure of the battery authentication key of a BQ27Z561 fuel gauge.

Keywords: Differential Power Analysis · HMAC · SHA256 · SHA1

1 Introduction

1.1 Motivation

The keyed hash authentication code HMAC specified in [14] is a symmetric authentication function commonly used for message or entity authentication. It requires the knowledge of a secret authentication key shared between the two parties: the generator of the HMAC and the verifier.

In a typical use case of entity authentication, some main device shall verify that an electronic accessory is original. It will consider each accessory as original that can proof the knowledge of a shared secret HMAC key in a challenge-response-protocol. In this use case, a counterfeit manufacturer would be highly interested in the knowledge of this key in order to enable its fake products to pass the entity authentication.

The counterfeit manufacturer can buy an original main device with original accessory and analyze the devices in her laboratory. Hence, she will not only be able to track the communication between main device and accessory, but also to mount physical attacks and side channel analysis in order to extract the key from one of the two devices. Side channel analysis of the HMAC function is a realistic threat for this use case. It motivated our interest in the topic.

J. Balasch and C. O'Flynn (Eds.): COSADE 2022, LNCS 13211, pp. 193–211, 2022.
https://doi.org/10.1007/978-3-030-99766-3_9

1.2 DPA

Differential power analysis (DPA) is a class of side channel attacks. The attacker measures the power profile of the targeted device during a crypto operation with a digital oscilloscope. DPA requires multiple identical crypto operations with randomized inputs, always using the same secret key. Furthermore, it requires that the inputs or outputs are known to the attacker. In the example of an accessory authentication, the attacker can misuse the challenge-response-protocol to trigger the accessory to do multiple HMAC computations for her measurement. A DPA attacker tries to gain information on the secret key by analyzing statistical dependencies between the power traces X and intermediate values $I = I(\texttt{plaintext}, \texttt{subkey})$ of the crypto algorithm depending on known data `plaintext` derived from the known input (or known output) and small portions `subkey` of the secret key K.

A DPA attack is either a profiled attack or a correlation power analysis (CPA). A profiled attack requires the access to a device with a known key. The attacker will first run a profiling measurement using this device, and try to identify intermediate values of the crypto algorithm suitable for a DPA. An intermediate of the form $I = I(\texttt{plaintext}, \texttt{subkey})$ is suitable for DPA if the profiling traces statistically depend on the values of I. She will generate a template for each identified intermediate, i.e. the average over all profiling traces with fixed intermediate value. The exploit will be a matching between means over exploitation traces with fixed input bytes (and unknown key K) and the templates.

A CPA does not require a profiling, but a leakage model for a set of suitable intermediates. A leakage model is a real valued function h modeling the power of gates and registers processing the intermediate value. The attacker will try to identify a subkey as the hypothesis `hyp` maximizing the correlation

$$\texttt{cor}(h(I(\texttt{plaintext}, \texttt{hyp})), X_x)$$

for at least one runtime x.

For devices without DPA protection, the Hamming weight `ham` (number of one-bits) is typically a good leakage model. An alternative leakage model is Hamming distance leakage, modeling the leakage due to overwriting a register or bus line with value I_0 by value I_1. The Hamming weight of the bitwise xor $I := I_0 \wedge I_1$ is called the Hamming distance between I_0 and I_1.

Profiled attacks are stronger than CPA. If a CPA is applicable, then a profiled attack is applicable as well. The inverse implication is not true, in general. However, the access to a device with known key is a strong prerequisite. Feasibility of a CPA attack is a stronger conclusion of a side channel analysis than feasibility of a profiled attack.

1.3 Known DPA Attacks on HMAC

We have found three references on "full-fledged" attacks on HMAC-SHA: Reference [7] describes a CPA attack based on a Hamming distance leakage model for the SHA256 intermediates $T1$, `Ch`, and `Maj` (to be defined in Sect. 2.4) and proves it's feasibility on an suitable own HMAC implementation on a Spartan-3E FPGA.

Reference [2] describes a CPA attack based on a Hamming weight leakage model for the SHA256 intermediates $T1$, $a \wedge b$, $a \wedge c$, $e \wedge f$, $\neg e \wedge g$ (to be defined in Sect. 2.4) and proves its feasibility on simulations.

Reference [3] is a bit exotic, since it describes a profiled attack on a fast hardware implementation of HMAC-SHA256 with a side channel measurement at a low sample rate. It specializes on the case where the computations (1) and (2) of Sect. 2.4 are performed in parallel and/or an attacker that cannot split the time line into points of interest for intermediates related to (1) and points of interest for intermediates related to (2). The reference provides a clever specification of 12-bit intermediates for template attacks abusing a leakage of the overwriting of a_t by a_{t+1} and e_t by e_{t+1}. In this aspect, the attack is similar to [7] with the difference that it requires a profiling stage instead of an explicit leakage model.

All full-fledged attacks in the literature require – in addition to the leakage of the working variables a to h of the SHA-256 specification [5] – the leakage of multiple ephemeral intermediates, or the ephemeral leakage due to the overwriting of a variable by its new value.

We have found one reference on DPA on HMAC-SHA256 targeting only the persistent intermediates a to h (to be defined in Sect. 2.4). However, this reference [9] only identifies one half of a full attack. Provided a Hamming weight leakage of the intermediates a-h in the first SHA256 rounds, it is suitable to disclose the "inner secret" $S^{\texttt{inner}}$ (to be defined in Sect. 2.2) with CPA. Since the reference is only a sketch on a power-point slide, we are going to describe this half attack in detail in Sect. 3.2.

Finally, we have found one reference describing a successful attack on an authentication device: Reference [8] describes an attack on real targets DS28E01 and DS2432 similar to [7]. The attacked targets use a custom, non-standard MAC specification. The attack is not applicable to HMAC.

1.4 Contribution

The motivation for this publication is that we have identified one product supporting an HMAC authentication that we were unable to break with any of the CPA attacks on HMAC that we found in the literature. Any of the attacks on HMAC-SHA256 listed in Sect. 1.3 is based on the leakage of at least one an ephemeral value (or on the ephemeral leakage of the overwriting of a variable) that did not leak in our analysis of a real target in Sect. 4.

However, we have identified a new CPA attack that we could successfully apply to disclose the secret key data of the analyzed product, see Sect. 5. In fact, our main contribution is the second half of a full attack for the disclosure of the "outer" HMAC secret $S^{\texttt{outer}}$.

In combination with the half attack of reference [9], we obtain a full-fledged attack with a principal advantage with respect to known full-fledged DPA attacks on HMAC: it only requires the leakage of "persistent" intermediate values that are used in several consecutive computation steps, in particular in copy operations, bitwise rotations, and additions. Each of these consecutive steps is potentially vulnerable to DPA. For implementations without sophisticated DPA protection, the Hamming weight leakage model likely applies for these intermediates. Our attack applies to HMAC-SHA1 and HMAC-SHA2.

1.5 Organization of the Paper

The attack description requires multiple definitions from the HMAC and SHA specifications. For the convenience of the reader, we recall all required definitions in Sect. 2. This section also precises the aim of DPA attacks on HMAC. Section 3 describes the known attack on the "inner" HMAC secret. Our new attack on the "outer" HMAC secret is presented in Sect. 4. In Sect. 5, we apply the new attack on a recent battery authentication product as a proof-of-concept.

2 HMAC-SHA1/SHA2

2.1 SHA1/SHA2 as Merkle-Damgård Constructions

The HMAC specification [14] requires an approved hash function, such as SHA1, or a member of the SHA2 family as specified in [5]. Due to the existence of practical collision attacks, HMAC-SHA1 is out-of-date for message authentication but still in use for entity authentication. Recent micro-controller systems use HMAC-SHA256, instead. SHA256 is a member of the SHA2 family. We mainly focus on HMAC-SHA256 and HMAC-SHA1 in this article.

SHA1 and SHA256 both are Merkle-Damgård constructions with a block size of 512 bits: they start with an initial hash value $H^{(0)}$, and the hashing of a sequence of blocks $M^{(0)}, \ldots, M^{(n-1)}$ is defined as a sequence of updates

$$H^{(i+1)} = \texttt{compress}(H^{(i)}, M^{(i)})$$

for some "one-way" compression function `compress`. Details on the SHA256 compression function will be provided in Sect. 2.4 Details on the SHA1 compression function will be provided in Sect. 2.5 The hash sum is $H^{(n)}$. For SHA256, the hash value $H^{(i)}$ has eight words à 32 bits. For SHA1, the hash value $H^{(i)}$ has five words à 32 bits.

2.2 HMAC-SHA1/SHA2 as Merkle-Damgård Tree

The standard [14] defines HMAC-SHA for any SHA1 or SHA-2 function SHA as

$$\texttt{HMAC}(K, \texttt{challenge}) = \texttt{SHA}((K \oplus \texttt{opad})||\texttt{SHA}((K \oplus \texttt{ipad})||\texttt{challenge})),$$

where `ipad` and `opad` are constants depending on the selected SHA function, and the symbol || is used for message concatenation. To become more specific, consider a typical entity authentication protocol, where the verifier sends a `challenge` to the entity to be authenticated, the entity computes the HMAC-SHA and sends it as `response` to the verifier. Typically, `challenge` and `response` are of the same size, i.e. 160 bits for HMAC-SHA1, and 256 bits for HMAC-SHA256. This response generation requires the compression of two message blocks $M^{(0)}$ and $M^{(1)}$ in each of the two SHA executions. In the inner SHA, to be computed first, the message block $M^{(0)}$ is $K \oplus \texttt{ipad}$, and the message block $M^{(1)}$ is the concatenation of `challenge` with a constant padding. We denote $\texttt{digest}^{\texttt{inner}}$ as the outcome of the inner SHA. In the outer SHA, the message block $M^{(0)}$ is $K \oplus \texttt{opad}$, and the message block $M^{(1)}$ is the concatenation of $\texttt{digest}^{\texttt{inner}}$ with the same constant padding. The outcome of the outer SHA is the `response`.

For both, the inner and outer SHA, the value $H^{(1)}$ only depends on the key K but not on the `challenge`. Therefore, most devices do this computation only once per secret HMAC key K and store the values $S^{\texttt{inner}} := \texttt{compress}(H^{(0)}, K \oplus \texttt{ipad})$ and $S^{\texttt{outer}} := \texttt{compress}(H^{(0)}, K \oplus \texttt{opad})$ permanently, but not the key K. We call $S^{\texttt{inner}}$ the **inner secret**, and $S^{\texttt{outer}}$ the **outer secret**. The HMAC-SHA function can be depicted as a "Merkle-Damgård tree" with an inner and an outer branch, see Fig. 1.

2.3 Aim of DPA Attacks on HMAC

The attacker, for example the counterfeit manufacturer of Sect. 1.1, would like to reveal the secret HMAC key K. If the device does not store K but only the pair $(S^{\texttt{inner}}, S^{\texttt{outer}})$ of the inner and outer secret, she will not have any chance to disclose K. But even if the device computes $S^{\texttt{inner}}$ and $S^{\texttt{outer}}$ in every challenge-response-authentication, the key K cannot be disclosed by a CPA attack, since the computation does not depend on any randomized data. In some exotic cases, K might be disclosed by an SPA attack, but this it not in the focus of this paper. On the other hand-side, the knowledge of the pair $(S^{\texttt{inner}}, S^{\texttt{outer}})$ is sufficient for the HMAC computation, and hence to pass a challenge-response-authentication. A counterfeit manufacturer who is able to disclose this pair can build fake accessories that will be considered as original by the original main devices. The disclosure of $(S^{\texttt{inner}}, S^{\texttt{outer}})$ is the aim of any DPA attack on HMAC-SHA.

Attacking the inner secret might demand for a completely different method than attacking the outer secret. An attack on $S^{\texttt{inner}}$ requires the leakage of intermediates $I = I(\texttt{subkey}, \texttt{plaintext})$ in the **inner compression**

$$\texttt{digest}^{\texttt{inner}} = \texttt{compress}(S^{\texttt{inner}}, \texttt{pad}(\texttt{challenge})),$$

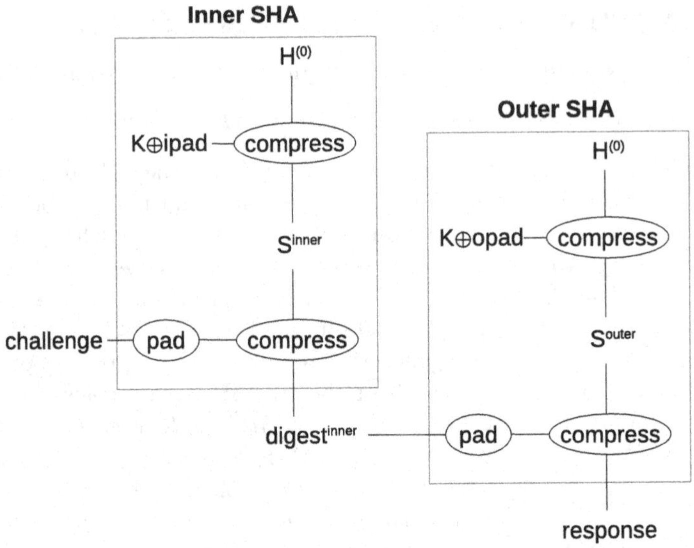

Fig. 1. HMAC function as Merkle-Damgård tree.

where `subkey` is a key information on $S^{\texttt{inner}}$, and `plaintext` is a known data byte derived from `challenge`. The attack is typically chosen-input and always unknown-output. An attack on $S^{\texttt{outer}}$ requires the leakage of intermediates $I = I(\texttt{subkey}, \texttt{plaintext})$ in the **outer compression**

$$\texttt{response} = \texttt{compress}(S^{\texttt{outer}}, \texttt{pad}(\texttt{digest}^{\texttt{inner}})).$$

The attack is known-output. It is known-input if and only if the attacker already knows $S^{\texttt{inner}}$. It is never chosen-input.

2.4 The SHA256 Compression Function

The SHA256 compression function `compress` first copies the initial hash value $H^{(0)}$ to eight **working variables** $a, ..., h$, then updates these working variable 64 times in the form

$$a_{t+1}, ..., h_{t+1} = \texttt{round\_function}(a_t, ..., h_t, W_t, K_t^{\{256\}}),$$

where the words $W_0, ..., W_{63}$ of the "message schedule" [5] only depend on $M^{(1)}$, and the 32-bit integers $K_0^{\{256\}}, ..., K_{63}^{\{256\}}$ (not to be mixed up with the key K) are round constants [5]. We have used subscript t to denote the value of a working variable $a, ..., h$ input to round $t = 0, ..., 63$, or output of round $t - 1$. The round function depicted in Fig. 2 sets $b_{t+1} = a_t$, $c_{t+1} = b_t$, $d_{t+1} = c_t$, $f_{t+1} = e_t$, $g_{t+1} = f_t$, $h_{t+1} = f_t$,

$$a_{t+1} = \Sigma_0^{\{256\}}(a_t) + \texttt{Maj}(a_t, b_t, c_t) + T1, \tag{1}$$

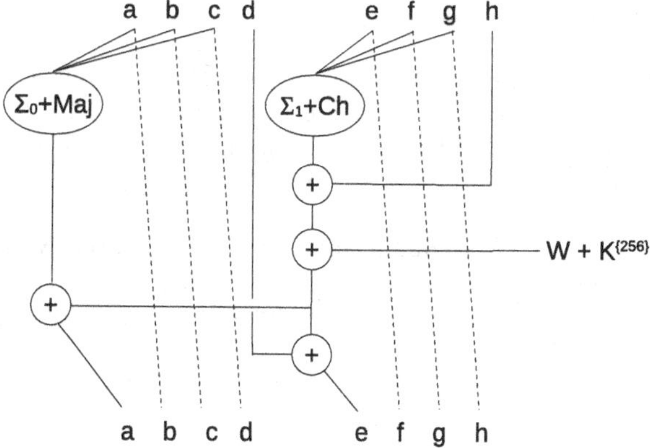

Fig. 2. SHA256 round function.

and

$$e_{t+1} = T1 + d_t, \tag{2}$$

where the intermediate $T1$ is defined as

$$T1 = h_t + \Sigma_1^{\{256\}}(e_t) + \mathtt{Ch}(e_t, f_t, g_t) + K_t^{\{256\}} + W_t. \tag{3}$$

Here, we have used the standard [5] functions

$$\Sigma_0^{\{256\}}(a) = \mathtt{ROTR}^2(a) \oplus \mathtt{ROTR}^{13}(a) \oplus \mathtt{ROTR}^{22}(a),$$

$$\Sigma_1^{\{256\}}(e) = \mathtt{ROTR}^6(e) \oplus \mathtt{ROTR}^{11}(e) \oplus \mathtt{ROTR}^{25}(e),$$

where ROTR denotes the bitwise right rotation,

$$\mathtt{Maj}(a, b, c) = (a \wedge b) \oplus (a \wedge c) \oplus (b \wedge c),$$

and

$$\mathtt{Ch}(e, f, g) = (e \wedge f) \oplus (\neg e \wedge g).$$

The final step of the `compress` function is the word-wise addition

$$H^{(2)} = H^{(1)} + (a_{64}, b_{64}, c_{64}, d_{64}, e_{64}, f_{64}, g_{64}, h_{64}). \tag{4}$$

Note that the values of the working variables a_{t+1} and e_{t+1} computed in round t still persist in rounds $t + 1$ to $t + 4$ if $t < 60$, where they are object to copy operations, and inputs to functions Σ_0, Maj, Σ_1, Ch, and/or to 32-bit additions. This persistence makes the hardware activity highly dependent on the values of the working variables a and e. These working variables are the "fat" intermediate targets for DPA attacks on HMAC-SHA256.

2.5 The SHA1 Compression Function

The SHA1 compression function operates with a 5-word intermediate hash value H and five working variables $a - e$. The standard [14] defines SHA1 specific round constants K_t and a SHA1 specific computation of the message schedule W_t. The compression function requires 80 updates of the form

$$a_{t+1}, ..., e_{t+1} = \texttt{round\_function}(a_t, ..., e_t, W_t, K_t).$$

For $0 \leq t \leq 19$, the round function has the form

$$a_{t+t} = \texttt{ROTL}^5(a_t) + \texttt{Ch}(b_t, c_t, d_t) + e_t + K_t + W_t \tag{5}$$

$$b_{t+1} = a_t \tag{6}$$

$$c_{t+1} = \texttt{ROTL}^{30}(b_t) \tag{7}$$

$$d_{t+1} = c_t \tag{8}$$

$$e_{t+1} = d_t \tag{9}$$

For $60 \leq t \leq 79$, the definition of the round function is identical except that Eq. (5) must be replaced by

$$a_{t+t} = \texttt{ROTL}^5(a_t) + (b_t \oplus c_t \oplus d_t) + e_t + K_t + W_t. \tag{10}$$

The remaining t values are not relevant for the subsequent considerations. The final step of the `compress` function is the word-wise addition

$$H^{(2)} = H^{(1)} + (a_{80}, b_{80}, c_{80}, d_{80}, e_{80}). \tag{11}$$

Note for SHA1 that up to bitwise rotation, an intermediate value a_t computed in round $t \leq 75$ still persists in rounds $t+1, ..., t+4$ and forms the input to multiple copy, add and logical operations in these rounds. This persistence makes the hardware activity highly dependent on the values of the working variable a. It is the "fat" intermediate target for DPA attacks on HMAC-SHA1.

3 Known Attack on the Inner Secret

3.1 DPA on Plaintext Plus Subkey

Before describing DPA on the HMAC secrets, first consider more generally attacks on a 32-bit `subkey`, exploiting a `plaintext` + `subkey` leakage, where `plaintext` is a known and variable 32-bit integer (required modifications if working with a word size of 64-bit should be obvious). We fix a byte size of 8-bits, and write $I[0]$ for the most significant byte of an intermediate I and $I[3]$ for the least significant byte.

A byte-by-byte attack on `plaintext`+`subkey` can efficiently be implemented as in the (python style) pseudo-code of Fig. 3, where the `plaintext` is considered as an array of length M, where M denotes the number of traces, and the trace set X as an array of shape (M,N), where N is the trace length. The attack starts

```
def disclose_subkey(plaintext, X, threshold):
    subkey = 0
    for byte in [3,2,1,0]:
        csq = chisq((plaintext + subkey)[byte], X)
        roi = where(csq > threshold)
        P = (plaintext + subkey)[byte]
        champ = disclose_subkey_byte(P, X, roi)
        subkey = subkey + (champ << 8*(3-byte))
    return subkey

def disclose_subkey_byte(P, X, roi):
    points = zeros(256)
    for x in roi:
        ch = zeros(256)
            for hyp in range(256):
                ch[hyp] = cor(ham((P+hyp) mod 256), X[:,x])
                winner = argmax(ch)
                points[winner] = points[winner] + 1
    return argmax(points)
```

Fig. 3. Pseudo-code for identification of best 32-bit subkey hypothesis

with the least significant byte 3 of the `subkey` and requires the disclosure of all less significant bytes, before disclosing a more significant byte.

In general, multiple plaintext dependent intermediates might leak but if the Hamming weight leakage of $I =$ `plaintext` $+$ `subkey` is the "dominant" leakage contribution, then the pseudo-code in Fig. 3 is suitable to disclose the `subkey`. The pseudo-code contains the function `chisq` for the computation of the chi-squared of an intermediate. Up to a constant factor, the chi-squared is the variance of the "set of means" divided by the mean of the "set of variances", where the set of means (also referred to as templates, or central moments of order 1) with respect to an intermediate I contains the means `mean`$[I]$ over all traces $X(m)$ with fixed $I(m) = I$. The set of variances (also referred to as central moments of order 2) with respect to an intermediate I contains the variances `var`$[I]$ over all traces $X(m)$ with fixed $I(m) = I$.

3.2 Attack on the Inner HMAC-SHA256 Secret

The slides [9] describe a DPA attack on HMAC-SHA256 that targets only the SHA256 working variables a to h (c.f. Sect. 2.4). It is a chosen input attack and therefore only applicable for the disclosure of $S^{\texttt{inner}}$. Since the reference [9] is only a sketch, we explain some details, here. The attack requires a leakage of a_t and e_t for $1 \leq t \leq 4$ and four different measurements with chosen challenges covering the first seven rounds of the inner compression.

In measurement 0, all four challenge words W_t are randomized. Then the attack on plaintext plus subkey described in Sect. 3.1 is applied on the constant "subkeys" $\alpha(a_0, ..., h_0, K_0^{\{256\}})$ and $\epsilon(a_0, ..., h_0, K_0^{\{256\}})$ defined by

$$a_1 = \alpha(a_0, ..., h_0, K_0^{\{256\}}) + W_0 \tag{12}$$

and

$$e_1 = \epsilon(a_0, ..., h_0, K_0^{\{256\}}) + W_0. \tag{13}$$

The functions α and ϵ can be defined explicitly using Eqs. (1), (2), and (3). However, explicit formulas are not relevant, here. By this DPA on measurement 0, the attacker obtains a_1 and e_1 for each challenge with $W_0 = 0$. Then, the attacker will perform measurement $t = 1, 2, 3$ with challenge words $W_0 = ... = W_{t-1} = 0$, and randomized words W_n for $n \geq t$. In this measurement, the values of $a_t, ..., h_t$ are constant. The attacker applies the DPA on plaintext plus subkey on the "subkeys" $\alpha(a_t, ..., h_t, K_t^{\{256\}})$ and $\epsilon(a_t, ..., h_t, K_t^{\{256\}})$ defined by

$$a_{t+1} = \alpha(a_t, ..., h_t, K_t^{\{256\}}) + W_t \tag{14}$$

and

$$e_{t+1} = \epsilon(a_t, ..., h_t, K_t^{\{256\}}) + W_t. \tag{15}$$

After the DPA on measurement t, the attacker can compute a_{t+1} and e_{t+1} for each challenge with $W_0 = ... = W_{t-1} = 0$. After step $t = 3$, the attacker knows $a_1, e_1, ..., a_3, e_3$ and can compute a_4, e_4 for each challenge with $W_0 = W_1 = W_2 = 0$, and can finally compute back from these values and W_3 to the inner secret $S^{\texttt{inner}} = (a_0, ..., h_0)$. The pseudo-code for this backward computation is displayed in Fig. 4. Due to the fact that it is difficult to avoid any leakage of the persistent working variables a_t and e_t, we believe that this attack is the strongest applicable attack on $S^{\texttt{inner}}$. The attacker [4] was able, for example, to disclose $S^{\texttt{inner}}$ of a real target (Solo Key) in this way, but finally failed to disclose $S^{\texttt{outer}}$ by applying one of the known attacks listed in the following subsection.

3.3 Attack on the Inner HMAC-SHA1 Secret

The core idea of the known attack described in Sect. 3.2 can be transferred from HMAC-SHA256 to HMAC-SHA1. We assume a Hamming weight leakage of a_t for $1 \leq t \leq 5$ as leakage model. Set

$$\gamma_t := \texttt{ROTL}^5(a_t) + \texttt{Ch}(b_t, c_t, d_t) + e_t + K_t.$$

The attack requires five measurements with chosen challenges. In measurement 0, all challenge words are randomized. The attacker discloses the constant "subkey" γ_0 by a DPA attack on plaintext plus subkey in $a_1 = \gamma_0 + W_0$. In measurement 1, challenge word W_0 is chosen zero and all other challenge words are randomized. Then, γ_1 is constant and can be disclosed by a DPA attack on plaintext plus subkey in $a_2 = \gamma_1 + W_1$. Continuing in this manner until measurement 4, the attacker

```
def compute_backwards(a1, a2, a3, a4, e1, e2, e3, e4):
    c3 = b2 = a1
    b3 = a2
    g3 = f2 = e1
    f3 = e2
    h3 = a4 - Sigma1(e3) - Ch(e3, f3, g3) - K256[3]
            - Sigma0(a3) - Maj(a3, b3, c3)
    e0 = f1 = g2 = h3
    d3 = e4 - Sigma1(e3) - Ch(e3, f3, g3) - K256[3] - h3
    a0 = b1 = c2 = d3
    h2 = a3 - Sigma1(e2) - Ch(e2, f2, g2) - K256[2]
            - Sigma0(a2) - Maj(a2, b2, c2)
    f0 = g1 = h2
    d2 = e3 - Sigma1(e2) - Ch(e2, f2, g2) - K256[2] - h2
    b0 = c1 = d2
    h1 = a2 - Sigma1(e1) - Ch(e1, f1, g1) - K256[1]
            - Sigma0(a1) - Maj(a1, b1, c1)
    g0 = h1
    d1 = e2 - Sigma1(e1) - Ch(e1, f1, g1) - K256[1] - h1
    c0 = d1
    h0 = a1 - Sigma1(e0) - Ch(e0, f0, g0) - K256[0]
            - Sigma0(a3) - Maj(a0, b0, c0)
    d0 = e1 - Sigma1(e0) - Ch(e0, f0, g0) - K256[0] - h0
    return a0, b0, c0, d0, e0, f0, g0, h0
```

Fig. 4. Pseudo-code for backward computation.

obtains the values $a_1, ..., a_5$ for each challenge with first four words zero. Using Eqs. (6) to (9), the attacker also gets the values of $b2, b3, b4, b5, c3, c4, c5, d4, d5$ and $e5$. Using Eq. (7), she can successively compute

$$
\begin{aligned}
e_4 &= a_5 - \mathtt{ROTL}^5(a_4) - \mathtt{Ch}(b_4, c_4, d_4) - K_4 \\
a_0 &= b_1 = \mathtt{ROTR}^{30}(c_2) = \mathtt{ROTR}^{30}(d_3) = \mathtt{ROTR}^{30}(e_4) \\
e_3 &= a_4 - \mathtt{ROTL}^5(a_3) - \mathtt{Ch}(b_3, c_3, d_3) - K_3 \\
b_0 &= \mathtt{ROTR}^{30}(c_1) = \mathtt{ROTR}^{30}(d_2) = \mathtt{ROTR}^{30}(e_3) \\
e_2 &= a_3 - \mathtt{ROTL}^5(a_2) - \mathtt{Ch}(b_2, c_2, d_2) - K_2 \\
c_0 &= d_1 = e_2 \\
e_1 &= a_2 - \mathtt{ROTL}^5(a_1) - \mathtt{Ch}(b_1, c_1, d_1) - K_1 \\
d_0 &= e_1 \\
e_0 &= a_1 - \mathtt{ROTL}^5(a_0) - \mathtt{Ch}(b_0, c_0, d_0) - K_0
\end{aligned}
$$

This yields the inner HMAC-SHA1 secret $S^{\mathtt{inner}} = (a_0, b_0, c_0, d_0, e_0)$.

4 New Attack on the Outer Secret

4.1 Attack on the Outer HMAC-SHA256 Secret

The values of a_{61}, e_{61} computed in round 60 still persist in rounds 61,62,63. The values of a_{62}, e_{62} computed in round 61 still persist in rounds 62,63. The values of a_{63}, e_{63} computed in round 62 still persist in round 63. Furthermore, as depicted in Fig. 5, the values of $a_{61}, ..., a_{64}$ and $e_{61}, ..., e_{64}$ still form the right input to the final word-wise addition. We can rewrite Eq. (4) as:

$$\texttt{response} = S^{\texttt{outer}} + (a_{64}, a_{63}, a_{62}, a_{61}, e_{64}, e_{63}, e_{62}, e_{61}).$$

The strategy is to attack the outer secret $S^{\texttt{outer}}$ using the knowledge of the `response` to each randomized challenge.

4.2 The Attack

Since $S^{\texttt{outer}} = H^{(1)}$, and $\texttt{response} = H^{(2)} = H^{(1)} + (a_{64}, ..., h_{64})$, we have:

$$a_{64} = \texttt{response}_0 - S_0^{\texttt{outer}} \tag{16}$$
$$a_{63} = b_{64} = \texttt{response}_1 - S_1^{\texttt{outer}} \tag{17}$$
$$a_{62} = b_{63} = c_{64} = \texttt{response}_2 - S_2^{\texttt{outer}} \tag{18}$$
$$a_{61} = b_{62} = c_{63} = d_{64} = \texttt{response}_3 - S_3^{\texttt{outer}} \tag{19}$$
$$e_{64} = \texttt{response}_4 - S_4^{\texttt{outer}} \tag{20}$$
$$e_{63} = f_{64} = \texttt{response}_5 - S_5^{\texttt{outer}} \tag{21}$$
$$e_{62} = f_{63} = g_{64} = \texttt{response}_6 - S_6^{\texttt{outer}} \tag{22}$$
$$e_{61} = f_{62} = g_{63} = h_{64} = \texttt{response}_7 - S_7^{\texttt{outer}} \tag{23}$$

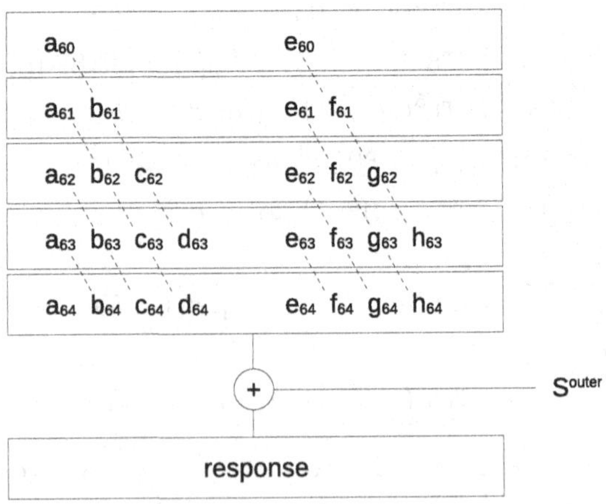

Fig. 5. Intermediates in last rounds of outer SHA256.

As leakage model, assume a Hamming weight leakage of the working variables a_{61} to a_{64} and e_{61} to e_{64} in the last 1, 2, 3, or 4 rounds. We set $\texttt{plaintext} := \texttt{response}_{\texttt{word}}$, and $\texttt{subkey} := 2^{32} - S_{\texttt{word}}^{outer}$ and apply the DPA attack on plaintext plus subkey described in Sect. 3.1 for each $\texttt{word}$ in 0, ..., 7. Each of the eight DPA attacks shall provide a word $S_{\texttt{word}}^{outer} = 2^{32} - \texttt{subkey}$ of the secret $S^{\texttt{outer}}$.

Note that this attack does not simply abuse an argument leakage in the final addition. Such a leakage would only provide a small contribution to the expected leakage of the working variables a and e.

4.3 Optimization and Fall-Back

Since a_{64} and e_{64} are less persistent than a_{61} to a_{63} and e_{61} to e_{63}, their leakage might be too small to disclose $S_0^{\texttt{outer}}$ and $S_4^{\texttt{outer}}$. However, this is no problem, if we are able to disclose $S_{\texttt{word}}^{\texttt{outer}}$ for $\texttt{word} \neq 0, 4$.

A first fall-back assumes that we already have disclosed $S^{\texttt{inner}}$. Then, we can compute the input $M^{(1,\texttt{outer})}$ to the outer compression. Even if we cannot choose the input, we can apply the attack described in Sect. 3.2 on the words $S_0^{\texttt{outer}}$ and $S_4^{\texttt{outer}}$. The disadvantage of this first fall-back is that it requires an additional measurement, covering the first rounds of the outer compression.

A smarter alternative that does not require an additional measurement works as follows: Assume that we have already disclosed $S^{\texttt{inner}}$ and the words $S_{\texttt{word}}^{\texttt{outer}}$ for $\texttt{word} \neq 0, 4$, and assume that the Hamming weight leakage model applies to $h_{63} = e_{60}$ and $d_{63} = a_{60}$ (in rounds 59–63). Then we can compute

$$\texttt{plaintext} := \texttt{response}_0 - \Sigma_0(a_{63}) - \texttt{Maj}(a_{63}, b_{63}, c_{63}) \\ - \Sigma_1(e_{63}) - \texttt{Ch}(e_{63}, f_{63}, g_{63}) - K_{63}^{\{256\}} - W_{63}$$

for each $\texttt{challenge}$, and apply the DPA attack on plaintext plus subkey for $\texttt{subkey} := 2^{32} - S_0^{\texttt{outer}}$, since due to Eqs. (1), (3), and (16), this sum equals e_{60}, which leaks by the assumption. In this way, we get $S_0^{\texttt{outer}} = 2^{32} - \texttt{subkey}$. We use this knowledge to compute a_{64} by Eq. (16), and hence h_{63} using Eq. (1) and (3). Then, we compute

$$\texttt{plaintext} := \texttt{response}_4 - \Sigma_1(e_{63}) - \texttt{Ch}(e_{63}, f_{63}, g_{63}) - K_{63}^{\{256\}} - W_{63} - h_{63}$$

for each $\texttt{challenge}$, and we apply the DPA attack on $\texttt{plaintext} + \texttt{subkey}$ for $\texttt{subkey} := 2^{32} - S_4^{\texttt{outer}}$. Due to Eqs. (2), (3), and (20), this sum equals a_{60} and leaks by the assumption. We finally get $S_4^{\texttt{outer}} = 2^{32} - \texttt{subkey}$.

4.4 Attack on the Outer HMAC-SHA1 Secret

The attack is applicable in an equivalent manner for HMAC-SHA1. We have

$$a_{80} = \texttt{response}_0 - S_0^{\texttt{outer}} \tag{24}$$
$$a_{79} = \texttt{response}_1 - S_1^{\texttt{outer}} \tag{25}$$
$$\texttt{ROTR}^{30}(a_{78}) = \texttt{response}_2 - S_2^{\texttt{outer}} \tag{26}$$
$$\texttt{ROTR}^{30}(a_{77}) = \texttt{response}_1 - S_3^{\texttt{outer}} \tag{27}$$
$$\texttt{ROTR}^{30}(a_{76}) = \texttt{response}_1 - S_4^{\texttt{outer}} \tag{28}$$

Note that $\texttt{ham}(\texttt{ROTR}^{30}(a)) = \texttt{ham}(a)$. Assumed that the Hamming weight leakage model applies for the intermediates $a_{76}, ..., a_{80}$, we can set $\texttt{plaintext} = \texttt{response}_{\texttt{word}}$ and apply the DPA attack on $\texttt{plaintext} + \texttt{subkey}$ on $\texttt{subkey} = 2^{32} - S_{\texttt{word}}^{\texttt{outer}}$ in order to disclose $S_{\texttt{word}}^{\texttt{outer}}$ for word in 0,..,4.

The intermediate a_{80} is again less persistent than $a_{76}, ..., a_{79}$ and the leakage might be too small for the disclosure of $S_0^{\texttt{outer}}$. In this case, the following optimization can be applied: Assume that we have already disclosed $S_{\texttt{word}}^{\texttt{outer}}$ for $\texttt{word} = 1, 2, 3, 4$. Then, we can compute

$$\texttt{plaintext} := \texttt{response}_0 - \texttt{ROTL}^5(a_{79}) - (b_{79} \oplus c_{79} \oplus d_{79}) - K_{79} - W_{79},$$

and for $\texttt{subkey} := 2^{32} - S_0^{\texttt{outer}}$, by Eq. (10), we get

$$\texttt{plaintext} + \texttt{subkey} = e_{79}.$$

Note that $\texttt{ham}(e_{79}) = \texttt{ham}(a_{75})$. If the Hamming weight leakage model applies to e_{79}, the DPA attack on $\texttt{plaintext} + \texttt{subkey}$ will finally reveal $S_0^{\texttt{outer}}$.

4.5 Preliminary Conclusion

We have presented a new attack on $S^{\texttt{inner}}$ with minimal leakage assumptions. The attack only requires the leakage of the "fat" variables a (and e). The combination with the attack [9] possibly provides the strongest generic attack method on HMAC-SHA1/SHA2.

5 Application to the BQ27Z561 Battery Authentication

5.1 Battery Authentication for Counterfeit Prevention

Battery authentication is required to distinguish a fake – and potentially dangerous – battery from an original one. Since battery counterfeits of popular mass products promise high benefits, battery authentication needs to counter a high attack potential. The BQ27Z561 fuel gauge IC [12] provides an HMAC-SHA256 based battery authentication. Texas Instruments specifies a proprietary 2-wire protocol called HDQ for sending commands to the fuel gauge. We wanted to figure out the required attack potential to disclose the authentication secrets $(S^{\texttt{inner}}, S^{\texttt{outer}})$ of a fuel gauge using DPA.

5.2 Measurement Setup

For the DPA measurements, we used the BQ27Z561EVM evaluation module [13]. Note that the command "AltManufacturerAccess() 0x0037 Authentication Key" specified for programming a new authentication key did not work for the fuel gauge on the evaluation module. Nevertheless, the device responded to the authenticate command. We concluded that the device had some default test authentication key not available from the public specifications. This was an ideal starting point for a black-box DPA. We used a self-made USB-to-HDQ adapter [11] for sending the authentication command with randomized `challenge` from the PC to the fuel gauge, and to provide a trigger signal to the oscilloscope in order to start the sampling of the power trace X. We removed resistors R5,R7,R17,R20 of the evaluation module to isolate the BQ27Z561 under test from the the other ICs on the PCB. We inserted a 0.6 Ohm shunt resistor between BAT+ and BAT to measure the current during the HMAC computation. We removed capacitor C3, which would suppress data dependent voltage variations at the test point. The voltage at the test point close to BAT was measured via a 220 nF capacitor as "voltage probe" (Fig. 6). The power traces were sampled with a LeCroy WavePro 7300 oscilloscope with 3 GHz bandwidth at a sample rate of 1 GS/s for all measurements.

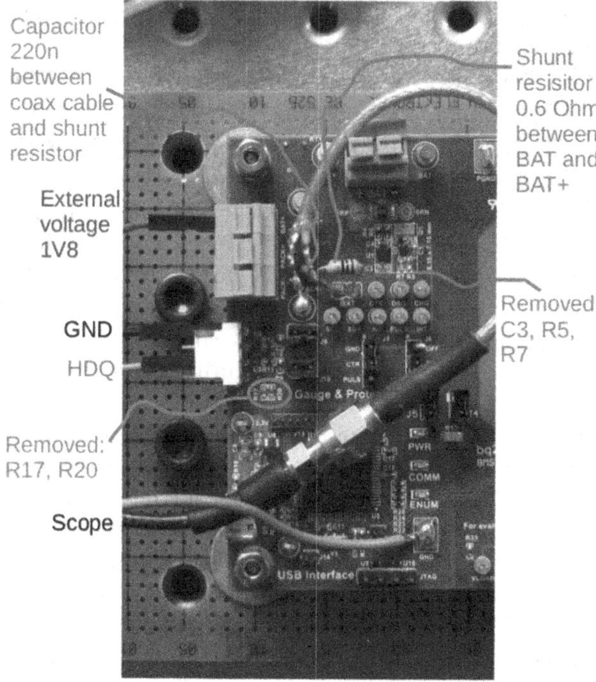

Fig. 6. Voltage probing.

5.3 Measurements

The power traces show a clock cycles structure with some variation ("jitter") in the clock cycle length of around 240 ns. Furthermore, they provide a clear SHA256 round structure within two blocks of 64 rounds – corresponding to the inner and outer compression within the HMAC-SHA256. All SHA rounds up to round 15 have an identical shape. From round 16 on, each round shows an additional activity, presumably related to the SHA-256 message schedule.

We made four measurements à 50 k traces and 2 million sample points per trace of the first seven rounds of the inner compression as required for the attack described in Sect. 3.2: measurement 0 with all challenge bytes randomized, measurement 1 with the first four challenge bytes zero, measurement 2 with the first eight challenge bytes zero, and measurement 3 with the first 12 challenge bytes zero. A fifth measurement of 50 k traces and 2 million sample points per trace covered the last seven rounds of the outer compression as required for our new attack method described in Sect. 4. The blue curve in Fig. 7 is an average over 50 k aligned traces covering five SHA256 rounds.

5.4 Disclosure of the Inner Secret

Denote $\texttt{roi}_{W_0}$ the set of sample points x where $\texttt{plaintext} := W_0$ has a significant (byte-wise) chi-squared leakage. The restriction of the average trace to $\texttt{roi}_{W_0}$ is colored magenta in Fig. 7.

As described in Sect. 3.2, we first tried to abuse this leakage and apply the attack of Sect. 3.1 on $\texttt{plaintext} + \texttt{subkey}$ for $\texttt{subkey} = \alpha(a_0, ..., h_0, K_0^{\{256\}})$ and $\texttt{subkey} = \epsilon(a_0, ..., h_0, K_0^{\{256\}})$ using measurement 0. To avoid a mismatch between α and ϵ, we had to find an α-sub-region and an ϵ-sub-region of $\texttt{roi}_{W_0}$. For the restriction $\texttt{roi}'_{W_0}$ of $\texttt{roi}_{W_0}$ to rounds $t = 0, 1$, this is challenging, because $\texttt{roi}'_{W_0}$ is very distributed and also covers the leakage of different ephemeral intermediates. For the restriction $\texttt{roi}''_{W_0}$ of $\texttt{roi}_{W_0}$ to rounds $t = 2, 3, 4$, it's easier: there, we could identify the sample points where the values a_1 and e_1 leak in the copy operations $b2 = a1$, $f2 = e1$, $c3 = b2$, $g3 = f2$, $d4 = c3$, and $h4 = g3$ (cf. Sect. 2.4). This allowed us to identify manually disjoint regions of interest $\texttt{roi}''_{\alpha_0}$ and $\texttt{roi}''_{\epsilon_0}$ as subsets of $\texttt{roi}''_{W_0}$.

The function $\texttt{disclose\_subkey}$ of the pseudo-code in Fig. 3 provided a clear champion α_0 (resp. ϵ_0) for the restriction of the 50k traces X of measurement 0 to $\texttt{roi}''_{\alpha_0}$ (resp. $\texttt{roi}''_{\epsilon_0}$). To optimize the attack for later-on, we extended this region of interest to rounds 1 and 2 using the gained "knowledge" of the word α_0 (resp. ϵ_0): we set $\texttt{roi}'_{\alpha_0}$ (resp. $\texttt{roi}'_{\epsilon_0}$) the set of sample points $x \in \texttt{roi}'_{W_0}$ such that the function $\texttt{disclose\_subkey\_byte}$ applied on the array X_x returned the known byte $\alpha_0[\texttt{byte}]$ (resp. $\epsilon_0[\texttt{byte}]$). In this way, we obtained the complete region of interest $\texttt{roi}_{\alpha_0}$ (resp. $\texttt{roi}_{\epsilon_0}$) as the disjoint union $\texttt{roi}'_{\alpha_0} \cup \texttt{roi}''_{\alpha_0}$ (resp. $\texttt{roi}'_{\epsilon_0} \cup \texttt{roi}''_{\epsilon_0}$).

For $t = 1, 2, 3$ we obtained $\texttt{roi}_{\alpha_t}$ (resp. $\texttt{roi}_{\epsilon_t}$) simply by shifting $\texttt{roi}_{\alpha_0}$ (resp. $\texttt{roi}_{\epsilon_0}$) t rounds to the right, and applied the attack $\texttt{disclose\_subkey}$ of the pseudo-code in Fig. 3 on measurement t restricted to $\texttt{roi}_{\alpha_t}$ (resp. $\texttt{roi}_{\epsilon_t}$). For each t, we obtained a clear champion α_t (resp. ϵ_t).

From these values and one known W_3 in measurement 3, we computed back to $S^{\texttt{inner}} = (a_0, ..., h_0)$. At this point, it was not possible to verify the correctness of $S^{\texttt{inner}}$ on a data level. However, we found a significant correlation of the input $\texttt{digest}^{\texttt{inner}}$ with samples X_x at the beginning of the outer compression which proved the correctness of the disclosed $S^{\texttt{inner}}$.

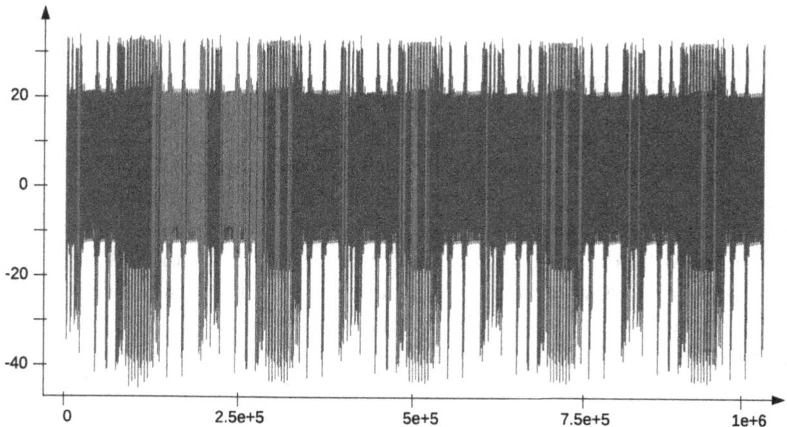

Fig. 7. Average trace (blue) and regions of interest for a_1 and e_1 (magenta). (Color figure online)

5.5 Optimizations

With the knowledge of $S^{\texttt{inner}}$, we could use rounds 5–9 as profiling traces with randomized challenge and randomized initial state in order to optimize the described attack. A first optimization is the selection of the regions of interest $\texttt{roi}_{\alpha,t}$ and $\texttt{roi}_{\epsilon,t}$. Computing them from traces with randomized initial state removes any bias due to dependencies of the fixed initial state in round $t = 0$.

A second optimization is principal component analysis (PCA) [1]. PCA is a method for optimizing the signal-to-ratio by projecting the $\texttt{length}(\texttt{roi})$-dimensional signal space to only a few principal components of the "signal covariance matrix". PCA is optimal, only, after a "pre-whitening" transformation [6]. After pre-whitening, the noise distribution is spherical symmetric and has standard deviation 1 (in each direction). This property remains after projection to the principal components.

Figure 8 shows for example the projection of the 256 means over traces with fixed intermediate $a_3[0]$ to the first three principal components, colored by the Hamming weight $\texttt{ham}(a_3[0])$. This picture clearly indicates three things: first, the means are perfectly sorted in the first principal component by their Hamming weight. This shows that the Hamming weight is a very good leakage model.

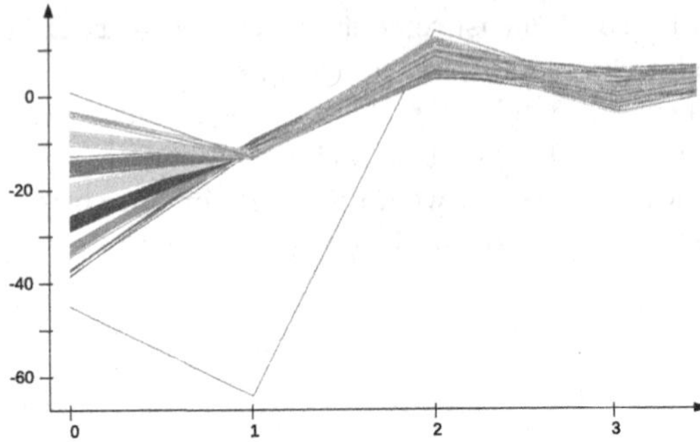

Fig. 8. Mean with fixed a_3 after PCA transformation colored by Hamming weight.

Secondly, the variance of means at this first component is big enough to have a good chance to disclose the Hamming weight already by a single trace template attack. Third, the means at the second principal component show that a value zero of $a_3[0]$ can be detected in a single trace in which it appears by a suitable template attack. The latter effect was however much less significant for other bytes. Therefore, we did not switch to template attacks.

Applying the described optimizations, we were able to implement a "profiled DPA with PCA" such that it revealed all bytes of $S^{\texttt{inner}}$ with 4×250 traces in the exploitation.

5.6 Disclosure of the Outer Secret

From the attack on $S^{\texttt{inner}}$ we already knew the regions of interest $\texttt{roi}_{a_t}$ and $\texttt{roi}_{e_t}$ for $t < 16$. Taking the time intervals of the message schedule into consideration, we could easily identify suitable $\texttt{roi}_{a_t}$ and $\texttt{roi}_{e_t}$ for $t \geq 16$, as well. We could therefore apply the attack on $S^{\texttt{outer}}$ described in Sect. 4 directly on the last 5 rounds of the outer compression. Applying similar optimization to those of Sect. 4.3, the attack could be realized with 250 traces.

5.7 Conclusion

We have shown that the combination of the known attack on $S^{\texttt{inner}}$ described in Sect. 3.2 and the new attack on $S^{\texttt{outer}}$ described in Sect. 4 is a realistic thread for authentication ICs. We conclude that counterfeit prevention should not solely rely on HMAC-SHA1/SHA2 authentication schemes without proven (hardware) security. As an alternative or fall-back, the implementer can choose hardware intrinsic authentication features for accessory authentication [10], where DPA is not applicable.

Acknowledgments. I would like to thank Sylvain Guilley, Colin O'Flynn, Yaacov Belenky, and the referees for their valuable feedback.

References

1. Archambeau, C., Peeters, E., Standaert, F.-X., Quisquater, J.-J.: Template attacks in principal subspaces. In: Goubin, L., Matsui, M. (eds.) CHES 2006. LNCS, vol. 4249, pp. 1–14. Springer, Heidelberg (2006). https://doi.org/10.1007/11894063_1
2. Belaid, S., Bettale, L., Dottax, E., Genelle, L., Rondepierre, F.: Differential power analysis of HMAC SHA-2 in the hamming weight model. In: SECRYPT 2013–10th International Conference on Security and Cryptography, Reykjavik, Iceland. Scitepress (2013). https://hal.inria.fr/hal-00872410
3. Belenky, Y., Dushar, I., Teper, V., Chernyshchyk, H., Azriel, L., Kreimer, Y.: First full-fledged side channel attack on HMAC-SHA-2. In: Bhasin, S., De Santis, F. (eds.) COSADE 2021. LNCS, vol. 12910, pp. 31–52. Springer, Cham (2021). https://doi.org/10.1007/978-3-030-89915-8_2
4. Collin, S.: Side channel attacks against the Solo key - HMAC-SHA256 scheme. Ph.D. thesis, UCL - Ecole polytechnique de Louvain (2020). http://hdl.handle.net/2078.1/thesis:26545
5. Dang, Q.: FIPS 180-2, Secure Hash Standard. Federal Information Processing Standards (NIST FIPS), National Institute of Standards and Technology, Gaithersburg, MD (2012)
6. Jutten, C., Herault, J.: Blind separation of sources, part I: an adaptive algorithm based on neuromimetic architecture. Signal Process. **24**(1), 1–10 (1991)
7. McEvoy, R., Tunstall, M., Murphy, C.C., Marnane, W.P.: Differential power analysis of HMAC based on SHA-2, and countermeasures. In: Kim, S., Yung, M., Lee, H.-W. (eds.) WISA 2007. LNCS, vol. 4867, pp. 317–332. Springer, Heidelberg (2007). https://doi.org/10.1007/978-3-540-77535-5_23
8. Oswald, D.: Side-channel attacks on SHA-1-based product authentication ICs. In: Homma, N., Medwed, M. (eds.) CARDIS 2015. LNCS, vol. 9514, pp. 3–14. Springer, Cham (2016). https://doi.org/10.1007/978-3-319-31271-2_1
9. Rohatgi, P., Marson, M.: NSA suite B crypto, keys, and side channel attacks. RSA Conference (2013). https://www.rambus.com/nsa-suite-b-crypto-keys-and-side-channel-attacks-2013-rsa-conference/
10. Schuhmacher, F.: Software-based self-testing for the authentication of car components. In: 18th escar Europe: The World's Leading Automotive Cyber Security Conference (2020)
11. Segrids GmbH: Software for IC programming, testing, debugging and hacking using python3, gcc and the arduino due (2021). https://github.com/segrids/testbench
12. Texas Instruments: bq27z561 - Technical Reference Manual (2018). https://www.ti.com/lit/ug/sluubo7/sluubo7.pdf
13. Texas Instruments: bq27z561EVM-011 EVM Single-Cell Impedance Track Technology - Users Guide (2018). https://www.ti.com/lit/pdf/sluubu0
14. U.S. Department of Commerce, National Institute of Standards and Technology: FIPS 198-1, The Keyed-Hash Message Authentication Code (HMAC). Federal Information Processing Standards (NIST FIPS), National Institute of Standards and Technology, Gaithersburg, MD (2008)

Masking

Provable Secure Software Masking in the Real-World

Arthur Beckers, Lennert Wouters(✉), Benedikt Gierlichs, Bart Preneel, and Ingrid Verbauwhede

imec-COSIC, KU Leuven, Kasteelpark Arenberg 10, 3001 Heverlee, Belgium
{arthur.beckers,lennert.wouters,benedikt.gierlichs,bart.preneel, ingrid.verbauwhede}@esat.kuleuven.be

Abstract. We evaluate eight implementations of provable secure side-channel masking schemes that were published in top-tier academic venues such as Eurocrypt, Asiacrypt, CHES and SAC. Specifically, we evaluate the side-channel attack resistance of eight open-source and first-order side-channel protected AES-128 software implementations on the Cortex-M4 platform. Using a T-test based leakage assessment we demonstrate that all implementations produce first-order leakage with as little as 10,000 traces. Additionally, we demonstrate that all except for two Inner Product Masking based implementations are vulnerable to a straight-forward correlation power analysis attack. We provide an assembly level analysis showing potential sources of leakage for two implementations. Some of the studied implementations were provided for benchmarking purposes. We demonstrate several flaws in the benchmarking procedures and question the usefulness of the reported performance numbers in the face of the implementations' poor side-channel resistance. This work serves as a reminder that practical evaluations cannot be omitted in the context of side-channel analysis.

Keywords: Side-Channel Analysis · Leakage Assessment · Masking in Software

1 Introduction

Cryptographic primitives are designed to thwart cryptanalytic attacks such as differential and linear cryptanalysis. Even though these cryptographic primitives are deemed theoretically and cryptanalytically secure, their real-world implementations can still be vulnerable to attack. Side-channel attacks are one example of such implementation attacks. The field of Side-Channel Analysis (SCA) studies how unintentional side-channel leakage, produced by a cryptographic primitive implemented on a specific platform, can be used to extract secret information (e.g. the cryptographic key). To mount such a side-channel attack one typically executes the cryptographic operations several times while acquiring side-channel information. Side-channel information can come in many shapes and forms and

J. Balasch and C. O'Flynn (Eds.): COSADE 2022, LNCS 13211, pp. 215–235, 2022.
https://doi.org/10.1007/978-3-030-99766-3_10

can, for example, be acquired by passively monitoring execution time, power consumption and electromagnetic (EM) emanations.

SCA research was instigated by Kocher et al. through their seminal work on Differential Power Analys (DPA) in 1999 [19]. Here the attacker exploits the dependency between the secret data being processed on the device and its power consumption. To mitigate these SCA attacks an implementer generally tries to break the relation between the power consumption and the secret data being handled by the device. A common technique to achieve this is the use of masking [6,14]. In a masked implementation the relation is broken by splitting up the sensitive intermediates in multiple random shares. Each of these shares is constructed such that on their own they are uncorrelated to the sensitive data. Depending on the masking scheme the implementation is given a security order. A masked implementation is said to be d^{th}-order secure if the implementation can withstand an attack exploiting up to d shares. Since the introduction of DPA different flavors of masking schemes have been proposed to counter SCA attacks. Masking schemes require randomness and the introduction of the shares comes with a large computational overhead especially when going to higher orders. The goal of many published schemes is therefore to minimize the randomness requirement and the execution time without compromising on security. Another aspect is to prove masking schemes secure in more realistic models. Many of the proposed schemes however focus on improving the timing and randomness requirement while neglecting to evaluate the practical side-channel security of their implementation. However, it has been shown many times that it is not easy to effectively protect an implementation with masking [3,9]. The estimated execution-time overheads lose their meaning if benchmarking is not performed rigorously. If the benchmarked implementation does not provide the claimed side-channel resistance it becomes impossible to judge the additional overhead involved in resolving the leakage. Said differently, there is no point in comparing the performance of two insecure implementations for which the additional overhead to secure them is unknown.

1.1 Contributions

In this paper we benchmark and evaluate the side-channel resistance of multiple software masked AES implementations published in a wide range of academic venues including Eurocrypt, Asiacrypt, CHES and SAC. The evaluated implementations are listed in Table 1. The evaluations and benchmarks are performed on the same ARM Cortex-M4 target platform. The implementations were evaluated for their side-channel security using test vector leakage assessment (TVLA) [13] and correlation power analysis (CPA) [5]. During our leakage assessment all of the evaluated implementations showed TVLA leakage and nearly all of them could be broken with a straightforward CPA attack in our security evaluation. Additionally, all schemes were benchmarked using multiple configurations of the platform's clock tree. Our analysis reveals several discrepancies between cycle counts measured by us and the cycle counts reported by the authors. To reduce the risk of benchmarking mistakes and guarantee the relevance of the proposed implementation we propose a set of recommendations which should be followed when publishing side-channel secure software implementations.

1.2 Related Work

In the academic literature a multitude of masking schemes and implementations have been proposed. We collected AES implementations for multiple of these masking schemes. An overview of the schemes for which we found an implementation either online or by contacting the authors can be seen in Table 1. These implementations will be the center of this work. These schemes were selected purely on the basis of a software implementation being available which could be ported to our target platform. All these schemes implement side-channel countermeasures which are solely based on masking. Implementations containing other countermeasures such as random delays or shuffling of the intermediates (e.g. the side-channel protected ANSSI implementation [4]) were not considered in this work.

Table 1. An overview of the evaluated implementations. Note that implementations for [8,10,24] are provided as part of [10].

Paper title	Published venue	Reference
Provably Secure Higher-Order Masking of AES	CHES 2010	[24]
Higher order masking of look-up tables	Eurocrypt 2014	[8]
All the AES You Need on Cortex-M3 and M4	SAC 2016	[25]
Consolidating Inner Product Masking	Asiacrypt 2017	[2]
First-Order Masking with Only Two Random Bits	CCS-TIS 2019	[15]
Side-channel Masking with Pseudo-Random Generator	Eurocrypt 2020	[10]
Detecting faults in inner product masking scheme	JCEN 2020	[7]
Fixslicing AES-like Ciphers	TCHES 2021	[1]

Masking aims at removing the dependency between the intermediate values and the secret key. This is achieved by splitting up the intermediate values into random shares. The number of shares determines the security order of the scheme. Ideally if one has d+1 shares an attacker needs to exploit leakage of d+1 shares in order to mount a successful attack. In their work [3] Balasch et al. showed how, if one does not pay close attention when implementing a theoretically secure masking scheme, a reduction in the security order can occur. This is because the leakage models on which the masking schemes are based assume independent leakage of the intermediate values. However, in software implementations the independent leakage assumption is often broken by transition based leakage. This for instance occurs when values stored in registers are overwritten leading to a recombination of the shares. The occurrence of transition based leakage can often be attributed to overwriting a register in the register file, but there are also other micro-architectural leakage mechanisms present in microcontrollers as was shown by McCann et al. [20].

Balasch et al. propose to increase the security order to compensate for these micro-architectural transition based leakages [3]. Alternatively, the masking scheme can be carefully implemented taking all potential sources of leakage into account. Such side-channel leakage simulators require meticulously engineered leakage models specific for each target platform. McCann et al. introduced ELMO [20], a leakage simulator with a specifically engineered leakage model for the Cortex-M0. This work was later extended by Shelton et al., which proposed Rosita [26] a tool that patches the underlying assembly instructions based on a target specific leakage model to reduce the side-channel leakage. Tools such as Elmo [20], Rosita [26] and CoCo [12] demonstrate that relatively basic microcontrollers have multiple hidden leakage sources that can be difficult to discover and compensate for.

The implementations evaluated in this work cover a wide variety of underlying masking schemes most of which are proven to be secure under the d-probing model introduced by Ishai-Sahai-Wagner [17]. In [24] the authors propose a generic higher-order boolean masking scheme for AES. The proposed scheme allows to construct masked implementations with an arbitrary security order. The software implementation for this scheme was provided by Coron et al. and served as a baseline to compare to their proposed schemes [10]. In [10] the authors also use boolean masking based on the ISW scheme. However, their main goal is to try and reduce the number of true random bits required by the scheme by using a combination of true and pseudo random number generators. The repository implementing [24] and [10] also contains implementations for the masking schemes introduced in [8]. Here a generalized table based masking scheme is proposed which can be extended to any security order. All the previous implementations were implemented in C in a straightforward and byte-oriented manner.

Schwabe and Stoffelen provide a highly optimized bitsliced AES-128 implementation protected with first-order boolean masking using Trichina AND gates [25]. Their optimised assembly implementation targets ARM Cortex-M3 and Cortex-M4 based microcontrollers. In [15] Gross et al. implement a first order boolean masking scheme. Their design includes a novel masked AND gate which allows for the reuse of randomness, reducing the number of true random bits required to two. Gross et al. provide a highly optimized assembly implementation for the ARM Cortex-M4 platform. Adomnicai and Peyrin further reduce the cycle count of this implementation by optimising the linear operations using a fixed-slicing construction [1]. The fixed-slicing implementation is based on the implementation provided in [15] and uses the same S-Box.

In addition to boolean masking based implementations we also evaluate two Inner Product Masking (IPM) based implementations. Out of all publications listed in Table 1 only the IPM work by Balasch et al. includes a practical side-channel evaluation [2]. The second IPM based implementation combines IPM with a fault attack countermeasure [7]. In this work we will only evaluate the side-channel resistance of the implementation. The implementation of [7] is publicly available and is written in C.

All the implementations evaluated in this work (see Table 1) were used as provided by the authors, without performing any modifications to the code besides adding GPIO triggers and cycle counters. The analysis performed on the collected traces is straightforward and straightforward to replicate using open-source side-channel toolboxes such as the ChipWhisperer project [21] or eShard's SCAred [11].

Note that most implementations are provided by the authors of the underlying masking scheme. Therefore, we assume that the respective authors verified the adherence of their implementation to their proposed masking scheme. Benchmarking results based on a flawed implementation would be meaningless and a thorough security evaluation requires auditing the code. Additionally, we note that some authors provide a disclaimer stating that the practical side-channel security of the provided implementation was not evaluated and that the implementation is provided for the purpose of benchmarking. However, throughout this work we will provide several examples of flawed benchmark results and argue that such results do not provide a realistic estimate for the additional overhead required to secure the implementation.

Finally, for one implementation the authors state in their paper: "We also provide [...] a masked implementation that is secure against first-order power analysis attacks" [25].

2 Side-Channel Analysis

This section covers SCA of open-source first order protected AES implementations. We start by detailing the used measurement setup followed by leakage assessment and CPA for each implementation.

2.1 Measurement Setup

All of the studied implementations are compiled for, and executed on the same STM32F415 (Cortex-M4) microcontroller, with the Cortex-M4 being the target platform for most of the studied implementations. Each implementation is compiled using the same toolchain[1], compiler optimizations were mimicked from makefiles provided by the respective authors. Consequently, most C based implementations were compiled using `-O3`, except for the IPM based implementations that were compiled using `-O1`. These compiler optimizations can have an impact on the side-channel security of the implementations, but also impact the benchmarking results discussed in Sect. 3. It is thus important to evaluate both the side-channel security and the performance of an implementation using the same compiler flags. As later discussed in Sect. 3, the execution time of a side-channel protected implementation may be meaningless if the implementation leaks side-channel information.

[1] `arm-none-eabi toolchain release 8-2019-q3`.

Additionally, each implementation is evaluated using the same clock tree configuration using an 8 MHz external clock and 24 MHz core operating frequency.

For the acquisition setup we used a NewAE CW308 UFO board in combination with a STM32F415 target board, a Mini-Circuits ZFL-1000LN+ amplifier and a Tektronix DPO7254C oscilloscope. All measurements were acquired using a sample rate of 200 MS/s with the oscilloscope's internal 20 MHz lowpass filter enabled. The oscilloscope's vertical range was adjusted for each implementation to minimize quantization noise. Similar results are likely achievable using the low cost and open-source ChipWhisperer-Lite side-channel evaluation board [22].

2.2 Leakage Assessment

We performed a fixed vs random TVLA for each of the evaluated implementations [13]. Each implementation was evaluated using the same fixed key, the same fixed plaintext was used for the fixed set during each evaluation. We used the fixed key and plaintext values suggested in [13].

We limit the scope of this evaluation to first order protected implementations as not all of the evaluated works include higher order implementations. Furthermore, Balasch et al. demonstrated that a straightforward implementation of an n-th order protected implementation protects against $n - 1$ order attacks [3]. While higher order software implementations are less likely to leak in the first order they are likely to exhibit multivariate leakage at an order lower than intended by the design. Given that some of the higher order implementations require many millions of CPU cycles the evaluation would quickly become impractical.

Figure 1 shows the TVLA results using 10,000 measurements for each implementation. The TVLA based leakage assessment provides a high degree of confidence that these first-order masked implementations do in fact produce first-order leakage on the target platform (Cortex-M4) using the measurement setup documented in Sect. 2.1. At this point in the evaluation it is clear that the evaluated implementations do not live up to their claims. However, while TVLA based leakage assessment is a useful tool it does not allow us to compare the side-channel security of these implementations or to draw conclusions on how straightforward it would be to extract the secret key.

Note that the implementation provided as part of [2] (Consolidating Inner Product Masking) was deemed to be leakage free up to 1M traces. We consider determining the exact reason for this discrepancy out of scope as too many variables are unknown and beyond our control. Note that when compared to [2] we are using a different lab environment, physical side-channel, measurement setup and compiler version. Put differently, the only similarities between our leakage assessments are the used C source code and the use of a Cortex-M4 based microcontroller as evaluation target.

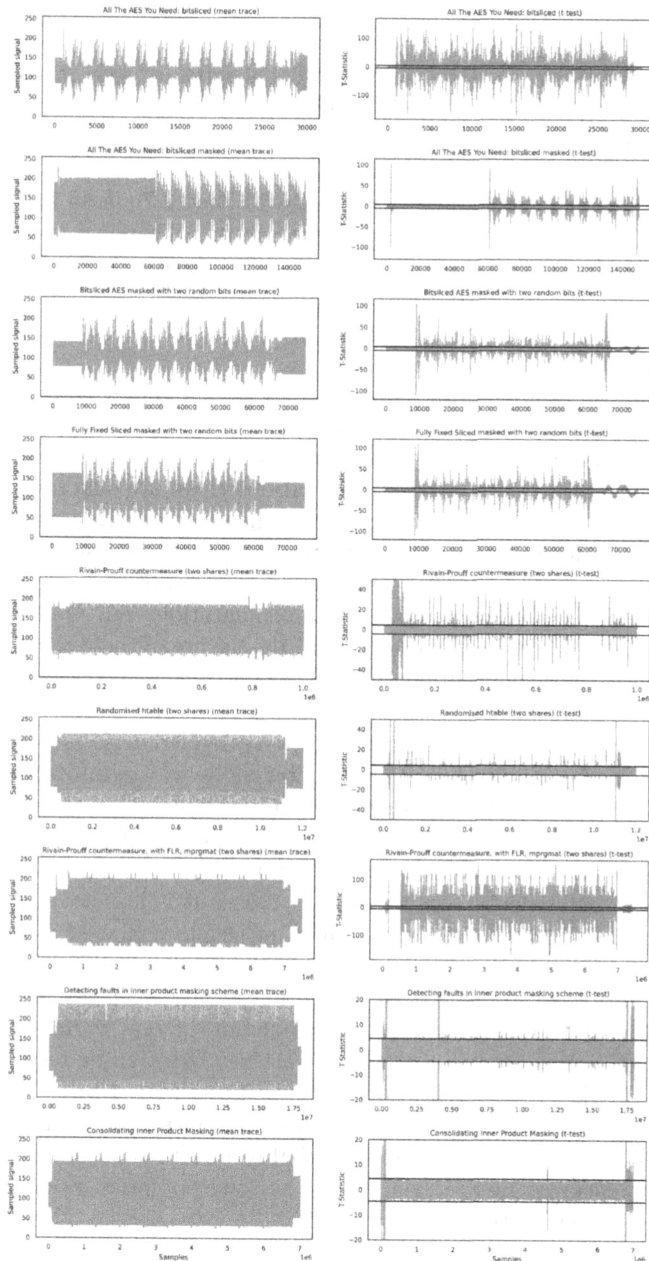

Fig. 1. TVLA results for the evaluated software implementations. The topmost plot contains the results for an unprotected bitsliced implementation. All other plots contain results for first order protected software implementations, yet exhibit clear first order leakage. This is evident from the T-statistic surpassing the ± 4.5 boundary marked by black horizontal lines. Note that big peaks towards the start and end in the T-statistic trace likely correspond to input and output leakage respectively.

2.3 CPA Attack Results

The most straightforward attack on unprotected software AES implementations is a CPA attack in which the leakage model is assumed to be the Hamming weight (HW) of the first round S-Box output or last round S-box input.

A first-order protected implementation should not be susceptible to such a first-order attack. However, as demonstrated in Sect. 2.2, these first-order protected implementations leak first-order information. Therefore, it makes sense for us to try and mount a first-order attack using the classical S-box output as the target intermediate. This type of unprofiled attack would arguably be the first thing any attacker would try, making it the bare minimum side-channel attack to protect from.

To evaluate the studied implementations we mounted first-order CPA attacks targeting both the first round S-box output and the last round S-box input. For the byte-oriented implementations (those provided by [2,7,10]) we target the first key byte. Among the evaluated implementations there are also several bitsliced implementations for which the attack strategy needs to be slightly modified. The bitsliced implementations process two AES-block simultaneously. In the bitsliced representation each 32-bit state register contains one bit of each of the state bytes from each block. Unprotected bitsliced implementations can often be attacked by targeting a single state bit. Nevertheless, the nature of these implementations results in more algorithmic noise as a single bit (out of 32) is being targeted. The implementations provided in [25] and [15] assume the use of AES in counter mode, therefore we also use the implementation provided in [1] as a counter mode implementation. Because of the use of counter mode we are limited to attacking a single bit in the first round. However, when carrying out an attack on the last round we can target two bits (one bit from each block being processed).

Figure 2 provides the results for each CPA attack. Even though we were able to attack most implementations with relative ease it is important to note that this does not mean that the underlying masking scheme is flawed. Neither does it show that one masking scheme is more secure than another. It does demonstrate that a straightforward software implementation of a theoretically secure masking scheme is unlikely to live up to its expectations in the real world.

These results demonstrate that the correct key byte can be recovered for six out of eight masked implementations using a first-order attack. Notably only the implementations where inner product masking is applied cannot be attacked with a classical CPA attack. This is probably due to mechanism behind the accidental unmasking. In Sect. 2.4 we discuss one potential leakage source for some of the implementations.

CPA Elaboration per Implementation. Figure 2 contains a few interesting and/or surprising results. Unsurprising is the fact that an unprotected, yet bitsliced implementation can be attacked with ease (topmost plot). This result is included as a reference. The protected bitsliced implementations require slightly

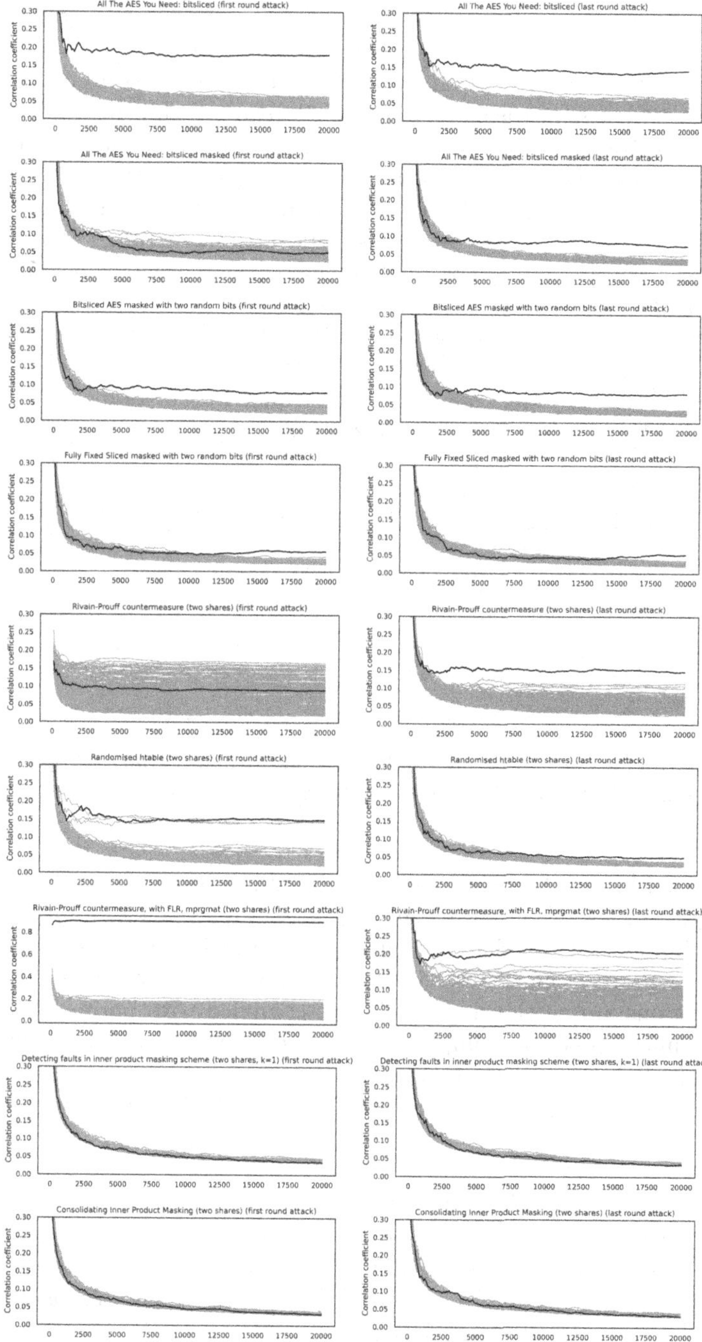

Fig. 2. CPA results for the evaluated software implementations. The plots show the evolution of the correlation coefficient (Y-axis) versus the number of traces (X-axis) used for the attack. The correlation coefficient for the correct key guess is shown in black.

more traces to result in a successful attack, but the exact same attack strategy applied for the unprotected implementation can be used.

Note that the attack on the bitsliced AES implementation from [25] (second row) was only successful (using at most 20,000 traces) while attacking the last round. This is most likely the result of transition based leakage occurring at the S-Box input as will be explained in Sect. 2.4. Additionally it is interesting to note that fixsliced implementations, which are based on the implementations masked with two random bits, require significantly more traces to recover the key. This may indicate that the original implementation provided in [15] contains an additional implementation mistake in the linear layers.

Interestingly, the SecMultFLR implementation provided by Coron et al. appears to not provide any side-channel protection in the first round (Fig. 2, 7th row). Figure 3 shows that the lack of side-channel protection can be partially attributed to the use of compiler optimizations.

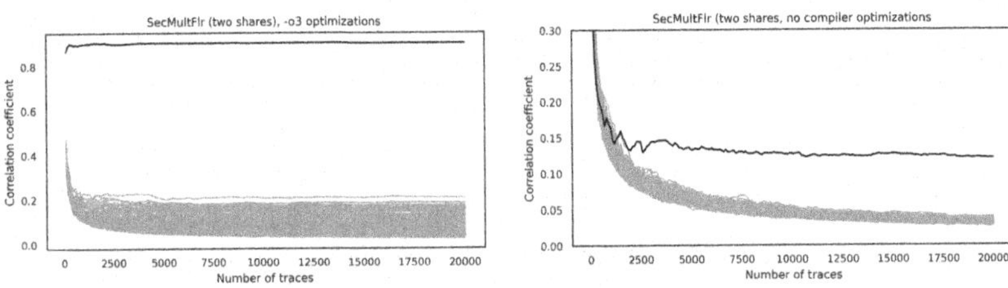

Fig. 3. CPA results when targeting the first round of the SecMultFlr implementation with (left) and without (right) compiler optimizations enabled.

Finally, neither of the IPM-based implementations appear to be vulnerable to the classical CPA attack up to 20,000 traces. This is likely because accidental recombinations of the shares, resulting in transition based leakage, do not directly reveal secret information in the IPM scheme. Note that both of these implementations are written in C and were compiled with optimizations. This shows that masking schemes implemented in software which do not suffer from security order reduction by transitional leakage are less prone to implementation mistakes and therefore an interesting field of study for future research.

2.4 Root Cause Analysis

From Fig. 2 it is clear that it is often easier to attack the last round S-box input compared to the first round S-box output. To investigate why this is the case we performed a manual root cause analysis for the boolean masked bitsliced AES implementation and the bitsliced AES implementation masked using two random bits.

In order to speed up our analysis we employed an emulator to pinpoint the different instructions which could potentially lead to a successful attack.

We emulated the leakage of register updates with both the Hamming weight and Hamming distance leakage model. In practice there are more subtle sources of leakage present in these microcontrollers which are not covered by our emulation of the leakage through register updates. McCann et al. [20] for example showed that a microcontroller can leak through recombinations between pipeline stages of buffer registers in the arithmetic logic unit (ALU). Leakage free emulated traces therefore do not guarantee a leakage free implementation but they are a good starting point. In our case the simple model proved to be sufficient to find a cause of leakage in both the boolean masked bitsliced AES implementation and the bitsliced AES implementation masked using two random bits. The fixsliced AES uses exactly the same S-box implementation as the bitsliced AES implementation masked using two random bits and therefore has the same implementation flaw.

Unsurprisingly the Hamming weight model did not show any leaking instructions. Leakage in the Hamming weight model would only occur if an instruction operated directly on an unmasked piece of data or under a biased randomness distribution, indicating a severe flaw in the masking scheme. In the Hamming distance model however multiple unintentional unmaskings were discovered for both the boolean masked implementation and the bitsliced AES implementation masked using two random bits. These leakages are a common flaw in first order boolean masked software implementations and occur when a register containing one share is overwritten by the other share leading to an unintentional recombination of the shares.

Listing 1.1 shows the part of the S-box code containing the unintended unmasking for the boolean masked bitsliced implementation. The Listing was taken from the public Github repository of the implementation [28]. The unintentional unmasking happens at line 1502 in the aes_128_ctr_bs_masked.s file. The intermediate S-box value $y3$ stored in register r9 (line 1482) gets overwritten by the previously calculated $y3m$, which was stored on the stack. Since it is a two share implementation the recombination of two shares will result in an unmasking of the data. The leakage resulting from the register overwrite is written out in full in Eq. (1)–(3) where y_{3p} is the unmasked intermediate S-box value.

$$HW\left[r9 \oplus [sp + 120]\right] \tag{1}$$

$$HW\left[y_{3m} \oplus y_3\right] \tag{2}$$

$$HW\left[y_{3p}\right] \tag{3}$$

Listing 1.2 shows the critical assembly instructions on line 1471 resulting in the observed leakage in the bitsliced AES implementation masked using two random bits. In this case the unmasking is more subtle in nature and one has to calculate back to the initial masking of the plaintext ($i_{0,P}$) and key ($k_{0,p}$) to demonstrate the accidental unmasking. The full backtracing of the unmasking is given by Eq. (4)–(8).

```
eor    r11,  r7, r11     //Exec y8 = x0 ^ x5; into r11
eor    r9, r6, r11 //Exec y3 = y5 ∧ y8; into r9
eor    r2,  r7,  r2     //Exec y9 = x0 ^ x3; into r2
str    r11, [sp, #100 ] //Store r11/y8 on stack
str    r8, [sp, #96  ] //Store r8/y10 on stack
str.w r5, [sp, #92  ] //Store r5/y20 on stack
eor    r11,  r5,  r2     //Exec y11 = y20 ^ y9; into r11
eor    r8,  r8, r11     //Exec y17 = y10 ^ y11; into r8
eor    r0,  r0, r11     //Exec y16 = t0 ^ y11; into r0
str    r8, [sp, #88  ] //Store r8/y17 on stack
eor    r5,  r4, r11     //Exec y7 = x7 ^ y11; into r5
ldr    r8, [sp, #1496] //Exec t2 = rand() % 2; into r8
str    r9, [sp, #84 ] //Store r9/y3 on stack
eor    r10, r10,  r8     //Exec u1 = u0 ^ t2; into r10
eor    r1, r10,  r1     //Exec u3 = u1 ^ u2; into r1
eor    r3,  r1,  r3     //Exec u5 = u3 ^ u4; into r3
eor    r3,  r3, r14     //Exec t2m = u5 ^ u6; into r3
and    r1,  r9, r12     //Exec u0 = y3 & y6; into r1
ldr    r10, [sp, #112 ] //Load y6m into r10
str    r12, [sp, #80  ] //Store r12/y6 on stack
and    r14,  r9, r10     //Exec u2 = y3 & y6m; into r14
ldr    r9, [sp, #120 ] //Load y3m into r9
and    r12,  r9, r12     //Exec u4 = y3m & y6; into r12
```

Listing 1.1. Assembly snippet of All the AES You Need

```
orr    r0, r12, r14   //Exec M1ORM2 = MASK1 | MASK2 into r0
eor    r2,  r7,  r9   //Exec y14 = i4 ^ i2 into r2
str.w r0, [sp, #112] //Store r0/M1ORM2 on stack
eor    r0,  r4, r10   //Exec y13 = i7 ^ i1 into r0
eor    r1,  r0, r14   //Exec hy13 = y13 ^ MASK2 into r1
eor    r3,  r4,  r7   //Exec y9 = i7 ^ i4 into r3
str.w r3, [sp, #108] //Store r3/y9 on stack
eor    r3,  r3, r14   //Exec hy9 = y9 ^ MASK2 into r3
str.w r1, [sp, #104] //Store r1/hy13 on stack
eor    r1,  r4,  r9   //Exec y8 = i7 ^ i2 into r1
eor    r6, r5, r6 //Exec t0 = i6 ∧ i5 into r6
str.w r3, [sp, #100] //Store r3/hy9 on stack
eor    r3, r6, r11 //Exec y1 = t0 ∧ i0 into r3
str.w r6, [sp, #96 ] //Store r6/t0 on stack
eor    r6, r3, r14 //Exec hy1 = y1 ∧ MASK2 into r6
eor    r7,  r6,  r7   //Exec y4 = hy1 ^ i4 into r7
```

Listing 1.2. Assembly snippet of First-Order Masking with Only Two Random Bits

In both implementations the unintentional unmasking occurs towards the start of the S-Box computation. This observation explains why the CPA attack targeting the last round S-box input is more successful.

$$HW\big[(r6) \oplus (r3 \oplus r14)\big] \tag{4}$$
$$HW\big[(t_0) \oplus (t_0 \oplus i_{0,M} \oplus M2)\big] \tag{5}$$
$$HW\big[i_{0,M} \oplus M2\big] \tag{6}$$
$$HW\big[(i_{0,P} \oplus M2 \oplus k_{0,P} \oplus M1 \oplus M2 \oplus M1 \oplus M2) \oplus M2\big] \tag{7}$$
$$HW\big[i_{0,P} \oplus k_{0,P}\big] \tag{8}$$

3 Benchmarking

While some authors did provide a disclaimer stating that the side-channel security of their implementations was not practically verified they also state that the masked implementation is provided for benchmarking purposes. Nevertheless, during the side-channel evaluation of the different implementations we noticed several discrepancies between observed and reported cycle counts.

In this section we provide a comparison between measured and reported cycle counts for all implementations and analyse a few discrepancies. Additionally, we provide insight into how seemingly small configuration changes can have a big impact on the cycle count, a metric often optimised for in the academic literature.

All execution time measurements were taken using the same STM32F415 Cortex-M4 microcontroller that was used during the side-channel evaluation and the same toolchain. As the evaluated implementations aim to be side-channel resistant we disabled both the data and instruction cache. Leaving these enabled might result in unintentional leakage, especially at higher CPU frequencies. With caches disabled the number of flash wait cycles will have a significant impact on the execution time. The number of flash wait cycles indicates the latency between requesting data from flash and the data arriving in the registers of the microcontroller. We provide measurements at clock frequencies of 24 MHz and 168 MHz to demonstrate the effect of flash wait cycles on the reported cycle count. The used platform does not require any additional flash wait cycles at 24 MHz, but requires an additional 5 wait cycles at 168 MHz. Implementations suffering from more pipeline stalls will thus be penalized in their cycle counts when the clock frequency is increased.

The internal random number generator was always clocked at 48 MHz, its maximal operating frequency. We measured the cycle count for each implementation using the Data Watchpoint and Trace (DWT) unit. As in the side-channel evaluation, all software implementations were compiled using the flags provided by the respective authors. Specifically, this means that most C implementations are compiled using `-O3` with the exception of the IPM implementation provided by Balash et al. which is compiled using `-O1` [2].

To compare the benchmarking results we used the same implementation parameters (e.g. number of shares) as those that were used by the respective authors, in some cases these parameters differ from those used during side-channel evaluation. The resulting cycle counts can be found in Table 2. Note that these cycle counts correspond to the execution of a single call to the implemented primitive. For most of the implementations this corresponds to one block of AES-128. However, for the bitsliced implementations (i.e. [1,15,25]) these cycle counts correspond to the encryption of two AES-128 blocks. Additionally, note that this table reports the number of random words collected, this number does not necessarily correspond to the number of random bytes used in the implementation.

The authors of each implementation report execution times or cycle counts in their respective publications, but the used evaluation platforms vary. We omit reported cycle counts in Table 2 if the used platforms cannot be directly compared. For example Rivain and Prouff provided cycle counts on a 8051-based platform in their original work and report 271k cycles for their three share assembly implementation [24]. It is not clear how the randomness was generated in, or provided to, this implementation. Nevertheless, Coron et al. provide their own implementation of the scheme proposed in [24] as a baseline for comparison in [10] and report a cycle count of 20.6M cycles for the three share variant. The implementations provided in [10] were benchmarked using an emulated Cortex-M3 running at 44 MHz, it is not clear which emulator was used exactly. Results from emulator based benchmarks are included in Table 2 and marked with an asterisk (*). We used the implementation provided in [10] during our benchmarks as the target platform closely matches ours. In Sect. 3.1 we demonstrate the near 76 fold increase in reported cycle-count can be largely attributed to the unrealistically low throughput TRNG used during the emulation process.

Similarly, the difference in measured and reported cycle count for the masked and bitsliced implementation provided in [25] is too big to be attributed to a small configuration or platform difference. The difference is probably due to a misconfiguration of the random number generator (RNG) during the benchmarking of the implementation. This issue will be explained in more detail in Sect. 3.1.

Table 2. Measured and reported cycle counts for the evaluated implementations.

Implementation	cycles (measured/reported)	randomness (RNG/PRNG)	clock frequency
[25]	17.5k/14.8k	328/-	24 MHz
	62.8k/-	328/-	168 MHz
[15]	6.8k/6.8k	2/-	24 MHz
	9.5k/-	2/-	168 MHz
[1]	6.2k/6k	2/-	24 MHz
	8.9k/-	2/-	168 MHz
[24] (n = 3)	651k/20.6M*	2880/-	24 MHz
	834k/-	2880/-	168 MHz
[8] (n = 3, randomized table)	9.099M/-	164,160/-	24 MHz
	13.639M/-	164,160/-	168 MHz
[8] (n = 3, randomized table word including common shares)	2.091M/-	34,032/-	24 MHz
	3.195M/-	34,032/-	168 MHz
[10] (n = 3, multiple PRG, secmultFLR)	3.608M/12M*	52/5120	24 MHz
	4.576M/-	52/5120	168 MHz
[2]	819k/-	1632/-	24 MHz
	1.272M/-	1632/-	168 MHz
[7] (n = 2, k = 1)	1.650M/-	2432/-	24 MHz
	2.283M/-	2432/-	168 MHz

3.1 Randomness Generation

Certain members of the STM32F4 family of microcontrollers have an internal TRNG. According to the public documentation the TRNG is based on multiple ring oscillators, the outputs of which are summed and used as the seed for a Linear Feedback Shift Register (LFSR) [27]. The seeded LFSR is clocked by a dedicated clock to generate 32-bit random words. The reference manual states that a new 32-bit random word is generated every 40 periods of the dedicated TRNG clock which operates at maximum 48 MHz. In addition to being independent of the main system clock, the TRNG will not operate correctly under certain clock tree configurations.

For the remainder of this discussion we assume that the TRNG is clocked at 48 MHz independent of the system clock. As the TRNG operates independently from the main clock the number of CPU clock cycles required to generate a random word can vary. When the operating frequency of the microcontroller is set to 24 MHz (i.e. half of the TRNG clock) it should take 20 MCU cycles to get a new random word. An increase in the CPU clock frequency will thus result in more CPU clock cycles to generate a random word.

This effect can be observed in Table 3, using a simple assembly loop we get a new random word every 21 CPU cycles, the same code will have to be executed more often at a higher operating frequency resulting in more CPU cycles to obtain a random word. Additionally, Table 3 provides an overview of the number of cycles required to generate a random word on different platforms running at multiple CPU clock frequencies.

Interestingly, Schwabe and Stoffelen report that their bitsliced and masked AES implementation takes 7422.6 cycles per block, of which 2132.5 cycles are used to collect the required randomness [25]. As the reported cycle counts are per block we can double them to obtain the number of cycles required for one call to their AES implementation which computes two blocks in parallel. Each call requires 328 words of randomness which, according to the reported numbers, requires 4265 cycles to collect. Looking back at Table 3 we would expect this process to take 6888 ($328 * 21$) cycles at the used 24 MHz CPU clock. Schwabe and Stoffelen made their git repository publicly available, allowing us to track down the issue that caused this cycle count discrepancy. Two recent commits (`910d446` and `56abc40`) slightly modified the clock tree configuration and the assembly code responsible for collecting randomness. Before those commits the TRNG could not operate as expected resulting in the randomness collection loop simply reading the TRNG status register and data register 328 times without actually obtaining random data. This admittedly easy to make mistake resulted in an overestimation of the TRNG throughput and the use of all zero masks, effectively resulting in an unmasked implementation. Nevertheless, it is commendable that five years after the initial commit the authors are still maintaining their repository and fixing issues.

Coron et al. used an emulator to estimate the cycle count of their implementations on a 44 MHz ARM-Cortex M3 processor [10]. The exact processor or emulator is not mentioned, but the authors report that one 32-bit random word is generated every 6000 CPU cycles. We are not challenging the numbers reported by their emulator, but it is important to use realistic numbers when comparing the use of a TRNG to that of a software PRNG in terms of cycle counts. As mentioned earlier, the STM32F4 TRNG produces a new random word every 40 clock cycles at 48 MHz. Similarly, the Microchip SAM D5x microcontrollers produce a new random word every 84 clock cycles over a wide range of clock frequencies (up to 120 MHz) [16]. This would mean that the TRNG used in [10] is 150 times slower compared to the TRNG used in the STM32F4 microcontrollers or 71 times slower compared to the SAM D5x microcontrollers.

As can be seen from Table 3 the XorShift PRNG used by Coron et al. does produce more random bits per cycle and scales better when the clock frequency on the STM32F4 is increased. Nevertheless, the use of unrealistic TRNG performance estimates results in an overestimation in the performance gained from using a software PRNG. In the extreme case these unrealistic performance estimates resulted in implementations which are more efficient (in terms of cycle count) on paper, but in fact less efficient in practice. For example, in [10] the authors claim that their three share implementation with multiple PRGs (secmultFLR) requires roughly half the number of cycles compared to the their reference implementation of [24]. From Table 2 it is clear that in practice their provided implementation requires roughly seven times more cycles compared to the reference implementation.

Table 3. Randomness generation cycle counts for different platforms and CPU clock frequencies.

platform	function	word length	cycles	clock frequency
STM32F415 Cortex-M4	polling opencm3	32 bit	27	24 MHz
		32 bit	147	168 MHz
	polling assembly	32 bit	21	24 MHz
		32 bit	147	168 MHz
	PRNG XorShift 96	64 bit	39	24 MHz
		64 bit	63	168 MHz
LPC55S69 Cortex-M33	polling assembly	32 bit	104	25 MHz
		32 bit	361	150 MHz
SAM D5x Cortex-M4	according to datasheet	32 bit	84	24 MHz
		32 bit	84	140 MHz

3.2 Benchmarking: Discussion and Conclusion

Cycle counts or execution time are popular metrics to optimise for in software implementations. New masking schemes and implementations often serve the purpose of outperforming previous work in such metrics, regardless of the real-world side-channel security. Unfortunately, results reported in the academic literature are often not directly comparable to other works or in certain cases impossible to reproduce. The need for a detailed description of the benchmarking setup is also evidenced when compiling the same implementation using different compiler versions. For example, compiling the RP implementation provided in [10] with toolchain version 7-2018-q2 results in an implementation that requires roughly 50k cycles more. In general, the masking community would benefit from a unified benchmarking process. Successful deployments of such processes were demonstrated by Kannwischer et al. as part of the PQM4 project [18] and by Renner et al. as part of the NIST Lightweight cryptography competition [23].

Table 2 demonstrates the necessity of using realistic platforms, realistic microcontroller configurations and providing detailed descriptions of the benchmarking setup. This is also evident by comparing the measured cycle counts when the clock frequency of the used platform is increased.

The use of a hardware TRNG peripheral adds another dimension to the benchmarking process. The implementer can carefully interleave the collection of randomness with other useful instructions instead of polling the TRNG status register in a blocking manner, this comes at a cost of increased implementation complexity. Similarly, some implementations waste randomness by discarding three out of four bytes produced by the TRNG. Alternatively, if cycle-count is the metric to be optimised we can also simply reduce the CPU clock frequency.

Specifically, for the STM32F415, we would be able to reduce the CPU clock frequency to 4 MHz while keeping the TRNG peripheral clocked at 48 MHz. As shown in Table 3, reducing the main CPU clock results in a trivial and meaningless reduction of the cycle count.

From this discussion it should be clear that benchmarking results depend on many factors, straightforward cycle-count comparisons without a detailed description can thus be considered meaningless. Furthermore, benchmark results for masked implementations that do not provide the claimed security level may not be meaningful, as securing the implementation will require additional unpredictable overhead.

4 Discussion and Conclusions

In this work we benchmark and evaluate the side-channel security of multiple masked software AES implementations based on a variety of masking schemes. Only two of the evaluated implementations namely [7] and [2] seem to live up to their promises. All other implementations were not side-channel secure in the claimed security order, or reported skewed benchmarking results in their respective publications.

This comes to show that a thorough side-channel evaluation is required when implementing a masking scheme. The side-channel evaluation will reveal potential implementation mistakes like a wrongly configured TRNG or dramatic over estimations of the TRNG overhead. Additionally, it will highlight micro-architectural leakage mechanisms present in the evaluation platform which are not captured by most theoretical leakage models. Compensating for these unexpected leakage sources can introduce a significant overhead. Madura et al. [26] report an overhead of up to 60% when rewriting a straightforward implementation to be free of T-Test leakage on the Cortex-M0 platform.

Most of the analysed works did not contain strong claims regarding the security of their implementations, but do offer security proofs for the used masking scheme. In those cases the provided implementations are used for benchmarks and comparisons with related work. We question the relevance of benchmarking results which do not take into account the additional unpredictable overhead required to secure the implementation.

Our work was enabled through the availability of the evaluated implementations, we want to commend the respective authors. Similar works without published implementations undoubtedly suffer from the same issues. Unfortunately, the absence of the implementations makes it impossible for anyone to evaluate and improve them.

In general, published implementations of masking schemes would benefit from a more rigorous approach to benchmarking and side-channel evaluation. Therefore, we provide a set of guidelines to be used when publishing a new side-channel secure implementation.

4.1 Recommendations

In this section we lay out some recommendations that can be used as a checklist for side-channel evaluations and benchmarks of masked software implementations. While many of these recommendations may appear obvious to an experienced practitioner they seem to be rarely applied in academic literature, as evidenced by this work.

- **Describe the side-channel setup in detail:** oscilloscope settings, filters, measurement method, probe location etc. In other words, provide all of the required information for someone to reproduce your setup. Commercially available and easily reproducible measurement setups exist (e.g. ChipWhisperer and accompanying target boards).
- **Perform a convincing side-channel leakage assessment:** An assessment should consist of two parts. First, the soundness of the side-channel measurement setup should be demonstrated by for instance performing TVLA with the masking randomness (TRNG/PRNG) disabled or by checking the Signal to Noise Ratio (SNR) of a known intermediate variable's leakage. Secondly TVLA should be performed with the countermeasures enabled. Perform a second evaluation with different fixed inputs if no leakage was detected [13] and provide the used fixed inputs.
  Note that leakage assessment is not meant to replace provable security but rather to complement it.
- **List the randomness requirement of the masking scheme.** Carefully indicate the number of bytes used for masking and the total number of random bytes acquired in the implementation.
- **Benchmark the randomness sources** used by the implementation separately. This allows to establish a trade-off between the use of TRNG and PRNG.
- **Use a realistic benchmarking platform.** Emulators are very useful tools, but as with any tool it has to be used correctly. The use of a real-world platform will provide more realistic results. Use a widely available platform for evaluation.
- **Provide all relevant platform settings:** clock setup, configuration of the caching mechanisms, flash wait cycles, TRNG clock frequency, etc.
- **Document the toolchain and compiler settings** used during the development and evaluation of the implementation.

Note that many of these recommendations can be easily addressed by providing a **public implementation**.

Acknowledgements. This work was supported in part by CyberSecurity Research Flanders with reference number VR20192203. In part by the Research Council KU Leuven C1 on Security and Privacy for Cyber-Physical Systems and the Internet of Things with contract number C16/15/058. In addition, this work was supported by the European Commission through the Horizon 2020 research and innovation programme under grant agreement Cathedral ERC Advanced Grant 695305, under grant agreement H2020-FETFLAG-2018-03-820405 QRANGE and under grant agreement H2020-DS-LEIT-2017-780108 FENTEC.

References

1. Adomnicai, A., Peyrin, T.: Fixslicing AES-like ciphers: new bitsliced AES speed records on ARM-Cortex M and RISC-V. IACR Trans. Cryptogr. Hardware Embedded Syst. **2021**(1), 402–425 (2020). https://doi.org/10.46586/tches.v2021.i1.402-425, https://tches.iacr.org/index.php/TCHES/article/view/8739
2. Balasch, J., Faust, S., Gierlichs, B., Paglialonga, C., Standaert, F.-X.: Consolidating inner product masking. In: Takagi, T., Peyrin, T. (eds.) ASIACRYPT 2017. LNCS, vol. 10624, pp. 724–754. Springer, Cham (2017). https://doi.org/10.1007/978-3-319-70694-8_25
3. Balasch, J., Gierlichs, B., Grosso, V., Reparaz, O., Standaert, F.-X.: On the cost of lazy engineering for masked software implementations. In: Joye, M., Moradi, A. (eds.) CARDIS 2014. LNCS, vol. 8968, pp. 64–81. Springer, Cham (2015). https://doi.org/10.1007/978-3-319-16763-3_5
4. Benadjila, R., Khati, L., Prouff, E., Thillard, A.: Hardened Library for AES-128 encryption/decryption on ARM Cortex M4 Architecture. https://github.com/ANSSI-FR/SecAESSTM32. Accessed 13 July 2020
5. Brier, E., Clavier, C., Olivier, F.: Correlation power analysis with a leakage model. In: Joye, M., Quisquater, J.-J. (eds.) CHES 2004. LNCS, vol. 3156, pp. 16–29. Springer, Heidelberg (2004). https://doi.org/10.1007/978-3-540-28632-5_2
6. Chari, S., Jutla, C.S., Rao, J.R., Rohatgi, P.: Towards sound approaches to counteract power-analysis attacks. In: Wiener, M. (ed.) CRYPTO 1999. LNCS, vol. 1666, pp. 398–412. Springer, Heidelberg (1999). https://doi.org/10.1007/3-540-48405-1_26
7. Cheng, W., Carlet, C., Goli, K., Danger, J.L., Guilley, S.: Detecting faults in inner product masking scheme IPM-FD: IPM with fault detection. J. Cryptogr. Eng. **11**, 119-133 (2020). https://doi.org/10.1007/s13389-020-00227-6, https://hal-cnrs.archives-ouvertes.fr/hal-02915673
8. Coron, J.-S.: Higher order masking of look-up tables. In: Nguyen, P.Q., Oswald, E. (eds.) EUROCRYPT 2014. LNCS, vol. 8441, pp. 441–458. Springer, Heidelberg (2014). https://doi.org/10.1007/978-3-642-55220-5_25
9. Coron, J.-S., Giraud, C., Prouff, E., Renner, S., Rivain, M., Vadnala, P.K.: Conversion of security proofs from one leakage model to another: a new issue. In: Schindler, W., Huss, S.A. (eds.) COSADE 2012. LNCS, vol. 7275, pp. 69–81. Springer, Heidelberg (2012). https://doi.org/10.1007/978-3-642-29912-4_6
10. Coron, J.-S., Greuet, A., Zeitoun, R.: Side-channel masking with pseudo-random generator. In: Canteaut, A., Ishai, Y. (eds.) EUROCRYPT 2020. LNCS, vol. 12107, pp. 342–375. Springer, Cham (2020). https://doi.org/10.1007/978-3-030-45727-3_12
11. eShard: SCAred. https://gitlab.com/eshard/scared. Accessed 16 Dec 2021
12. Gigerl, B., Hadzic, V., Primas, R., Mangard, S., Bloem, R.: Coco: co-design and co-verification of masked software implementations on CPUs. In: 30th USENIX Security Symposium (USENIX Security 21). USENIX Association, Aug 2021. https://www.usenix.org/conference/usenixsecurity21/presentation/gigerl
13. Gilbert Goodwill, B.J., et al.: A testing methodology for side-channel resistance validation. In: NIST Non-invasive Attack Testing Workshop, vol. 7, pp. 115–136 (2011)
14. Goubin, L., Patarin, J.: DES and Differential power analysis the "duplication" method. In: Koç, Ç.K., Paar, C. (eds.) CHES 1999. LNCS, vol. 1717, pp. 158–172. Springer, Heidelberg (1999). https://doi.org/10.1007/3-540-48059-5_15

15. Groß, H., Stoffelen, K., Meyer, L.D., Krenn, M., Mangard, S.: First-order masking with only two random bits. In: Proceedings of ACM Workshop on Theory of Implementation Security Workshop, TIS@CCS 2019, London, UK, November 11, 2019, pp. 10–23 (2019). https://doi.org/10.1145/3338467.3358950
16. Inc., M.T.: SAM D5x/E5x Family Data Sheet (2020). https://ww1.microchip.com/downloads/en/DeviceDoc/SAM_D5xE5x_Family_Data_Sheet_DS60001507F.pdf. Accessed 3 Dec 2020
17. Ishai, Y., Sahai, A., Wagner, D.: Private circuits: securing hardware against probing attacks. In: Boneh, D. (ed.) CRYPTO 2003. LNCS, vol. 2729, pp. 463–481. Springer, Heidelberg (2003). https://doi.org/10.1007/978-3-540-45146-4_27
18. Kannwischer, M.J., Rijneveld, J., Schwabe, P., Stoffelen, K.: PQM4: Post-quantum crypto library for the ARM Cortex-M4. https://github.com/mupq/pqm4
19. Kocher, P., Jaffe, J., Jun, B.: Differential power analysis. In: Wiener, M. (ed.) CRYPTO 1999. LNCS, vol. 1666, pp. 388–397. Springer, Heidelberg (1999). https://doi.org/10.1007/3-540-48405-1_25
20. McCann, D., Oswald, E., Whitnall, C.: Towards practical tools for side channel aware software engineering: 'grey box' modelling for instruction leakages. In: 26th USENIX Security Symposium (USENIX Security 2017), pp. 199–216. USENIX Association, Vancouver, BC, August 2017. https://www.usenix.org/conference/usenixsecurity17/technical-sessions/presentation/mccann
21. NewAE Technology Inc.: ChipWhisperer. https://github.com/newaetech/chipwhisperer. Accessed 16 Dec 2021
22. O'Flynn, C., Chen, Z.D.: ChipWhisperer: an open-source platform for hardware embedded security research. In: Prouff, E. (ed.) COSADE 2014. LNCS, vol. 8622, pp. 243–260. Springer, Cham (2014). https://doi.org/10.1007/978-3-319-10175-0_17
23. Renner, S., Pozzobon, E., Mottok, J.: A hardware in the loop benchmark suite to evaluate NIST LWC ciphers on microcontrollers. In: Meng, W., Gollmann, D., Jensen, C.D., Zhou, J. (eds.) ICICS 2020. LNCS, vol. 12282, pp. 495–509. Springer, Cham (2020). https://doi.org/10.1007/978-3-030-61078-4_28
24. Rivain, M., Prouff, E.: Provably secure higher-order masking of AES. In: Mangard, S., Standaert, F.-X. (eds.) CHES 2010. LNCS, vol. 6225, pp. 413–427. Springer, Heidelberg (2010). https://doi.org/10.1007/978-3-642-15031-9_28
25. Schwabe, P., Stoffelen, K.: All the AES you need on cortex-M3 and M4. In: Avanzi, R., Heys, H. (eds.) SAC 2016. LNCS, vol. 10532, pp. 180–194. Springer, Cham (2017). https://doi.org/10.1007/978-3-319-69453-5_10
26. Shelton, M.A., Samwel, N., Batina, L., Regazzoni, F., Wagner, M., Yarom, Y.: ROSITA: towards automatic elimination of power-analysis leakage in ciphers. In: 28th Annual Network and Distributed System Security Symposium, NDSS 2021, virtually, 21–25 February 2021. The Internet Society (2021). https://www.ndss-symposium.org/ndss-paper/rosita-towards-automatic-elimination-of-power-analysis-leakage-in-ciphers/
27. STMicroelectronics: RM0090 Reference manual (2019). https://www.st.com/resource/en/reference_manual/dm00031020-stm32f405-415-stm32f407-417-stm32f427-437-and-stm32f429-439-advanced-arm-based-32-bit-mcus-stmicroelectronics.pdf. Accessed 3 Dec 2020
28. Stoffelen, K.: aes-armcortexm. https://github.com/Ko-/aes-armcortexm. Accessed 30 Sep 2020

Systematic Study of Decryption and Re-encryption Leakage: The Case of Kyber

Melissa Azouaoui[1], Olivier Bronchain[2(✉)], Clément Hoffmann[2], Yulia Kuzovkova[1], Tobias Schneider[1], and François-Xavier Standaert[2]

[1] NXP Semiconductors, Eindhoven, The Netherlands
[2] UCLouvain, ICTEAM/ELEN/Crypto Group, Louvain-la-Neuve, Belgium
olivier.bronchain@uclouvain.be

Abstract. The side-channel cryptanalysis of Post-Quantum (PQ) key encapsulation schemes has been a topic of intense activity over the last years. Many attacks have been put forward: Simple Power Analysis (SPAs) against the re-encryption of schemes using the Fujisaki-Okamoto (FO) transform are known to be very powerful; Differential Power Analysis (DPAs) against the decryption are also possible. Yet, to the best of our knowledge, a systematic and quantitative investigation of their impact for designers is still missing. In this paper, we propose to capture these attacks with shortcut formulas in order to compare their respective strength in function of the noise level. Taking the case of Kyber for illustration, we then evaluate the (high) cost of preventing them with masking and the extent to which different parts of an implementation could benefit from varying security levels. We finally discuss tweaks to improve the situation and enable a better leveling of the countermeasures. Our conclusions confirm that current solutions for side-channel secure PQ key encapsulation schemes like Kyber are unlikely to be efficient in low-noise settings without (design or countermeasures) improvements.

Keywords: Side-channel attacks · Post-quantum cryptography · Key encapsulation mechanism · Fujisaki-Okamoto transformation · Masking

1 Introduction

Many Post-Quantum (PQ) Key Encapsulation Mechanisms (KEMs), including third-round finalists of the NIST post-quantum standardization effort, rely on the Fujisaki-Okamoto (FO) transform [15]. It allows building a Chosen-Ciphertext (CCA) secure scheme from a Chosen-Plaintext (CPA) secure Public-Key Encryption (PKE) scheme. This transform first decrypts the ciphertext c with the underlying CPA-secure PKE to retrieve the message m. Then, it re-encrypts (in a deterministic manner) m to obtain a ciphertext c'. By construction, any ciphertext c that has not been generated by the CPA-secure encryption

J. Balasch and C. O'Flynn (Eds.): COSADE 2022, LNCS 13211, pp. 236–256, 2022.
https://doi.org/10.1007/978-3-030-99766-3_11

scheme will result in a case where $c' \neq c$ (up to a negligible probability). In such a case, the CCA-secure KEM returns a random message which cannot be exploited by the adversary. Yet, while the FO transform is well suited to reach mathematical security, several recent works showed that the situation strongly differs when physical attacks are considered [25,29,32,34]. In such a context, leakage about intermediate computations makes it possible to circumvent mathematical security guarantees. Roughly, an adversary can then use a chosen-ciphertext attack against the part of the scheme that is only CPA secure. For example in [29], the adversary carefully crafts ciphertexts such that the decrypted message m leaks a bit of a secret key coefficient. Since this message m is used as input for the deterministic re-encryption, the adversary then only has to distinguish between an encryption of 0 or 1 given leakage of the computation. To do so, she can target all the intermediate computations within the (long) deterministic re-encryption jointly, which can include hundreds, thousands or even millions of intermediate bytes/words. Furthermore, this leakage is easy to exploit, whether being via standard techniques (e.g., template attacks with dimensionality reduction) or machine learning based cryptanalysis.

Echoing the situation in symmetric cryptography, such an attack actually corresponds to the strongest (state comparison) one in the taxonomy of [30, Slide 1.7]. In terms of design, [30] also recalls that symmetric decryption ensuring CCA security with leakage requires a two-pass design where the validity of the ciphertexts is verified before being decrypted (e.g., thanks to a MAC).

In addition to these attacks targeting the re-encryption, Differential Power Analysis attacks (DPAs) that target the leakage in the first (guessable) parts of a secret computation are also possible. In the case of PQ KEMs, such attacks naturally apply to the part of the decryption that takes place before the re-encryption. As usual, they can be extended from a standard DPA to analytical attacks exploiting even the hard-to-guess parts of the computation thanks to belief propagation, leading to strong key recoveries [26,27].

In parallel to the efforts regarding the identification of attack vectors, countermeasures against side-channel attacks have also been adapted to the PQ setting. As one of the leading protections, masking has received particular attention and, for example, first- and higher-order masked implementations of Saber and Kyber have been proposed [4,7,14,19]. To the best of our knowledge, masked implementations of PQ schemes so far mostly considered an uniform protection level, where all the parts of the computations embed the same number of shares. Again echoing the situation in symmetric cryptography, these works naturally question the possibility to consider so-called leveled implementations, where different parts of the computations have different security levels, for example based on the number of operations exploitable via side-channel leakage [5].

Based on this state-of-the-art, the objectives of the paper are threefold:

First, we propose a model for both (i.e., SPA and DPA) attack paths. For each of them, we derive a shortcut formula (i.e., a generic expression for the minimal number of traces needed for a successful attack) that takes as parameters the number of shares in the masking scheme, the level of noise in the leakage (measured as the mutual information between the shares and the leakage λ) and the (cipher-specific) amount of operations for which the leakage is exploitable. These shortcut formulas enable a first (simplified) approximation of attack complexities to compare side-channel attacks according to the above parameters.

Second, we illustrate these formulas at the example of CRYSTALS-Kyber [2]. This specific choice of KEM is motivated by the already large literature dedicated to its side-channel analysis and countermeasures. We derive our model parameters based on state-of-the-art implementation results from [7] and, in order to enable a comparative study of the attack paths, additionally express the cost needed to protect the different subparts of the Kyber computations.

Third, we use our results to discuss masked implementations of Kyber and the possibility to leverage the leveled implementation concept for PQ KEMs. We show that for unmasked implementations, the re-encryption becomes the preferred attack vector as the noise level increases (since it enables very strong horizontal attacks). But somewhat surprisingly, we also show that as the number of shares (hence, the target security level) increases, the impact of the re-encryption in the overall security vs. efficiency tradeoff tends to vanish, which significantly limits the interest of leveled implementations.

As a conclusion, we first recall that getting rid of the FO-transform in a PQ KEM such as Kyber would require a way to identify "well structured ciphertexts" without re-encryption, as performed in the symmetric cryptographic setting thanks to a leakage-resilient MAC. We note that this is a hard problem in itself. At this stage, it is not clear whether simple filtering heuristics can be sufficient [34], and the more formal solution of relying in a zero-knowledge proof (which we briefly discuss in Sect. 6) is quite expensive. In this respect, our results show that the performance margin available to (heuristically or formally) get rid of the FO-transform is quite limited. This conclusion derives from the observation that as the number of shares increases, the cost of protecting the (CPA-secure) decryption and the re-encryption becomes increasingly balanced in Kyber. In other words, improving the efficiency of side-channel secure Kyber implementations would not only require to get rid of the FO-transform, but also to increase the performance gap between its protected (CPA-secure) decryption and re-encryption. Candidates for this purpose include improving the efficiency of this decryption (especially the compression part), reducing the complexity of its masking and taking advantage of hardware tweaks (e.g., exploiting different noise levels in the decryption and re-encryption). We believe a similar challenge appears in related PQ KEMs relying on the FO-transform (e.g., Saber [3]).

2 Background

We next recall the necessary background for the rest of the paper. We first describe shortcut formulas for side-channel attacks based on Information Theoretic (IT) metrics. We continue with a short description of CRYSTALS-Kyber [2].

2.1 Information Theory for Side-Channel Attacks

Side-channel attacks allow recovering cryptographic secrets by observing the leakages $\boldsymbol{L}$ from an implementation. All side-channel attacks (whether based on a divide-and-conquer or analytical strategy) include an extraction phase where they collect information about guessable intermediate computations. A standard strategy to estimate the number of traces required to recover leaking target intermediate values with confidence is to use information theoretic metrics such as the Mutual Information (MI) [11,13,31]. Next, we recall the simple relations that we are going to leverage in order to derive shortcut formulas. We start with unprotected variables, continue with masked variables and finally discuss the impact of attacks exploiting multiple intermediate computations.

Unprotected Variables. In order to evaluate the number of independent leakages N required to recover a (sub)-secret X, one can use the relation:

$$N \approx \frac{c}{\mathrm{MI}(X;\boldsymbol{L})}, \tag{1}$$

where c is a small constant that depends on the size of the intermediate variable and the target success rate (we will set it to the Shannon's entropy such that $c = \mathrm{H}(X)$ for simplicity), and $\mathrm{MI}(X;\boldsymbol{L})$ is the Mutual Information between the target variable X and the leakage vector $\boldsymbol{L}$.

Roughly, the attack complexity is inversely proportional to the MI, which is itself inversely proportional to the noise variance of the leakages [24]. In the following, we will use the MI between target intermediate computations and their leakage as a parameter of our evaluations, and denote it as λ.

Masked Variables. In order to protect implementations against SCA, masking is a countermeasure that has been extensively studied. It consists in representing a sensitive variable X as d shares $(X^0, X^1, \ldots, X^{d-1})$ such that any set of $d-1$ shares remains independent of X. The operations are then applied to the shares of X instead of on X directly. When implemented securely (i.e., under some noise and independence conditions), it guarantees an exponential security increase at the cost of quadratic performance overheads [9,12,13,22,28]. Concretely, this security amplification is reflected by a reduction of the MI:

$$\mathrm{MI}(X;\boldsymbol{L}) \approx \prod_{i=0}^{d-1} \mathrm{MI}(X^i;\boldsymbol{L}) = \lambda^d, \tag{2}$$

leading to an increased attack data complexity captured by:

$$N \approx \frac{c}{\lambda^d} \cdot \tag{3}$$

Targeting Multiple (Independent) Operations. Side-channel attacks are not limited to the exploitation of a single intermediate computation and its corresponding leakage. Multiple operations can be exploited jointly. The simplest way to do so is when multiple intermediate computations relate to the same guessable secret. In this case, a natural abstraction is to model their leakages as providing independent information on the secret, as captured by the Independent Operations' Leakages (IOL) proposed in [17]. It leads to the approximation:

$$\mathrm{MI}(X; \boldsymbol{L}) \approx \sum_{j} \mathrm{MI}(var_j(X); \boldsymbol{L}) \approx \#var \cdot \lambda^d, \tag{4}$$

where $var_j(X)$ is one of the $\#var$ variables depending only on X.

For example in the case of block-ciphers, an attack can be performed by exploiting leakage (e.g., with Gaussian templates) at the input of the Sbox and at its output and combining information from both. This will double the information about X (hence $\#var = 2$) compared to an attack exploiting only its output (with $\#var = 1$). It turns out this simple setting will be quite frequently observed (and generalized) in our following investigations.

Cautionary Notes. The above formulas are admittedly simplified and may ignore a part of the leakages. First, it is also possible to exploit the leakages of operations that are not exploitable via a divide-and-conquer DPA, for example using analytical strategies [33], as considered by [26,27] in the PQ setting. Second, masked multiplications with d shares imply quadratic overheads, e.g., they require computing d^2 partial products which may leak as well. Yet, as modeled in [18], the leakage of intermediate values that do not relate to the same guessable secret does not simply add up as in the previous IOL case and rather implies a constant gain in the attacks; and the leakage of partial products in masked multiplication is dominated by the leakage of the tuples as the noise level of the implementation increases. So simply stated, while the following shortcut formulas could be refined to take into account advanced attacks, they are a convenient first step to study the large design space of masked PQ KEMs up to small constants.

2.2 CRYSTALS-Kyber

Arithmetic and Notations. We denote the polynomial ring $\mathbb{Z}_q[X]/(X^n + 1)$ as $\mathbb{R}_q$. We denote polynomials with lower case such that $f \in \mathbb{R}_q$. As a result, the polynomials are of the form:

$$f = f_0 + f_1 \cdot X^1 + \ldots + f_{n-1} \cdot f^{n-1}, \tag{5}$$

where $f_i \in \mathbb{Z}_q$ is the i-th coefficient of the polynomial. We denote vectors and matrices with bold letters. For example, $\boldsymbol{v} \in \mathbb{R}_q^k$ is a vector of k polynomials such that $\boldsymbol{v}[i] \in \mathbb{R}_q$ for all $0 \leq i < k$. Hence, $\boldsymbol{v}[i]_j$ refers to the j-th coefficient of the i-th polynomial in $\boldsymbol{v}$. Additionally, $\boldsymbol{A} \in \mathbb{R}_q^{k \times k}$ is a matrix of polynomials with size $k \times k$. For CRYSTALS-Kyber, the prime q is chosen such that polynomial multiplications can be performed very efficiently via the Number-Theoretic Transform (NTT). Concretely, the NTT is first applied to the polynomials such that:

$$\hat{f} = \mathrm{NTT}(f) = \hat{f}_0 + \hat{f}_1 \cdot X^1 + \ldots + \hat{f}_{n-1} \cdot X^{n-1}, \tag{6}$$

where $\hat{f}$ (resp., $\hat{f}_0$) denotes the NTT domain representation of f (resp., f_0). NTT(·) is efficiently applied with a butterfly algorithm [10,16]. The multiplication between two polynomials can then leverage their representations in the NTT domain such that:

$$c = a \cdot b = \mathrm{NTT}^{-1}(\hat{a} \circ \hat{b}), \tag{7}$$

where $\circ$ is the coefficient-wise multiplication.

CRYSTALS-Kyber PKE. We first detail the underlying CPA-secure PKE scheme denoted as Kyber.CPAPKE, which relies on the hardness of Module-LWE [23]. Kyber.CPAPKE encryption and decryption are recalled in Algorithm 1 and Algorithm 2, respectively. There, $\hat{\boldsymbol{s}}$ denotes a secret key, pk a public key containing a vector of polynomials $\hat{\boldsymbol{t}}$ and a random matrix of polynomials $\hat{\boldsymbol{A}}$, m the 256-bit message, σ a 256-bit random seed used to derive deterministically the randomness from a pseudo-random generator and CBD_η denotes the sampling, from a uniform random string, of a centered binomial distribution with parameter η. Comp_q and Decomp_q are respectively compression and decompression functions such that $\mathrm{Decomp}_q(\mathrm{Comp}_q(x, d_x), d_x) \approx x$. Both PRF, KDF, G and H are hash functions with various output lengths based on the Keccak permutation. For more details about these algorithms, we refer to their specifications in [2].

Algorithm 1 Kyber.CPAPKE.Enc(pk,m,σ)

Input: Public key $pk := (\hat{\boldsymbol{t}}, \hat{\boldsymbol{A}})$ with $\hat{\boldsymbol{t}} \in \mathbb{R}_q^k$ and $\hat{\boldsymbol{A}} \in \mathbb{R}_q^{k \times k}$, message $m \in \{0,1\}^n$, random coin $\sigma \in \{0,1\}^{256}$.
Output: Ciphertext $c := (c_1, c_2)$.

- **for** i in $[0, \dots, k-1]$ **do**
  - $\boldsymbol{r}[i] := \mathrm{CBD}_{\eta_1}(\mathrm{PRF}(\sigma, i))$
  - $\boldsymbol{e}_1[i] := \mathrm{CBD}_{\eta_2}(\mathrm{PRF}(\sigma, i + k))$
- $e_2 := \mathrm{CBD}_{\eta_2}(\mathrm{PRF}(\sigma, 2 \cdot k))$
- $\hat{\boldsymbol{r}} := \mathrm{NTT}(\boldsymbol{r})$
- $\boldsymbol{u} := \mathrm{NTT}^{-1}(\hat{\boldsymbol{A}}^T \circ \hat{\boldsymbol{r}}) + \boldsymbol{e}_1$
- $v := \mathrm{NTT}^{-1}(\hat{\boldsymbol{t}}^T \circ \hat{\boldsymbol{r}}) + e_2 + \mathrm{Decomp}_q(m, 1)$
- $c_1 := \mathrm{Comp}_q(\boldsymbol{u}, d_u)$
- $c_2 := \mathrm{Comp}_q(v, d_v)$
- **return** (c_1, c_2)

Algorithm 2 Kyber.CPAPKE.Dec($\hat{\boldsymbol{s}}$,c)

Input: Secret key $\hat{\boldsymbol{s}} \in \mathbb{R}_q^k$, ciphertext $c := (c_1, c_2)$.
Output: Message m.

- $\boldsymbol{u} := \mathrm{Decomp}_q(c_1, d_u)$
- $v := \mathrm{Decomp}_q(c_2, d_v)$
- $\hat{z} = \hat{\boldsymbol{s}}^T \circ \mathrm{NTT}(\boldsymbol{u})$
- $w := v - \mathrm{NTT}^{-1}(\hat{z})$
- $m := \mathrm{Comp}_q(w, 1)$
- **return** m

CRYSTALS-Kyber KEM and FO-transform. CRYSTALS-Kyber leverages the FO-transform [15,20] to build a CCA-secure KEM from a CPA-secure PKE. The resulting Kyber.CCAKEM encapsulation and decapsulation algorithms are described respectively in Algorithm 3 and Algorithm 4. More precisely, Kyber.CCA KEM.Dec first retrieves a message candidate m' by decrypting the ciphertext c thanks to Kyber.CPAPKE.Dec and the secret key. Then, it computes c' by re-encrypting m' using the encryption $c' =$

Kyber.CPAPKE.Enc(pk, m', σ'). It then only outputs the correct symmetric key material K if c is equal to c'. As a result, the resulting scheme is protected against chosen-ciphertext attacks: as soon as an adversary attempts to use a forged ciphertext, the resulting re-encrypted c' will differ from c (up to a negligible probability).

We note that for such a construction to be correct, the randomness used during the (re)-encryption should be deterministically generated from a random coin associated with the plaintext. Otherwise, the ciphertexts c and c' could differ even though they are both correct ciphertexts of the same message m.

Algorithm 3 Kyber.CCAKEM.Enc(pk)

Input: Public key $pk := (\hat{t}, \hat{A})$
Output: Ciphertext c, encap. secret K.

$m \leftarrow \{0,1\}^{256}$
$m := \mathrm{H}(m)$
$(\bar{K}, \sigma) := \mathrm{G}(m||\mathrm{H}(pk))$
$c :=$ Kyber.CPAPKE.Enc(pk, m, σ)
$K := \mathrm{KDF}(\bar{K}||\mathrm{H}(c))$
return (c, K)

Algorithm 4 Kyber.CCAKEM.Dec(c, sk)

Input: Ciphertext $c := (c_1, c_2)$, secret key $sk := (\hat{s}, pk, \mathrm{H}(pk), z)$.
Output: Decap. secret K.

$m' :=$ Kyber.CPAPKE.Dec($\hat{s}, c$)
$(\bar{K}', \sigma') := \mathrm{G}(m'||\mathrm{H}(pk))$
$c' :=$ Kyber.CPAPKE.Enc(pk, m', σ')
if $c = c'$ **then**
  return $K := \mathrm{KDF}(\bar{K}'||\mathrm{H}(c))$
else
  return $K := \mathrm{KDF}(z||\mathrm{H}(c))$

Concrete Parameters. Finally, we give the parameters used by CRYSTALS-Kyber for the third round of the NIST PQC standardization process [2] in Table 1, for the different versions corresponding to different security levels.[1]

Table 1. Summary of Kyber parameters (from [2]).

	n	k	q	η_1	η_2	d_u	d_v
Kyber512	256	2	3329	3	2	10	4
Kyber768	256	3	3329	2	2	10	4
Kyber1024	256	4	3329	2	2	11	5

3 Shortcut Formulas for SPA and DPA

As stated in the introduction, there exists two main attack paths against PQ KEMs based on the FO-transform. In this section, we derive shortcut formulas for their data complexity. For this purpose, we use the illustration of Fig. 1, which is a simplified graphical representation of Algorithm 4.

[1] Namely, NIST security levels 1, 3 and 5 for which any attack requires comparable computational resources to attacks against AES-128,AES-196 and AES-256 [1,2].

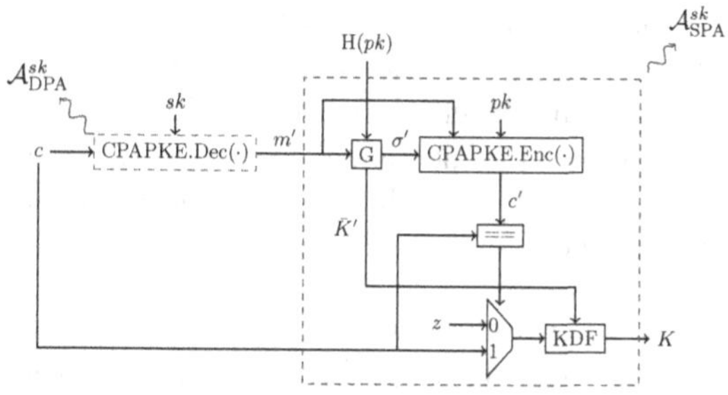

Fig. 1. Attack paths against Kyber.CCAKEM.Dec(c, sk) (Algorithm 4).

3.1 $\mathcal{A}^{sk}_{\text{DPA}}$: DPA Against CPAPKE.Dec

Description. A DPA attack against PQ KEMs can be performed in a similar way as classical (divide-and-conquer) DPA against block-ciphers. In this case, $\mathcal{A}^{sk}_{\text{DPA}}$ targets directly each of the secret key coefficients $\hat{s}_i$ independently. To do so, she asks for the decryption of legit ciphertexts c's and records the corresponding traces. She then exploits every operations that directly involve $\hat{s}_i$, as she would target the Sbox's input and output in the case of a block-cipher.

For illustration, in the case of CRYSTALS-Kyber, this adversary targets each $\hat{\boldsymbol{s}}_i$ independently by observing the leakage of $\hat{\boldsymbol{s}}^T \circ \text{NTT}(\boldsymbol{u})$ (see Algorithm 2, line 3) where $\boldsymbol{u}$ is known and random. Indeed, she obtains leakage of the coefficient-wise operations $\hat{\boldsymbol{s}}_i \circ \hat{\boldsymbol{u}}_i$ as detailed in Eq. 7.

Shortcut Formula. Because this attack targets each of the coefficients independently, the resulting shortcut formula can leverage the approximations given in Subsect. 2.1. Namely, we can estimate the data complexity of $\mathcal{A}^{sk}_{\text{DPA}}$ with:

$$N_{Dec} \approx \frac{\alpha_{Dec}}{\lambda^{d_{Dec}}}, \tag{8}$$

where d_{Dec} is the amount (#) of shares used to protect the CPAPKE.Dec and $\alpha_{Dec} = \frac{c}{\#var}$ is the cipher-dependent constant reflecting the # of operations that can be exploited via DPA (and the constant c), discussed for Kyber in Sect. 5.

Other DPA Attacks. As already mentioned in Subsect. 2.1, advanced adversaries could additionally exploit the leakages in NTT^{-1} thanks to belief-propagation [26,27]. By exploiting the leakage of hard to guess intermediate variables, such advanced attacks can reduce the data complexity by additional constant factors, which could be reflected by adapting α_{Dec} [18].

3.2 $\mathcal{A}^{sk}_{\text{SPA}}$: SPA Against Re-encryption

Description. The SPA adversary $\mathcal{A}^{sk}_{\text{SPA}}$ targets leakages from all operations that directly depend on the decrypted message m' [25,29,32,34]. In short, these attacks are chosen-ciphertext attacks against the part of the KEMs that are only CPA-secure. This is made possible despite the FO-transform by exploiting the leakage of m' as a plaintext-checking oracle. This can be done simply by observing whether m' is equal or not equal to a reference message. In order to recover the full secret key sk, multiple forged ciphertexts (and corresponding oracle accesses) are required. We denote their number as $\#\mathcal{O}$.

Shortcut Formula. In order to predict the data complexity of such an SPA adversary, we first observe that by targeting the leakage of the re-encryption, it is possible to exploit multiple independent variables that directly depend on m'. We denote the number of these operations as $\#var$. Again leveraging the approximations of Subsect. 2.1, the number of traces required to succeed in detecting whether m' is equal to the reference is then estimated as:

$$N_{Enc} \approx \frac{\alpha_{Enc}}{\lambda^{d_{Enc}}}, \tag{9}$$

with $\alpha_{Enc} = \frac{c' \cdot \#\mathcal{O}}{\#var}$. Here again, the number of exploitable operations $\#var$ is cipher-specific. The same holds for the number of required oracle accesses $\#\mathcal{O}$. Those values will be specified for the case of Kyber in the next section.

4 Generic Intuitions

In this section, we discuss the case of masked implementations of PQ KEMs. We assume a designer aiming at an implementation that can resist attacks of complexity γ (which therefore corresponds to the security level) on a platform with physical security parameter λ (which, as outlined in Subsect. 2.1, can be viewed as a measure of the implementation's noise level). More precisely, we first study the case where a designer selects the same number of shares to protect the decryption and the re-encryption, and show that such a strategy requires a large number of shares. Then, we quantify the effect of using different number of shares for decryption and re-encryption and discuss its impact regarding the relative cost of the re-encryption in the overall implementation.

4.1 Masking can be (very) Expensive

Next, we estimate the number of shares required to protect against both decryption and re-encryption attacks such that $d = d_{Enc} = d_{Dec}$. To do so, the target security level γ should be smaller than the attack complexities N derived in Sect. 3 such that:

$$\gamma \leq \alpha \cdot \frac{1}{\lambda^d}, \tag{10}$$

with $\alpha = \min(\alpha_{Enc}, \alpha_{Dec})$. As a result, the required number of shares to protect the entire implementation is defined by:

$$d \geq \log_\lambda \left(\frac{\alpha}{\gamma}\right) \tag{11}$$

$$\geq \frac{\log_{10}(\alpha) - \log_{10}(\gamma)}{\log_{10}(\lambda)}, \tag{12}$$

up to $\lceil \cdot \rceil$ to ensure that d is an integer (for readability, we omit the rounding for the rest of the section). Based on this equation, we report the number of shares for various settings in Fig. 2. As expected from Eq. 12, the parameter that has the strongest influence on the number of shares is the noise λ, which corresponds to the slope of the curves. For example, moving from $\lambda = 0.1$ to $\lambda = 0.01$ reduces the number of shares by a factor 2 since $|\log_{10}(\lambda)|$ is increased similarly. The number of shares also depends on the attack parameter α, but to a lower extent (since this factor is constant in d). For example, reducing α by a factor 10 implies the need for $1/\log_{10}(\lambda)$ additional shares to compensate.

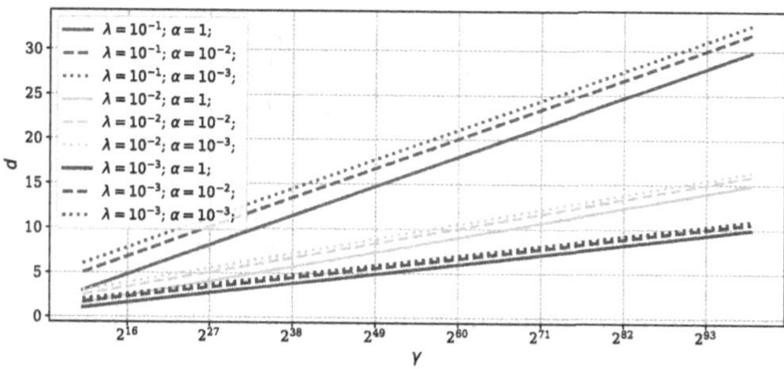

Fig. 2. Impact of the attack parameters α and the noise level λ on the number of shares d in function of the target security level γ.

The combination of these two effects is at the basis of the somewhat paradoxical conclusions in the following sections. On the one hand, large number of operations (which are observed for PQ KEMs) make side-channel attacks very strong in the absence of countermeasures. On the other hand, the impact of reducing this number of leaking operations vanishes as the target security level (and number of shares) increases, since it is then increasingly dominated by the amplified noise. For the rest, the figure also recalls that with low-noise devices, the number of shares needed to reach high security against side-channel attacks, and therefore the implementation overheads, can be prohibitive [8].

4.2 Leveling Moderately Helps

State-of-the-art analyses of PQ KEMs indicate that SPA attacks targeting re-encryption are very powerful. This is for exampled witnessed by the "curse of re-encryption" discussed in [32]. Concretely, the origin of this curse mainly lies in the different number of exploitable operations that decryption and re-encryption may have. A natural target to mitigate this issue is to use a different number of shares for these two parts of a KEM. By doing so, we could expect to reduce the overall cost of an implementation by protecting less its stronger (i.e., CPA decryption) part. In order to model such a leveling, we assume that masking leads to overheads that are quadratic in d and express the cost of protecting one component as $\zeta = \beta \cdot d^2$, where β is the cycle count of an unprotected implementation. Note that the quadratic cost overheads are naturally dependent on the fraction of linear and non-linear operations in the algorithm to protect. But concrete results recalled in Appendix A show that this trend is observed even for low number of shares in the case of Kyber.[2] More precisely, we are interested in the proportion ζ_{Enc}/ζ_{Dec} of time that is spent to protect re-encryption and decryption. A large ratio means that the re-encryption is the dominating the overall cost. Hence, removing re-encryption would lead to significant performance improvements in this case. A small ratio means the opposite. Next, we study this ratio according to attack parameter α, target security level γ as well as the implementation complexity β.[3] This proportion can be given by:

$$\zeta_{Enc}/\zeta_{Dec} = \frac{\beta_{Enc}}{\beta_{Dec}} \cdot \frac{d^2_{Enc}}{d^2_{Dec}} \tag{13}$$

$$= \frac{\beta_{Enc}}{\beta_{Dec}} \cdot \frac{(\log_{10}(\alpha_{Enc}) - \log_{10}(\gamma))^2}{(\log_{10}(\alpha_{Dec}) - \log_{10}(\gamma))^2}, \tag{14}$$

thanks to the expression of the number of shares in Eq. 12. For increasing security target γ, this ratio converges such that:

$$\lim_{\gamma \to \infty} \zeta_{Enc}/\zeta_{Dec} = \frac{\beta_{Enc}}{\beta_{Dec}}. \tag{15}$$

We observe that as γ increases, the proportion of time spent between the two blocks converges towards the ratio of their performances when implemented without side-channel protections. In other words, the gap between the number of shares needed to compensate different number of exploitable operations vanishes with the security level. This equation is illustrated in Fig. 3. For low security, the re-encryption dominates the overall cost of the secure implementation. By contrast, it is no more the case for large security levels.

Interestingly, even if the idea of leveling we analyze in this work looks quite similar to the one leveraged in symmetric cryptography [5], its impact is much lower. The best factor that a designer could hope to gain in the case of a PQ

[2] For both CPAPKE.Enc and CPAPKE.Dec, lattice arithmetic can be efficiently masked with linear complexity. However, both include polynomial comparison, polynomial compression and binomial noise sampling which require boolean-to-arithmetic and/or arithmetic-to-boolean masking conversions implying quadratic overheads. In the case of Kyber, these conversions dominate the overall cost of protected implementations even for small masking order.

[3] β is strongly connected to α in the case of PQ KEMs where the leakage of most operations can be exploited. Yet, it could be more different in other cases.

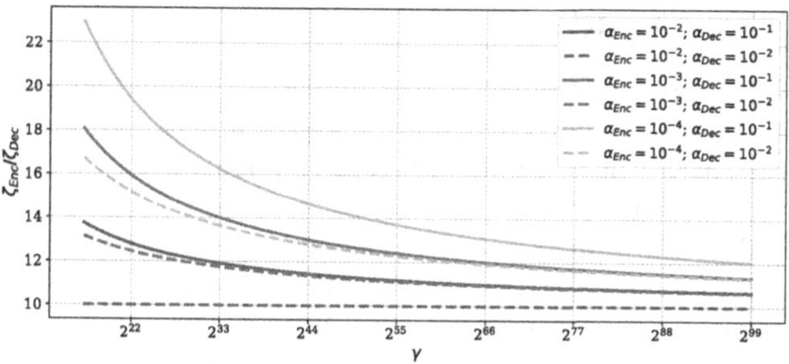

Fig. 3. Ratio between the cost of decryption and re-encryption ($\beta_{Enc}/\beta_{Dec} = 10$).

KEM that is strongly protected against side-channel attacks is $\approx 1+\beta_{Enc}/\beta_{Dec}$. But in fact, the explanation is also quite natural. The main factor making the leveling process very effective in the symmetric case is the possibility to amortize the cost of a highly masked implementation for long messages. In the case of a PQ KEM, the size of the messages is fixed. Admittedly again, these conclusions are based on generic formulas that may be over simplifying and their concrete impact depends on the exact complexity of concrete PQ KEMs. We next show that a specialization to Kyber leads to these conclusions as well.

5 Applications to CRYSTALS-Kyber

We now aim to characterize the parameters of the SPA and DPA attack paths more concretely. For this purpose, we first introduce a slightly finer-grain analysis than the shortcut formulas in the previous section. Its goal is to enable a discussion of how stable our conclusions are in front of technology-dependent variations. We next quantify the operation counts in the specific case study of a software CRYSTALS-Kyber implementation from [7]. We finally use these concrete values to revisit the generic intuitions of the previous section.

Preliminaries. Before these discussions, we mention two preliminary steps towards specializing our shortcut formulas to Kyber. The first one is to observe that the c constant in Sect. 3 will be different for the two attack paths. In the $\mathcal{A}^{sk}_{\mathrm{DPA}}$ case, one aims to recover 12-bit values (key coefficients in NTT domain), leading to $c = 12$. In the $\mathcal{A}^{sk}_{\mathrm{SPA}}$ case, one only wants to recover a 1-bit value (i.e., to distinguish the leakage of a message from the leakage of another message), leading to $c' = 1$. The second step is to determine the number of oracle accesses $\#\mathcal{O}$ required for the SPA to succeed. For Kyber, this number is worth $\#\mathcal{O} = k \cdot n \cdot 3$, as given in Table 3 of [32], based on the analysis in [21].[4]

[4] The basic $\mathcal{A}^{sk}_{\mathrm{SPA}}$ aims to recover a single coefficient of s per oracle access. But it can be extended to target b coefficients of the secret at once, which essentially works by targeting b bits of the decrypted message rather than a single one.

5.1 Finer Grain Analysis

Equations 8 and 9 in the previous section implicitly assume that all the intermediate variables they target leak the same amount of information λ. However, it may not be the case in practice, for different (implementation-specific) reasons. The simplest one, that we will characterize next, is that the operations may not all manipulate the same amount of bits per cycle. For example, in a software implementation of Kyber, an efficient implementation of the hash function Keccak will typically be obtained by bitslicing. In this case 32 bits would be manipulated per cycle. By contrast, the 12-bit arithmetic operations will generally lead to 12 bits manipulated by cycle. Assuming a Hamming weight leakage model, where one can roughly approximate $\mathrm{MI}(X; \boldsymbol{L})$ by $\log_2(n)$ when X is an n-bit value, it means that the leakage of 32-bit operations will be $f = \frac{\log_2(32)}{\log_2(12)}$ time larger than the one of 12-bit operations. A completely accurate fine-grain characterization of how the different operations of an implementation of Kyber leak is outside the scope of this work (and would go against the simplicity goal of shortcut formulas). Yet, in order to assess the potential impact of such a characterization, we will next consider two leakage parameters: λ_{32} for 32-bit operations and λ_{12} for 12-bit operations. By default, we will further assume that $\lambda_{32} = f \cdot \lambda_{12}$ with $f = \frac{\log_2(32)}{\log_2(12)}$. As a result, Eqs. 8 and 9 will be updated as:

$$N_{Dec} \approx \frac{12}{\#var_{Dec} \cdot \lambda_{12}^{d_{Dec}}}, \tag{16}$$

since there are no Keccak instances in Kyber.CPAKEM.Dec, and:

$$N_{Enc} \approx \frac{3 \cdot k \cdot n}{\#var_{Enc}^{12} \cdot \lambda_{12}^{d_{Enc}^{12}} + \#var_{Enc}^{32} \cdot \lambda_{32}^{d_{Enc}^{32}}}. \tag{17}$$

In the next subsection, we therefore focus on evaluating the number of 12-bit and 32-bit operations that can be exploited in the different sub-computations that are found in the Kyber decryption and re-encryption algorithms.

5.2 Concrete Attack Parameters

DPA Against Decryption. The $\mathcal{A}_{\mathrm{DPA}}^{sk}$ adversary exploits the leakage generated by the first few operations in the decryption involving the private key $\hat{\boldsymbol{s}}$ (Algorithm 2 - Line 3). It aims to recover the NTT representation of the private key $\boldsymbol{s}$. More precisely, $\mathcal{A}_{\mathrm{DPA}}^{sk}$ exploits leakage from the product between the two vectors of polynomials $\hat{\boldsymbol{u}} \in \mathbb{R}_q^k$ and $\hat{\boldsymbol{s}} \in \mathbb{R}_q^k$ where $\hat{\boldsymbol{u}}$ is known by the adversary (since derived from the ciphertext). In the specific case of Kyber, the polynomial-wise base multiplications $\hat{\boldsymbol{u}}[i] \circ \hat{\boldsymbol{s}}[i]$ is performed by computing coefficient-wise operations $\hat{\boldsymbol{u}}[i]_{2j} \cdot \hat{\boldsymbol{s}}[i]_{2j}$, $\hat{\boldsymbol{u}}[i]_{2j} \cdot \hat{\boldsymbol{s}}[i]_{2j+1}$, $\hat{\boldsymbol{u}}[i]_{2j+1} \cdot \hat{\boldsymbol{s}}[i]_{2j}$ and $\hat{\boldsymbol{u}}[i]_{2j+1} \cdot \hat{\boldsymbol{s}}[i]_{2j+1}$ for $0 \leq i < k$ and $0 \leq j < n/2$. As a result by requesting one single decryption, $\mathcal{A}_{\mathrm{DPA}}^{sk}$ can directly exploit, thanks to dedicated attacks such as [8], the leakage from the multiplication of every coefficient in $\hat{s}$ with two know coefficients in $\hat{\boldsymbol{u}}$. Hence in this case $\#var_{Dec} = 2$.

SPA Against Re-encryption. As mentioned above, the $\mathcal{A}_{\text{SPA}}^{sk}$ adversary exploits the leakage of the deterministic re-encryption to gain knowledge on the message m' decrypted by Kyber.CPAPKE.Enc [29]. Next, we evaluate the number of operations in Kyber of which the leakage can be jointly exploited to gain information on m' during the re-encryption. We first estimate the number of operations performed on 32-bit words (i.e., for hash functions). Then, we estimate the number of operations on 12-bit words (i.e., arithmetic operations).

- $\#var_{Enc}^{32}$. The re-encryption involves many calls to hash functions depending directly on the decrypted message m'. The first call to a hash function depending on m' is G in $\text{G}(m'||\text{H}(pk))$ (see Algorithm 4 - Line 2). The others are made within the re-encryption with Kyber.CPAKEM.Enc (Algorithm 1). There, $(1+2\cdot k)$ calls to $\text{PRF}(\cdot,\cdot)$ are performed in order to sample $\boldsymbol{e}_1$, $\boldsymbol{r}$ and e_2 with $\text{CBD}_\eta(\cdot)$. As a result, $(2+2\cdot k)$ calls to hash functions can be exploited by the $\mathcal{A}_{\text{SPA}}^{sk}$ adversary. All of them are based on the Keccak[1600] permutation [6].[5] For each of the calls to the hash functions, because of the input and output length, one single call to Keccak[1600] is performed.[6] Keccak[1600] requires 24 rounds alternating between linear and Sbox layers. Each rounds implies about 320 operations on 32-bit words. As a result, $\mathcal{A}_{\text{SPA}}^{sk}$ exploits jointly the leakage of $\#var_{Enc}^{32} \approx (2+2\cdot k)\cdot 24\cdot 320$.
- $\#var_{Enc}^{12}$. To model the information that can be extracted from the NTT and NTT^{-1} operations, we assume that each of the intermediate stages in the butterfly algorithm provides independent leakages. As a result, the adversary can exploit the leakage of $n\cdot\log_2 n$ operations for each of the calls to NTT or its inverse. Kyber.CPAPKE.Enc includes $2+k$ NTT calls, leading to a total of $n\cdot\log_2 n\cdot(2+k)$ operations on 12-bits from the NTT.

Besides, Kyber.CPAPKE.Enc also uses 12-bit element-wise operations such as the base multiplication ($\circ$) and additions. The base multiplication implies $2\cdot n$ operations and the polynomial addition only n. In Algorithm 1, the variable $\boldsymbol{u}$ is computed thanks to k^2 base multiplications and k^2 vector additions since $\hat{\boldsymbol{A}} \in \mathbb{R}_q^{k\times k}$ and $\hat{\boldsymbol{r}} \in \mathbb{R}_q^k$. Similarly, k base multiplications and $k+2$ additions are needed to derive $\boldsymbol{v}$. Kyber.CPAPKE.Enc also includes $(2k+1)\cdot n$ calls to CBD, $(k+1)\cdot n$ calls to Comp. The final comparison consists in $(k+1)\cdot n$ coefficient-wise operations. Overall, the adversary can exploit a total of $(3k^2+8k+5)\cdot n$ leaking element-wise operations.

Hence in the following, we take $\#var_{Enc}^{12} \approx n\cdot(3k^2+8k+5+\log_2 n\cdot(2+k))$.

5.3 A Look at Unprotected Implementations

In Fig. 4, we report the data complexity of attacks against an unprotected ($d=1$) implementation of Kyber768. The x-axis corresponds to physical noise

[5] Expect for the Kyber 90s versions.

[6] The only exception is for its call in $\text{CBD}_\eta(\text{PRF}(\cdot,\cdot))$ of Algorithm 1 if $\eta=3$ (for Kyber512). Indeed, in such a case, $\text{CBD}_3(\cdot)$ requires 1526 random bits. This requires two executions of Keccak[1600] since 1526 is larger than the rate of $\text{PRF}(\cdot,\cdot)$.

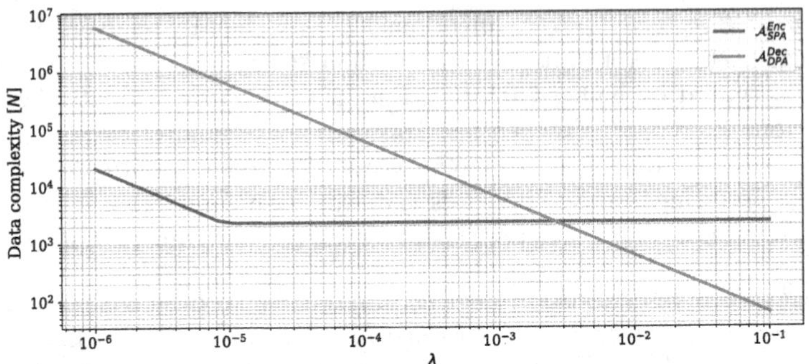

Fig. 4. Data complexity of attacks against unprotected Kyber768.

parameter λ. The y-axis reports the data complexity N which is derived from Eq. 8 for the $\mathcal{A}^{sk}_{\text{DPA}}$ adversary and from Eq. 9 for the $\mathcal{A}^{sk}_{\text{SPA}}$ adversary, with the concrete parameters estimated above. We can observe that for low noise levels (i.e., large λ values), the DPA attack path leads to stronger attacks. But as the noise increases, the SPA becomes the preferred attack path. Its complexity remains constant for a wide range of noise levels (up to λ values of 10^{-5} per leakage sample), as reflected by the plateau region of the curve. This is because a single oracle access is then sufficient to recover the key, leading to a successful attack in $\#\mathcal{O} = 3 \cdot n \cdot k$ traces. Concretely, for small λ values, the $\mathcal{A}^{sk}_{\text{SPA}}$ requires $(\#var^{32}_{Enc} \cdot f + \#var^{12}_{Enc}) \cdot 12/(\#var_{Dec} \cdot \#\mathcal{O}) \approx 2.8 \cdot 10^2$ less traces than the $\mathcal{A}^{sk}_{\text{DPA}}$, providing a quantitative view on the "curse of re-encryption".

5.4 Generic Intuition Revisited

In this subsection, we finally revisit the intuitions put forward in Sect. 4 with concrete parameters corresponding to a software implementation of Kyber. We aim to derive the implementation cost needed to reach a given security level γ. Concretely, this requires to optimize the number of shares d_{Dec}, d^{12}_{Enc} and d^{32}_{Enc} in Equations 16 and 17 based on the numbers given in Appendix A. We used a grid search for this purpose, considering only integer number of shares.

Masking is (very) Expensive. The cycle counts of a protected implementation of Kyber768 is reported in Fig. 5. It confirms the large overheads needed to reach high physical security, especially in case of low noise levels. For example, 10^9 cycles are required to reach a 2^{32} security for a noise $\lambda = 0.1$. With a larger noise $\lambda = 0.01$, similar overheads would lead to a security level $\gamma = 2^{74}$. Our results consolidate and quantify the intuition that masking PQ KEMs like Kyber can only be done at realistic cost under sufficient noise levels. Those may not be directly available in low-end embedded microcontrollers (where $\lambda = 0.1$ is a typical value, see [8] Fig. 10), and therefore suggest relying on secure microcontrollers with noise engines or hardware implementations for this purpose.

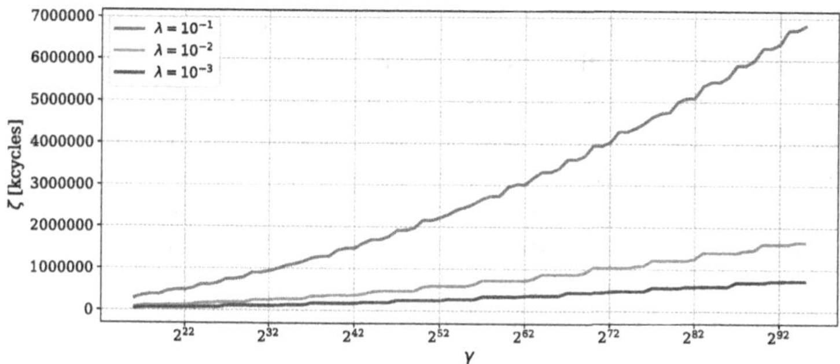

Fig. 5. Cost (kcycles) of Kyber768 for noise parameter λ and security level γ.

Levelling Still Moderately Helps. Figure 6 contains the estimated ratio between the cost of encryption and decryption for the minimal d_{Enc} and d_{Dec} leading to a given security level γ. The steps on the curves are due to the grid search on d_{Enc} and d_{Dec} which only considers integer number of shares. Overall Fig. 6 also confirms that the impact of the re-encryption in the overall implementation cost decreases as the security level increases. For example, for high security levels, the protected re-encryption is about 12 times slower than the protected decryption for Kyber 768.

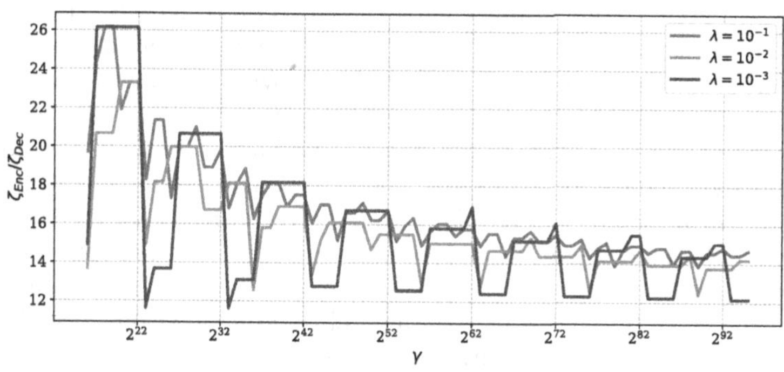

Fig. 6. Ratio between the cost of decryption and re-encryption for Kyber768.

6 Discussion and Challenges

The generic analysis in this work enables clarifying the challenges for improving the side-channel security of PQ KEMs. It first confirms that the re-encryption used in the FO transform is an important and hard-to-contain source of leakage. For an unprotected implementation, it gives rise to a very large amount of easy-to-exploit leakage samples. As a result, an SPA against this part of a PQ KEM becomes the best attack as soon as the noise in the implementation increases. Our results also show that the direct application of higher-order masking to prevent such attacks can lead to very expensive implementations. We are unaware of a CPA to CCA FO-like transform that would avoid this (or a similar) issue.

An intuitive design goal following these observations would be to limit the use or even to get rid of the FO transform. Heuristic solutions for this purpose, such as rejecting certain easy-to-exploit ciphertext structures (e.g., with low Hamming weight) or adding redundancy in the plaintext or the key are unlikely to solve the problem in a generic manner [34]. The standard solution used to obtain CCA security with leakage in symmetric cryptography (i.e., to MAC the ciphertext with a careful verification mechanism [5]) is not applicable in the public-key setting. A generic replacement of this solution would be to rely on zero knowledge proof techniques on top of the CPA encryption, in order to avoid using the secret key before verifying the validity of the resulting ciphertext during its decapsulation. By quantifying the performance gap between the decryption and re-encryption parts of a masked KEM, our results clarify the limited budget that such a zero-knowledge proof can use to beat the security vs. performance tradeoff of a uniformly masked implementation. For Kyber, it roughly corresponds to a factor 10 in clock cycles (which ignores the increase of ciphertext size).

Overall, we therefore put forward the paradoxical observation that the FO transform leads to very strong attack vectors agains unprotected PQ KEMs, but that the impact of getting rid of this transform in order to leverage a leveled implementation vanishes as the security level increases. The latter is mostly due to the eventually comparable complexities of a protected decryption and re-encryption, which cannot be amplified by an amortization over long messages like in the symmetric encryption setting. Hence, improving the side-channel security vs. efficiency tradeoff of PQ KEMs like Kyber will not only require to mitigate the leakages due to re-encryption, but also to find a way to make the protected decryption significantly more efficient. Our shortcut formulas directly indicate optimizations that could play a role in this direction, for example reducing the number of exploitable operations reflected by the α parameters in our formulas or leveraging different noise levels in decryption and re-encryption (i.e., playing with the f parameters of Subsect. 5.1). Alternatively, finding solutions to optimize the masking complexity of the decryption would also be beneficial. In absence of such advances, ensuring a sufficient noise level in order to limit the number of shares in PQ KEMs appears as the only practical option.

Eventually, while the interest of shortcut formulas lies in their ability to identify design trends, the counterpart of this genericity naturally lies in the limited details they provide about fine-grain implementation-specific issues. Evaluating the impact of the previous optimizations based on concrete case studies and experiments is therefore an interesting scope for further investigations.

Acknowledgments. François-Xavier Standaert is a senior research associate of the Belgian Fund for Scientific Research (F.R.S.-FNRS). This work has been funded in parts by the European Union through the ERC consolidator grant SWORD (project

724725) and by the Walloon Region through the FEDER project USERMedia (convention number 501907-379156).

A Masked Kyber.CCAKEM.Dec

In Table 2, we show the performance values for masked Kyber.CCAKEM.Dec for different masking orders based on [7] but with an optimized comparison. These values are provided for the STM32F407G (ARM Cortex-M4) MCU and up to order 6, since the maximum stack size on the target MCU is 112 KiB (for SRAM1). Starting from *2nd* order, the implementation requires more than 13.5 KiB of stack size for each subsequent order. The *7th* order masked code requires at least 114 KiB of stack.

Table 2. Performance numbers for masked Kyber.CCAKEM.Dec and its subroutines (values are in kCycles).

Operation	Order					
	1st	2nd	3rd	4th	5th	6th
`crypto_kem_dec`	3 178	57 141	97 294	174 220	258 437	350 529
`indcpa_dec`	200	4 203	7 047	13 542	20 323	27 230
`unpack`	24	30	36	43	50	56
`poly_arith`	89	119	148	598	713	790
`compression`	87	4 054	6 863	12 901	19 561	26 384
`indcpa_enc`	2 024	18 879	32 594	53 298	75 692	104 191
`decompression`	118	291	537	889	1 267	1 745
`gen_at`	391	391	391	391	391	391
`poly_getnoise`	1 217	17 727	31 069	49 390	70 856	98 435
`prf`	706	11 483	19 577	30 318	43 541	60 640
`cbd`	510	6,243	11 492	19 071	27 314	37 794
`poly_arith`	302	453	603	2 627	3 172	3 643
`ntt`	66	99	131	585	670	817
`invntt`	70	105	140	1 008	1 274	1 410
`comparison`	693	32 293	54 725	102 922	156 075	210 518
`hashg (SHA3-512)`	98	1 639	2 801	4 489	6 456	8 794
`hashh (SHA3-256)`	113	113	113	113	113	113
`kdf`	13	13	13	13	13	13

References

1. Alagic, G., et al.: Status report on the first round of the NIST post-quantum cryptography standardization process. National Institute of Standards and Technology (2019)
2. Avanzi, R., et al.: CRYSTALS-Kyber algorithm specifications and supporting documentation. NIST PQC Round, vol. 3, p. 4 (2019)
3. Basso, A., et al.: Saber algorithm specifications and supporting documentation. NIST PQC Round, vol. 3, p. 44 (2019)
4. Van Beirendonck, M., D'Anvers, J.-P., Karmakar, A., Balasch, J., Verbauwhede, I.: A side-channel-resistant implementation of SABER. ACM J. Emerg. Technol. Comput. Syst. **17**(2), 10:1–10:26 (2021)
5. Bellizia, D., et al.: Mode-level vs. implementation-level physical security in symmetric cryptography. In: Micciancio, D., Ristenpart, T. (eds.) CRYPTO 2020. LNCS, vol. 12170, pp. 369–400. Springer, Cham (2020). https://doi.org/10.1007/978-3-030-56784-2_13
6. Bertoni, G., Daemen, J., Peeters, M., Van Assche, G.: The keccak reference (2011)
7. Bos, J.W., Gourjon, M., Renes, J., Schneider, T., van Vredendaal, C.: Masking kyber: first- and higher-order implementations. IACR Trans. Cryptogr. Hardw. Embed. Syst. **2021**(4), 173–214 (2021)
8. Bronchain, O., Standaert, F.-X.: Breaking masked implementations with many shares on 32-bit software platforms or when the security order does not matter. IACR Trans. Cryptogr. Hardw. Embed. Syst. **2021**(3), 202–234 (2021)
9. Chari, S., Jutla, C.S., Rao, J.R., Rohatgi, P.: Towards sound approaches to counteract power-analysis attacks. In: Wiener, M. (ed.) CRYPTO 1999. LNCS, vol. 1666, pp. 398–412. Springer, Heidelberg (1999). https://doi.org/10.1007/3-540-48405-1_26
10. Cooley, J.W., Tukey, J.W.: An algorithm for the machine calculation of complex fourier series. Math. Comput. **19**, 297–301 (1965)
11. de Chérisey, E., Guilley, S., Rioul, O., Piantanida, P.: Best information is most successful mutual information and success rate in side-channel analysis. IACR Trans. Cryptogr. Hardw. Embed. Syst. **2019**(2), 49–79 (2019)
12. Duc, A., Dziembowski, S., Faust, S.: Unifying leakage models: from probing attacks to noisy leakage. In: Nguyen, P.Q., Oswald, E. (eds.) EUROCRYPT 2014. LNCS, vol. 8441, pp. 423–440. Springer, Heidelberg (2014). https://doi.org/10.1007/978-3-642-55220-5_24
13. Duc, A., Faust, S., Standaert, F.-X.: Making masking security proofs concrete. In: Oswald, E., Fischlin, M. (eds.) EUROCRYPT 2015. LNCS, vol. 9056, pp. 401–429. Springer, Heidelberg (2015). https://doi.org/10.1007/978-3-662-46800-5_16
14. Fritzmann, T., et al.: Masked accelerators and instruction set extensions for post-quantum cryptography. IACR Cryptology ePrint Archive, p. 479 (2021)
15. Fujisaki, E., Okamoto, T.: Secure integration of asymmetric and symmetric encryption schemes. In: Wiener, M. (ed.) CRYPTO 1999. LNCS, vol. 1666, pp. 537–554. Springer, Heidelberg (1999). https://doi.org/10.1007/3-540-48405-1_34
16. Gentleman, W.M., Sande, G.: Fast fourier transforms: for fun and profit. In: American Federation of Information Processing Societies: Proceedings of the AFIPS 1966 Fall Joint Computer Conference, San Francisco, California, USA, 7–10 November 1966. AFIPS Conference Proceedings, vol. 29, pp. 563–578. AFIPS/ACM/Spartan Books, Washington D.C. (1966)

17. Grosso, V., Standaert, F.-X.: Masking proofs are tight and how to exploit it in security evaluations. In: Nielsen, J.B., Rijmen, V. (eds.) EUROCRYPT 2018. LNCS, vol. 10821, pp. 385–412. Springer, Cham (2018). https://doi.org/10.1007/978-3-319-78375-8_13
18. Guo, Q., Grosso, V., Standaert, F.-X., Bronchain, O.: Modeling soft analytical side-channel attacks from a coding theory viewpoint. IACR Trans. Cryptogr. Hardw. Embed. Syst. **2020**(4), 209–238 (2020)
19. Heinz, D., Kannwischer, M.J., Land, G., Pöppelmann, T., Schwabe, P., Sprenkels, D.: First-order masked kyber on ARM cortex-M4 (work in progress) (2021)
20. Hofheinz, D., Hövelmanns, K., Kiltz, E.: A modular analysis of the Fujisaki-Okamoto transformation. In: Kalai, Y., Reyzin, L. (eds.) TCC 2017. LNCS, vol. 10677, pp. 341–371. Springer, Cham (2017). https://doi.org/10.1007/978-3-319-70500-2_12
21. Huguenin-Dumittan, L., Vaudenay, S.: Classical misuse attacks on NIST round 2 PQC. In: Conti, M., Zhou, J., Casalicchio, E., Spognardi, A. (eds.) ACNS 2020. LNCS, vol. 12146, pp. 208–227. Springer, Cham (2020). https://doi.org/10.1007/978-3-030-57808-4_11
22. Ishai, Y., Sahai, A., Wagner, D.: Private circuits: securing hardware against probing attacks. In: Boneh, D. (ed.) CRYPTO 2003. LNCS, vol. 2729, pp. 463–481. Springer, Heidelberg (2003). https://doi.org/10.1007/978-3-540-45146-4_27
23. Langlois, A., Stehlé, D.: Worst-case to average-case reductions for module lattices. Des. Codes Crypt. **75**(3), 565–599 (2014). https://doi.org/10.1007/s10623-014-9938-4
24. Mangard, S., Oswald, E., Standaert, F.-X.: One for all - all for one: unifying standard differential power analysis attacks. IET Inf. Secur. **5**(2), 100–110 (2011)
25. Ngo, K., Dubrova, E., Guo, Q., Johansson, T.: A side-channel attack on a masked IND-CCA secure saber KEM implementation. IACR Trans. Cryptogr. Hardw. Embed. Syst. **2021**(4), 676–707 (2021)
26. Pessl, P., Primas, R.: More practical single-trace attacks on the number theoretic transform. In: Schwabe, P., Thériault, N. (eds.) LATINCRYPT 2019. LNCS, vol. 11774, pp. 130–149. Springer, Cham (2019). https://doi.org/10.1007/978-3-030-30530-7_7
27. Primas, R., Pessl, P., Mangard, S.: Single-trace side-channel attacks on masked lattice-based encryption. In: Fischer, W., Homma, N. (eds.) CHES 2017. LNCS, vol. 10529, pp. 513–533. Springer, Cham (2017). https://doi.org/10.1007/978-3-319-66787-4_25
28. Prouff, E., Rivain, M.: Masking against side-channel attacks: a formal security proof. In: Johansson, T., Nguyen, P.Q. (eds.) EUROCRYPT 2013. LNCS, vol. 7881, pp. 142–159. Springer, Heidelberg (2013). https://doi.org/10.1007/978-3-642-38348-9_9
29. Ravi, P., Roy, S.S., Chattopadhyay, A., Bhasin, S.: Generic side-channel attacks on CCA-secure lattice-based PKE and KEMs. IACR Trans. Cryptogr. Hardw. Embed. Syst. **2020**(3), 307–335 (2020)
30. Standaert, F.-X.: Towards and open approach to secure cryptographic implementations (invited talk). In: EUROCRYPT I. LNCS, vol. 11476, p. xv (2019). https://www.youtube.com/watch?v=KdhrsuJT1sE
31. Standaert, F.-X., Malkin, T.G., Yung, M.: A unified framework for the analysis of side-channel key recovery attacks. In: Joux, A. (ed.) EUROCRYPT 2009. LNCS, vol. 5479, pp. 443–461. Springer, Heidelberg (2009). https://doi.org/10.1007/978-3-642-01001-9_26

32. Ueno, R., Xagawa, K., Tanaka, Y., Ito, A., Takahashi, J., Homma, N.: Curse of re-encryption: a generic power/EM analysis on post-quantum KEMs. IACR Cryptology ePrint Archive, p. 849 (2021)
33. Veyrat-Charvillon, N., Gérard, B., Standaert, F.-X.: Soft analytical side-channel attacks. In: Sarkar, P., Iwata, T. (eds.) ASIACRYPT 2014. LNCS, vol. 8873, pp. 282–296. Springer, Heidelberg (2014). https://doi.org/10.1007/978-3-662-45611-8_15
34. Xu, Z., Pemberton, O., Roy, S.S., Oswald, D.F.: Magnifying side-channel leakage of lattice-based cryptosystems with chosen ciphertexts: the case study of kyber. IACR Cryptol. ePrint Arch. **2020**, 912 (2020)

Handcrafting: Improving Automated Masking in Hardware with Manual Optimizations

Charles Momin(✉), Gaëtan Cassiers, and François-Xavier Standaert

UCLouvain, ICTEAM, Crypto Group, Louvain-la-Neuve, Belgium
{charles.momin,gaetan.cassiers,francois-xavier.standaert}@uclouvain.be

Abstract. Masking is an important countermeasure against side-channel attacks, but its secure implementation is known to be error-prone. The automated verification and generation of masked designs is therefore an important theoretical and practical challenge. In a recent work, Knichel et al. proposed a tool for the automated generation of masked hardware implementations satisfying strong security properties (e.g., glitch-freeness and composability). In this paper, we study the possibility to improve their results based on manual performance optimizations for the AES algorithm. Our main conclusion is that as the target architecture becomes more serial, such a handcrafted approach gains interest. For example, we reach latency reductions by a factor six for 8-bit architectures. We conclude the paper by discussing the extent to which such optimizations could be integrated in the tool of Knichel et al. As a bonus, we adapt a composition-based verification tool to check that our implementations are robust against glitches & transitions, and confirm the security order of exemplary implementations with preliminary leakage assessment.

Keywords: Side-Channel Attacks · Masking Countermeasure · Efficient Hardware Implementations · AES Rijndael · Formal Verification

1 Introduction

Side-channel attacks relying on the exploitation of physical information leakage such as the power consumption or the electromagnetic radiation of cryptographic implementations are an important security threat. The masking countermeasure is a standard answer to this threat [CJRR99]. Its underlying principle is to compute over secret-shared intermediate variables that are individually independent of the secret data manipulated by a device. For this purpose, the designs to protect are typically split in small operations (e.g., AND and XOR gates) which are then replaced by gadgets able to compute securely over shared data.

The evaluation of masked implementations is a tricky task. On the one hand, the security of small gadgets may not directly extend to their combination, leading to so-called composition issues [CPRR13, BBD+16]. On the other

J. Balasch and C. O'Flynn (Eds.): COSADE 2022, LNCS 13211, pp. 257–275, 2022.
https://doi.org/10.1007/978-3-030-99766-3_12

hand, physical defaults such as glitches can break the independence assumptions needed for masking to be secure [MPG05, NRS11]. These issues can also be combined leading to additional challenges [FGP+18, MMSS19]. This state-of-the-art has motivated an increased interest for the automated verification of masked implementations [BBD+15, BGI+18, BBC+19, KSM20]. The automated generation of these implementations therefore appears as the natural next steps, and first efforts in this direction can be found in [BDM+20, KMMS22].

In this paper, we are in particular interested in the work of Knichel et al., which introduced a tool, AGEMA, allowing inexperienced engineers to generate masked implementations from unprotected ones [KMMS22]. At high-level, the tool leverages the Hardware Private Circuits (HPC) scheme introduced in [CGLS21] and variations thereof. The HPC scheme provides strong composition properties in the presence of hardware defaults such as glitches and comes with the fullVerif tool which allows checking if the requirements needed for the composition theorems to hold are respected in practice. By combining AGEMA and fullVerif, Knichel et al. made a significant step towards improving the usability of masking schemes in hardware. Yet, and as usual when considering automation, these advances also raise the question whether the implementations obtained compete with manually optimized ones. In other words, can all the architecture-level optimizations that an experienced designer would exploit be automated, and if not, what is the performance gap that they lead to?

We contribute to this question by presenting the results of different masked hardware implementations of the AES, designed to take advantage of the inherent pipeline of complex blocks based on the HPC2 gadgets. In particular, we first point out that AGEMA's generated implementations are suboptimal in terms of latency. We propose an optimization strategy and demonstrate that using it gives better result for the implementation of specific blocks such as the AES S-box. Second, we propose optimized masked AES implementations based on 8-bit, 32-bit and 128-bit loop architectures. We show that the latency of our handcrafted designs is significantly improved w.r.t. the ones generated by AGEMA in the 8-bit case, while the gains tend to vanish for the larger architectures. Concretely, our results therefore provide improved masked implementation results for the AES-128 algorithm based on a state-of-the-art masking scheme. More generally, we also use our investigations to discuss tracks that could be used to improve the performances of automatically generated masked implementations for tools like AGEMA. Eventually, and as an additional contribution, we analyze the security of our implementations, first in the robust probing model with glitches and transitions using the fullVerif tool, which we modified to verify the transition-robustness conditions introduced in [CS21].[1] We finally confirm these results by means of leakage detection tests on exemplary implementations.

Related Works. Many hardware masking schemes are proposed in the literature. For example, the proposals in [CRB+16, GMK17] aim at similar goals as HPC, with less formal composability guarantees. Our focus is on the HPC scheme

[1] The verification of the transition-robustness has been integrated in the latest version of fullVerif at https://github.com/cassiersg/fullverif.

because it has been selected for automation in [KMMS22], but we believe our main conclusions regarding automation are mostly independent of this choice.

Paper Structure. The paper is organized in 3 parts. First, we describe the AES-128 algorithm and recall some specificities about the HPC2 masking scheme. We also provide brief explanations about the fullVerif and AGEMA tools. Next, we detail the construction of the protected S-box as well as the three AES architectures considered in this work. Finally, performance metrics and basic side-channel analysis results are presented.

2 Background

Advanced Encryption Standard. The Advanced Encryption Standard (AES) is a symmetric key algorithm standardized by the NIST in 2001. Its variant AES-128 operates on 128-bit state with 128-bit secret key. Both the state and the key can be represented as 4×4 matrices of 16 bytes each. The algorithm is composed of 10 rounds, each one being composed of 4 different operations. First, the `SubByte` operation is a non-linear substitution operating on each byte independently. Second, the `ShiftRows` operation is a cyclic shift of 1, 2 or 3 positions of each byte in the last three rows. Third, the `MixColumns` operates over each column of the state independently. The later are considered as polynomials with coefficients over $GF(2^8)$ and are multiplied modulo $x^4 + 1$ by the fixed polynomial 03 $\times^3$ +01 $\times^2$ +01 $\times$ +02. Finally, the `AddRoundKey` operation adds the round key by performing a bitwise XOR operation. It has to be noted that the `MixColumns` operation is not performed in the 10-th (i.e., last) round and an `AddRoundKey` is performed before the first round.

Each round key is derived with a key scheduling algorithm applied at each round on the previous round key. First, the last column is rotated by one byte up. Next, the SubByte operation is applied on each byte of the resulting column and the round constant is added using a bitwise XOR operation. The first column of the new round key is obtained by applying a bitwise XOR between the column obtained after the round constant addition and the first column of the key. Finally, the new value of the i-th column is obtained by bitwise XORing the i-th column of the key and the $i-1$-th column of the new round key.

HPC2 Masking Scheme. The hardware private circuits introduced in [CGLS21] come in two flavors: we next focus on the HPC2 variant. In addition to being glitch-robust, its gadgets are proven trivially composable at any order using the Probe Isolation Non Interference (PINI) framework [CS20]. The HPC2 scheme operates over GF(2) (i.e., bitwise) and requires state-of-the-art amount of randomness for its non-linear operation (i.e., AND2 gates). Precisely, each AND2-HPC2 gadget requires $d(d-1)/2$ bits of randomness where d is the number of shares in the design. A specificity of this gadget is its latency asymmetry: if the first input sharing enters the gadgets at cycle t, the second input sharing is expected to enter the gadget at cycle $t+1$ and the output is produced at cycle $t+2$. Other gadgets performing basic operations have been designed (e.g., XORs & MUXes).[2] The HPC2 masking scheme requires no refresh gadget, and the affine/linear gadgets do not require randomness and have no latency.

fullVerif. The open source tool fullVerif is an automated composition-based program that can verify that the assumptions of the HPC2 security proofs are fulfilled by a Hardware Description Language (HDL) design. In order to be checked by fullVerif, the modules' definitions as well as their ports should be annotated with specific verilog attributes. These attributes indicates signal's properties such as their types (i.e., *sharing*, *control* or *randomness*) or their sizes and time validity to the tool. Different composition strategies can be specified for each module in the design. The tool works based on a netlist of the architecture together with a simulation file in order to build a dataflow graph. The latter is then used to proceed to different security checks as listed in [CGLS21].

AGEMA is an open source tool presented in [KMMS22]. It automatically generates masked hardware netlists based on unprotected HDL implementations and relies on specific annotations of the IO ports at the top level of the hierarchy in order to identify which part of the circuit should be masked. Working on top of a synthesized netlist of the full architecture, it propagates the signals annotations across the hierarchy before implementing the masked parts of the circuit. It offers the choice between different masking schemes relying on the PINI property (among which HPC2), as well as different optimization strategies depending on the chosen masking scheme. To ensure the proper synchronization of the signals across the hierarchy, the tool relies on two approaches: pipelining (i.e., introducing registers to synchronize all the inputs of each masked gadgets) or clock gating (i.e., modulating the registers' clock signals). As shown in [KMMS22], pipelining implies more area cost while achieving better throughput; clock gating allows reducing the global cost but results in implementations with larger latency.

3 Architectures Descriptions

We now describe our optimized constructions. First, we introduce a generic latency optimization methodology for pipeline blocks based on the HPC2 AND gadget. It is applied to a bit-level AES S-box, reducing its latency by 25 %. Second, our three AES architectures are detailed, differing by their level of parallelism, and more particularly the number of S-boxes instantiated in the design. Precisely, we next consider an architecture using one S-box instance (8-bit serial), 4 S-box instances (32-bit serial) and 20 S-box instances[3] (128-bit serial).

3.1 Masked AES S-box Implementation

Because of its significant cost both in logic and randomness, the masked implementation of the non-linear `SubByte` layer requires a particular attention. First,

[2] All the gadgets are available in a public verilog library at https://github.com/cassiersg/fullverif/tree/release/lib_v.

[3] 16 S-boxes for the rounds computation and 4 for the key schedule.

taking into account the constraint that the HPC2 masking scheme instantiates gadgets operating over GF(2) only, we need a bit-level S-box representation. We follow the design choice of [KMMS22] for this purpose, and use the S-box design proposed by Boyar and Peralta [BP12]. It is only composed of basics operation over GF(2) (i.e., XOR2, AND2 and NOT gates). To the best of our knowledge, it is the known representation with the lowest number of AND2 gates. Precisely, it only requires 34 AND2 gates and its naive implementation using the HPC2 gadgets results in an S-box with 8 cycles latency.

Due to the asymmetry at their inputs, naively replacing basic unprotected operations in complex circuit with HPC2 gadgets may result in a sub-optimal area and latency. For example, two different implementations (i.e., unprotected and masked) of an AND3 gate are shown Fig. 1. While the area and latency for the two unprotected implementations are identical, they differ for the protected ones. On the left, 4 additional registers are required to ensure the circuit functionality, and the computation is performed in 4 cycles. On the right, only 2 registers are required and the computation is performed in 3 cycles. Such area and latency overheads are incurred by implementations (such as AGEMA) that add a register on one of the inputs of the AND2 gadget to achieve symmetric latency (which simplifies the design process).

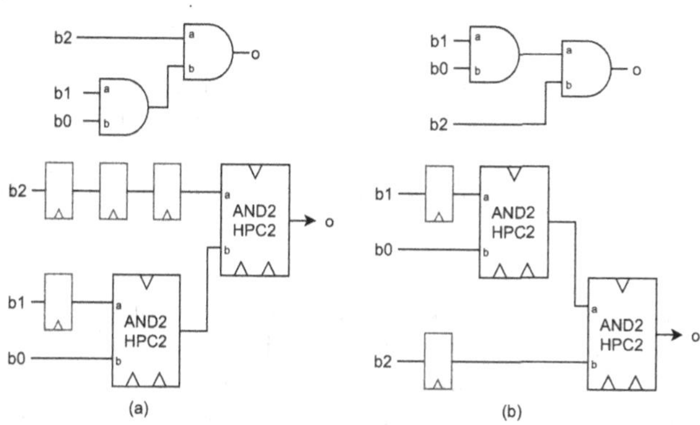

Fig. 1. Example of AND3 gate implementation using HPC2 gadgets.

Based on this observation, it may be tempting to look for optimal symmetric-latency gadget-based circuits for more complex operations (e.g., AND3 gates). However, using a composition of such larger gadgets is still not optimal. For example, two implementations of an AND5 operation are shown in Fig. 2. On the left, the implementation directly instantiates twice the optimized AND3 construction of Fig. 1 and requires 10 additional registers to compute the results in 6 cycles. On the right, a more optimized implementation only requires 3 additional registers and performs the computation in 4 cycles. Instead of the "larger gadgets" approach, we optimize directly the latency of a full logic block (the full S-box), which helps reducing the number of registers in our designs.

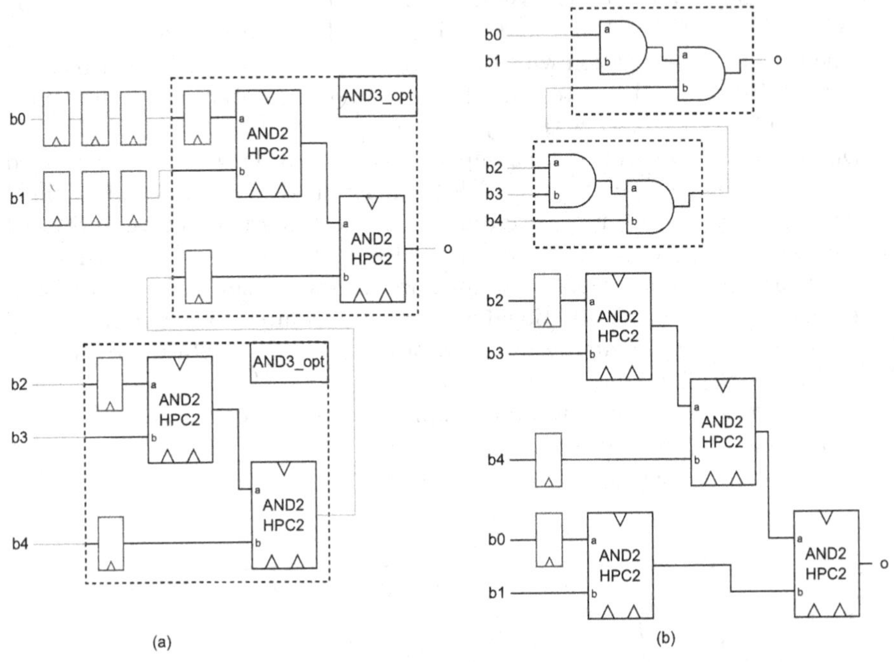

Fig. 2. Example of AND5 gate implementation using HPC2 gadgets.

Generic Block Latency Optimization Algorithm. The optimization of a block is efficiently performed as follows. Starting from the input signals of the logic block to optimize, the information about the exact time of validity of each signal is propagated across the circuitry, level by level. For some gadgets that have more than one input, the latency requirements of all the inputs may not be met. In such cases, a solution is to insert registers on the input path in order to meet the timing constraints. In the specific case where the latest signal (i.e., the signal being valid with the largest latency) is connected to the input port with the lowest timing requirement (i.e., the input port at which a signal is first entering the gadget), then the input connections are switched. This optimization naturally leads to a solution with a reduced amount of additional registers while keeping the same functionality as the original circuit.

This (easy to automate) procedure has been used in order to generate the architecture of the implementations (b) on Fig. 1 and Fig. 2. It leads to significant improvements for the AES S-box implementation. Considering a latency-equalized version of the AND2-HPC2 gadget from [CGLS21] (as in Fig. 1), the implementation of the Boyar-Peralta S-box requires $156d$ additional registers and operates in 8 cycles. With our optimization, it only requires $94d$ additional registers and operates in 6 cycles.

3.2 8-Bit Serial Implementation

As depicted in Fig. 3, the 8-bit serial implementation takes as input the shared value of the key `sh_key` and the (unshared) plaintext `pt`. The later is first represented as a valid sharing by concatenating $d-1$ zero shares to each bit. The architecture of this implementation is organized around two mains blocks: the `KeyHolder` and the `StateHolder` which store and order the processing of the round key and of the state. The blocks feed each byte serially during the `SubByte` and `AddRoundKey` layers. Unless otherwise noted, each bus in the architecture is 8-bit wide. In addition, one S-box is instantiated with the block `MSKSbox`. The block `MSKmc` is a combinatorial logic that implements the `MixColumns` operation for a full column (i.e., 4 bytes) and consists in d instances of the unprotected `MixColumns` operation logic, where each instance processes one state share.

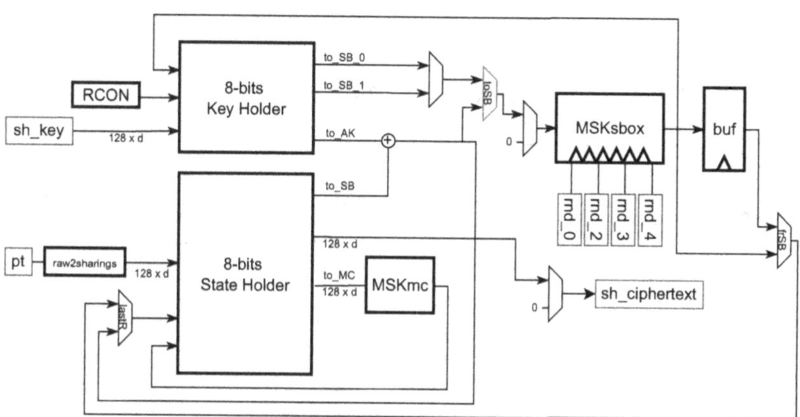

Fig. 3. Global Architecture of the 8-bit serial implementation.

The shared state and round key are stored in dedicated shift registers of shared bytes, as shown in Fig. 4 and Fig. 5. The rounds are computed serially by performing the `SubByte` and `AddRoundKey` operations byte per byte. The state is processed row per row (i.e., starting with the bytes 0,4,8,12 and ending with the bytes 3,7,11,15). The four S-box executions occurring during the key scheduling are interleaved between the processing of the state. To do so, the mux `toSB` in Fig. 3 is used to feed the S-box instance with a shared byte coming either from the key, either from the `AddRoundKey` result. This interleaving of key scheduling and round processing necessitates the insertion of a buffer at the output of the S-box to avoid loosing data in cases where the output of the S-box is valid and a key byte is provided at its input. Indeed, in such cases, the shift register holding the state is stalled, making any feedback from the S-box to the state holder impossible. We rely on the pipeline structure of the S-box instance to reduce the overall latency of the execution. That is, we do not wait for full S-box execution to be finished before feeding the S-box with valid data. Instead, we feed it at each clock cycle when its input data is available. Considering the latency of our S-box design, the full `AddRoundKey`, `SubByte` and the key scheduling operations of a round are performed in $\mathsf{SB}_{lat} + 16 + 4 = 26$ cycles.

The `ShiftRows` operation is performed in a single cycle by enabling the data flowing through the state holder with an appropriate routing defined by the MUXes `sh-i` (depicted in green in Fig. 4). Finally, the `MixColumns` operation is performed in 4 cycles, using the MUXes `mc-i` to route the signals back from the `MC` instance (depicted in red in Fig. 4). The last `AddRoundKey` operation is performed byte per byte in 16 cycles, using the mux `lastR` in Fig. 3 to bypass the S-box instance. Overall, the latency of a full execution of our 8-bit implementation is equal to $9 \times (26 + 1 + 4) + (26 + 1) + 16 = 322$ cycles.[4]

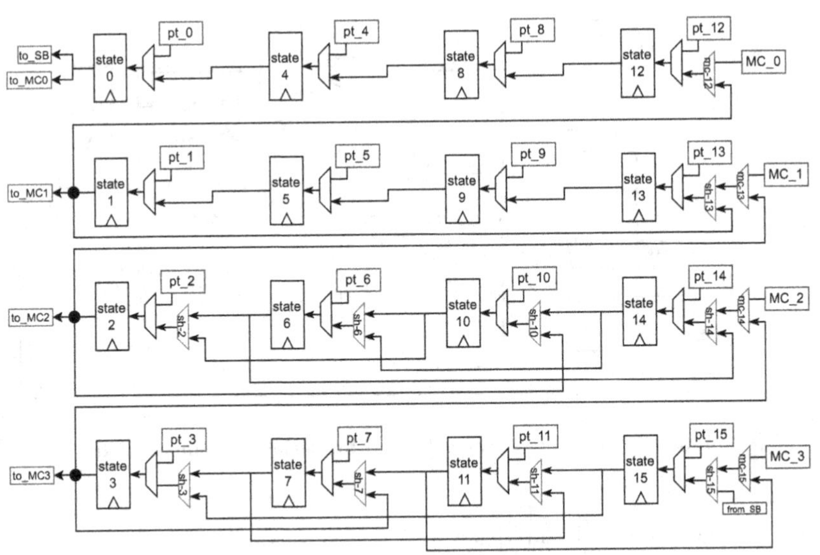

Fig. 4. 8-bit implementation: architecture of the state holder.

[4] A MUX located at the output of the global core is used to control the proper release of the valid ciphertext. This is not strictly required in the context of our work, however practical integrations will likely add a logic block computing the recombined ciphertext. Without our output gating, this would lead to leaking unmasked internal states of the AES, defeating the masking countermeasure.

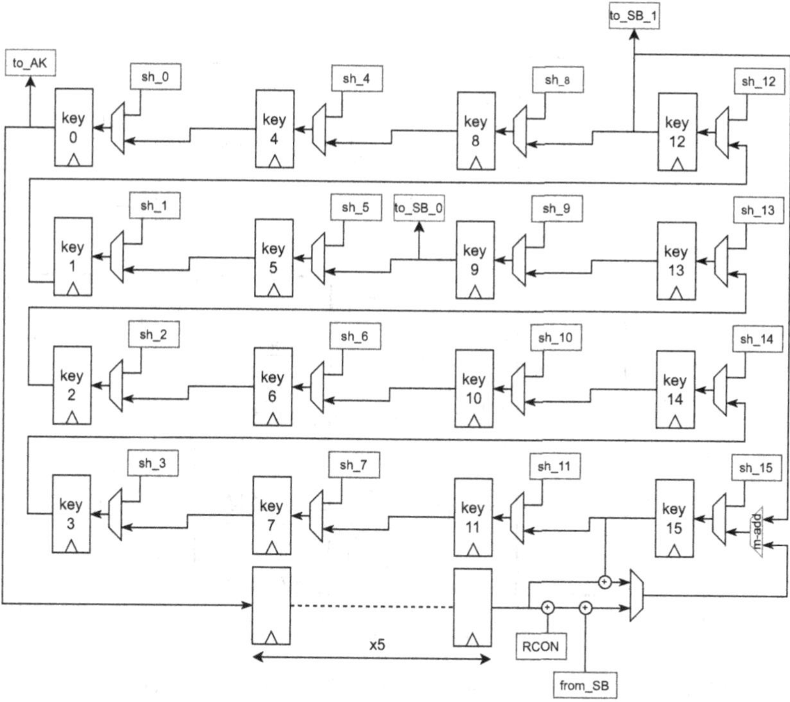

Fig. 5. 8-bit implementation: architecture of the key holder.

3.3 32-Bit Serial Implementation

The 32-bit serial architecture is also organized around two main blocks containing the values of the state and the key. As for the 8-bit serial architecture, the data is stored in 16 register blocks, each of them holding a shared byte value. A round is computed serially, 32 bits per 32 bits. To do so, four S-boxes are instantiated in the architecture. The latter are fed either with the result of the `AddRoundKey` layer (represented in Fig. 7) or by the `KeyHolder` (in order to perform the key schedule), as controlled by the `toSBi` MUXes (see Fig. 6). Finally, a dedicated combinatorial logic block is used to compute the masked `MixColumns` operation on a full column.

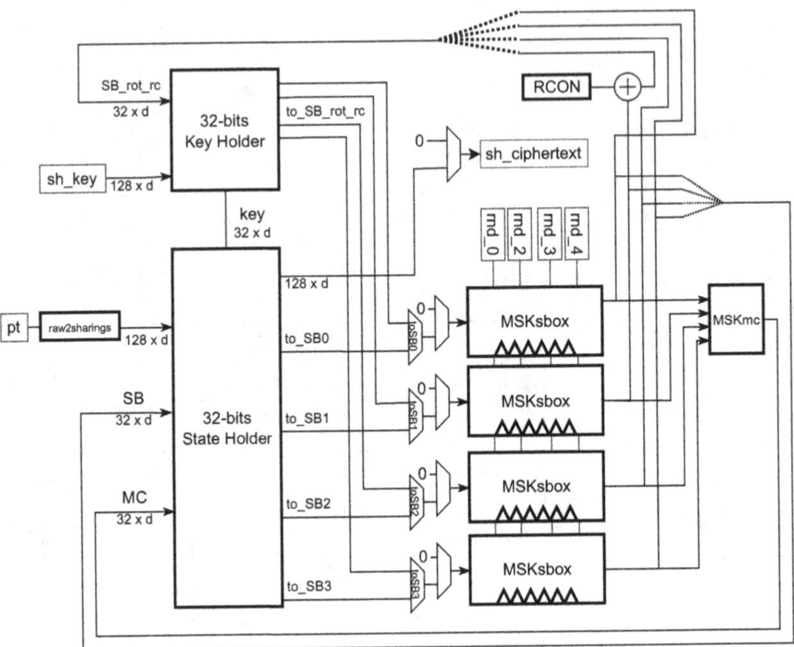

Fig. 6. Global Architecture of the 32-bit serial implementation.

Both the `StateHolder` and the `KeyHolder` are organized as four shift registers (see Figs. 7 and 8). The `AddRoundKey` operation is performed with combinatorial logic before sending the signals `to_SBi` to the S-boxes. Under this mode of computation, the MUXes `loopi` (depicted in green in Fig. 7) are routing the data in a loop manner over the shift registers. In such a way, 4 cycles are sufficient to feed the S-boxes with the full state. The positions of the `to_SBi` signals (i.e., on byte indexes 0, 5, 10 and 15) have been carefully chosen to perform the `ShiftRows` operation at the same time as feeding the S-boxes without using a dedicated clock cycle. For full round computations (i.e., all except the last), the output of the S-boxes is directly routed to the `MSKmc` block before entering back the `StateHolder`. In the last round, the MUXes `mc-i` are used to bypass the `MixColumns` layer. The last `AddRoundKey` operation is performed by enabling the `loopi` MUXes as well as the key addition.

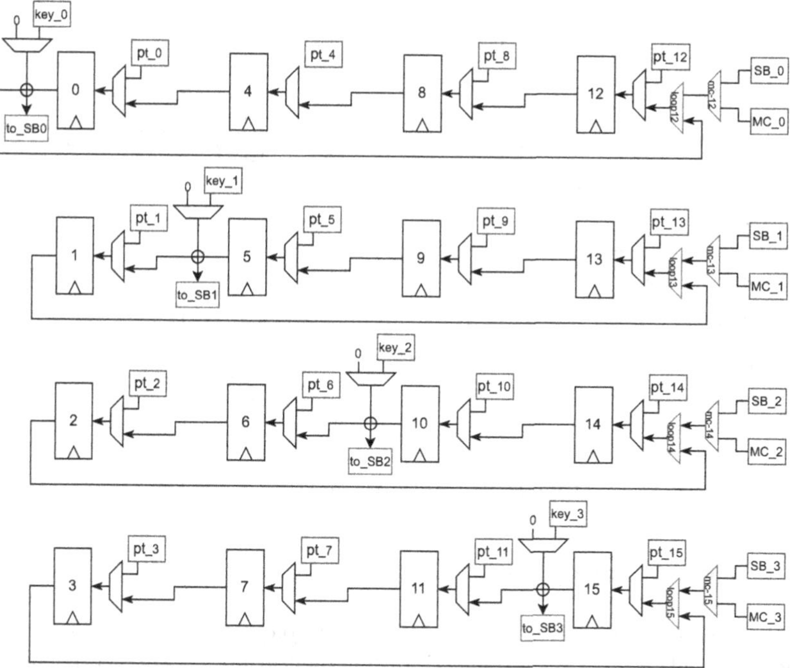

Fig. 7. 32-bit implementation: architecture of the state holder.

The key schedule is performed in parallel to the round computation, by interleaving appropriately the feeding of the S-boxes with key bytes. More precisely, the fourth column of the key is sent to the S-boxes during the last cycle of the `MixColumns` computation of the previous round. We take advantage of the S-box latency to perform the key schedule algorithm in the time lap required to compute the `MixColumns` operation. For this mechanism to work properly, the encryption execution starts by feeding the S-boxes with key material during the first cycle. The rotation operation is performed via direct routing and does not require dedicated clock cycle as shown in Fig. 6. The addition of the round constant is performed in parallel to the rotation. Once the `SubByte` operation is performed, the new key value is computed column per column during four cycles. To this end, the dedicated MUXes `addi` (depicted in red in Fig. 8) are configured in such a way that `SB_rot_rc` (the output of the S-box) is added to the first column of the round key. Configuring the `addi` MUXes, the other columns of the new round key are then computed by serially adding them to the new column. The latency of a full encryption is therefore $1 + 10 \cdot (4 + 6) + 4 = 105$ cycles.

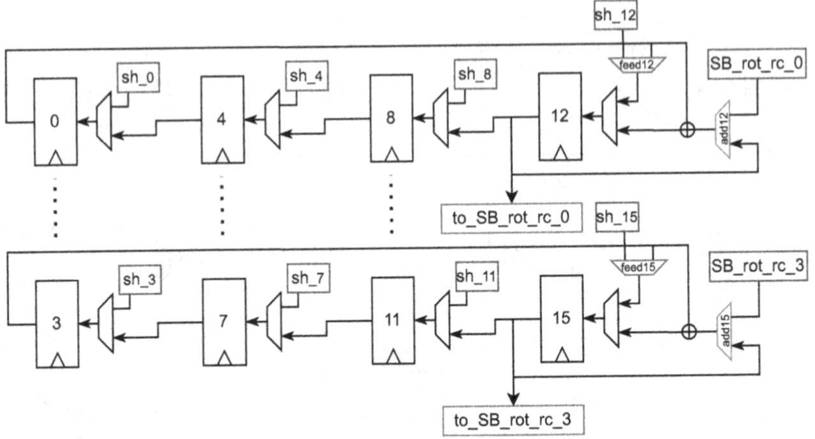

Fig. 8. 32-bit implementation: architecture of the key holder.

3.4 128-Bit Serial Implementation

Compared to the 8-bit serial and 32-bit serial implementations, the organization of the architecture of the 128-bit serial implementation is more straightforward. As depicted in Fig. 9, it contains all the logic necessary to operate on a full 128-bit state, as well as the logic required to perform the key scheduling in parallel to the round computation. In more details, the state and the key sharing `sh_key` are stored in a register. After the `AddRoundKey` layer, the state in directly routed to the `SubByte` logic composed of 16 S-box instances. Directly following the latter, the `ShiftRows` operation is performed at the routing level before entering the logic for the `MixColumns` operation, itself composed of four independent blocks, each operating on one individual column of the shared state. Depending on the round counter, MUXes are used to feed back to the state register the results either after the `ShiftRows` operation, or after the `MixColumns` operation.

For the key scheduling, four S-box instances are used order to process the 4 bytes of the fourth column of the key in parallel. As for the `ShiftRows` layer, the rotation occurring is performed as the routing level, requiring no additional logic. Finally, combinatorial XOR gadgets are placed at the output of the S-box in order to finalize the round key. The resulting round key is fed back to the key holder register. For this 128-bit architecture, it therefore follows that the latency of a full encryption is $10 \cdot (6 + 1) = 70$ cycles.

4 Implementation Results

In this section, we present the post-synthesis ASIC implementation results obtained for the different architectures and compare them with results obtained with AGEMA generated implementation. All the syntheses have been performed using Genus Synthesis Solution (Cadence) using the TSMC-N65 design kit.

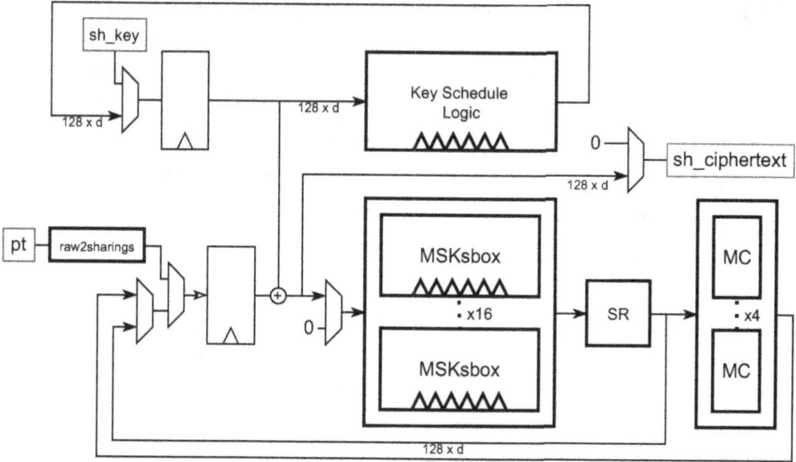

Fig. 9. Global Architecture of the 128-bit serial implementation

We complete these results with a brief discussion of physical security guarantees based on both formal verification and experimental leakage assessment.

4.1 Masked S-box Implementations

Starting with the S-box implementation results depicted in Table 1, our implementation performs a computation in 6 cycles, which is 25% faster than the 8 cycles obtained by AGEMA for both pipeline and clock-gating synchronization strategies. This is a direct effect of the input ports switching for AND2-HPC2 gadgets described in Sect. 3.1. Compared to the S-box with pipelined synchronization, our implementation is approximately 20% smaller (see Table 2). The first reason for this is the reduced number of synchronization registers thanks to the lower latency. A second reason for this difference lies in the implementation of the AND2-HPC2 gadget used by AGEMA: they require more registers than what is required, i.e., $4d(d-1)+3d$ per multiplication gadget, while our implementation (which comes from fullVerif's library) only instantiates $2d + 7/2 \times d(d-1)$ registers per multiplication. Since both implementations are fully pipelined, they reach a throughput of one S-box evaluation per cycle.

The comparison with the S-box generated with the clock-gating synchronization strategy is interesting. On the one hand, it avoids all synchronization registers, but on the other hand, clock gating logic is added, and the multiplication gadgets are more expensive, as discussed above. The increased cost of the multiplication gadgets dominates for $d \geq 3$, while for $d = 2$ the AGEMA implementation is a bit smaller than ours. In addition to having a higher latency, the AGEMA clock-gated S-box has a much lower throughput.

Table 1. ASIC TSMC-N65 S-box implementation results (post-synthesis).

Instance	Share [count]	Seq. area [GE]	Area [GE]	Latency [cycle]	Throughput [exec/cycle]
AGEMA c.g.*	2	2009	2972	8	0.125
AGEMA c.g.*	3	4625	6822	8	0.125
AGEMA c.g.*	4	8329	12290	8	0.125
AGEMA pipe.†	2	3024	3981	8	1
AGEMA pipe.†	3	6168	8360	8	1
AGEMA pipe.†	4	10400	14356	8	1
New	2	2273	3213	6	1
New	3	4831	6705	6	1
New	4	8354	11515	6	1

* Clock-gating synchronization mechanism.
† Pipeline synchronization mechanism.

Table 2. ASIC TSMC-N65 S-box implementation results comparison (post-synthesis).

Instance	Shares	Area [%]*	Latency [%]*	Area [%]†	Throughput [%]†
New	2	+8	−25	−19	+0
New	3	−2	−25	−20	+0
New	4	−6	−25	−20	+0

* Compared to AGEMA with clock-gating synchronization.
† Compared to AGEMA with pipeline synchronization.

4.2 Masked AES Implementations

The previous differences are amplified when considering a full encryption core, as shown in Tables 3 and 4. Starting with the 8-bit serial architecture, our new implementation has a 6.4 times lower latency than the ones generated with AGEMA for both synchronization mechanisms. This is due to the fact that the hand-crafted control mechanism takes full advantage of the pipeline architecture of the S-box without adding superficial pipeline levels, speeding up the computation of the `SubByte` operation by processing up to 6 bytes of the same AES encryption in parallel instead of 1. Regarding the throughput, the 8-bit pipelined AGEMA implementation is better then ours: it is able to optimally use the S-box pipeline while our implementation dedicates cycles to other operations.

As for the area, our new implementation is roughly 2.6 times smaller than the one generated with pipeline synchronization. This difference is mainly due to the very large number of registers needed to achieve a complete round pipeline for the full AES state and round keys in the AGEMA pipelined implementation. Compared to the implementations synchronized with clock-gating, the area of our new architecture is slightly higher, but are of the same order of magnitude. In more details, the overheads observed for the 8-bit implementations vary from

Table 3. ASIC TSMC-N65 AES encryption implementation results (post-synthesis).

Instance	Share [count]	Seq. area [GE]	Area [GE]	Latency [cycle]	Throughput [exec/cycle]
AGEMA 8-bit c.g.*	2	4068	9356	2043	0.00049
AGEMA 8-bit c.g.*	3	7678	16319		
AGEMA 8-bit c.g.*	4	12375	24919		
AGEMA 8-bit pipe.†	2	25055	30338	2043	0.0044
AGEMA 8-bit pipe.†	3	38667	47302		
AGEMA 8-bit pipe.†	4	53382	65921		
New 8-bit	2	4790	10634	322	0.0031
New 8-bit	3	8571	17591		
New 8-bit	4	13315	25915		
New 32-bit	2	11139	19598	105	0.0095
New 32-bit	3	22399	36776		
New 32-bit	4	37511	59217		
AGEMA 128-bit c.g.*	2	40198	63613	99	0.010
AGEMA 128-bit c.g.*	3	92909	143100		
AGEMA 128-bit c.g.*	4	167376	254948		
AGEMA 128-bit pipe.†	2	86317	109725	99	0.091
AGEMA 128-bit pipe.†	3	161789	211969		
AGEMA 128-bit pipe.†	4	259307	346880		
New 128-bit	2	47597	73699	70	0.10
New 128-bit	3	99859	148129		
New 128-bit	4	171274	249011		

* Clock-gating synchronization mechanism.
† Pipeline synchronization mechanism.

14 % to 4 % (for 2, 3 and 4 shares) and are caused by the synchronization registers used in our implementations. In particular, besides the registers introduced in the S-box, $48d$ registers are used in the global architecture ($40d$ in the key schedule, as shown in Fig. 5, and $8d$ in the global datapath, as depicted in Fig. 3).

For the 128-bit implementations, we also achieve a latency reduction and a throughput increase compared to the AGEMA implementations, but the gain is much smaller than in the 8-bit case. Our implementation is slightly larger than the AGEMA clock-gated one, while the pipelined one is larger than ours.

Finally, we also report the result of a 32-bit implementation (an architecture that was not given in [KMMS22]). It performs a full encryption in 105 cycles, which is similar to what is achieved by the round-based implementation generated by AGEMA. On top of that, its area turns out to be significantly lower than what is achieved for round-based architectures, making it an interesting alternative when the area vs. latency trade-off is considered.

Table 4. ASIC TSMC-N65 AES enc. implem. results comparison (post-synthesis).

Instance	Shares	Area [%]*	Latency [%]*	Area [%]†	Throughput [%]†
New 8-bit	2	+14	−84	−65	−30
New 8-bit	3	+8	−84	−63	−30
New 8-bit	4	+4	−84	−60	−30
New 128-bit	2	+16	−30	−33	+10
New 128-bit	3	+4	−30	−30	+10
New 128-bit	4	−2	−30	−28	+10

* Compared to AGEMA with clock-gating synchronization.

† Compared to AGEMA with pipeline synchronization.

4.3 Physical Security

We use a two-step methodology to validate the $d-1$-th order security.

As a first step, we use the fullVerif tool to validate that the implementation satisfies the HPC conditions [CGLS21]. Those conditions guarantee glitch-robust probing security, but give no assurance against transition leakage. To also take into account the latter, we relied on the "Optimized composition approach" presented in [CS21], which ensures security against both glitches and transitions. In our context, this approach requires the insertion of a pipeline bubble in the S-box between each AES rounds. In such pipeline bubbles, the data processed by the S-boxes should not depend on any sensitive input.

We extended fullVerif to check this property. Concretely, using the identification of non-sensitive pipeline bubbles, the new verification algorithm builds groups of executions that are not separated by such bubbles for each S-box (in full genericity, for each PINI but non-affine gadget). Then for each execution in each group, it checks that none of the input sharings is computed using an output sharing of a gadget in the same group, which is implemented as a path existence check in the computation graph.

The second step leverages the TVLA testing methodology in order to validate practical security and rule-out issues that cannot be caught by fullVerif such as those due to (post-)synthesis optimizations. Namely, we used fixed vs. random T-tests as a preliminary leakage assessment [GGJR+11]. The measurements were performed on a Sakura-G board running at 6 MHz. We conducted the acquisitions with a PicoScope 5244D sampling at 500 MS/s with 12-bit resolution. As in [KMMS22], each randomness bit was generated on-the-fly by a randomly seeded independent instance of the 31-bit maximum length LFSR presented in [Alf98]. As shown in Fig. 10 for the 8-bit implementation, leakage can be observed starting at second order with 2 shares (1 M traces for both test orders) and at the third order with 3 shares (10 M traces for all test orders).

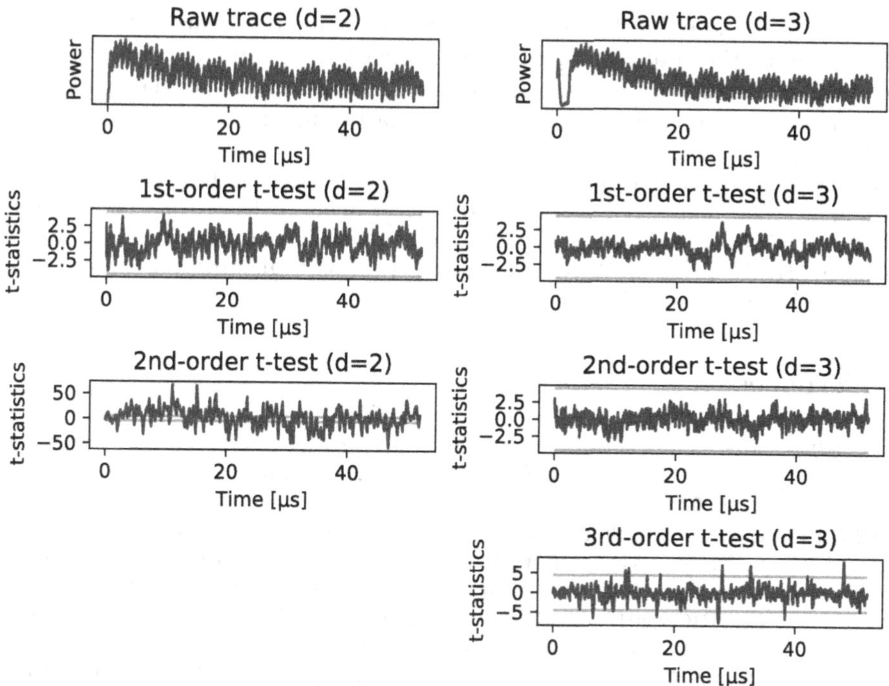

Fig. 10. Fixed vs random T-test results (AES-128, 8-bit serial architecture).

5 Conclusion

While the automated generation of masked hardware performed by AGEMA is a significant advance towards improving the usability of masking for non-expert designers, our results show that there remains room for further performance optimizations and therefore raise the question whether our handcrafted improvements could be integrated in AGEMA. For example, when dealing with asymmetric gadgets like the ones developed in the HPC2 scheme, a first approach could be to implement the optimization method based on the input switching described in Sect. 3.1. We believe that such a feature should be easily implemented in AGEMA by working with high-level netlists containing information about the timings of signals' propagation. Such timings may be either provided in the HDL by the use of annotations (as done for the fullVerif tool) or hard-coded in the tool. As another easy-to-integrate option, relying on the AND2 gadget implementation proposed in [CGLS21] could also be considered, as the latter requires less registers and enables asymmetric optimizations.

By contrast, which strategy to follow in order to automatically take advantage of the pipeline nature of the masked architectures is less clear. Indeed, our architecture optimizations are based on a deep understanding of the operations to be performed (e.g., how the S-box can be re-ordered). Automating them would *a minima* require to analyze the precise control logic of the core.

Finally, we note that besides the aforementioned performance optimizations, implementing the automated generation of annotations compliant with fullVerif may be an interesting addition to AGEMA, in order to facilitate the verification of compositional properties that generated masked implementations exploit.

Acknowledgments. Gaëtan Cassiers and François-Xavier Standaert are respectively Research Fellow and Senior Associate Researcher of the Belgian Fund for Scientific Research (FNRS-F.R.S.). This work has been funded in part by the ERC project number 724725 (acronym SWORD) and by the Walloon Region through the Win2Wal project PIRATE (convention number 1910082).

References

Alf98. Alfke, P.: Efficient shift registers, lfsr counters, and long pseudo-random sequence generators (1998). http://www.xilinx.com/bvdocs/appnotes/xapp052.pdf

BBC+19. Barthe, G., Belaïd, S., Cassiers, G., Fouque, P.-A., Grégoire, B., Standaert, F.-X.: maskVerif: automated verification of higher-order masking in presence of physical defaults. In: Sako, K., Schneider, S., Ryan, P.Y.A. (eds.) ESORICS 2019. LNCS, vol. 11735, pp. 300–318. Springer, Cham (2019). https://doi.org/10.1007/978-3-030-29959-0_15

BBD+15. Barthe, G., Belaïd, S., Dupressoir, F., Fouque, P.-A., Grégoire, B., Strub, P.-Y.: Verified proofs of higher-order masking. In: Oswald, E., Fischlin, M. (eds.) EUROCRYPT 2015. LNCS, vol. 9056, pp. 457–485. Springer, Heidelberg (2015). https://doi.org/10.1007/978-3-662-46800-5_18

BBD+16. Barthe, G., et al.: Strong non-interference and type-directed higher-order masking. In: CCS, pp. 116–129. ACM (2016)

BDM+20. Belaïd, S., Dagand, P.É., Mercadier, D., Rivain, M., Wintersdorff, R.: Tornado: automatic generation of probing-secure masked bitsliced implementations. In: Canteaut, A., Ishai, Y. (eds.) EUROCRYPT 2020. LNCS, vol. 12107, pp. 311–341. Springer, Cham (2020). https://doi.org/10.1007/978-3-030-45727-3_11

BGI+18. Bloem, R., Gross, H., Iusupov, R., Könighofer, B., Mangard, S., Winter, J.: Formal verification of masked hardware implementations in the presence of glitches. In: Nielsen, J.B., Rijmen, V. (eds.) EUROCRYPT 2018. LNCS, vol. 10821, pp. 321–353. Springer, Cham (2018). https://doi.org/10.1007/978-3-319-78375-8_11

BP12. Boyar, J., Peralta, R.: A small depth-16 circuit for the AES S-Box. In: Gritzalis, D., Furnell, S., Theoharidou, M. (eds.) SEC 2012. IAICT, vol. 376, pp. 287–298. Springer, Heidelberg (2012). https://doi.org/10.1007/978-3-642-30436-1_24

CGLS21. Cassiers, G., Grégoire, B., Levi, I., Standaert, F.-X.: Hardware private circuits: from trivial composition to full verification. IEEE Trans. Comput. **70**(10), 1677–1690 (2021)

CJRR99. Chari, S., Jutla, C.S., Rao, J.R., Rohatgi, P.: Towards sound approaches to counteract power-analysis attacks. In: Wiener, M. (ed.) CRYPTO 1999. LNCS, vol. 1666, pp. 398–412. Springer, Heidelberg (1999). https://doi.org/10.1007/3-540-48405-1_26

CPRR13. Coron, J.-S., Prouff, E., Rivain, M., Roche, T.: Higher-order side channel security and mask refreshing. In: Moriai, S. (ed.) FSE 2013. LNCS, vol. 8424, pp. 410–424. Springer, Heidelberg (2014). https://doi.org/10.1007/978-3-662-43933-3_21

CRB+16. De Cnudde, T., Reparaz, O., Bilgin, B., Nikova, S., Nikov, V., Rijmen, V.: Masking AES with $d+1$ shares in hardware. In: Gierlichs, B., Poschmann, A.Y. (eds.) CHES 2016. LNCS, vol. 9813, pp. 194–212. Springer, Heidelberg (2016). https://doi.org/10.1007/978-3-662-53140-2_10

CS20. Cassiers, G., Standaert, F.-X.: Trivially and efficiently composing masked gadgets with probe isolating non-interference. IEEE Trans. Inf. Foren. Secur. **15**, 2542–2555 (2020)

CS21. Cassiers, G., Standaert, F.-X.: Provably secure hardware masking in the transition- and glitch-robust probing model: better safe than sorry. IACR Trans. Cryptogr. Hardw. Embed. Syst. **2021**(2), 136–158 (2021)

FGP+18. Faust, S., Grosso, V., Pozo, S.M.D., Paglialonga, C., Standaert, F.-X.: Composable masking schemes in the presence of physical defaults & the robust probing model. IACR Trans. Cryptogr. Hardw. Embed. Syst. **2018**(3), 89–120 (2018)

GGJR+11. Goodwill, B.J.G., et al.: A testing methodology for side-channel resistance validation. In: NIST non-invasive attack testing workshop vol. 7, pp. 115–136 (2011)

GMK17. Gross, H., Mangard, S., Korak, T.: An efficient side-channel protected AES implementation with arbitrary protection order. In: Handschuh, H. (ed.) CT-RSA 2017. LNCS, vol. 10159, pp. 95–112. Springer, Cham (2017). https://doi.org/10.1007/978-3-319-52153-4_6

KMMS22. Knichel, D., Moradi, A., Mullër, N., Sasdrich, P.: Automated generation of masked hardware. IACR Trans. Cryptogr. Hardw. Embed. Syst. (2022)

KSM20. Knichel, D., Sasdrich, P., Moradi, A.: SILVER – statistical independence and leakage verification. In: Moriai, S., Wang, H. (eds.) ASIACRYPT 2020. LNCS, vol. 12491, pp. 787–816. Springer, Cham (2020). https://doi.org/10.1007/978-3-030-64837-4_26

MMSS19. Moos, T., Moradi, A., Schneider, T., Standaert, F.-X.: Glitch-resistant masking revisited or why proofs in the robust probing model are needed. IACR Trans. Cryptogr. Hardw. Embed. Syst. **2019**(2), 256–292 (2019)

MPG05. Mangard, S., Popp, T., Gammel, B.M.: Side-channel leakage of masked CMOS gates. In: Menezes, A. (ed.) CT-RSA 2005. LNCS, vol. 3376, pp. 351–365. Springer, Heidelberg (2005). https://doi.org/10.1007/978-3-540-30574-3_24

NRS11. Nikova, S., Rijmen, V., Schläffer, M.: Secure hardware implementation of nonlinear functions in the presence of glitches. J. Cryptol. **24**(2), 292–321 (2011)

Author Index

Azouaoui, Melissa 236

Batina, Lejla 3
Beckers, Arthur 215
Bronchain, Olivier 236

Cassiers, Gaëtan 257
Chancel, G. 125

Egger, Maximilian 75

Fournaris, Apostolos P. 3

Galliere, J.-M. 125
Genêt, Aymeric 164
Gierlichs, Benedikt 143, 215

Hoffmann, Clément 236

Kaluđerović, Novak 164
Kerkhof, Maikel 29
Kong, Yinan 3
Kuzovkova, Yulia 236

Lippert, Florian 75

Mangard, Stefan 100
Maurine, P. 125
Momin, Charles 257
Mukhtar, Naila 3

Nasahl, Pascal 100

Papachristodoulou, Louiza 3
Perin, Guilherme 29, 49
Picek, Stjepan 29, 49
Preneel, Bart 143, 215

Schamberger, Thomas 75
Schilling, Robert 100
Schneider, Tobias 236
Schuhmacher, Frank 193
Sigl, Georg 75
Standaert, François-Xavier 236, 257

Tebelmann, Lars 75

Verbauwhede, Ingrid 215

Wouters, Lennert 143, 215
Wu, Lichao 29, 49

Printed in the United States
by Baker & Taylor Publisher Services